The Love Commandments

The Love Commandments:
Essays in Christian Ethics and Moral Philosophy

GENE OUTKA, EDMUND N. SANTURRI, WILLIAM WERPEHOWSKI,
DAVID LITTLE, TIMOTHY P. JACKSON, JOHN H. WHITTAKER,
JEAN PORTER, RONALD M. GREEN, JOHN P. REEDER, JR.

Edited by EDMUND N. SANTURRI and WILLIAM WERPEHOWSKI

WIPF & STOCK · Eugene, Oregon

Wipf and Stock Publishers
199 W 8th Ave, Suite 3
Eugene, OR 97401

The Love Commandments
Essays in Christian Ethics and Moral Philosophy
By Edmund N. Santurri and William Werpehowski
Copyright©1992 by Edmund N. Santurri and William Werpehowski
ISBN 13: 978-60899-156-3
Publication date 10/1/2009

for
Rachel, Alissa Marie, Anne, Stephen, and James.

Contents

Introduction　ix

GENE OUTKA
Universal Love and Impartiality　1
    Section One: A Theocentric Case for Universal Love　6
    Does Universal Love Include the Self? 6　Does Universal Love Lead to Impartiality? 10
    Section Two: Four Asymmetries Between One's Relation to One's Neighbor and One's Relation to Oneself　17
    Is Impartiality a Goal I Should Strive to Attain? 17
    Is Impartiality a Goal I Can Attain? 44　Should I Value My Particular Identity and Personal Projects? 48　Does What I Can Do For Anyone Else Differ Unavoidably From What I Can Do For Myself? 60
    Section Three: The Case Reviewed　72
    What Similarities Between Neighbor and Self Does Universal Love Legitimate? 74　What Differences Between Neighbor and Self Does Universal Love Accommodate? 79　What Fundamental Subjects Remain Unaddressed? 88　NOTES　92

EDMUND N. SANTURRI
Who Is My Neighbor? Love, Equality, and Profoundly Retarded Humans　104
    Introduction 104　Theological Considerations 111
    Philosophical Considerations 120　NOTES 132

WILLIAM WERPEHOWSKI
"Agape" and Special Relations　138
    Introduction 138　A Theological Consensus 139
    Consensus Challenged 141　Two Objections 143
    The Problem With Universalist Derivation 145
    The Neighbor to be Loved 148　Conclusion 152　NOTES 153

DAVID LITTLE
The Law of Supererogation   157
    Introduction 157   Permissive Acts, Universalizability, and 'Subjective Duty' 163   NOTES 179

TIMOTHY P. JACKSON
Christian Love and Political Violence   182
    Introduction 182   Stanley Hauerwas and the Peaceable Kingdom 183   Reinhold Niebuhr and Prophetic Christianity 187   Paul Ramsey and Love Transforming Justice 192   Juan Segundo and Liberated Ethics 194   Separatism, Apology, and Political Idolatry 199   Moral Conflict and Putting Charity First 204   Conclusion 212   NOTES 214

JOHN H. WHITTAKER
"Agape" and Self-Love   221
    Preference, Freedom, and the Concern for Basic Needs 223   Self-Love 227   *Agape* and the Love of God 233   NOTES 238

JEAN PORTER
Salvific Love and Charity: A Comparison of the Thought of Karl Rahner and Thomas Aquinas   240
    Salvific Love 241   Charity 246   Morality and Grace 252   NOTES 258

RONALD M. GREEN
Kant on Christian Love   261
    NOTES 277

JOHN P. REEDER, JR.
Analogues to Justice   281
    The Moon Anarres 282   The Circumstances of Justice 284   Well-Being and Liberty on Anarres 288   Extensive Benevolence and Distributional Policies 294   Utopias and Options 296   NOTES 299   REFERENCES 304

Introduction

The essays in this volume consider the meaning of the Christian injunction to love one's neighbor as oneself from various perspectives and in the light of several discrete topics. Their common theme is the working understanding that the meaning of neighbor-love or *agape* is located and configured in relation to conceptions of self-love and the love of God. Different descriptions and assessments of these two forms of love establish contexts that present both possibilities and limits for any account of love of neighbor. Some essays focus on the complex interrelation among all three loves, while others attend to a particular pair; an abiding interest in this collection, in any case, is to pursue a critical description of *agape* through examination of the loves that bear upon and encompass it. The examination includes the use of classical discussions in Christian tradition by thinkers such as Thomas Aquinas, John Calvin, Sören Kierkegaard, Reinhold Niebuhr, Karl Barth, Paul Ramsey, and Karl Rahner. It pays attention, moreover, to a set of central and time-honored themes in Christian ethics, including the moral significance of self-sacrifice, the universal scope of *agape*, the meaning of "neighbor," the nature of Christian identity, the justification of the use of political violence, and the relation between love and justice. Finally, the work contained herein employs and refers to resources in contemporary moral philosophy that serve well both general and particular concerns of Christian ethical reflection.

This Introduction orients the reader to individual essays, to aspects of the abiding interest, and to certain questions which the contributors pose. Thus, we hope to encourage understanding and to spur critical thinking on the issues at hand.

I: AGAPE AND IMPARTIALITY

Gene Outka opens this volume with what is perhaps the most extensive and significant study of the normative content of neighbor-love since the publication of his own book on the topic.[1] In its breadth and depth, the essay anticipates in important ways a number of themes encountered in the contributions that follow. Some significant connections are noted below.

After commending the claim that human creaturely love is *universal* in scope, given the inclusive and unconditional character of the love of God to which Christians are to bear witness, Outka concludes that a theocentric case for universal love can properly encompass both neighbor-love and self-love. The primary purpose of Outka's study is to evaluate the proposals that "there should be *no disparity* between our consideration of others and our consideration of ourselves," and that we should "commend *impartially* in our neighbor's case and in our own, whatever attitudes and actions we judge the law of love to require, extol, permit, and forbid."

The basic difficulty with an appeal to impartiality, as Outka notes, is that its implications move in directions that both coincide with and depart from traditional accounts of the law of love. On one side, impartiality has to do with interpersonal consistency: any action or trait of character judged to be right for one person must be judged to be right for any similar person similarly circumstanced. So no person ought to make arbitrary exceptions on his or her own behalf; but since the human self *does* tend to make such exceptions for one's own good to the exclusion of the good of others, impartial consistency can work to foster both self-criticism and a stance of fair detachment from self-interest. Here we have a real alliance between the Christian injunction to love the neighbor and a "theoretically unambitious sense of impartiality." The latter requires that the self question its drift toward special pleading, and reach out to consider the good of others who share with oneself a divinely bestowed dignity. On the other side, one may object that appeals to impartiality concede to self-love either too much or too little. It yields too much in one case by cutting against Christian proposals that love of neighbor demands altruistic *self-giving*. In the light of these proposals, impartial regard for those beloved of God, *including oneself*, appears anomalously like morally sanctioned *self-withholding*. In another case the problem is descriptive rather than normative. A strategy that stresses impartial regard fails to respond adequately to the *fact* that we do invariably favor ourselves selfishly. Even interpersonal consistency makes for too weak a demand. What is called for instead is an "ameliorative strategy" that compensates "for our tendency to go soft when we consider our own case, to be easy on ourselves and hard on others." But this sort of strategy runs up against, rather than fitting in neatly with, an impartialist stance.

An interpretation of Christian love of neighbor that favors impartiality may concede too little to the love of self in two different ways as well. First, it can be said that counting the self as one and only one (perhaps, indeed, as *merely* one) disregards the depth of a theologically appropriate self-regard. Impartiality may fail to accommodate the value one should give to his or her particular life. Inasmuch as that life and its projects are given by God as a unique opportunity, faithfulness before God requires that it be affirmed as such. Commitment to a norm of impartiality, with its pressures toward a kind of impersonality, can occasion "a bona fide temptation . . . when I allow it to disperse my energies so that my way of life remains forever unfocused, distracted, bereft of identifiable direction." Second, impartiality cannot accommodate or can even mask the fact that there are real differences between what I can do for myself and what I can do for others. One cannot, for example, transmit moral perfection, let alone religious faith, to another. Yet we are likely to ascribe a measure of self-responsibility regarding our own moral cultivation, and to acknowledge at least that whatever religious good I sincerely will for others, God cannot be lost to *me* against *my own* will. The recommendation of impartiality may seem not so much to take these differences into account as to change the subject.

Thus Outka identifies four "unlikenesses or asymmetries between one's relation to one's neighbor and one's relation to oneself." 1) Normatively, we *ought* to be more other-regarding than our impartial attention to all, including the self, can allow. 2) Descriptively, we simply *are* far more preoccupied with ourselves than with others, and merely commending the even-handedness of impartiality reflects a refusal to take this fact seriously. 3) Normatively, we *ought* to honor the importance of our own determinate character far more than impartiality permits: "I *should* not just go into the hopper with everyone else." 4) Descriptively, there actually *are* real differences between what I can accomplish for myself and what I can accomplish for others that render a standard of impartiality either misleading or somewhat beside the point.

Outka's careful scrutiny of these asymmetries progresses toward a critical redescription of the Christian norm of universal love. General and more specific background beliefs (concerning, e.g., the connection between self-love and love of God, the implications of the promise of redemption for ethics, etc.) are critically tested and revised with respect to one another. These beliefs also are tested and revised with respect to more particular, considered moral judgments (e.g., the ways in which the self's resistance to manipulation by others is proper). The substantive content of universal love is similarly scrutinized and modified in light of background beliefs and considered judgments. What emerges is a provisional case for a "reflective equilibrium" that justifies Outka's concluding account of universal love. Along the way, the comparison with impartiality serves to expose alliances and to heighten contrasts with *agape*.[2]

II: WHO IS MY NEIGHBOR?

Outka's work covers one issue that emerges from the claim that the Christian law of love is universal in scope: does such universal love include the self? As he acknowledges, however, other controversies surround this claim. One of them has to do with "boundaries." Do certain features of "humanity" or "personhood" more or less successfully identify the neighbor to be loved? Do they establish qualifications that limit love's applicability to some humans but not to others, and/or extend it to some nonhumans? How do these features relate to the normative view that all human beings possess an equal moral worth? Of course, one may go on to ask: should substantive qualifications for moral regard of human beings be part of Christian theological ethics? One can recall the instructive misdirection of Jesus' answer to the lawyer who, "seeking to justify himself," asked "who is my neighbor?" (Luke 10:29) The parable of the Good Samaritan and the subsequent question, "who proved neighbor?" has been interpreted as a caution against the specification of necessary and sufficient conditions giving title to neighbor-love.

> One thing the story teaches might be stated like this: when in doubt, do not consult your categories of which human beings have what status; rather, respond in a neighborly way to a human being in need of help and see whether, during that response, you clarify your perception of what that being is. When in doubt, do not first classify and categorize; be neighborly toward the stranger in question and then see how your classifications are affected.[3]

In his essay, Edmund N. Santurri addresses this range of questions with reference to the class of profoundly retarded humans. Making extensive use of biblical, theological, and philosophical sources, Santurri enters the debate between "humanists" and "rationalists." The former affirm that membership in the human community is sufficient for guaranteeing equal moral worth within the universal scope of *agape*; the latter argue that some measure of rational capacity is decisive for qualifying human beings as human persons, entitled as such to full moral status.

Santurri concludes that the rationalist case as developed in contemporary philosophy fails to win the day over the humanist alternative. The vision of "the biblical tradition and Christian love properly understood" also moves to the idea that "all humans count as neighbors to be loved, whatever their characteristics or circumstances, . . . simply because they are members of the human community." The author points to the abiding presence of severely retarded humans "in various practices that constitute our human way of life." The retarded "are born of us, look like us, and interact with us in a wide assortment of distinctive communal settings. They are beings with whom we have deeply significant historical and social relations." For rationalists to overlook these facts or count them as irrelevant is to risk abstraction born of being "held in the grip of a theory." With this appeal to activities constitutive of a human way of life, Santurri himself may make a bow in the direction of the Good Samaritan story mentioned earlier. While from one vantage point membership in the human community is a criterion for equal consideration, from another it emerges as such from reflection on the sorts of practices that include, among others, the profoundly retarded—practices, we may say, by which Christians and other folks prove neighbor to them.

Some contemporary Christian ethicists have inquired into the identity of the "neighbor" in another way. They have expressed reservations about the "universal" character of the concept, especially as it reflects the heritage of Enlightenment liberalism. It would appear that that heritage calls for the stripping away of particular human identity in the name of generic features such as "rationality" or "agency." Accordingly, the proper Christian theological context framing the law of love may be lost. A second, related worry is that *agape*, conceived in "Enlightenment" or "Kantian" fashion, cannot readily accommodate special, more local, and preferential human ties. Critics challenge that such ties of friendship, family, and the like that are so important to our everyday lives, become something of an anomaly or embarrassment in the light of universal, "disinterested" love. At least, so regarded, they would seem to have to bear a burden of proof that appears unnecessary.

In "*Agape* and Special Relations," William Werpehowski considers the second problem as he develops an interpretation of the idea of the "neighbor" that preserves its universal applicability within an explicitly theological framework. Thus the neighbor is not a denuded "rational agent," but a creature of God, a sister or brother for whom Christ died, and a possible companion in beatitude. These three descriptions impart a perspective that works to transform and complete certain special relations. Love of the one God who creates, redeems, and fulfills finally grounds the intelligibility of these descriptions—the extraneous conceptualities do not.

III: SUPEREROGATION

David Little's essay addresses some of the paradoxes that appear in the writings of John Calvin, but that are also typical of much other Christian and non-Christian ethical reflection. On the one hand, Calvin sees acts of Christian love as those properly performed "with eager readiness" and "not as if constrained by the necessity of the law." On the other hand, works of supererogation, in which notable altruism and self-giving are displayed, are "lawlike." For Little, Calvin's latter claim makes sense in two ways. First, one can speak of supererogatory acts as "in some sense universalizable according to a set of rules that governs the application of the term." Second, "it is appropriate to associate the idea of 'duty,' albeit a 'permissive' or 'subjective' duty, with supererogation." How are we to understand these claims?

For Little, the key is a distinction between what he categorizes as "mandatory oughts" and "permissive oughts." The former refers to certain duties of justice, such as a duty of mutual aid,[4] or obligations established in virtue of standing within a particular role (e.g., a parent) or by certain social conventions (e.g., promise-making). In contrast, the latter category concerns moral matters, analogous to contexts of gift-giving, for which there necessarily remains a "privilege of benefaction." Yet this privilege is allied with a moral "ought" which, even with its "permissiveness," can include moral liability for non-performance of certain supererogatory acts. In the case of requests for small favors, for example, it is true *both* that doing the favor is left up to the would-be benefactor, *and* that this is something that anyone in a similar situation (including, of course, the agent in question) "ought to do, or face strong censure." Little argues that the degree of permissiveness that we assign to different sorts of beneficent acts may vary, from the "low" permissiveness of a trivial favor to the "high" permissiveness of ultimate self-sacrifice. But across this range of supererogation, a set of objective and universalizable criteria concerning costs to the agent, benefits to the recipient, and so on, operate regarding the limits or extent of permissiveness. The range of supererogatory acts is aptly described as a "moral duty" in a wide sense and in a narrow sense. The wide sense applies to the universalizably binding requirement "to exercise the privilege of benefaction—one way or the other." In the narrow sense, the moral agent is liable to moral blame for non-performance in certain cases. Now these "oughts" are not strictly mandatory in being the response to a *moral demand*; rather, they are distinguished as fitting responses to an *appeal* that implicitly acknowledges the privilege of benefaction.[5]

In conclusion, Little offers a Christocentric explanation for the claim that some loving acts may be grasped as non-mandatory "subjective duties." He reminds us that "a Christian might personally feel 'bound in gratitude' to return the benevolence manifested in Christ's life and death by undertaking to display benevolence, in turn, to God and fellow human beings." But such a binding quality is compatible with free and unexacted response, for this is the appropriate way to witness to and express love for a gracious divine Benefactor. We find here a complex coincidence of *gratuitous action* in the context of *loving indebtedness* to the divine love, and, therefore, an instructive connection drawn between love of God and love of neighbor.[6]

IV. LOVE AND POLITICAL VIOLENCE

Timothy Jackson defends the Christian tradition of the "just war," as represented in the work of Paul Ramsey, over the pacifism of Stanley Hauerwas, Reinhold Niebuhr's Christian realism, and Juan Luis Segundo's liberationist stance. His protests to the contrary notwithstanding, Hauerwas is taken to be a political sectarian or separatist in fact if not in principle. That is, the Hauerwas viewpoint does not appear consistently to recognize the proper role which the nation-state must play in establishing a tolerable peace. Niebuhr, as a critic of pacifism, fails to gain a principled control over his realism in the name of neighbor-love; thus, his ethic tends to drift toward mere consequentialism. Segundo so radically contextualizes decisions about the use of violent force that any determinate normative impact that traditional notions like love and justice might have on these decisions is dubious at best. Jackson finds that Ramsey properly understands that political activity, even when violent, may be a licit and a morally limited instrument of the highest values of love of God and neighbor. So "violent love," as Jackson puts it, "is not a contradiction in terms."[7]

But Jackson also notes that "postmodern" critics such as Judith Shklar, Richard Rorty, and others can say that this judgment is too sanguine. Christian love, far from being simply compatible in principle with violence licitly if regretfully employed, often engenders violence of various sorts without, if you will, "just cause." Jackson responds to three distinct forms of this postmodern challenge. They include: 1) the "meritarian objection" that so-called "selflessness" disguises the hatred of the weak for the strong; 2) the "naturalist objection" that the life of Christian charity exacts too high a price intrapsychically by forcing a denial of other human goods; and 3) the "liberal objection" that it "generates a self-righteousness that encourages dogmatism and aggression." Jackson's defense blends conceptual clarification with constructive theological insight, and works to the conclusion that *agape*, even in its legitimate violent employment, may be normatively self-eliciting.

V: SELF-LOVE, LOVE FOR GOD, AND SALVATION

John Whittaker's study of *agape* and self-love is a sort of commentary on Kierkegaard's treatment of the matter in *Works of Love*. "When it is said: 'You shall love your neighbor as yourself,' therein is contained what is presupposed, that every man loves himself." Yet it is not the purpose of this command "to proclaim self-love as a prescriptive right"; rather, "it is its purpose to wrest self-love away from us human beings. This implies loving oneself; but if one must love his neighbor *as himself*, then the command, like a pick, wrenches open the lock of self-love and thereby wrests it away from a man." The point is not "to teach a man not to love himself" but instead "to teach him proper self-love."[8] Kierkegaard concludes:

> The law is, therefore, you shall love yourself in the same way as you love your neighbor when you love him as yourself. Whoever has any knowledge of men will certainly admit that whenever he has desired the capacity of moving others to relinquish self-love, he has also frequently been constrained to wish that it were possible to teach them to love themselves.[9]

The three parts to this analysis are: 1) a presupposed sense of self-love; 2) its status as a sort of preliminary basis for discerning the character of neighbor-love; and 3) a transformed normative notion of self-love. Whittaker considers each thoroughly on the way toward a concluding account of the relation between self-love and the grateful love of God.

He establishes, first of all, that there is a presupposition that we all in fact love ourselves. "We love ourselves by wanting to be happy, to be fulfilled, to be complete. *And we do not abandon this wish.*" Then Whittaker analyzes different senses of this sort of love in order to establish a basis for understanding the commandment to love one's neighbor as oneself. The commandment, he proposes, calls us to love others in the same way that we love ourselves "when we long for an unspecified fulfillment." This interpretation is fitting because the presupposition is that *everyone* loves oneself, and the only sense in which every one of us does so is the sense in which one longs "for fulfillment of *some* kind, specified or unspecified." Self-love, then, represents a permanent bond of attachment to ourselves, even when we are disappointed in ourselves and in our invested desires; but the love command "wrenches open the lock of self-love and wrests it away" from ourselves by making that permanent bond a paradigm for that refusal to abandon concern *for the neighbor* that is constitutive of *agape*.[10] Conforming to the second great commandment is a matter of "maintaining a certain disposition, struggling to sustain an accepting attitude toward others in the face of obstacles, extending approval to them as far as one can in good conscience, and preserving a willingness to forgive them for what one takes to be their wrongdoings."

While the love command presupposes self-love, the disposition to love the neighbor is a *new creation*, and not merely the extension of an existing disposition. Consequently, it brings with it a transformed notion of self-love; for in fact we do not, in our self-preoccupation, our insecurity, and our self-doubt, love ourselves as we *ought*. We ought and need to trust that the "unquenchable longing for . . . happiness has been answered in an unknown way, that one is an heir to ultimate well-being, and that one can rely on this hope even without knowing how to define its object." Trust of this sort may come in the assurance of faith in the divine promise of "satisfaction for the unfocused desire that underlies all our hopes." The love of God, as source and goal of that promise, includes in that case the affection of gratitude for the assurance of fulfillment. Whittaker infers, in a way reminiscent of Little, that gratitude for a gift may and must be manifested by "repeating the generosity" in one's loving approach toward the neighbor.

In writing about the self and its preoccupation with itself, and of how trust in God frees the self to turn to the neighbor, Whittaker addresses themes characteristic of the tradition of the Reformation. This is no surprise, given the Kierkegaardian cast of his essay.[11] In contrast, Jean Porter's work on salvific love and charity in the thought of Rahner and Aquinas attends to issues of importance for Roman Catholic moral theology. Specifically, her defense of the use of the language of the theological virtues, especially charity, reflects the traditional Catholic insistence that the sphere of grace completes, and does not destroy, the sphere of (human) nature.[12] Porter takes that language both to preserve the particularity of the Christian vision of the good life and, as it is a language of *virtue*, to indicate characteristic enactments of that vision that help to display its intelligibility. She makes the point, in condensed form, this way: "Why should anyone want salvation? We point to examples of those who are living the life of charity, in order to show that they have something that other people might reasonably want; or conversely, we point to examples of sinfulness in order to show that sin is really a misfortune, even though appearances are sometimes to the contrary." What is presumed here is a field of human discernment continuous with the supernatural love of God, however it may be elevated by it.

En route to her defense of the language of charity, Porter gives a bracingly clear analysis of Rahner's theological anthropology and its relation to salvific love. For him the human intentionality toward God, as the ground of an infinite horizon of self-transcendence, is "pre-thematically" present "whenever a person goes out of himself or herself in genuine love to affirm the reality and integral value of another person." Thus, an act of genuine neighbor-love is also an act in which the person "says Yes to God in the depths of his or her personal being." Every instance of loving the neighbor is also an instance of loving God, and "every act of the love of God is also formally an act of the love of the neighbor." Now Thomas Aquinas's view differs crucially from Rahner's in that, for Aquinas, charity adds something qualitatively different to the moral life. The life of the justified person "looks different from the life of the morally good person; the former acts in different ways and expresses different motivations and feelings than does the latter." In contrast, Rahner holds that salvific love "does not necessarily add any new element to the moral life as now experienced."

Recall that Outka, in his third "asymmetry," inquires about the implications of a positive assessment of a person's particular identity that can be offered within a theocentric framework ("I should not just go into the hopper with everyone else."). Whittaker also works from a sort of positive assessment presupposed in the second love commandment. He proceeds to present a distinctively Christian depiction of how love of God conditions self-regard and one's self-assessment. Porter's study of Rahner and Aquinas, in its turn, explores and exposes the formal presuppositions of these two projects. She suggests that a standpoint like Rahner's, which makes "moral goodness" and "salvific love" perfectly coextensive, excludes the possibility of making discriminations that display typical forms of Christian identity. For Aquinas, charity or loving fellowship with God is a character-trait concept; using it enables specification of the theocentric framework within which one is operating (what sort of God is this to whom I am lovingly related?), and permits descriptions of characteristic Christian actions, emotions, and dispositions. These descriptions ideally lend a kind of reasonableness to Christian vision by "tethering" the particular framework to everyday life. Outka and Whittaker use analogous concepts with a related function that shows what differences the love of God makes for morality. For Outka, it is the self's "obedient willing" before God, and for Whittaker it is the posture of grateful trust. Without notions such as these, we cannot effectively begin to talk about Christian identity, be it more or less self-possessed, or more or less grateful, or whatever.

VI: LOVE, BENEFICENCE, AND BENEVOLENCE

Outka's interest in points of convergence and divergence between impartiality and Christian universal love is paralleled somewhat by the contributions of Ronald Green and John Reeder. Green looks at Immanuel Kant's specific attempts to interpret the second love commandment, while Reeder gives a close analysis of the relationship between justice and the social practice of benevolence. For the first author, a conception of impartiality is essential to the most defensible understanding of Kant's interpretation of love as a duty of beneficence; for the second, an impartial moral disposition of benevolence requires norms which specify the fitting distribution of social goods. This is true even when it is assumed that citizens of a society are not motivated to make claims in the name of what is *owed* them.

Seeking to dispel standard views of Kant as a moral rigorist hostile to human affections, Green distinguishes between a pure case of moral motivation and a moral ideal of concrete human action. The former in Kant's thought locates the basis of moral worth in acting from, and not merely in accord with, a sense of moral duty. The latter, however, for Kant includes the commendation to cultivate sympathetic feelings "and to use them as so many means to participating from moral principles and from the feelings appropriate to these principles." The issue has to do with a priority relation based on a presumption about what is and what is not under the control of the human will and, therefore, of what can and what cannot be subject to moral praise and blame. *Duties* can be commanded. *Feelings* more nearly happen to us, and hence are not the proper objects of praise and blame apart from a prior sense of duty. So Kant will want to say both that a duty to love one's neighbor is logically impossible, when love is regarded merely as a matter of feeling, and that we have "a duty to participate actively in the fate of others." Feelings of sympathy *may* enable us to do "what the thought of duty alone would not accomplish."

However surprising this nuance might be, Kant's general view of Christian love, as Green portrays it, is hardly so; such love "represents an injunction to the most perfect fulfillment of rationally understood moral duty. It involves respecting the dictates of the Categorical Imperative in their fullest and most complete sense." Green concedes that this will be seen by many to be an impoverished understanding of the love commandment, especially in view of Kant's rejection of any essential bearing that love of God may have for it. Nonetheless, the Kantian tendency to identify love of neighbor with a positive obligation of beneficence ("to promote . . . the happiness of others who are in need, and this without hope of gaining anything by it") and the manner of Kant's justification of this obligation raise instructive issues about the interconnections of neighbor-love and self-love. Much of Green's work in his essay is devoted to explicating these connections.

The final contribution to this volume provides a thoughtful and imaginative analysis of the relation between love and justice. Conceiving "love" in terms of what Hume calls extensive benevolence, according to which a person "has the same degree of concern for the interests of others as for one's own," John Reeder explains how social arrangements on the fictional planet "Anarres" eschew presuppositions we might typically make in contemporary considerations of liberal individualist justice.[13] In her imaginative tale about Anarres, novelist Ursula LeGuin details the ways in which conflicts of interest among citizens, while extending to certain differences in preferred ways of life, do not include the desire of each individual for a greater rather than a lesser share of the fruits of cooperation; rather, generosity prevails. What is more, a common trust in one another enables benevolence to be motivationally effective, in that persons do not need the desire to do what is just to be superimposed upon their set of preferences. The so-called subjective "circumstances of justice," then, are not in force on Anarres.

Still, benevolence or universal love requires distributional specification even as it transcends the distributional arrangements of justice. Reeder shows that on Anarres, under ordinary circumstances of scarcity and social productivity, a principle of equal contribution and return applies, suitably adjusted for individual capacity and interest. In effect, citizens give to and receive from one another equal attention to the good life of each. In addition, the desire for more rather than less equality in social shares overrides even the desire for a greater total social product which is still distributed along egalitarian lines. Rewards based on incentives are ruled out, and the people of Anarres prefer less for each for the sake of greater equality of shares. The system of distribution of benefits and burdens of social cooperation departs from utilitarian schemes which maximize total or average satisfaction, and from egalitarian proposals such as John Rawls's difference principle, in which significant social inequalities are justified if they benefit the worst off members of society.[14]

These reviews of contrasting distributional approaches help to establish one of Reeder's crucial points. It is that the disposition of universal love or mutual benevolence underdetermines the distributional arrangements which would express it. The disposition leads one to desire everyone's good (including one's own) with an equal intensity. But the initial egalitarian starting point does not tell you which distributive principles to adopt. In principle, either the utilitarian, or the Rawlsian, or the Anarresian distributions are compatible with the disposition. This position suggests that the differing background beliefs we have about persons and the character of human relationships underlie noteworthy contrasts.

VII: CONCLUSION

It is our hope that readers of these essays will be disposed to pursue further the subjects and questions raised by the authors. They have tried to lay open to view the salient issues and to display patterns of critical conversation that animate reflection on the love commandments. But to expose issues about relations between self-love, neighbor-love and the love of God is not to resolve them once and for all. Conversations, moreover, are open ended. Our collective efforts will have served their purpose if others are encouraged to take part in the exchange.

WILLIAM WERPEHOWSKI

NOTES

1. Gene Outka, *Agape: An Ethical Analysis* (New Haven and London: Yale University Press, 1972).

2. I analyze the idea of reflective equilibrium as it pertains to theological ethics in *Social Justice, Social Selves* (Ph.D. diss., Yale University, 1981). See also Ronald F. Thiemann, *Revelation and Theology* (Notre Dame: University of

Notre Dame Press, 1985), and Francis Schussler Fiorenza, *Foundational Theology* (New York: Crossroad, 1984).

3. Hessel Bouma, Douglas Diekma, Edward Langerak, Theodore Rottman, Allen Verhey, *Christian Faith, Health and Medical Practice* (Grand Rapids: Eerdmans, 1989), p. 210.

4. See John Rawls's treatment of a duty of mutual aid in *A Theory of Justice* (Cambridge: Harvard University Press, 1971), pp. 338f.

5. Cf. Outka's discussion in this volume of supererogation in connection with his first normative "asymmetry."

6. Cf. William F. May, *The Physician's Covenant* (Philadelphia: Westminster Press, 1983), pp. 129-30.

7. See also Outka's treatment in this volume of what he calls the "self-other, other-other distinction" as it bears on the debate between pacifists and proponents of "justified killing."

8. Sören Kierkegaard, *Works of Love* (New York: Harper & Row, 1962), pp. 38-39.

9. *Ibid.*, p. 39.

10. Cf. Paul Ramsey, *Basic Christian Ethics* (New York: Charles Scribner's Sons, 1950), pp. 99-100.

11. See especially Martin Luther's classic treatise, "The Freedom of A Christian," in *Luther: Selected Political Writings*, J. M. Porter, ed. (Philadelphia: Fortress Press), pp. 25-35.

12. Consider, e.g., Thomas Aquinas, *Summa Theologiae* II-II, q. 23, aa. 7-8 (Chicago: Encyclopedia Britannica, 1952).

13. I discuss individualist justice and its relation to Christian political ethics in "Political Liberalism and Christian Ethics," *The Thomist* 48/1 (1984): 81-115.

14. See Rawls, *A Theory of Justice*, pp. 75-83.

Contributors

Ronald M. Green is the John Phillips Professor of Religion and adjunct professor of Business Ethics, Tuck School, Dartmouth College, Hanover, New Hampshire.

Timothy P. Jackson is an assistant professor in the Department of Religious Studies, Stanford University, Stanford, California.

David Little is senior scholar at the U.S. Institute of Peace, Washington, D.C.

Gene Outka is Chair of the Department of Religious Studies at Yale University, New Haven, Connecticut.

Jean Porter is an associate professor in the Department of Theology, University of Notre Dame, Notre Dame, Indiana.

John P. Reeder, Jr., is a professor in the Department of Religious Studies, Brown University, Providence, Rhode Island.

Edmund N. Santurri is a professor in the Department of Religion, Saint Olaf College, Northfield, Minnesota.

William Werpehowski is an associate professor in the Department of Religious Studies and an assistant director of the Center for Peace and Justice Education, Villanova University, Villanova, Pennsylvania.

John H. Whittaker is a professor and director of the Religious Studies Program, Louisiana State University, Baton Rouge, Louisiana.

Gene Outka

Universal Love and Impartiality

Those who take the Bible as authoritative for their identity as religious believers do not debate *whether* they should love God with heart, mind, and strength, or love their neighbors as themselves.

> Some practical doctrines, such as the "law of love" in Christianity, are held to be unconditionally necessary. They are part of the indispensable grammar or logic of the faith. There are, for example, no circumstances in which Christians are commanded not to love God or neighbor.[1]

Of course *what* the law of love enjoins demands careful attention. Determinate directions are clearly set. To love God is actively to refer all things to God, to prefer nothing to God in one's affections and goals. To love one's neighbor is to aid a person or persons in distress. No special deliberation is needed to judge in many cases what actions are appropriate. Without agonizing one may, for instance, go regularly to worship and take food and clothing to the homeless shelter. Similarly, certain prohibitions are clearly seen to specify what violates a life of love. Adultery, for example, harms all of those affected and breaks especially a promise to the innocent spouse. Lying manipulates the one(s) deceived, and undermines the conditions for a good community. To ignore such prohibitions may show self-indulgence and self-aggrandizement, and not that one has neglected to deliberate enough.

Yet to engage in commentary and debate about what the law of love enjoins does not always represent culpable evasion. The determinate directions that the great commandments set also generate questions widely discussed by writers in the Christian tradition. How is each of the three loves identified—love for God, love of neighbor, and love of self—like and unlike the others? What connections are essential, which differences fitting? Moreover, a comprehensive account of neighbor-love faces large substantive and distributive considerations. Which needs and choices of the neighbor should we generally meet and support? Which neighbors should we aid when we cannot aid them all? Finally, the tradition hands down an amalgam of specific judgments about what the law of love requires, exhorts, permits, and forbids. Such judgments display varying kinds and degrees of reliance on the Bible, and reflect developments within later Christian communities as well as encounters with surrounding cultures. The range of these judgments includes prohibitions more contested and contestable than adultery and lying, e.g., from usury to euthanasia. Many call for extended critical thought. Which should be reaffirmed? Which revised? Which abandoned?

My inquiry here is meant to pay reflective homage to the law of love as a practical doctrine to which Christians are necessarily committed. It centers on essential connections and fitting differences among the three loves that the great commandments identify. Such a restriction is important to note but obviously insufficient; the vastness of the remaining subject demands that I select only certain questions on which to focus. The questions that I select, and the way that I shall examine them, are as follows.

I take as a point of departure one of the oldest convictions present in the tradition (associated above all with Augustine, and despite important variations, met also in Bernard of Clairvaux and Jonathan Edwards). The conviction is this. That God is the *Summum Bonum* is a truth that obtains for neighbor and self alike. Nothing is higher than God; nothing is commensurable with God. Yet I find that as I love God supremely, I rightly love my neighbor and myself.

Two aspects of this conviction concern me. First, to love God supremely includes the recognition that any transfer of one's absolute attachment and devotion from God to one's neighbor or to oneself ends in idolatry. Some of the effects of this fitting difference between love for God and the other two loves I shall identify as I continue. I am concerned especially to place the discussion of the other two loves within what I call a theocentric frame of explanation and evaluation.[2] Second, we find also positive connections among the three loves. There *can* be proper or legitimate neighbor-love *and* self-love when one loves God supremely. One such connection again concerns me especially. Love for God—as the most basic and comprehensive human love of all—includes fidelity to God in loving whom God loves. (This fidelity reflects a deeper assumption that God's love is prior and determining, and that such priority should receive acknowledgment not only in doctrines of grace, but in the overall account of the law of love.) Many Christians affirm that God's love toward human beings is universal in scope, for all people are created, sustained, and redeemed by God. Thus, our love should correspond as far as possible to this universal scope.

The conclusion that our love should be correspondingly universal in scope supports the view that there can be proper or legitimate neighbor-love and self-love. For such love means at least that we should exclude neither our neighbors nor ourselves as subjects of attention and care. Yet the conclusion leaves open a number of questions that prove crucial to examine. Does universal love also mean that there should be *no disparity* between our consideration of others and our consideration of ourselves? To put it positively, should we commend *impartially* in our neighbor's case and in our own, whatever attitudes and actions we judge the law of love to require, extol, permit, and forbid? But what then should we say about the unease many Christians evidence with even-handed verdicts that take the self's own well-being equivalently into account? How can such verdicts accommodate a stress on self-giving and self-denial? Should we love neighbor and self dissimilarly rather than similarly, or perhaps sometimes one and sometimes the other?

I examine these and related questions by dividing my inquiry into three sections.

In Section One (subsections 1-2) I introduce a theocentric case for saying that universal love plausibly extends to neighbor and to self. I then identify a proposal to construe universal love in terms of impartiality. According to this proposal, one should love others neither less nor more than oneself. So a love that gives more weight to others than to self is disallowed, or at least is not required. The proposal by virtue of its forthrightness serves to concentrate our thoughts. It prompts us specifically to reflect about two matters that will occupy us throughout the inquiry.

First, what different senses of inclusiveness or universality of scope can we distinguish that remain compatible with an insistence that one should love others neither less nor more than oneself? From the one side, we will see that the proposal itself must be given nuance when we trace more technical meanings that impartiality acquires in various ethical theories put forward by modern philosophers. For example, to say that giving more weight to others than to oneself is not required proves to be compatible with commending acts of supererogation, where the agent laudably does more than duty requires. Thus, not all accounts of impartiality demand that I love myself exactly as I love my neighbor. Secular proponents of impartiality permit at least one sort of distinction between what I may do for others and what I may do for myself. From the other side, those for example who regard nonviolence as essential to any way of life that purports to be Christian build this conviction into their account of inclusiveness, an account they apply to self and neighbor alike. They offer a kind of normative impartiality of their own, at least with respect to nonviolence. The distinction on which they dwell is not between self and neighbor, but between church and world. In brief, attending to impartiality yields discoveries about different senses of inclusiveness.

Second, why are so many uneasy nonetheless with saying that one should love others neither more nor less than oneself? I contend that there is a point to such unease, or rather several points. Here questions about the status and relation of neighbor-love and self-love come into sharp focus. Here too the proposal to interpret universal love in terms of impartiality serves as a disciplined point of reference in relation to which various sources of unease can be sorted out and subsequently compared. The objections to impartiality that I shall identify help to account for possible differences between neighbor-love and self-love. Yet I realize that paying explicit heed to self-love carries particular hazards. The "as yourself" clause in the second love command has generated a daunting amalgam of judgments of its own. Debate about it often assumes special intensity. Now I emphatically do not wish to isolate judgments about self-love from those about neighbor-love; but I think we improve a general account of the law of love when we reckon with differences as well as affinities. We must go on to ask whether any or all of these differences are themselves compatible with a universal love that includes a place for proper neighbor-love and self-love.

In Section Two (subsections 3-6) I contend that the unease with impartiality reveals possible unlikenesses or asymmetries between one's relation to one's neighbor and one's relation to oneself. The asymmetries differ among themselves as do the objections to impartiality that they promote. Again, however, the objections are all specifications of the unlikeness theme, and may help to account for differences between neighbor-love and self-love. I distinguish and pair four objections.

Two objections find impartiality deficient because it authorizes too much attention to the self's own well-being. The first objection is predominantly normative. Impartiality fails to accommodate radically other-regarding elements in Christian love or *agape*: including stress on going the second mile, on self-giving and cross-bearing, on turning the other cheek so that one refuses to resist evil or to engage in self-defense. The second objection is predominantly descriptive. Impartiality fails to take seriously enough the self's *de facto* preoccupation with its own wants and ambitions. We are naive to suppose that appeals to even-handedness, including theoretical ones, substantially alter this preoccupation. What is needed is an ameliorative strategy: sacrificial love.

The remaining pair of objections finds impartiality deficient because it neglects to acknowledge distinctive and legitimate self-regarding considerations. Like the first, the third objection is predominantly normative. Impartiality fails to honor the importance of personal identity, including one's determinate character. What we honor within a theocentric frame is one's obedient willing before and for God. Such willing means that I should value my particular identity and personal projects. The fourth objection is predominantly descriptive. Impartiality fails to accommodate a fixed and structural difference between what I can do for another and what I can do for myself. To be accountable to God as an agent establishes an ineliminable imbalance between neighbor-love and self-love. This imbalance does not imply however that we are essentially unrelated to one another.

In Section Three (subsections 7-9) I return to the case for universal love with which I began. Distinguishing among asymmetries and the objections to impartiality they promote may throw light on questions we too rarely consider in one place. Do objections to impartiality succeed? And if they do, will they prove fatal to universal love as well? Or can we effect a reconciliation? Can we affirm universal love as a way to love God, and our neighbors and ourselves in God? And can we affirm the asymmetries as marking suitably different ways to love God, and our neighbors and ourselves in God?

Let me append three remarks that further identify overall features and limits in what I undertake.

First, I shall consider modern Christian interpretations of the law of love, and occasionally refer as well to earlier accounts found in the tradition. The material examined and the questions pursued extend and revise what I presented in an earlier study of twentieth century Protestant and Roman Catholic theological literature on love.[3]

Second, as in my earlier study, I shall treat not only the first but also the second love command as part of a determinately religious and theological body of belief and practice. It is, of course, indisputable that many in our wider society see the second love command as a moral injunction standing on its own. Some view it as a maxim of popular wisdom, a salutary exhortation whose force requires no reference to its origins or interpretations within Judaism or Christianity. Others, notably professional philosophers, sometimes employ it as part of a theoretical argument to close, or at any rate narrow, the gap between prudential and moral requirements. They proceed in effect from self-love to neighbor-love. I already love myself and so in the wake of this antecedent natural fact (construed in various ways) I avoid arbitrariness and inconsistency only if I love my neighbor as well. They justify this case on rational grounds, to be accepted as valid by everyone irrespective of the particular communities to which they belong. Both the popular usage and the theoretical employment are significant, but they lie outside my concerns in this inquiry. I am interested now in what it means *normatively* to say *within* a theocentric frame that the second love command applies to all human beings. The frame as I interpret it reflects beliefs shared by those who identify with the historical Christian community. Naturally, I hope that some of the normative reflections prove helpful to those beyond this community, but I shall not discuss whether the second love command applies on grounds acceptable to all—believers and nonbelievers alike. The normative universalism I examine does not require us to show that people everywhere, in all communities, have had the same justificatory procedures or value system. It is enough here to affirm that "humanity at large is the neighbor given to the church."[4]

Third, I shall however refer at various times to modern moral philosophers who address instructively some of the questions posed about impartiality. These references will remain selective and ad hoc. They enrich our reflection about normative questions. But I hope to incur no large philosophical debts that require independent analysis and defense. The references will be confined, for example, to moral judgments where the claims of other persons as well as oneself are already assumed to carry weight.

The last two remarks mean, in short, that I carry out two kinds of activity: (a) intramural conversations within the tradition about how to interpret the law of love most adequately; (b) extramural explorations with modern secular morality where comparisons hold especially illuminating prospects for the tradition.

Section One
A Theocentric Case for Universal Love

1. DOES UNIVERSAL LOVE INCLUDE THE SELF?

1.1. *The expansion of love outward*. Let us start with the claim that the law of love is universal in scope: it contains nonpreferential and nonexclusive features that authorize reverence and care for *every* human being. We find a representative instance of the claim in the Pastoral Letter on War and Peace written by the American Catholic Bishops:

> At the center of the Church's teaching on peace and at the center of all Catholic teaching are the transcendence of God and the dignity of the human person. The human person is the clearest reflection of God's presence in the world; all of the Church's work in pursuit of both justice and peace is designed to protect and promote the dignity of every person.[5]

Many controversies surround this claim. Let me mention three. One concerns boundaries. Must certain features be present for the claim to hold? For example, does a fetus qualify? Another controversy concerns scope itself. Why must the dignity of *every* person be protected and promoted? Why cannot other-regard be genuine without being universal in scope? Still another controversy concerns multilateral cases. When two or more persons are affected by one's action, does the claim furnish any guidance? What especially of situations where the well-being of various persons conflict and choice is unavoidable?

The Bishops do not address the first two controversies in their document. But it seems obvious that they would include the fetus and would view restricted other-regard as incomplete (though a gain over egoism). They do wrestle explicitly with one set of multilateral cases: how can military policies and practices respect the dignity of numerous persons in many nations? However we assess the Bishops' specific policy judgments, their commitment to inclusiveness is striking, for they strive to encompass the adversary, the outsider, and the interrogator. Indeed, they insist that "how we treat our enemy is the key test of whether we love our neighbor."[6] And they rehearse the debate about whether only nonviolence as a way of life passes this key test.[7] How, except for nonviolence, can we include the adversary and, more generally, the outsider in any way that is demonstrably serious? Or may we resist unjust attack, by violent means if strictly necessary, to save innocent third parties? Ought we to resist, so as to avoid by our inaction, effectively favoring an unjust aggressor over an innocent bystander? May we resist to save ourselves?

I shall return to such questions, but for now, by alluding to them, what I wish to stress is this. That the debate occurs at all (and has occurred persistently through the centuries) indicates how far the pressures extend toward a love that is universal in scope. Such pressures go back to an informal yet cumulative case for expansion of love outward that we detect in many New Testament and early church writings. Unsystematically but influentially, this expansion calls into question various conventional judgments from that period.

Let us take as examples two conventional judgments that are effectively challenged. The first judgment is this: only those who are friends, coreligionists, members of a specific class, community, state, or empire should receive our time and care. The result can be a ferociously limited other-regard: those within the relations with which we identify are entitled to our regard, while those outside exist (or are treated as though they exist) wholly for the sake of those inside. We may either ignore entirely or do anything whatever to outsiders if this serves to protect or otherwise strengthen our bonds with those inside. The Christian confession that all human beings are included in the range of Jesus' redemptive activity, and that we should ourselves attest to that activity, challenges, over time but at a deep level, any unreserved in-group particularism. The challenge also arises from various accounts of creation in which all persons are held to share in God's image.

The second judgment is this: even when we care about those to whom we are not initially related by ties of blood, class, or other special affiliation, we should limit our affection to those who show themselves prepared to reciprocate in kind. Thus we should demand approximate equivalence in the goods (understood in suitably personal and not only material terms) we give and receive. Sometimes this demand is viewed as the positive counterpart to an equivalence in the evils we suffer and requite. This judgment is also challenged. "For if you love those who love you, what reward have you? Do not even the tax collectors do the same?" (Matthew 5: 46; see also Luke 6: 32-34)* *Agape* then includes unilateral efforts to establish and enhance personal relations marked by closeness and social relations marked by concord. It does not await, anticipate, or demand a response in kind, though it desires and hopes for such a response, and takes actual attainment as the fruition it seeks. It will, moreover, strive for reconciliation that forsakes negative equivalence: "When reviled, we bless; when persecuted we endure, when slandered we try to conciliate" (I Corinthians 4:12b-13). The refusal to make reciprocity a condition for care about another's well-being points likewise toward universal love.

Such pointing does not mean that universal love is commended self-consciously, as express teaching. The enjoinder to expand our

---

*All Scripture references are from the Revised Standard Version.

love is not strictly an insistence that we should love everyone. And we know that many early Christians concentrated on love among those who explicitly shared a confession of faith. Yet to challenge the conventional judgments that I have identified removes two stumbling blocks to commending universal love. Moreover, when we link such challenges with two other injunctions found in the New Testament, the move to commend universal love expressly is an extrapolation that it is natural to make. The first injunction is found at the end of the parable of the Good Samaritan (Luke 10: 29-37): "Go and do likewise." That is, actively help even those who are not members of your community and who have no natural claim on your assistance, for they too are fit recipients of neighbor-love. The second injunction is to "love your enemies and pray for those who persecute you" (Matthew 5: 43). That is, care about those who do not wish you well, who themselves actively dislike or oppress you. You should extend your love to those who refuse to reciprocate, not because they stand outside your circle and pay you no heed, but because the interest they take in you is the most unwelcome of all. They are hostile.

The extrapolation is made in later tradition. That love is universal in scope receives explicit acknowledgment by Jerome and detailed discussion by Augustine. In those centuries two more explicitly theoretical warrants are often cited: a largely Stoic emphasis on the community of reason and a largely Christian emphasis on common Adamic descent.[8] The first is incorporated into a doctrine of creation. We share a common status as distinctive creatures of God. We possess rational powers unique in creation. The status is given. It is not ours to establish or undo. Love for God includes revering this status given by God. The second warrant brings together fall and redemption. We share a common plight as creatures who sin against God. The plight is remedied by God's redemptive acts that occur after creation. We come to know that we have value that is conferred upon us. Whether these acts apply to all human beings is a contested subject in Christian thought. But again, for those who affirm that all human beings are included in the range of Jesus' redemptive activity, love for God includes revering the relational status this activity establishes. In a contemporary statement such as that of the Bishops, the appeals to creation and redemption tend to converge. When the Bishops use the language of dignity that applies without exception to "every person," the warrants they offer stem from both creation and redemption.

From either side, the status is, as it were, God-derived. It is independent of particular merit or other excellences we employ to distinguish and compare persons. Worth is worth, or, dignity is dignity in relation to God. And congruent with this is the insistence that the first great commandment precedes and governs the second, even though the second is "like it." A generalization by Jonathan Edwards attests to such governance: "It is sufficient to render love to any created being virtuous, if it arise from the temper of mind wherein consists a disposition to love God supremely."[9]

1.2. Extension to the self.   This cumulative theocentric case for universal human worth seems to answer a question it is also natural by this time to ask. If all talk of meriting the status is misplaced, why should I exclude myself? It appears that if the status is truly universal, it will include me. Or again, the same expansionist pressures, that challenge both unreserved in-group particularism and the demand for reciprocity in kind, will also extend to me. And the estimate Edwards gives applies *both* to neighbor-love and self-love, provided that neither love turns idolatrous. In brief, we are to love our neighbors and ourselves not as any of us are simply to ourselves but as all of us are finally to God.

Viewed in this light, suppose we accept provisionally that universal love prevents us from excluding ourselves. I want now to consider what normative significance such acceptance has for human action and interaction, as we attest, on our own level and with our own capacities, to the inclusive love God discloses in creation and redemption. In the next subsection, I begin with a judgment that takes what seems the least circuitous path, from excluding no one to considering neighbor and self alike.

2. DOES UNIVERSAL LOVE LEAD TO IMPARTIALITY?

2.1. From universal scope to impartial appraisal.   The path I have in mind goes from universal love to impartiality. Claims made along the way run roughly as follows. (a) Two beliefs within a theocentric frame especially ground the judgment that the dignity of every person includes neighbor and self. First, to say that we share a status as distinctive creatures, a status independent of particular merit or other excellences that differentiate us from each other, is to say that the dignity attached to this status is already there. It is not producible—I do not produce it in my neighbor's case, and my neighbor does not produce it in my case. Second, to say that dignity is dignity in relation to God is traditionally linked to a conviction that God is our *Summum Bonum*. To forge this link means that we know something about each person's good, and what we know cannot be only about the neighbor's good. It must be about one's own good as well. (b) We should then endeavor to include fully both neighbor and self in the judgments that we formulate to protect and promote such dignity. (c) To include both fully is to include both equally. We should accord equal dignity or equal worth to the neighbor as a human being and to the self as a human being. At least insofar as "neighbor-love" and "self-love" *mean* the protection and promotion of such dignity, the normative weight they carry is equivalent. The neighbor's well-being and the self's well-being are equally worthy of protection and promotion. For no one of us objectively—as a subject with dignity already there, as a subject of providential action—matters more than anyone else. Put positively, one person's well-being is as valuable as another's. (d) We should adopt a general strategy of disallowing disparities between neighbor and self. Again, put positively, we should appraise impartially the neighbor's well-being and the self's well-being.

These claims do not follow one another in any strictly deductive order of dependence. But they hang together intelligibly enough to repay close examination. It is the last claim about impartial appraisal that especially concerns me. To be even entertained as acceptable, the claim must rest on two beliefs about the dignity of every person. First, such dignity authorizes us sometimes to distinguish between equal consideration and equivalent treatment. The needs people have, for example, may differ, and we honor rather than violate the dignity in question when we treat others or ourselves differently in order to meet varying needs. We may then similarly distinguish between impartial appraisal and impartial treatment. Second, such dignity at other times requires us to conjoin equal consideration and equivalent treatment. Frequently our basic needs at least do not differ. Impartiality plays a crucial role, as we will see, in compelling us to recognize that unless morally relevant differences exist between people, it is correct to charge us with inconsistency or arbitrariness when we treat them differently. In such cases we can readily conjoin impartial appraisal and impartial treatment. Yet the affirmation of dignity gives normative content to impartial appraisal that such impartiality does not otherwise necessarily have. For the affirmation leads us to evaluate all persons positively, to appraise each person as irreducibly valuable. And this evaluation may seem to us vacuous apart from certain treatments that are always demanded or forbidden in all human interaction. That is, we bring specific estimates of what we should always or never do to people when we believe that they have worth. We may disagree about particular estimates. We may wish to revise some of those we inherit. But we do not disagree that estimates of this kind are appropriate. The estimates center on noncomparative attention to what treatments every person's dignity requires and prohibits. It is on these estimates that impartiality must rest if we are to entertain it as acceptable. We then avoid the standard complaint that to be impartial or fair, treating like cases alike, allows us to do nothing positive whatever, or to do what is injurious, provided we practice consistency. One of coach Vincent Lombardi's football players is alleged to have said of him: "He treated us all the same. Like dogs." Similarly, no comparative unfairness exists if a legal system denies a defense attorney to everyone.[10] The impartialty with which we are concerned is closer to substantive fairness. In the parlance of constitutional theory, it requires substantive due process, not merely procedural due process. Consequently, it is not subject to the charge that it permits inhumaneness or indifference, so long as it is uniformly followed.

To foreclose this charge allows the claim about impartial appraisal to place a definite proposal before us about the relation between self and others. We can begin to see what the proposal is by noting that many modern philosophers take the move from universalism to impartiality to be correct in essential respects. For example, various utilitarians and neo-Kantians agree in this. Their accounts of morality are requisitely universal in scope. Indeed, in the case of utilitarianism, the constituency of morality includes but may not be restricted to all human beings. It may extend to all creatures capable of suffering. Such accounts remain distinct, to be sure, from theocentrically grounded universal love. For one thing, the moral judgments they offer are universal in their reach, but they deliberately omit all references to God. Moreover, utilitarians and neo-Kantians differ importantly among themselves, and this is a further fact we must not ignore. We should nonetheless take note of a point on which they firmly agree: they commend impartiality between self and others in human interaction. So R. M. Hare argues that we should be

> impartial between our own and other people's preferences, not altruistic in its correct sense of giving *more* weight to the preferences of others. We have to treat everybody as one, including ourselves: to do unto others *as* we wish they should do to us . . . and love our neighbours *as* (not more than) ourselves. We get no extra weight for our own preferences because we are doing the moral thinking, but they get equal weight with those of others in so far as we are affected parties.[11]

Alan Gewirth also maintains:

The agent must . . . be impartial as between himself and other persons when the latter's freedom and well-being are at stake, so that he ought to respect their freedom and well-being as well as his own. . . . The equality required . . . runs in both directions. It does not require that an agent surrender his own freedom or well-being for the sake of his recipients. They have a right to a parity of generic goods with him but not to a disparity in their favor any more than in his own.[12]

Again, I shall bracket various internal points of controversy that surface in these statements, e.g., that Hare appeals to preferences whereas Gewirth appeals to freedom and well-being, that Gewirth invokes a *right* to generic goods, and so on. My interest now centers on their mutual adherence to impartiality between self and others. An altruism that gives more weight to others than to the self is thereby disallowed, as Hare indicates; any disparity in favor of others is not required, as Gewirth insists.

These two quotations summarize the claim about neighbor and self that impartiality mandates. It is a no-nonsense claim, quickly made but seriously plausible. It bears on our inquiry as follows. We should commend in our neighbor's case and in our own whatever attitudes and actions we judge the law of love to require, extol, permit, and forbid. Neighbor and self alike should be subjects of attention and care. We should not require that we give more weight to the neighbor's well-being as altruism does. Or at a minimum, we should always permit parity between neighbor and self.

2.2. *An informal alliance.* To address this claim, we must first say more about impartiality. In modern discussions, impartiality is not one determinate view, but a class of views. What unites them as a class is that they commonly stress the requirement of universalizability or interpersonal consistency. Any action or trait of character that I judge to be right for one person I must judge to be right for any similar person similarly circumstanced. There should be "similar treatment for similar cases," again assuming that all persons are positively valued.

This appeal to consistency traditionally possesses normative force without our having to incorporate it into any particular ethical theory. It appears frequently as a "role-reversal test" exemplified in the golden rule. Even critics of impartiality like Bernard Williams acknowledge that the role-reversal test "is a basic item of ethical thinking."[13] It is employed in a theoretically unambitious way by biblical writers to condemn self-partiality above all.[14] Consider Nathan's reproof of David (2 Samuel 11-12). David recognizes that he has done something evil—when he sends Uriah to certain death in battle so that he can marry Uriah's wife—only after he condemns a similar action in another case that Nathan puts to him. Similarly, a prophet like Amos (2:6; 3:1-2; 7:7; 9:7) "gains the attention of his audience by pronouncing a judgment on the crimes of neighboring nations, a judgment to which his hearers doubtless gladly assent. Thereupon he turns upon the Israelites, requiring them to judge themselves by the same standard that they use in judging others."[15] And Paul finds that one is condemned by the very same judgments one pronounces on others. "Therefore you have no excuse, O man, whoever you are, when you judge another; for in passing judgment upon him you condemn yourself, because you, the judge, are doing the very same things" (Rom. 2:1).

We are frequently advised to associate appeals to impartiality as interpersonal consistency with general appeals to justice, fairness, even-handedness, and indeed to the second love command itself. For these various appeals often do similar normative work in their everyday employments. This work has three closely related aims. First, it supplies a reason to object when *anyone* makes an arbitrary exception on his or her own behalf, the neighbor or the nation as well as the self. Second, insofar as I am disposed toward greater partiality to myself than to my neighbor for no good (i.e., impersonally specifiable) reason, it provides a vantage point for identifying *this* disposition especially. We should notice that all of the biblical cases cited above are directed against this sort of partiality. In short, the work typically serves to foster self-criticism. Third, I am thereby encouraged to view myself with greater objectivity. "In a sense, the requirement is that you love your neighbor as yourself: but only as much as you love yourself when you look at yourself from outside, with fair detachment."[16] To strive to achieve fair detachment is often itself a "work of love."

Those within the Christian tradition employ such appeals routinely to make normative judgments. The appeals are not simply imposed from outside. We find a broad but important alliance therefore between the second love command and a theoretically unambitious sense of impartiality as interpersonal consistency. Neither the neighbor nor the self is excluded from normative consideration, though critical attention focuses on self-partiality. So far, this is compatible with universal love. Yet the alliance is a rough and ready affair, however significant it proves to be in practice. We still must consider rigorous versions of the claim that impartiality is the most plausible way to construe our love of others and of ourselves. This requires that we examine how, in modern discussion, impartiality is incorporated into positive ethical theories.

2.3. Modern interpretations of impartiality. Let us see then how impartiality acquires more technical meanings in modern moral philosophy. I shall consider the two meanings associated with the two defenses of impartiality already mentioned. The first is linked with utilitarianism; the second stands closer to Kantian conceptions and often issues in some species of contractualism. As we have noted, both give the self equal weight with others under the terms set by impartial moral deliberation.

Hare subscribes to the formula which utilitarians made famous: we ought to count ourselves as one but no more than one, and never accord ourselves a privileged position. The counting he elucidates in terms of the agent's imaginative identification with other people's preferences. I as an agent should consider what I would prefer if I were in the position of another (with another's desires and aims) as well as what it would be like if I were the other person affected.

The utilitarian account of impartiality grows distinctive and controversial at three points that concern us most directly.

First, imaginative identification, when it is ideally complete, involves the agent imagining that he or she would be *all* the people affected by a given action. The preferences of others should stand equally close to the agent as his or her own. "Equally close" means here that the agent should actually acquire the preferences of others; they are all to be felt by, so to say, taking them into oneself. Such absorptive identification is like that kind of Ideal Observer theory which "postulates one omniscient, impartial, and benevolent observer—he might be called the World Agent—who acquires everybody's preferences and puts them all together."[17] An identifying observer of this kind differs from a detached observer who imagines that he or she is *none* of the persons affected by a given action, but who surveys them all dispassionately, from outside. Both the identifying observer and the detached observer are customarily distinguished in turn from that figure in contractarian thought (exemplified by John Rawls) who is both agent and recipient and who imagines he or she is *one* of the people doing the identifying, but does not know whom.[18]

Second, utilitarianism that involves absorptive identification motivated by benevolence is linked to a doctrine of negative responsibility. Negative responsibility holds that "I must be just as responsible for things that I allow or fail to prevent, as I am for things that I myself . . . bring about."[19] Stringent demands are placed on agents actively to promote welfare overall, and not simply to refrain from diminishing it. Only human finitude unambiguously limits these demands. Williams contends that negative responsibility at the hands of utilitarianism takes impartiality to an extreme point. Impartiality now means that no relevant difference remains between whether I bring about the changes that produce the most welfare or whether someone else does. What matters is the outcome itself. And here utilitarianism's well-known commitment to consequentialism comes into play. Supreme value is assigned to whatever states of affairs optimize welfare. Utilitarian impartiality "abstracts from the identity of the agent, leaving just a locus of causal intervention in the world...."[20]

Third, the absence of definite boundaries between the demands on oneself and the demands on others means that the decisions any given agent makes are indeterminately affected by the decisions of others. And one's own decisions are constantly subject to change, depending on changes in the total causal nexus. For it is the actual state of the nexus itself that constitutes the criterion of moral evaluation. To be impartial is to assess continuously the actual state of the nexus, and to determine one's own choices accordingly. Critics of utilitarianism find that this criterion alienates the agent from his or her own actions and convictions. One's personal integrity is jeopardized.[21]

A second defense of impartiality displays Kantian ancestry and often draws on the idea of a contract. Its concern is to locate principles and rules that are impartially acceptable among persons who stand related to one another at one and the same time as agents and as recipients. For the principles now in question it is assumed that all are concerned to reach agreement. What is needed are principles no one who is reasonable can reject. The agreements reached must be informed, uncoerced, and general.[22] They require equal relations among all the parties, between oneself and others, and among others. In order to meet this requirement, some thinkers like Rawls construct reflective agreement behind a "veil of ignorance." Our agreement must precede knowing precisely how we will personally fare. It is rational when we all subscribe to principles formulated to ensure that our prospects of being *anyone* in the outcome are equal. However, the principles to which we subscribe need not include benevolence; and they exclude altruism. As for the conditions in which we subscribe to the principles, Rawls thinks that to combine "mutual disinterest and the veil of ignorance" is simpler and clearer than the alternative of "benevolence plus knowledge," but that it achieves the same purpose. It "forces each person to take the good of others into account."[23]

Yet neo-Kantian attempts to force each person to take the good of others into account are typically held to honor the separateness of persons in a way utilitarianism does not. So "the idea of the contractual element, even between these shadowy and abstract participants, is in part to make the point that there are limitations built in at the bottom to permissible trade-offs between the satisfactions of individuals."[24] What matters at a basic level are actions and policies, and not only the outcome itself. Such actions and policies serve as fundamental moral constraints whose aim is to give each person's interests equal weight. Because the contract depends on the agreement of all persons, it does not assign supreme value to whatever actual states of affairs optimize welfare. It avoids what David A. J. Richards takes as a consequence of utilitarianism's focus on the state of the total causal nexus, "viz. sacrificing the satisfaction of certain persons' basic wants in order to advance other persons' desires more, or refusing to satisfy certain persons' desires at all in order better to advance the desire of other persons later on...."[25]

The utilitarian and neo-Kantian construals show how impartiality is nuanced in accordance with particular ethical theories. What impartiality means is affected by the distinctive features of the systems which incorporate it. This is no less true with the meanings it can be given within Christianity, though Christian ethics is not a system in a comparable sense. Certainly one can learn from the points I located within these construals whether or not one subscribes to them. I shall return to such points in the subsections ahead.

It is time now to complicate the account so far given. I shall distinguish different kinds of objections to the move from universal love to impartiality. I do this by exploring four possible asymmetries between one's relation to one's neighbor and one's relation to oneself.

Section Two
Four Asymmetries Between One's Relation to One's Neighbor and One's Relation to Oneself

3. IS IMPARTIALITY A GOAL I SHOULD STRIVE TO ATTAIN?

Two objections find impartiality to be deficient because it authorizes too much attention to the self's own well-being. The first of these is predominantly normative. Impartiality fails to accommodate the characteristic Christian stress on self-denial and cross-bearing, on a love that goes the second mile and turns the other cheek. To weigh the good of neighbors equally with one's own may prove demanding to be sure. But it is less demanding than altruistic dedication to the good of others. And the latter dedication is the kind of normative aysmmetry proposed.

3.1. Two judgments: a fifty-fifty division rejected; and a self-other, other-other distinction accepted. From the vantage point of this first normative asymmetry, *agape* is distinguished by its partiality toward the neighbor. Paul Ramsey writes:

> [Henry] Sidgwick nevertheless defined "justice as treating similar cases similarly." ... Nothing could be clearer than that Christian ethics must judge quite insufficient such fifty-fifty division of the ground between a man and his neighbor.... The meaning of Christian love may be stated in sharp opposition to Sidgwick: It means "treating similar cases *dissimilarly*," regarding the good of any other individual as *more* than your own," when he and you alone are involved.... Without entering further into the idea of justice so important for social ethics, it should be clear that just as any who are "but men" are apt to exercise partiality when judging their *own* cause, so Christian love (which is self-love inverted) judges with partiality the *neighbor's* cause, treats his own case as exceedingly dissimilar from one's own.[26]

This passage identifies two judgments shared by proponents of the normative asymmetry (we may call them Christian altruists, and focus on Ramsey as their representative).

First, they contrast neighbor-love with a "fifty-fifty division of the ground between a man and his neighbor." The latter they associate with impartiality. In general they take impartiality to demand that I love myself exactly as I love my neighbor. And more specifically they take this demand to issue in at least one of two strategies. (a) I endorse a comprehensive tit-for-tat, where I correlate in a strict way carefully calculated risks and sacrifices with probable benefits and rewards. (b) I endorse a stipulation Alan Donagan enunciates: "One does not fail to respect another as a rational creature by declining to procure a good for him, if that good can be procured only by relinquishing an equal or greater good for oneself."[27] Whatever good I procure for another is then ruled by the stipulation, without disproportionate inconvenience to me. Both strategies are judged inadequate in a tradition whose canonical writings include the parable of the Good Samaritan, the account of Jesus washing the feet of his disciples, the injunction to love your enemy, the teaching that love does not insist on its own way, Paul's instruction to "let no one seek his own good, but the good of his neighbor" (I Corinthians 10:24), and the cross itself as the paradigm of Christian existence. *Agape* will seek to transcend the calculating quality that a comprehensive tit-for-tat legitimates. And it will foster a riskier strategy where one's own good is concerned than a stipulation about proportionate convenience mandates.

Second, altruists such as Ramsey also argue that my neighbor should often be viewed from two discrete vantage points. The first is self-other. That is, I view the well-being of a single neighbor *vis-à-vis* my own well-being. The second is other-other (a more accurate but too cumbersome reference for this is "self-other-others"). Here I view the well-being of a single neighbor *vis-à-vis* the well-being of another or other neighbors. We should distinguish the situation where my neighbor and I alone are involved (a bilateral one) from the situation where third parties are involved (a multilateral one), because the actions that count as *agapeic* may well diverge in respect to each. Historically, this divergence seems to focus above all on resistance to evil. Ramsey holds that what I ought to do to resist "an onrushing enemy or an assassin lying in wait" (Augustine's examples) who poses a threat to my life differs from what I ought to do when such an enemy or assassin poses a threat to the life of a third innocent party.

In the other-other situation, I view both the enemy or assassin and the innocent party as indisputably my neighbors. But if I do nothing the one innocent neighbor may be fatally affected by the unprovoked aggression (we may suppose) of another neighbor. Is it more loving to intervene on behalf of the innocent neighbor? Ramsey in continuity with a major segment of the Christian tradition answers affirmatively. The answer in favor of intervention to protect the innocent often broadens into acceptance of responsibility for the well-being of the social order overall. Such responsibility includes support of constraints, including force, even deadly force, and provision of public defense against armed, unjust aggression. This answer does not by any means yield a ready acceptance of killing. I should acknowledge that the aggressor remains my neighbor by doing only what is strictly necessary to prevent the aggression. My aim is to incapacitate, and often this stops feasibly short of any serious injury. Tear gas is better than bullets. Yet in a self-other situation, I should not similarly resist on my own behalf. Ambrose summarizes the case for rejecting private self-defense by insisting that

> [the wise person] when he meets an armed robber . . . cannot return his blows, lest in defending his life he should stain his love toward his neighbor. The verdict on this is plain and clear in the books of the Gospel. . . . What robber is more hateful than the

persecutor who came to kill Christ? But Christ would not be defended by the wounds of the persecutor, for He willed to heal all by his wounds."[28]

Ramsey here sides with Ambrose. He laments Aquinas' greater allowance of self-defense. He insists however that Aquinas continues importantly to recognize the assailant as a neighbor by formulating what later is called the rule of double effect.[29]

Both judgments—the rejection of a fifty-fifty division, and the acceptance of a self-other, other-other distinction—merit detailed scrutiny. To attempt to provide it, I offer two kinds of comparison. The first is between the Christian altruism sketched so far and nuanced secular accounts of impartiality. The second is between such altruism and another distinct segment of the Christian tradition. These comparisons will enhance our understanding of the first normative asymmetry and of impartiality.

3.2. *Christian altruists and secular impartialists.* We noticed that altruists take impartiality to demand that I love myself exactly as I love my neighbor. The two strategies in which they take this demand to issue disallow *any* disparity between self and others.

I think it indeed makes sense to claim that these two strategies—a comprehensive tit-for-tat and a stipulation that all assistance to others must be limited to actions involving no disproportionate inconvenience to oneself—cannot be harmonized with other-regarding elements in *agape*. Yet I also think we find in nuanced accounts of impartiality room for normative maneuver that is wider than the account of impartiality so far given suggests. The two strategies identified under the first judgment fail to exhaust the range of possibilities for which nuanced accounts of impartiality allow. Any contention that impartiality *must* involve a kind of calculating tit-for-tat, for example, is simply incorrect. Certainly we cannot reduce the role-reversal test to such calculation. Moreover, the stipulation about no disproportionate inconvenience does not mean that impartialists must forbid dissimilar treatment that positively promotes the neighbor's well-being, provided that I as an agent consent to undertake it.

This last point is illumined when we consider the assessment of so-called works of supererogation usually offered in impartialist accounts. For the assessment is positive. It thereby qualifies any stipulation about no disproportionate inconvenience. Gewirth for instance denies that impartiality renders the saint's or hero's supererogatory principle inconsistent. "When a person performs heroic actions. . ., he consents to these deprivations of his life and liberty, so that they are not cases of his acting in violation of his own generic rights."[30] Such self-sacrifice is "an act of grace" on the agent's part, and so not a strict duty. But it is not censurable as an act of generic inconsistency. Instead, it is seen as laudable. Once again we observe how many proponents of impartiality are concerned above all to prevent the agent from making an inconsistent exception *in his or her own favor*. Christian interpreters of the law of love or *agape* share this concern, as I have argued.

Impartialists often reason then about supererogation roughly as follows. Impartiality *permits* dissimilar treatment on the neighbor's behalf and in fact regards it as praiseworthy. However, impartiality still does not *require* such dissimilar treatment. To be sure, impartiality requires that the agent give "reasonable assistance" to someone exposed to (say) perilous physical harm. The requirement is seriously meant. It also specifies conditions such as need, proximity, capability, and last resort.[31] Yet to require acts of grace on every agent's part is unfitting. For a requirement warrants reproach from *others* when one fails to meet it. But to refrain from acts of grace is not a fit subject of reproach from others. One can choose not to perform such acts and incur no blame. One may reproach *oneself* for failure, but that is all.

To draw a line between what is a fit subject for interpersonal reproach and what is not proves difficult in practice. For many persons and in many cases, the matter is endlessly disputed. Even certain proponents of impartiality are prepared to ask, for example, why the type of sacrifice that displays supererogatory virtue we rightly find so laudable should remain "optional." Why not require it? They finally defend its optional status because the claims of impartial morality ideally conceived must undergo relaxation. Human nature normally has limits that it is better to tolerate than to denounce as wrong. Toleration is the price we pay to make moral claims "motivationally effective." Such claims do not exhaust what persons care about.[32] Moreover, less demanding requirements than those Mother Teresa, for instance, follows achieve the greatest utility because their widespread inculcation is more likely.[33] Given the normal limits of human nature, we then content ourselves with saying that I as an agent am free to relinquish my claims if I so choose for the sake of genuine benefits to the neighbor.

In short, our findings about the first judgment lead us to conclude that not all accounts of impartiality demand that I love myself exactly as I love my neighbor. These findings reduce the range of clear disagreements between a nuanced account of impartiality and the normative asymmetry under review. How far the reduction extends remains uncertainty, however, until we consider the second judgment altruists make, namely, that we should distinguish self-other and other-other relations. And about this judgment, complexities abound. I think we must disentangle the following questions.

(a) Let us ask first about supererogation. We saw that the positive assessment of supererogation impartialists give provides more normative latitude for promoting the good of the neighbor than critics of impartiality assume. This positive assessment likewise furnishes one reason to distinguish self-other and other-other relations. But it is not a reason on which altruists depend when they themselves make the distinction. To clarify what is at stake requires us to consider the place supererogation occupies in Christian ethics. No single answer will do. For Christian assessments of supererogation reveal a complicated history of their own. Rival verdicts surface. The position altruists take must be identified as we go.

The simplest way to proceed is to return to the defense of supererogation that impartialists allow and to compare this defense with rival Christian verdicts. Secular defenders of supererogation permit disparities between self and others that promote the good of other people and that rest on agent-consent. One such defender, David Heyd, cites as typical cases of supererogation actions that are saintly and heroic (e.g., martyrdom, the sacrifice of one's life to secure one's friends' survival), that are charitable, generous, and giving, that show kindness and consideration, that display forgiveness, mercy, and pardon, and that involve volunteering.[34] These cases he finds intelligible only when we refuse to reduce the supererogatory to the obligatory. But Heyd also argues that supererogation and duty remain logically interdependent. Two features characterize this interdependence. *Correlativity* "means that acts of supererogation derive their special value from their being 'more than duty requires'; i.e., they have meaning only relatively to obligatory action."[35] *Continuity* means that a supererogatory action "has to be *morally* good, its value being of the same *type* that makes obligatory action good and valuable."[36] The feature of continuity excludes from the category of supererogation those Nietzschean personal ideals and aesthetic values that are non-obligatory and non-moral. Finally, the accent falls, as we saw, on agent-allowance. The disparity is only not forbidden. It is not required. That supererogatory actions are left open to the discretion of agents in a way obligations are not implies that I as an agent possess some wider latitude over my own actions than I possess over the actions of others. What such latitude implies in turn is that while I can relate to others as one who (let us assume) performs supererogatory actions, I lose the liberty to relate *in the same way* in other-other relations. When I consider relations that my neighbors have with each other, I more suitably confine my evaluations and expectations within the boundaries of the obligatory.

Cases doubtless recur within the Christian tradition that resemble the one endorsed by secular defenders where supererogation and duty remain both distinct and interdependent, a point to which I shall return. Yet two considerations dispose many in the tradition to draw back from the sort of defense of supererogation that impartialists allow.

First, for Christians to be neighbors in the fashion of the Good Samaritan assuredly means that we are to promote good and not simply refrain from diminishing it. Among Protestants especially we sometimes encounter a sense of infinite liability.[37] No specified limits constrain what we are to do on behalf of others. Does this mean that to promote good is not at the discretion of the agent in the way secular defenders assume? Is such promotion required? For many it is required. Hospitals must be built, prisoners visited and preached to, the hungry fed and the homeless sheltered, orphans reared, and so on. To attend to such matters cannot be consigned to the realm of optional ideals. All in the Christian community are enjoined to attend; and interpersonal reproach for failure to attend is fitting.

Second, I said that Christian assessments of supererogation reveal a complicated history of their own. It is noteworthy that "historically speaking, Christian theology is the origin both of the concept and of the formulation of . . . supererogation."[38] Yet concern tended to concentrate not simply on the promotion of good for other people, but on the specified end of the *agent's* salvation. Aquinas, for instance, distinguishes precepts and counsels in this way: "a commandment implies obligation, whereas a counsel is left open to the option of the one to whom it is given."[39] Secular defenders of the doctrine can follow him this far. He goes on, however, to write: "the commandments [are] about matters that are necessary to gain the end of eternal bliss. . ., the counsels are about matters that render the gaining of this end more assured and expeditious."[40] The counsels also have to do with the agent's perfection, where one's attention to God is undivided, one is preoccupied totally with God. Here the counsels "are supererogatory, because although necessary to perfection, they are superfluous for salvation."[41] In this latter case, of "evangelical counsels" in particular, all persons find them expedient, but not all are effectively inclined to perform them. Some people are ill-disposed (and blamelessly so) to observe, e.g., the counsels of perpetual poverty and perpetual virginity.[42] The Protestant Reformers denounce supererogation as (in John Calvin's words) "patched together out of terrible sacrileges and blasphemies. . . ."[43] And the Anglican authors of The Thirty-Nine Articles similarly repudiate any claim that there can be "voluntary works besides, over and above God's commandments."[44] Such a claim is held to foster arrogance and impiety. When one has done all that is commanded, one still remains an unprofitable servant (Luke 17:10).

Both considerations help explain the paucity of notice that supererogation receives from altruists. Dedication to the good of others is required. As for specifically theological debates, Ramsey refers favorably to Martin Luther's opposition to "counsels of perfection."[45] Any doctrine appears suspect that focuses on the agent's performance as an ingredient in one's own life of salvation and/or perfection. A third consideration operates as well. Ramsey shows no interest comparable to secular defenders of supererogation in the promotion of good as the context in which to distinguish self-other and other-other relations. His examples to which we referred earlier take *resistance to evil* as the context in which such a distinction arises.

(b) Let us ask next therefore about the reasons altruists have for making the distinction between self-other and other-other relations in the context of resistance to evil. Since supererogation is a reason they do not appropriate, we have not so far further reduced the range of disagreement between impartialists and altruists. And as we will see, we come now to the place where their respective normative verdicts clash most centrally.

According to altruists, why in a self-other situation should I not resist on my own behalf? One reason Ambrose identifies. "Christ would not be defended by the wounds of the persecutor." If I am to imitate Christ, I cannot defend my life by returning the blows an armed robber inflicts upon me. Another reason may be extracted from the first quotation from Ramsey. He observes that because persons are instinctively apt to exercise partiality when judging their own cause, we should judge with partiality the neighbor's cause. I take it that this means that I am to lean against the likelihood of self-deception when I judge my own cause in a self-other situation by giving the other the preference. Perhaps the armed robber has legitimate grievances. Perhaps I am less innocent than I presume to be. Perhaps my manner constituted a provocation. The first reason evokes debates within the tradition about what imitation of Christ means, and indeed whether we should follow him at a distance rather than imitate him directly.[46] The second reason is formidable in its own right. I shall have more to say about it when I consider the first descriptive asymmetry, the second on our list.

When secular impartialists turn from the self's promotion of good to the self's resistance to evil, the normative room they permit shrinks markedly. They allow or even require me in a self-other situation to resist on my own behalf. In self-other relations this turn alters our attention from what the self may do *qua* agent to what the self may do *qua* recipient. Again, often we cannot divide these respective points of attention precisely. But we need to retain a distinction. The reason, as Thomas Nagel puts it, is this. "Moral principles don't simply tell victims what they may and may not do. They also tell victims what sort of treatment they may and may not object to, resist, or demand."[47] What then does impartiality tell victims? In short, can impartiality also accommodate a love that turns the other cheek?

The self who promotes good, it is assumed, acts freely or voluntarily, on his or her own initiative, to further the well-being of the neighbor. The self who turns the other cheek, it is also assumed, acts as a recipient. Though a recipient certainly *elects* not to resist, he or she responds nevertheless to an action *initiated* by the neighbor. Gewirth takes the condition of being a recipient to justify in certain circumstances suspending a general prohibition against killing and other harms, a prohibition which his account of impartiality otherwise upholds. The circumstances of self-defense are again the obvious case in point. Suppose I am physically assaulted by my neighbor. This assault is judged to be morally wrong. If I defend myself by physically assaulting this same neighbor, my defensive response is judged not to be similarly wrong, if my response is "directly an attempt not to inflict a basic harm, but rather to prevent such an infliction or to restore an equilibrium of mutual nonharm. . . ."[48] To prevent an infliction is not on a par with the infliction itself. I may use means of prevention that are as severe as the harm my neighbor tries to inflict. These means may include killing, although only when there is no other way to make the prevention succeed. Is my response one that impartiality requires or only allows? Gewirth often says "may" and "permits." Yet in circumstances of self-defense he adds "may even require."[49]

In self-other relations where the self is a recipient we find then normative verdicts that simply clash. At the very least, impartialists allow responses that altruists disallow. This latter judgment by no means completes the range of verdicts widely accepted in the tradition. The Bishops, for example, remind their readers that the Second Vatican Council continues to preserve the individual's fundamental right of defense.[50] My main point here is that nuanced accounts of impartiality challenge if not reject the injunction to turn the other cheek.

(c) Let us ask finally about other-other relations. We noted earlier that in the case of one innocent neighbor threatened by the unprovoked aggression of another neighbor, Ramsey thinks it is more loving to intervene on behalf of the innocent than to practice nonresistance. Two warrants he finds are these. (i) He believes the imitation of Christ continues. "When it was a question of injustice done to persons other than himself. . ., Jesus did not remain at his ease lifting up their faces to additional blows or supporting by silence their compulsion to go the second mile."[51] Ramsey proceeds to define justice "as what Christian love does when confronted with two or more neighbors."[52] And the change from pacifism generally practiced in the early church to later Christian participation in armed conflict is not degeneration. We need not take the church's accommodation to Constantine's empire as a fall from moral purity. "[U]nderneath the obvious reversal of tactic, the general strategy of Christian love continued without abatement and without any alteration in its fundamental nature."[53] (ii) Ramsey also reiterates that one can be more "impartial and clear-headed about justice" in other-other or multilateral relations than when one judges in one's own case.[54]

It thus appears that in contrast to self-other relations where normative judgments diverge, in other-other relations impartialists and altruists often agree. To bring love and justice together in other-other situations the way altruists do leads to normative verdicts that can overlap with the ones proponents of impartiality advance. Important disputes clearly remain. Ramsey maintains on occasion that one should "insist with utter severity" in other-other relations that "what is due to others is never simply just payment but full forgiveness. . . ."[55] To require forgiveness in this way removes an element of agent-discretion on which, as we saw, a theory of supererogation insists. Ramsey also defends non-combatants from direct and intentional attack without exception. Such absolute immunity is not something that utilitarians at least are prepared to grant.[56] Absolutists, however, who defend the normative asymmetry between neighbor-love and self-love demonstrate that in other-other relations altruists may seek to distinguish the shedding of blood from the shedding of innocent blood, even if they unconditionally prohibit the latter.

The case that altruists make for distinguishing self-other and other-other relations is subject to contrary pressures. From the one side, secular impartialists wish to allow or even require the self to resist evil in self-other as well as other-other situations. From the other side, certain Christians wish to require non-resistance (or entirely nonviolent resistance) to evil, in other-other as well as self-other relations. In 3.2., we have rehearsed debates from the first side. We now turn to the second.

3.3. Christian altruists and the historic peace churches. Another sort of comparison with altruism comes from a discrete segment of the Christian tradition. The "historic peace churches," such as the Mennonites, the Hutterites, the Quakers, and the Brethren, and their modern proponents and interpreters (e.g., John Howard Yoder and Stanley Hauerwas), extend the normative verdict that Ambrose renders in self-other relations to other-other relations as well.[57] Both churches and individual proponents vary in what they emphasize. I shall refer mainly to Yoder, but acknowledge that his views are not identical to those that Quakers and the Brethren espouse, for example. The peace churches characteristically stress nonviolence as an essential ingredient in any way of life that purports to be Christian. For them, any acceptable depiction of *agape* must incorporate nonviolence.

Let us proceed as before by comparing answers to the two judgments altruists make. The first judgment assumes that impartiality means the absence of disparity between self and others. Those in the peace churches certainly join altruists in opposing the two particular strategies in which this judgment is thought to issue. Yet we saw that nuanced accounts of impartiality also need not support these two strategies. What complicates matters now is that those in the peace churches commend, in effect, an absence of normative disparity between self and others, at least when confronting questions of nonviolence. On such questions they seem to put forward their own version of impartiality. How this is so will become clearer if we turn to the second judgment that altruists make: the distinction between self-other and other-other relations. I shall consider the same three questions about this distinction that I disentangled in 3.2.

(a) Let us then first consider supererogation. That secular impartialists assess it positively furnishes one reason to support a distinction between self-other and other-other relations. We noted that their assessment permits disparities between self and others that promote the good of other people and that rest on agent-consent. Those in the peace churches extol the promotion of good and agent-consent, but not in a way that permits similar disparities. We can summarize their views as follows.

Agent-consent finds favor chiefly as part of an insistence that the church is a voluntary community. In short, the values of the free church tradition predominate. Unlike the civil society whose membership is generally involuntary, membership in the church should be genuinely voluntary. People must consent to communal authority and freely participate in communal life. They must also be able to leave the community freely. No one *has* to be a believer. Yet a condition of uniform stringency applies to those who voluntarily commit themselves to membership in the church and who remain in the community. Nonviolence is affirmed as constitutive of a common way of life. Those within are to hold this affirmation in concert. To take up the sword for any reason is seen as faithless, a defection from the only pattern accepted as authoritative.

Supererogation plays no acknowledged part in this way of life then, at least with respect to nonviolence. No distinction is drawn between what is required and censurable when unmet, and what is permitted and praised when performed. Rather, as Yoder maintains, "every member of the body of Christ is called to absolute non-resistance."[58] Thus, as a member, my adherence to this calling is a fit subject of interpersonal praise and blame in accordance with standards binding on the entire community. And similarly, the manner of life of the brother or sister *is* my business.[59] Reproach for failure is appropriate whether one is on the giving or receiving end. In the sense of mutual reproof and discipline, no normative asymmetry obtains between my relation to my neighbor and my relation to myself.

(b) It follows that in self-other situations I should not resist on my own behalf. The reason Ambrose identifies—that Christ would not be defended by the wounds of the persecutor—is right. He is right also to believe that I should imitate Christ. Those in the peace churches see in this imitation, however, a pattern binding on the entire community. The pattern collapses a morally relevant distinction between self-other and other-other situations. They endorse instead a distinction between church and world. Nonviolence applies in an equally binding way to oneself and to others, within the community of faith. Thus, believers err when they "try to preach a kind of ethics which will work for non-Christians as well as Christians."[60] Those outside the community may consistently endorse and live in terms of "the police function of the state," for this function coincides with the biblical view of the state as comprising realistic arrangements under the "old aeon."[61] But those inside the community should live by what is "specifically Christian," and so by the terms of the "new aeon."

(c) Christian altruists like Ramsey go wrong when they hold that in other-other situations it is more loving to intervene on behalf of the innocent than to practice non-resistance. Those in the peace churches see as flawed exegesis Ramsey's effort to justify such intervention by continuing to appeal directly to the imitation of Christ. For example, Jesus rebukes his disciple for wielding the sword on Jesus' behalf (Matthew 26: 51-54; Luke 22: 49-51; John 18:10-11). This rebuke is taken as part of the pattern for all who follow Jesus, and not as Jesus' own honoring of the difference between what he allows to be done to himself and to persons other than himself. They assume that Jesus would have said nothing essentially dissimilar if the disciple had been betrayed and unjustly arrested. They also assume that the teachings of the Sermon on the Mount bind all of his followers.[62]

If the actions that count as *agapeic* do not diverge in respect to self-other and other-other vantage points, and if nonviolence is always *agapeic* (again, for all those within the community of faith), believers should not try to distinguish between the shedding of blood and the shedding of innocent blood. This conclusion applies to those other-other relations that comprise the church's proper engagements with the world. In general, believers should not permit those outside the community to alter the community's own commitments. Neighbor-love, whether inside or outside the community, should not find expression in actions that violate the community's nonviolent way of life. The actions judged to be in violation include interventions on behalf of innocent third parties. So even when a neighbor outside is attacked unjustly and plainly *wants* to be defended, by violent means if necessary, that want should not be satisfied. Those outside the community of believers do not stop being neighbors on that account. The love that the community extols remains universal in scope. Indeed, the Bishops' contention—that how we treat our enemy is the key test of whether we love our neighbor—receives emphatic endorsement.

Moreover, the community of believers should sustain ongoing relations with the wider society that are consistent with its own commitments. Adherents offer varying verdicts about what such consistency demands. Some advocate strict separation. One example is the group of sixteenth century Hutterites who had been granted asylum on the estates of Count Leonard of Lichtenstein.[63] When Austrian authorities threatened to extradite them, the well-meaning Count offered them protection by coercive measures, including defense by arms. Instead, the Hutterites proceeded to relocate, as an entire community. They sought a nobleman who would grant them toleration without protection. Only then could they respond to intruders in what they judged to be a consistent way. Other adherents advocate a more active involvement with the society in which they find themselves. They do no permit believers to use deadly force and public defense. But they are unwilling to retreat to the ghetto or the desert (how far they actively forgo protection is uncertain, and raises a "free rider" question I cannot discuss here). They stand willing to challenge establishments and to labor for humane cultural change. Yoder depicts their overall perspective as follows: "It is clear in the New Testament that the meaning of history is not what the state will achieve in the way of a progressively more tolerable ordering of society, but what the church achieves through evangelism and through the leavening process."[64] All of their involvements in the wider society must be governed by the conviction that the church will be the salt that savors society only if it cares first and foremost about the integrity of its own witness.

3.4. *Exploring the limits universal love establishes.* We have uncovered complicated areas of agreement and disagreement between altruists and secular impartialists on the one hand, and altruists and those in the peace churches on the other. I began this subsection with a standard contrast: impartiality requires weighing the good of others equally with one's own, and the normative asymmetry requires altruistic dedication to the good of others. Altruists assume that impartiality issues in two strategies they deem unacceptable. Later, however, I qualified this contrast by noting that nuanced secular accounts of impartiality need not reduce to either of these strategies. One way such accounts generate normative room for maneuver is by allowing and indeed commending supererogatory actions. This commendation of supererogation provides one reason to distinguish between self-other and other-other situations. Later still I noted that those in the peace churches call this distinction into question and put forward, in effect, a kind of normative impartiality of their own.

I sought to enhance our understanding of both the first normative asymmetry and of impartiality by developing the comparisons. Though I cannot resolve the points at issue among all three groups, I do want now to discuss how we are to relate a commitment to universal love to these areas of agreement and disagreement.

Universal love as we sketched it at the beginning means that in a theocentric frame both our neighbors and ourselves should at least be subjects of genuine attention and care. Basil Mitchell summarizes what is crucial for present purposes: "The love of others, which the Christian ethic demands, involves an active concern for their well-being, and that in turn implies a clear conception of what is best for them, which must, in consistency, be also in essentials what is best for ourselves."[65]

To accept this summary establishes certain limits. Altruism cannot be endorsed unqualifiedly, *if* endorsement signifies that the self does not matter. To require or even permit unlimited disparities between neighbor and self leaves us no essentials to honor in common. Still, the summary is not self-interpreting about substantive matters. To identify, for example, what content to ascribe to "well-being," to what is best for neighbor and self, is not obvious. Certainly conceptions of what is best for persons when we accord them equal consideration can be influenced and sometimes governed by religious commitments. Such commitments themselves were seen to vary however. Those in the peace churches can interpret well-being to reflect their own account of the obedient life to which self and others are similarly called. Altruists can interpret well-being differently, or at least weigh its features differently when conflicts are adjudicated in other-other relations.

Faced with these complexities, I shall try to probe the limits that universal love establishes, to ascertain more clearly which views among those we have considered are compatible with universal love. But I cannot proceed deductively, from universal love to these views. That the summary I cited is not self-interpreting rules out any such procedure. I shall instead "cross-fertilize." That is, I probe limits and I specify how the views themselves may within these limits provide varying kinds of content to universal love. Sometimes I get no further than to refine issues at stake. At other times (particularly in 3.5. ahead) I advance proposals of my own, proposals to develop the account of universal love along the lines that seem to me most plausible.

One matter need not detain us. Altruists are right to reject the two strategies I identified under the first judgment they make. Again, *agape* will seek to transcend the calculating quality that a comprehensive tit-for-tat legitimates. And it will foster a riskier strategy where one's own good is concerned than a stipulation about no disproportionate inconvenience mandates. We can be grateful to altruists for alerting us to these strategies. Any absence of disparity between self and others on which we take universal love to insist must avoid them both. Because secular impartialists can also avoid them, however, we clarify an important matter but still face the more difficult issues. These issues arise under the second judgment that altruists make—the distinction between self-other and other-other relations. And once more I shall consider the three same questions about it that I discussed earlier.

(a) The first question concerns supererogation. I said I would return to the point that cases recur within the Christian tradition resembling the one endorsed by secular defenders—where supererogation and duty remain distinct and interdependent. The earlier defense of supererogation we examined concerned the promotion of good. Such promotion a Christian ethic plainly enjoins. Yet, whatever a Christian ethic enjoins, does it likewise require? To "require" here assumes that *mutual* reproof and discipline is fitting when failures occur. (The only latitude this assumption allows is a practical one: we can further the well-being of others in such varied ways that it may make little sense to reprove someone for donating money to a hospital rather than a school, or vice versa. Because we can more readily identify violations of prohibitions against doing harm, we often reserve explicit reproof for determinate violations.) Or can we find instances where we *insist* on a fuller kind of agent-discretion, where we praise for performance but view reproach for nonperformance as unacceptable rather than simply impractical? Neither alternative obviously violates universal love. Yet to insist on such agent-discretion allows for supererogation.

Cases of supereogation mentioned previously included actions that are saintly, heroic, charitable, generous, and forgiving. Again, some Christians view all such actions as required. Others treat certain actions at any rate as agent-relative in this sense: I can require them of myself in a way I should not require them of others, though others can similarly require them of themselves. Certain frequently cited examples of supererogation seem to me controversial; others indeed appear to be indisputable. I give one example of each.

The controversial example involves a radically other-regarding way of life that Mother Teresa personifies. On the one hand, consider whether both of these statements are right: Mother Teresa would not be Mother Teresa if *we* required her to be. Mother Teresa would not be Mother Teresa if *she* failed to require herself to be. While the injunction to promote good is addressed to all, its successful execution depends in this case on what she accomplishes that exceeds what we think she is obliged to accomplish. At least interpersonal reproach for failure is not quite suitable. On the other hand, consider that some versions of a Christian ethic see her as required to do what she does as a community-defined duty. Should other Christians not reproach themselves for failing to live in the other-regarding way she does? Her way seems surely more than a personal preference or vocational choice.[66] The injunction under which she lives cannnot then be consigned to the realm of optional ideals.

The indisputable example involves donation of vital organs made possible in modern medical practice. It is common to insist that a person who donates a vital organ from his or her body to benefit a neighbor should do so only by virtue of free and informed consent. Indeed, Ramsey himself questions whether one's own consent should override concern for one's bodily integrity, especially if the consent is secured under pressure from the beneficiary, from family or physicians, or from the community at large. He worries in general that such pressure may support views that make any person merely part of, or systemically subservient to, the larger society. At the very least, therefore, one should not be reproached by others if one declines to be a donor. This verdict seems to apply to Christians as well as to non-Christians. Donation of a vital organ is a gift. And Ramsey is prepared to say that "gifts are not rights to be claimed or duties to be imposed...."[67]

We may take the insistence in the case of organ donation—that gifts are not rights or duties—as important support for the argument that we can and should make a place for supererogation. We can do so without violating universal love. To gather more general support we must give affirmative replies to the following lines of inquiry.

To begin, we must ask whether there exists a kind of voluntariness that agents *qua* agents distinctively enjoy. Some in the tradition find support for this in Christianity's pervasive willingness to affirm (as Tertullian does for example) "a special sphere of liberty ordained to human beings to test their virtue."[68] And often we may attach particular value to what one does in open-ended circumstances, where one's genuine options are manifold. We must then go on to ask whether such a sphere includes two sorts of agent-discretion *vis-à-vis* rights to be claimed. (i) There is agent-discretion about whether claims or rights are relinquished. That is, any claims or rights which we believe the equal worth of every person to establish are rights and claims that only each agent is then free to relinquish. At a minimum, the agent may relinquish his or her own claims or rights, but is *not similarly free* to relinquish the claims or rights of others. (ii) There is agent-discretion in certain cases even about whether we may say that some attitudes and actions are present or absent. The thought here is that to require people to do certain things (let alone to force them) changes inexorably what these things are. It is self-defeating, for example, when recipients transmute gratitude for gifts freely given into claims that these are owed. So it makes sense to praise certain attitudes and actions when we find them but not to reprove when we miss them.

Further, and in more explicitly religious terms, we must ask whether particular agents are called to undertakings not required of everyone. Here we return to the distinction between precepts that bind us all and counsels that do not. Various Roman Catholic moralists in the modern period endeavor to uphold the distinction without perpetuating all of the elements in medieval formulations to which earlier Protestants objected.[69] For instance, Bernard Häring defends the general notion of an individual "vocation" manifested through the movement of special grace. Though he excludes "all coercion and judgment from without," he allows "that God can directly present a counsel to an individual with all the force of command."[70] For the individual to oppose such a counsel is to be more than merely imperfect; it is to sin. Such sin is, however, internal to the agent's own history. The agent-discretion at stake here is not simply the exercise of human autonomy. It points rather to the inner life of the individual who responds to God's inner guidance. This person sees himself or herself as positively obliged, but in a way that does not similarly oblige others. To grant the possibility of a special calling means that universal love must be more than a set of uniform requirements. Such love must accommodate a distinction between self and others that corresponds to *this* distinction between counsels and precepts. This distinction passes the universalizability test in that an agent can say that anyone so circumstanced should do what he or she does. No issue of inconsistency or contradiction necessarily arises. Yet, by definition, a special calling lacks blanket applicability, even to others within the church. And the way of life it elicits has irreducibly (though never exhaustively) to do with one's own love for God.

(b) The second question concerns the first half of the distinction between self-other and other-other relations, in the context of resistance to evil. To promote good is to resist natural and moral evils in a sense. Yet such promotion usually assumes considerable room for taking initiative. But in the case of this second question, agent-discretion diminishes. We must ask what universal love allows or requires when the *self* is an unwilling *recipient* of actions someone else initiates. Suppose this "someone else" is my enemy, whose actions toward me are evil. Love of enemy is a requirement in a Christian ethic. It is not supererogatory. To conclude otherwise would violate universal love.[71] We face a potential collision here, for the scope of universal love also includes the self. Can we honor inclusiveness in both directions?

The views of secular impartialists and those in the peace churches I canvassed suggest that we can honor inclusiveness in different ways. Secular impartialists honor it by holding that in circumstances of self-defense where one acts as a recipient one is allowed or even required to prevent an infliction of harm rather than to suffer it. The means of prevention may be, if strictly necessary, as severe as the harm the neighbor tries to inflict. Because such impartialists claim that a defensive response to a wrongful physical assault by one's neighbor is not similarly wrong, they would deny that one's prevention should be described as repaying evil with evil. Those in the peace churches honor inclusiveness in a radically different manner. They require nothing more or less of the self than of anyone else in the Christian community. The defense that Ambrose and Ramsey prohibit to the self is prohibited on the neighbor's behalf as well. Seemingly heroic intervention can compromise the freedom of the innocent to respond in faithful witness. Nonviolence may well end in sacrifice for self and other innocents alike, at any rate in the eyes of the world, because or whenever their neighbors still live like predators. Those in the community of faith have religious grounds to hope that their neighbors will change, but at all costs they themselves should not change.

Altruists tend to link *self*-sacrifice and nonviolence in the case they offer for distinguishing self-other and other-other relations. Those in the peace churches commend nonviolence in both self-other and other-other relations, and so do not stress self-sacrifice as such. They thereby decline to forge this distinctive link. Again, the distinction they stress is not between self and others, but between church and world.

(c) The third question concerns the second half of the distinction between self-other and other-other relations, in the context of resistance to evil. A perennial subject of debate for Christians is whether to intervene to protect the innocent, the victimized, the weak and defenseless in other-other relations, when this may include the use of deadly force. We have rehearsed the conflicting attempts that altruists and those in the peace churches make to provide scriptural warrants for their respective verdicts. Both sides agree that inclusion of the enemy is the key test of whether we love our neighbor. Altruists are willing to prefer the enemy in a self-other situation, and in general to seek ways to honor the enemy's humanity. But in other-other situations, they oppose any movement from seriously including the enemy to automatically preferring the enemy. One reason for their opposition lies in their knowledge that sometimes the innocent party is not an enemy and the guilty party is an enemy. In such cases, to refuse to intervene on behalf of the innocent is to favor the guilty by default. Or at least inaction seems less loving in certain situations where conflict among third parties proves unavoidable, and where we can discriminate morally among the parties. Those in the peace churches wish to apply their conception of life well-lived—obedient witness—to all parties. So their own sort of normative impartiality enjoins them to allow innocent third parties to trust in God when attacked. Their allowance does not make them responsible, as they see the matter, for outcomes they do not intend. But their chief concern is fidelity in every direction to the terms of obedient witness. They find it odd to treat as absolute for others a value (even physical survival) they regard as relative in their own case.

Since both altruists and those in the peace churches aspire to honor inclusiveness in other-other situations, we must distinguish concern about the integrity of the church's witness from judgments about what normative content integrity demands. To decide between the two accounts requires us to weigh especially two kinds of consideration.

The first is the weight to be given to *human* calculations of responsibility, in the case of agents and of recipients. Should we actively prefer those who suffer injustice because the perpetrators bear the onus of responsibility? Should our preference ever extend to violent actions on the sufferers' behalf? Or should we remain agnostic about ascriptions of responsibility (which are painfully fallible by any reckoning), and adhere consistently to nonviolence in all directions? To give some weight to human calculations of responsibility is not thereby to give indiscriminate authority to others that allows any intended recipient simply to determine what conduces to his or her well-being. It is unfair to charge altruists with giving the latter sort of authority to recipients. The categories of innocence and defenselessness and victimization carry more objective weight than this. Those who are victims may accede, after all, to miserable treatment. They may lack awareness of injustice. Still the categories themselves assume some capacity for determining who is and is not responsible, and a readiness to discriminate, at the point of action, on the basis of such determinations.

The second is the moral relevance of a post-fallen world. Consider the following conversation from Charlotte Brontë's *Jane Eyre*. Jane says: "If people were always kind and obedient to those who are cruel and unjust, the wicked people would have it all their own way: they would never feel afraid, and so they would never alter, but grow worse and worse."[72] Jane's friend Helen quotes the New Testament in reply: "Love your enemies; bless them that curse you; do good to them that hate you and despitefully use you."[73] Those in the peace churches are content to live with Helen's reply. Altruists also wish to keep faith with Helen's reply, as we have seen. Yet they do not simply rest content with it. In other-other situations they think there is something in Jane's observation. We seem so constituted that her melancholy description proves too often accurate to be ignored. Many (especially the physically strong and the socially powerful) are inclined to follow a policy of "all the traffic will bear." They will take what they can; they will bully, cajole, and intimidate, unless they are opposed and made accountable. We find their numbers not only outside, but inside the church. Altruists by no means sanction an "anything goes" policy in response. As we also have seen, they adhere absolutely to a prohibition against the direct and intentional killing of innocent life. But the alternatives they see available to Christians in a post-fallen world dispose them sometimes to reckon actively with unwelcome impingements on their innocent neighbors' peace. Their intervention likewise reflects concern for the moral discipline and transformation of aggressors.

Reflection by Christians on what kinds of responses to evil love requires or permits bears the marks, unavoidably, of anguishing struggle. They cannot abandon texts that partly serve to define their identity. For example: "To him who strikes you on the cheek, offer the other also; and from him who takes away your cloak do not withhold your coat as well. Give to every one who begs from you; and of him who takes away your goods, do not ask them again" (Luke 6: 29-30). We are exhorted here to acquiesce and even further the aims of physical assailants, thieves, and beggars. It is unsurprising that those in the peace churches sometimes conflate nonviolence and nonresistance, as our earlier account of their views indicated. Yet at some juncture many Christians draw back from wholesale acquiescence to whatever the neighbor may happen to want. We find, in fact, a continuum of positions enunciated by Christian writers through the centuries on the kinds of responses to evil that love requires or permits: (i) nonresistance; (ii) nonviolent resistance (e.g., perhaps those nonviolent critical stances toward the establishment to which I referred earlier, certainly the active but nonviolent opposition to injustice exemplified by Gandhi and Martin Luther King, Jr.); (iii) violent resistance limited by the principle of discrimination (e.g., the just war teaching that any direct and intentional killing of noncombatants is absolutely forbidden, even on pain of losing the war itself); (iv) violent resistance limited by the principle of proportion (i.e., the good consequences of violent resistance must always outweigh the evil consequences); (v) unlimited violent resistance.[74]

Although (v) is excluded as a possible option, we have seen how proponents of the normative asymmetry can espouse nonviolence, even nonresistance, in self-other relations when the self is unjustly attacked. To this extent they seem to agree with those in the peace churches against secular impartialists. But in other-other relations they can espouse violent resistance at least to the point of (iii) above. To this extent their differences with secular impartialists narrow, sometimes to the vanishing point, while their differences with those in the peace churches increase, sometimes to the breaking point.

3.5. Love, resistance, and the incompleteness of altruism. To assess what limits universal love establishes in the context of this first asymmetry proves hardest at the point where one struggles to locate what kinds of responses to evil that love requires or permits. I want finally to offer certain remarks by way of assessment.

There are two large questions which our account leads us to distinguish. First, can resistance to evil form any part of a way of life that purports to be Christian? Second, does the answer we give to the first question hold similarly for neighbor and self?

To answer the first question, we must obviously say what we take "resistance" to mean. The text from Luke that I cited above suggests passive compliance with the neighbor's actions and aims. Yet many Christians refuse to isolate such a text from the larger narrative that includes, for instance, Jesus' driving the money-changers from the temple. They are also forced to extrapolate, because the narrative leaves them with normative gaps they are bound to seek to fill even when they believe that the narrative implies an entire pattern of thought governing specification. In consequence, they have produced impressive strategies, such as those of Martin Luther King. Evil is to be actively and not only passively resisted. The target of resistance is the evil and not the person. We should strive to convert rather than defeat opponents, and to disavow hatred and bitterness in the process.[75]

An active though nonviolent resistance exceeds pure passive compliance to the demands of others. Such resistance means that we should refrain from issuing to anyone (including ourselves) a "blank check."[76] That is, we should not in love always acquiesce to *anything* the other wants (or demand from another anything we want). For suppose my neighbor wants me to serve as a victim of sadistic practices or to indulge every momentary whim he or she happens to have. Certain persons who extol nonresistance without qualification set themselves up for such possibilities to be raised as cogent objections. Once raised, however, the usual response is that some lines must be drawn after all, some sorts of resistance are warranted. Even Yoder rejects "a weak acceptance of the intentions of the evil one, resignation to his evil goals":

> The services to be rendered to the one who coerces us—carrying his burden a second mile, giving beyond the coat and cloak—are to his person, not to his purposes. The "resistance" which we renounce is a response in kind, returning evil for evil. But the alternative is not complicity in his designs. The alternative is creative concern for the person who is bent on evil, coupled with the refusal of his goals.[77]

To avoid complicity in someone's designs, to refuse his or her goals, seem to be cases of resistance to evil. What is forbidden is resistance that responds to coercion by doing evil. Yet we face controversy about which actions count as "doing evil" in response. Secular impartialists could argue, as we saw, that it begs the question to characterize a response in kind as returning evil for evil.

I propose that among these agreements and disagreements we make our general way as follows.

(a) To ascribe final, irreducible authority to the Bible, we need not deny that reflection on resistance may lead us to extrapolate. It is not frivolous speculation for Christians to ask, for example, what neighbor-love might require of the Good Samaritan if he had arrived on the scene "while the robbers were still at their fell work."[78] Should he be willing to risk interference rather than the victim's welfare? Moreover, I think we should attempt a larger kind of risk in the scope of our reflection. Too often we focus on those cases of human interaction where actual or threatened physical violence looms as a definite possibility, to be either affirmed or rejected. We attend too little to the far more extensive number of cases where no one meaningfully envisages physical violence, not the agent, the recipient, or affected third parties, but where resistance in a wider sense looms as a definite possibility. To attend to the latter encourages us to interpret the law of love comprehensively, in accordance with the claim noted earlier that moral principles do more than tell agents what they may or may not do; they also tell victims what sorts of treatment they may and may not object to, resist, or demand. I shall suggest below that we expand our discussion to ask what reasons might count as loving ones for resisting *at all*. It proves illuminating to consider this question in relation to cases where physical violence is not at issue, but nonviolent wrong-doing may be.

(b) Altruists seem to me right to confront the alternatives they see available in a post-fallen world. In this they do not obviously depart from the Biblical narrative. I should acknowledge that I find myself a realist in the tradition of Augustine, and share Jane Eyre's worries to this extent: we can make matters worse if we are always *obedient* to those who are cruel and unjust. Such realism leads one to discriminate among the appraisals that those in the peace churches *and* secular impartialists offer. Those in the peace churches are correct to distinguish concern for the person bent on evil and refusal of that person's goals. Yet they go wrong when they abstract this distinction from other-other situations in which we are often immersed. The person bent on evil may temporarily rob us of our ability to keep the distinction as intact as we would like when that person's goal is harm to an innocent third party. Not to oppose this goal, by constraint if necessary, can betray the innocent unjustly. Such betrayal seems worse, if our hand is forced. Secular impartialists are correct to point out that neighbors who initiate evil actions bring unwanted choices in their train, choices for which neighbors bear comparatively greater responsibility. Yet impartialists are unduly sanguine when they announce that the goal is "to restore an equilibrium of mutual nonharm." We should not call such responses merely restorative. To do so is too complacent. Defensive responses to evil of the kind they describe never become *all right*. Such responses at most are more loving than inaction, but they stand as sad disciplinary measures in a fallen world. Seen in the light of the new aeon they remain defective. They should leave us dissatisfied and tireless in our search of higher possibilities.

(c) What I have said in the previous paragraph (b) mainly supports the answer altruists give to the first large question whether resistance to evil forms any part of a way of life that purports to be Christian. But altruists err, I believe, in their answer to the second large question. For they deny that the answer to the first question holds similarly for neighbor and self. I contended earlier that to require or even permit unlimited disparities between neighbor and self leaves us no essentials to honor in common and thereby transgresses the limits that universal love establishes. I suggest that we now expand our discussion to ask what reasons count as loving ones for resisting *at all*. This encourages us to interpret the law of love comprehensively, reflecting on cases where physical violence is not at issue, but nonviolent wrongdoing may be. This also puts us in a better position to assess whether the self should ever resist on its own behalf.

We noted that even those in the peace churches draw back from issuing a blank check. Yet we must still indicate why we should draw lines, when love is our measure. Three reasons are often cited to authorize our refusal to acquiesce without qualification.[79] First, for the neighbor's own sake I should not conflate his or her legitimate needs and actual wants. To try to disentangle needs and wants is admittedly fraught with risks. Many wrongs have been committed in the name of a putatively enlightened paternalism. Still, we must retain some room to tell the neighbor a truth out of love for example, a truth the neighbor does not want to know, even when the telling may itself provoke unwanted suffering on all sides. Second, for the sake of affected third parties, I should oppose certain actions the neighbor intends or performs. Here other-other considerations supply the rationale. Third, for my own sake I should oppose certain actions the neighbor intends or performs.

The first two reasons provide considerable room for normative maneuver. Contrast the following cases. It is one thing for my friend to ask me to serve as a character witness for him when he is on trial for embezzlement. Though this requires me to fly to California at great inconvenience and financial cost to myself, my regard for him leads me to comply. It is another thing if my friend asks me to bribe the prosecution's star witness and take him back to Connecticut with me until the trial is finished. It would be wrong for me to comply (or serve as a character witness!). The first two reasons for refusing to issue a blank check can account for why it would be wrong. I should resist my friend's request both for his own sake and for the sake of an affected third party. I do my friend no favor if I support his corruption by acquiescing to his request. And the effort to bribe and otherwise involve the star witness in withholding the truth makes him an instrument of my friend's plans.

Proponents of the normative asymmetry have these first two reasons at their disposal. Such reasons prove supple enough in general to provide other-regarding warrants for self-benefitting actions. W. G. Maclagan's defense of altruism, for example, includes the claim that others find disciplinary value for themselves (albeit value they may not seek) when an agent declines to permit them to treat his or her own happiness with indifference. And overall the conditions for a good community are realizable only when its members learn to respect interests beyond their own.[80]

These two reasons remain indispensable (for proponents of universal love and impartiality and not only of the normative asymmetry). We still must ask whether the first two reasons are incomplete without the third. Neither has essentially (from the ground up) to do with my own well-being. Hence, let us inquire whether I should ever resist on my own behalf. To give an affirmative answer to this question requires us to refer to the self's well-being directly, not derivatively from other-regard as the altruist does. It is to say that concern about the self's own well-being is a substantive religious and moral claim *along with* concern about neighbors. To return to our case: concern about the self's well-being may lead us to conclude that by asking me to bribe and cooperate in withholding the truth, my friend treats me as his instrument as well. I should add this to the set of reasons for judging that it would be wrong to comply. My friend's request instrumentalizes twice.

To introduce this third reason to resist requires extreme care. Of course the phrase "on one's own behalf," hardly less than "self-love," carries multiple and sometimes incompatible meanings. It may mean little more, for example, than feathering my own nest, possessiveness, self-indulgence, etc. But it may also mean honoring my religious and moral commitments because my sense of my own good or well-being is inextricably tied to such commitments. This latter meaning surfaces when Alexander Solzhenitsyn writes:

> There is one simple step a simple courageous man can take—not to take part in the lie, not to give his support to false actions. Let this principle [sc. the lie that masks the method of violence] enter the world and even dominate the world—*but not through me.*[81]

Precisely because of my commitments, it matters to me that *I not do something* and not only that *something not happen*. "On one's own behalf" can also mean that rather than refuse, I cooperate, in the always vigorous tradition of opportunism, with lies and false actions, joining the forces that hold the greatest promise of actually dominating the world, however corrupt these forces are.

Any acceptable sense of resisting "on one's own behalf" cannot include instances where the charge readily applies that one is simply self-serving, opportunistic, and the like. In general we must construe this third reason to resist in a way that remains as congruent as possible with the first two. I offer now one list of more ordinary instances where the charge does not apply and the congruence is achieved.

I introduce this list by identifying what I as an agent culpably do. And once again I draw this list from the countless cases of human interaction where physical violence is not at issue. The instances are familiar but no less crucial for all that: when I as a surgeon neglect to obtain informed consent because the operation I perform increases not the patient's recovery prospects (nil in any case) but my own income; or I as an employer knowingly and avoidably permit hazardous working conditions and see to it that my employees remain ignorant of such conditions. Or more generally: I know that another person would decline to interact with me if he or she were aware of the use to which I intended to put our interaction, and I keep silent about my intention, so that the interaction can take place.[82] Finally, in my personal relations, I seek the company of others, and am prepared to be cooperative, but always for the sake of an audience. Others are important only as sounding-boards for my projects and as listeners to my problems.

Let me next alter and further specify these same instances to refer to what I as a recipient warrantably resist, object to, or demand:

I want to have a voice in determining how I am to spend my remaining days; or I want to know if the asbestos I routinely handle can harm me; or I am left exposed and vulnerable in an interpersonal "transaction" whose significance I cannot interpret correctly without the knowledge deliberately withheld; or I refuse to be merely another's "audience" because my own history and quests are distinctively, noninstrumentally mine (for better or for worse), and I wish them to be acknowledged as such. This device helps to show that I should object whenever one of the participants in an interaction is reduced to a wholly menial status, whether I or someone else is on the receiving end.

I anticipated what links these instances together when I alluded to "instrumentalization." Part of discerning the evil to be resisted centers, I wish to argue, on one person using another purely as a means or instrument. We often associate the sense of instrumentalization with Immanuel Kant's second formulation of the Categorical Imperative which retains astoundingly wide appeal: "Act in such a way that you always treat humanity, whether in your own person or in the person of any other, never simply as a means, but always at the same time as an end."[83] I shall not delve into exegetical problems about what Kant himself meant by this formulation.[84] One plausible, although shorthand way to take it is this. No person's importance is to be reduced to or exhausted by his or her importance for another person or group. Persons are irreducibly valuable *in themselves*. Each person's well-being constitutes a terminal point for another's attitudes and actions. I propose that we specify the basic likeness in worth that universal love assumes partly along these lines, as one way for it to do discernible normative work.

Another and more theological way of specifying the basic likeness in worth comes, as it happens, from Ramsey himself. Some years ago he took up the question of whether a Christian black person could legitimately resist a white oppressor. He answered that

> no one who bears the human countenance has the right to hide this from us. He has no right to stand hat in hand and not show forth the human countenance to the full measure that it is upon him. He has no right to deprive any one or all of his fellow men of the challenge to covenant which his creation constitutes. . . . His inalienable right of fellow humanity is at the same time his inalienable duty to fellow man. He can never renounce this without going frontally against covenant imprinted upon him in creation and depriving another of the right not to be without him. It is not permitted him to allow another to be without him.[85]

This answer takes us beyond altruism, it seems, as we have construed it here. Universal love enjoins us to honor anyone, neighbor and self, who bears the human countenance.

4. IS IMPARTIALITY A GOAL I CAN ATTAIN?

4.1. *The weight of self-partiality.* In this subsection I consider the second objection which finds impartiality deficient because it authorizes too much attention to the self's own well-being. This objection is predominantly descriptive. Impartiality fails to take seriously enough the self's *de facto* preoccupation with its own wants and ambitions.

The preoccupation points to an asymmetry between myself and my neighbor on which Christian thinkers often dwell. Something akin to a phenomenological account is required to do justice to this difference. The concern shifts our attention from whether impartiality is *desirable* to whether it is *likely*. What is challenged is the assumption that impartiality is a simple possibility, waiting straightforwardly to be realized, briskly commended without further ado. Impartialty is then not so much a goal to be transcended as an achievement we lack assurance we can attain. Yet to ignore this absence of assurance is itself perceived by proponents of the second asymmetry as a failure to be other-regarding enough.

Consider an ordinary datum. The self experiences unease about its ability to be impartial whenever its own well-being is directly at stake. The traditional insistence that one is not to be one's own judge and jury finds a natural home here. John Locke gives voice to this insistence:

> I easily grant, that *Civil Government* is the proper Remedy for the Inconveniences of the State of Nature, which must certainly be Great, where Men may be Judges in their own Case, since 'tis easily to be imagined, that he who was so unjust as to do his Brother an injury, will scarce be so just as to condemn himself for it.... [86]

Here also we may distinguish between other-other and self-other relations. I as an agent find it easier to be impartial when I am not one of the parties whose well-being I must directly weigh. So I am able to furnish requisitely balanced advice to a divorcing couple, both of whom are my friends but who are deeply at odds about what a fair distribution of their property and other resources should be. Yet when I am in the midst of my own divorce, my balance notoriously recedes. Hurt and bitterness may drive me to strike the hardest bargain I can devise; guilt and remorse may dispose me to give away my store. I am properly loath to trust myself. Or again, I deliberate with other tenured faculty members over which of two younger colleagues we shall recommend for tenure. Whatever conflicts our discussion reveals, we can strive for a level of objectivity unavailable to the younger colleagues themselves. If I am one of the younger colleagues I invite derision at best if I demand to be given a formal vote about my own promotion.

Why is it easier to be impartial in other-other than in self-other relations? Why should there be real and not merely notional difficulties in attaining the degree of self-transcendence that makes impartiality possible? A standard answer is that I am instinctively partial in my own case. The answer is familiar enough in modernity. Nietzsche and Freud are among the most influential secular diagnosticians of our endemic self-absorption.[87] A generalized context of suspicion is now so well established that moralists who ignore it risk self-parody. Yet such suspicion is not created by modern sensibilities. Historical cases among Christian writers abound. And thus this standard answer receives comprehensive formulation in Christian depictions of the fall. The characteristic human situation is one in which the self sees "through a glass darkly," plagued by the possibility of self-deception and rationalization. We do well always to view skeptically the self's protestations of virtue. I cannot hope to explore these depictions adequately. While they display psychological acumen equal to that of the more modern prophets of suspicion, the ultimate explanatory and evaluative frame they provide is theocentric, not anthropocentric. It is one's relation or disrelation to God that matters first and last. So the tendency to self-enclosure and self-preoccupation which bedevils us is understood above all as unbelief or pride or idolatry. Yet its effects appear in human interaction as well. Each self tends to give itself priority, and we grossly underestimate the power of this tendency if we think it can be easily or completely overcome.

Such estimates of the characteristic human situation explain in part why many Christian writers (especially Protestant ones) refuse to accord the "as yourself" clause the status of a second command alongside or equal in normative weight to love of neighbor. Self-love needs no such encouragement; it is ludicrous to imagine we must commend it. Luther typifies this refusal. He takes as a constant datum that

> because of the defect of his nature, man loves himself above everything else, he seeks himself in everything, and loves everything for his own sake, even when he loves his neighbor or his friends, for he seeks only his own therein.[88]

Luther concludes explicitly from this estimate of our defective nature that the love we have for ourselves does not depend on how well or ill we fare in comparison to others. Even if we are poor or dull our self-concern stands intact. "Nobody is such a nonentity that he does not love himself, and the love he has for others is not like the love he has for himself."[89]

4.2. The ameliorative strategy. Does such a sobering analysis yield any practical counsel? Those who accept the analysis and turn cynical dismiss self-sacrifice as a trap, and proceed to protect and promote their own well-being alone as intelligently as they can. Those who accept both the sobering analysis and the law of love, however, must proceed in some other way. One practical strategy they often adopt is ameliorative in character. We should *compensate* for our tendency to go soft when we consider our own case, to be easy on ourselves and hard on others. So Reinhold Niebuhr writes: "To disapprove your own selfishness more severely than the egoism of others is a necessary discipline if the natural complacency toward the self and severity in the judgment of others is to be corrected."[90] There is asymmetry in the measures required if we are to combat this mixture of complacency and censoriousness effectively. So we should deliberately proceed to give more weight to the well-being of others in order to offset our preference for our own.

This ameliorative strategy finds qualified favor with Hare, provided that it is kept at the level of intuitive thinking where ordinary prima facie principles, acquired by education and imitation, hold sway. A practical asymmetry may be warranted because, as he acknowledges, selfishness regularly tempts us more than altruism does. But for Hare, intuitive thinking is never self-supporting. It must be governed by the epistemologically prior level of critical thinking.[91] At this prior level we select prima facie principles and resolve conflicts between them. Here is the point at which our thought resembles an archangel or an "ideal observer." Any practical asymmetry is now excluded. This level yields only a verdict of strict impartiality.

More thoroughgoing defenders of an ameliorative strategy like Niebuhr find human limits and the power of self-interest too pervasive to trust themselves to think sufficiently like archangels. "No man will ever be so intelligent as to see the needs of others as vividly as he recognises his own. . . ."[92] Our rational powers can attain "no impartial perspective, from which to view, and no transcendent fulcrum, from which to affect human action. . . . Even the most rational men are never quite rational when their own interests are at stake."[93] Only practical compensation, and not a more balanced strategy, can defeat a partiality to ourselves that goes so far down. To engage in thought experiments, where we conceive of ourselves as archangels or as contractors behind a veil of ignorance, may witness to an inchoate sense of justice that saves us from a cynical retreat to egoism. But beyond this their power to illumine appears minimal. At least a view that starts from inordinate self-interest (including the way self-interest biases us on behalf of groups with which we identify) casts more light on the conflict-ridden world we know from every newspaper. And an ameliorative strategy of preferring the other proves more effective in realizing a measure of impartiality in that world.

4.3. The point and the limits of Christian realism. How shall we assess this second asymmetry? Those who challenge the assumption that impartiality is a simple possibility show insight that many ethical theorists lack. A warning is issued to the effect that our attempts to represent and identify with others prove deeply and permanently difficult. The elements of the naive, the sanguine, and the complacent in our practical thought are exposed as recalcitrant data. A darker feature intrudes as well: the sin located in our endemic partiality to ourselves. By making ourselves the center of existence we do injustice to others by subordinating them to our self-absorbed pursuits.

Yet this difference between our relations to ourselves and our relations to others and the ameliorative strategy which accompanies it, despite the undeniable insight its proponents display, does not exhaust the features with which we should reckon. It is preferable, I would argue, to limit the ameliorative strategy to a central Christian stress on beginning with one's own contributions to evil. I am enjoined to look first at the evil within myself. I am not to start with the evil that assails me, and the possible culpability to be charged to others.[94] But, then we should go on to distinguish between our looking *first* at the evil we do rather than suffer and our supposing we can *never* perceive the evil of others *at all* for fear of bias. This distinction is not one which the asymmetry canvassed in this subsection prepares us adequately to recognize. Yet the distinction carries important implications. To recall a teaching of Jesus (Matthew 7:3-5; Luke 6:41-42), only after we attend to the evil we ourselves do will we be able to see the evil of others clearly, and help effectively. That this sequence is held to be a practical possibility suggests that more than fear of bias may operate in our calculations. And unless more may operate, we could never minimally trust ourselves (a) that we possess some effective ability to recognize our own evil (an ability Jesus appears to assume), or (b) that we may place any limits on the ameliorative strategy because we can recognize the evil of others. Without some ability to recognize our own evil, the fear of bias itself loses its point. Without some ability to recognize the evil of others, the ameliorative strategy by itself turns into unchecked permissiveness. For if we follow the strategy literally, we would yield all our claims on all occasions and not only many claims on many occasions.

The possibility of trusting ourselves demands, I grant, a moderately hopeful appraisal of the powers of practical reason. Such reason is not *merely* the servant of self-interest, though often self-interest taints it, more often than most of us acknowledge. Its fallible, self-interested deployments depress us, but it *can* be perspicuous, sometimes even when it considers claims that involve the self as well as others. Insofar as this possibility takes us beyond a sheer distrust of ourselves to seek justice even when we are one of the affected parties, it lends some support to impartiality as a normative standard. The standard is no longer simply unrealizable. It is always difficult but it is not always impossible.

5. SHOULD I VALUE MY PARTICULAR IDENTITY AND PERSONAL PROJECTS?

I turn next to two objections that find impartiality deficient because it neglects to acknowledge distinctive and legitimate self-regarding considerations. In this subsection I take up the first of these two. It is predominantly normative. Impartiality fails to accommodate the value I should give to my particular life.

5.1. A determinate character of one's own.   We can acquire an initial sense for the value now at issue by introducing a passage from Henry James' novel, *The Bostonians*. One character, a lifelong activist on behalf of social causes named Miss Birdseye, James describes as follows:

> She had a sad, soft, pale face, which . . . looked as if it had been soaked, blurred, and made vague by exposure to some slow dissolvent. The long practice of philanthropy had not given accent to her features; it had rubbed out their transitions, their meanings. The waves of sympathy, of enthusiasm, had wrought upon them in the same way in which the waves of time finally modify the surface of old marble busts, gradually washing away their sharpness, their details. In her large countenance her dim little smile scarcely showed. It was a mere sketch of a smile, a kind of instalment, or payment on account; it seemed to say that she would smile more if she had time, but that you could see, without this, that she was gentle and easy to beguile.

She always dressed in the same way: she wore a loose black jacket, with deep pockets, which were stuffed with papers, memoranda of a voluminous correspondence; and from beneath her jacket depended a short stuff dress. The brevity of this simple garment was the one device by which Miss Birdseye managed to suggest that she was a woman of business, that she wished to be free for action. She belonged to the Short-Skirts League, as a matter of course; for she belonged to any and every league that had been founded for almost any purpose whatever. This did not prevent her being a confused, entangled, inconsequent, discursive old woman, whose charity began at home and ended nowhere, whose credulity kept pace with it, and who knew less about her fellow-creatures, if possible, after fifty years of humanitary zeal, than on the day she had gone into the field to testify against the iniquity of most arrangments.[95]

This is in some respects a pitiless judgment. It serves nonetheless to suggest the corruptions to which both impartiality and altruism are disposed. Miss Birdseye lacks two qualities at least which James reveres. First, she possesses no determinate character of her own. She has allowed her individual identity to be swallowed up by her other-regarding commitments. Second, she possesses no cumulative knowledge of human life, with its ambiguous twists and turns, its unending resistance to philanthropic solutions. She is in the grip of an ideal which robs her of an ability to see that intramundane redemption is unavailable.

It is the first of these qualities that is especially commended now. Individual identity is positively valued. What this means in modern discussions we can begin to discern when we consider recent attacks on impartiality by philosophers, most notably Bernard Williams. The attacks contain suggestions from which a normative case on behalf of self-regarding considerations may be developed, a case arguably absent in elaborated versions of impartiality.

Both the utilitarian and neo-Kantian accounts of impartiality sketched earlier are targets for criticism. Utilitarian accounts fail especially, it is alleged, to honor the separateness of persons. As we saw, who acts to produce a desirable outcome, and especially whether I so act, seem indifferently assimilated into a verdict about the outcome itself. Neo-Kantian accounts are thought to do better in honoring the separateness of persons, but still not to do nearly well enough in honoring the individual identities of persons. These accounts, as we also observed earlier, take impartiality to require arrangements that are above all interpersonally acceptable. The accounts sometimes posit mutual disinterest and the veil of ignorance that extrude self-partiality. We are to subscribe to principles which equalize our prospects of being *anyone* in the outcome. Yet the character of persons as moral agents such accounts impose is itself, so critics hold, unacceptably impoverished and abstract. To have character, the agent must be a particular *someone*, with personal projects and commitments, one's own life to lead. These projects and commitments require the agent to take an internal view of his or her life. They are not satisfactorily accommodated by the notion of a rational life-plan which implies only an external view, "something like a given rectangle that has to be optimally filled in."[96]

Whether these attacks fairly represent utilitarian or neo-Kantian accounts is an intricate question we must bypass. The attacks assume importance here because, as I said, they suggest how individual identity is to be positively valued. Two possible lines of development follow.

First, to lead one's own life, there must be projects and commitments that give meaning to that life and that are essential to personal integrity. These projects and commitments need not succumb to problematic self-absorption. Many may have genuinely other-regarding content. They nonetheless should place limits on what the claims of impartial morality can reasonably demand; when conflicts arise, impartial morality should not always triumph. "There can come a point at which it is quite unreasonable for a man to give up, in the name of the impartial good ordering of the world of moral agents, something which is a condition of his having any interest in being around in the world at all."[97]

Second, attention to the importance one's projects and commitments have can generate ideals of individual excellence and personal well-being that exclusively other-regarding ideals are seen to jeopardize. Altruism more than impartiality now comes under fire. Susan Wolf calls those who live solely in accordance with other-regarding ideals "moral saints." They embody a way of life she finds at once undesirable and imperialistic. "A moral saint will have to be very, very nice. It is important that he not be offensive. The worry is that, as a result, he will have to be dull-witted or humorless or bland."[98] Such moral saints are unattractive because they lack personal distinctiveness and the capacity to enjoy what is enjoyable in human life. Yet the threat that other-regarding morality poses to one's personal life seems particularly formidable. Morality appears voracious in that its demands are too regularly thought to be stronger and higher than nonmoral ones; the latter it always subsumes or demotes.

What is called into question, given the unattractiveness and the voraciousness, is "the assumption that it is always better to be morally better."[99] For Wolf, we reach a justified limit in how much altruistic morality we can abide. A life well-lived includes the realization of nonmoral values (e.g., we read novels, play the oboe, and improve our backhand) as well as moral ones (e.g., we feed the hungry, heal the sick, and raise money for The United Way). Hence, the good life, i.e., "the point of view of individual perfection,"[100] and the moral life, i.e., the exclusive devotion to further the well-being of others and of society as a whole, are not interdefinable. The moral life is part of the good life, but not all of it, or even the dominant part.[101] And the two can and do conflict. When conflicts occur, no hierarchical system will do where morality stands always at the top.[102]

5.2. A theocentric case for valuing one's particular life. The attacks on impartiality and altruism and the positive evaluation of individual identity just outlined complicate attempts to interpret the law of love. To wrestle with these complications proves nonetheless worthwhile. I shall proceed again within the frame of theocentric explanation and evaluation. Here especially the first love command will be brought explicitly to bear. I shall first indicate the sort of positive assessment of particular identity that can be offered within a theocentric frame. I shall then ask how this assessment allows us to analyze Miss Birdseye's condition. The analysis that results will also permit us to appraise the two lines of development already introduced.

I choose a positive assessment of particular identity found in the writings of Karl Barth. That we encounter this assessment at all in his writings is striking, because he often resists as vigorously as Luther does conceiving self-love as a command alongside neighbor-love. Self-giving is the paradigmatic meaning that Barth most frequently gives to *agape*. Moreover, we cannot accuse him of ignoring the darker possibilities of inordinate self-assertion. But I would argue that Barth's account of a positive assessment of particular identity provides insight into what self-regarding considerations carry legitimate normative force. And further, these considerations amount to one acceptable sense of "self-love." To withhold this phrase from them confuses more than it clarifies, Barth's own verbal stipulation to the contrary notwithstanding. In short, they should receive their due as capturing one appropriate meaning of self-love under theocentric control.

The sense that Barth extols appears in his general discussion of "respect for life." Such respect requires "an affirmation of life," and in addition, one's "resolute will" to be oneself.[103] This resolute will in turn includes "each man's respect for the individuality in which he may 'be alive' before and for God."[104] Again, "before God, and as the one whom God addresses, every man is *sui generis*, an original, and he must will to be this."[105] And finally, "the object of the commanded respect and affirmation is indeed the life which God has granted to every man in its uniqueness and individuality."[106]

What demands respect and affirmation is not natural self-assertion, where one attempts to claim uniqueness by oneself, to will to live for oneself. The object of one's respect and affirmation has rather to do and necessarily to do with one's relation to God. This relation involves the surrender of natural self-assertion. It is then that one regains oneself as created and addressed by God. Barth appeals to the New Testament passages where we are told that to seek to save one's life is to lose it, and to lose one's life for the sake of Jesus and the gospel is to save it. In another passage following these (Barth finds the link significant), it is asked what one gains (even the whole world) if one loses one's soul, and what one can give in exchange for one's soul (e.g., Matthew 16:24-26). Barth says that the "soul" here refers to the life one lives "by the Spirit of God."[107] I should see my life so lived as having value that cannot be interchanged with anyone or anything else in the world. And then, but only then, I can properly say that I am summoned to be myself.

> "Become what you are," means therefore: "Grow into your character, accept the outline of your particular form of life, the manner of existence which in your special struggle of the Spirit against the flesh will emerge more clearly as your own, as the one which is intended for you, as the form of the life allotted and lent to you by God. . . . To will to be in this form is not, therefore, a subjective or egocentric but an obedient willing, in perfect humility but also in perfect courage, no less distinct from indolent inertia than from the arrogant soaring of Icarus, and carrying with it the promise of fulfilment."[108]

To value my particular life cannot be inordinate self-assertion, unless I presumptuously suppose that other persons are not similarly called. To value my particular life cannot be arbitrary self-assertion, since the form of life allotted defines the character I am summoned to make my own.

We meet here with an energetic belief in personal providence to be sure. But if we share this belief, it seems natural to utilize terms like "self-love" and "self-regard" to show constructive as well as destructive possibilities. The former possibilities assume that obedient willing does not crush the self. We need not accept a Nietzschean insistence that we must get rid of God to avoid self-annihilation. And while destructive possibilities are undeniably present, we need not reserve the terms only for them. I am to value my projects and commitments not because they are mine in an exclusionary or egocentric sense. I am to see them as deriving from God. God and not other persons is their ultimate source. And I am actively to refer them all back to God. Valuing them is therefore one way to honor God.

5.3. Pride and sloth as two kinds of faithlessness. Let us now ask how this positive assessment of particular identity allows us to analyze Miss Birdseye's condition. I noted earlier that she permits her own identity to be swallowed up by her other-regarding commitments. How shall we interpret this phenomenon within a theocentric frame? We have already considered in prior subsections how universal love calls us to overturn inordinate self-assertion. The difficulty now is that inordinate self-assertion does not appear to depict Miss Birdseye's condition, unless we resort to explanatory devices that prove forced and unconvincing. It seems that we have to do with destructive possibilities of another sort.

What is Miss Birdseye's condition? The other-regarding commitments she undertakes consume her time, resources, and psychic energy. They erase any boundaries her own integrity may require her to maintain. Her character is left indeterminate. Can we then specify within a theocentric frame what goes wrong when such boundaries are erased? I suggest the following.

Barth recognizes, as we saw, that obedient willing is no less distinct from "indolent inertia" than from "arrogant soaring." This recognition recalls a strand of the tradition where the sins of sloth and not only pride receive serious attention. Sloth refers to a peculiar state of the self, one governed by passivity and torpor. Though it encompasses inaction and laziness, its operations range further. It includes activities, but activities without direction or focus. Its most typical operation is the dispersal of whatever energies the self has at its disposal. And so a life dominated by sloth acquires no discernible shape. In describing such a life, one is at a loss to find abiding aims, or definite views, or permanent loyalties. One who lives such a life lacks particularity, some characteristic personal center. He or she prefers to hide rather than to take the pains that development of particularity demands. Sloth involves a mysterious but culpable absence of intra-psychic vitality. It violates that "agency" that each of us has religious and moral reasons to honor.

Two questions now arise. (a) What is the status of sloth compared to pride? (b) What are the patterns of involvement with other people that someone dominated by sloth exhibits? Let me respond to each question briefly.

(a) The claim that sloth can tempt us, and not only pride or will-to-power, is explored especially by contemporary feminist writers. Valerie Saiving, for example, offers these instances of going wrong that no account of pride or will-to-power can adequately encompass: "triviality, distractibility, and diffuseness; lack of an organizing center or focus; dependence on others for one's own self-definition. . ., in short, underdevelopment or negation of the self."[109]

To agree with this claim means that indolent inertia and arrogant soaring remain distinct temptations. We miss too much on each side that deserves attention in its own right when we try to reduce one to the other. Indeed, both are genuine temptations in the sense that when we succumb to either, we sin. For we need not view Miss Birdseye as sheerly a victim. She remains a responsible agent; she is complicit in her self-evacuation. Judgment is then appropriate in each case. Thus, we find Susan Nelson Dunfee prepared to insist that

> human sinfulness is not just the sin of pride, but is also the sin of hiding; that the God who judges human pride must also judge human hiding and passivity, not by demanding a sacrifice of the self, but by beckoning the forgiven self to affirm her full humanity through grasping and claiming her call to freedom.[110]

Let us say then that the absence of self-direction corrupts, and not only selfishness, acquisitiveness, possessiveness. To dwell on the latter "Promethean" sins offers an incomplete picture, where sensitivity to inordinate self-assertion is the exclusive subject. Sloth requires us to enlarge the canvass. It shows another kind of corruption, one that stands in dialectical tension with Promethean excesses. It is the kind that allows us to understand Miss Birdseye. Although she is hardly lazy, she drifts from one cause to another. And she differs from those who assert themselves in ways that do injustice to others and those who use their benevolence as a means of controlling others.

(b) Both kinds of corruption find expression in involvements with other people. We discussed earlier how inordinate self-assertion does so. We shall consider now how sloth does so.

It is possible to lose oneself in the lives of others. Involvements with them leave one without a determinate character of one's own. Miss Birdseye appears to fit this description more than any other. Often it may be *easier* to attend to others in order to find anonymity there. Perhaps then it is easier for Miss Birdseye to lose herself in acts that are always public and ideological. To find anonymity may be understood as part of a larger pattern in which one disavows or represses the agency one has as a human being, and takes other finite objects with a seriousness only God should have. Sensuality is an instance of the pattern to which Christians show recurrently acute awareness, sometimes with unfortunate results. Other instances may involve institutions and causes, or other persons to whom one attaches oneself in idolatrous devotion.[111]

We may therefore view Miss Birdseye's condition as one instance of a general temptation to escape from oneself and to worship humanity. Other-regarding as well as self-regarding commitments can receive such idolatrous devotion. One can love humanity in the wrong way by following indiscriminately whatever causes and claims others set for one. Service to others then assumes the timbre of servitude. She seeks to make herself only a means to other peoples' ends.

This general temptation illuminates a range of experience that we have reason to take as bona fide. Miss Birdseye, though a fictional character, lives out a way of life that is not idiosyncratic. The temptation is one to which many actual persons succumb. Feminist writers do not stand alone in bearing witness to this.

Yet we should also introduce complications to our account of the temptation that serve to identify related possibilities and to forestall a conclusion we might otherwise draw. I mention four such complications: two attest to the intricacies of human waywardness; the other two attest more hopefully to a denial that other-regarding and self-regarding commitments must always collide. We need not conclude that the more we are other-regarding, the less we can be self-regarding, or vice versa.

First, not all unfocused activity is free of self-preoccupation in the fashion of Miss Birdseye. One can live a predominantly distracted life that remains self-absorbed. To be ineffectual is not necessarily to be unselfish. Second, not all self-denigration leads to idolatrous devotion to others. One may efface oneself in order to be all the more powerful, to dominate others. Third, not all radically other-regarding commitments lead to a life devoid of character. We must find ways to distinguish a Miss Birdseye from a Mother Teresa. That we see *ex post facto* a certain difference in their lives is apparent. Mother Teresa's dedication to others does not require her activity to be unfocused or her character to be indistinct. Her features retain their distinctiveness. Fourth, not all radically other-regarding commitments lead to idolatrous devotion to others. It is possible, as we saw, to contrast service and servitude. The former is founded on a realistic love of others. Here one attends to their weal and woe and yet looks frankly at their failures and vices, apprehends them honestly as fallible and sinful. The latter is founded on idealization and sentimentality. Here one indeed makes them idols, is willing to do virtually anything to secure their approval, assumes their needs and goals count more before God than one's own.

Suppose we accept these answers. Pride and sloth remain distinct temptations and they assume different patterns in human interaction. Suppose too we grant that complications like those I mentioned identify other crucial possibilities with which we must reckon. We can go on, I think, to locate one common source of both temptations within a theocentric frame of explanation and evaluation. To locate such a source supports the view that other-regarding and self-regarding commitments need not always collide.

The source is *faithlessness* to God.[112] It is faithless for me to suppose in my pride that I objectively matter more than other persons. My obedient willing, the particular history and prospects for which I am uniquely responsible, does not entitle me to prefer it in the sense that I believe or act as if I believe that my life has greater value before God and in my interactions with others. I am to affirm that God-relatedness obtains for all others as it obtains for me.

It is likewise faithless for me to suppose in my sloth that God-relatedness obtains only for my neighbors and that I am to regard my particular life of obedient willing as of no account or to neglect the manner of existence given distinctly to me. I should instead actively affirm my own calling, and resist the thought that I am interchangeable with others. My concern about others becomes a bona fide temptation to my obedient willing when I allow it to disperse my energies so that my way of life remains forever unfocused, distracted, bereft of identifiable direction.

We can connect therefore an awareness that we are tempted both to pride and to sloth with the judgment that "the dignity of every person" applies to the self as well as the neighbor. The connection is this. In maintaining such a judgment I must guard against two ways of going wrong and must assess impartiality accordingly. On the one side, that I am tempted to assert myself inordinately leads me to view with favor many of the concerns associated with impartiality. The role reversal test for example is one recourse I assuredly appropriate, whatever its deficiencies as a comprehensive standard.[113] To be willing to put myself in another's shoes—though not to claim that I ought or can do so completely—enables me to see more of both the rationalizations my pride generates and the commonalities in human life. On the other side, that I am tempted to lose myself in directionless activities, sometimes in the multiple and conflicting demands of other persons, leads me to oppose those impersonalizing pressures that certain interpretations of impartiality exert—pressures that can increase the temptation through a misguided highmindedness. I *should* not just go into the hopper with everyone else.[114] (This judgment differs from descriptive doubts about whether I *can* do so, considered in the previous subsection and to be considered again, though very differently, in the next.) I should revere the distinctiveness of my own obedient willing as well as the commonalities of human life.

5.4. Impartialists and saints. Finally, I shall draw on what has been said about Miss Birdseye to appraise the two lines of development identified by critics of impartiality.

As noted, the critics argue first that if I am to lead my own life, I must have projects and commitments that give my life meaning and that prove essential to my personal integrity. Impartiality is alleged to threaten these.

My prior remarks about pride and sloth suggest that such an argument addresses one way to go wrong and neglects to explore the other way. It can be positively appraised as one part of an attack on sloth. For the concern about obedient willing includes, as we have seen, an honoring of individual distinctiveness. This honoring surely assumes both the separateness and individual identity of persons. It is one thing imaginatively to identify with others. It is another thing when my identification with my neighbors is so complete that the boundaries between myself and others cease to make the normative difference that honoring distinctiveness requires. A concern for distinctiveness militates too against my taking a purely external view of my life. No impersonally specified set of projects and commitments ought to capture exhaustively the way in which I view them and carry them out.

Yet it is uncertain how far the critics are prepared to jettison the concerns associated with impartiality, concerns that may be summoned to oppose pride as inordinate self-assertion. Do they intend to undermine altogether the importance of imaginative identification with others for example, even after one agrees that it should be incomplete? I noted that the critics allow that many of one's projects and commitments may have other-regarding content. Whether such content is thought to be in any sense necessary however is another question, and one often ignored. But if it is not necessary, how are we to discriminate laudable personal projects from other kinds? Talk of the requirements for leading one's own life is by itself unacceptably indeterminate. Caligula appears after all to be a "particular somone"; so does Stalin.[115] To mention such figures may be a *reductio ad absurdam*. It serves nevertheless to register the difficulties in seeing how any sort of interest might not subordinate other-regarding considerations, how the requirements disallow self-indulgence and self-aggrandizement. One possible basis for disallowance is again the role-reversal test, which as I said much earlier is accepted by both advocates and critics of impartiality. Such an appeal to consistency acquires normative force without incorporation into a positive ethical theory. Yet what amounts to the critics' passing verbal endorsement of the role-reversal test is hardly enough. We need to know why the test has normative force when we employ it in a theoretically unambitious way to reprove self-partiality. Too often the critics of impartiality fail to specify what constraints the test imposes in light of their own acceptance of it.

The second line of development that the critics identify stresses ideals of individual excellence and personal well-being that other-regarding ideals jeopardize. Here the "moral saint" is viewed as too nice, inoffensive, humorless, and bland to be a desirable subject for imitation. Yet the figure thus depicted is liable to criticism within a theocentric frame as well. The grounds for criticism are two.

First, a life of obedient willing can include many human excellences that go beyond the specifically moral ones in question. This is because God as the object of one's obedient willing is infinitely richer than morality as conceived here. Since God "is lover of beauty," Robert Merrihew Adams maintains, "as well as commander of morals," submission of one's life to God "may in some cases ... encompass an intense pursuit of artistic excellence in a way that maximal devotion to the interests of morality, narrowly understood, cannot" (his examples include Johann Sebastian Bach and Fra Angelico).[116] And more generally we may say that in Judaism and Christianity the sense of the person indivisibly responsible to God does not readily lend itself to the clear divisions between religion and morality that characterize so many modern discussions.[117]

Second, the limits of morality are recognized when we refer once again to the priority of the first great command. Wholehearted devotion to God induces humility before God, for example. But we err badly if we confuse this humility with self-abnegation before other human beings.[118] Humility before God is compatible with the defiance of human wickedness in high places. "Humility, as something beyond the real demand of correct self-appraisal, was specially a Christian virtue because it involved subservience to God. In a secular context it can only represent subservience to other men and their projects."[119] We likewise err if we bestow such wholehearted devotion on morality. To do so would be a form of idolatry.[120] Mitchell cites the Victorian Age as precisely such an instance of misplaced devotion. "The Victorians idolized morality, giving it that supreme importance which they were increasingly unable to accord to God."[121]

Miss Birdseye seems at one with the Victorians. She and Mother Teresa differ not in the quantity of time and energy they give to others, but in their basic attachments, manifested above all perhaps in the absence or presence of a prayer-life.

These two grounds for criticism lead us to ask whether the very notion of a moral saint is itself wrongly conceived. Adams argues that such a notion fails to correspond to what religious people usually understand saints to be. He provides an alternative phenomenological account. Saints are apt to be truthful rather than simply nice, controversial rather than inoffensive, joyous rather than humorless, attractive rather than bland. Their attractiveness derives from their holiness, and this holiness consists in a charisma or power that manages to convey in exceptional measure the presence of God. They give of themselves unstintedly to be sure, yet they take an intense and frank interest "in their own condition, their own perfection, and their own happiness."[122] Both their self-giving and their self-interest are founded in "a trust in God to provide for their growth and happiness."[123]

This understanding of saints accords with the depiction of obedient willing within a theocentric frame that I have tried to develop (and that is so whether or not one retains theological or other misgivings about sainthood as a status bestowed through actual canonization). Love for God can heighten rather than evacuate particular identity; one's self-awareness becomes focused rather than distracted. A life well-lived in this way will certainly include the realization of nonmoral values, and there will be delights more profound than those that bland optimism affords. Love for God subtends or affects all one's goals and projects, not simply the moral ones. Yet the nonmoral values will be ordered; and for this Wolf's account makes no provision. Her examples could suggest a specious version of liberal individualism in which "whatever one is into," however narrow or acquisitive or frivolous, is embraced indiscriminately.[124] The nonmoral values will also be in circuit with moral values to an extent her account ignores. Moreover, the importance of the conflict on which she and others dwell—whether it is unreasonable to permit impersonal moral demands always to win when they collide with the projects and commitments that give meaning to one's life—recedes for saints as Adams depicts them. On the one side, that their relation to God gives their lives meaning is too apparent to them to make the question of such meaning urgent on its own. They lack this reason to be anxious to press their own claims. On the other side, their relation to God they know in a community that links this relation necessarily to love of their neighbors. Moral and nonmoral values on modern reckonings are interlaced from the start. Saints who love their neighbors will not display the strictly donor-mentality that Wolf's moral saints do. They will however be both free and bound to care about the particular lives of others, and for the same reasons they care about their own.

6. DOES WHAT I CAN DO FOR ANYONE ELSE DIFFER UNAVOIDABLY FROM WHAT I CAN DO FOR MYSELF?

6.1. Sheer capabilities. Now I take up the second objection that finds impartiality deficient because it neglects to acknowledge distinctive and legitimate self-regarding considerations. This objection is predominantly descriptive. Impartiality fails to accommodate certain structural and fixed differences between my relation to myself and my relation to others.

Kant's account of these differences serves to introduce the points I wish to consider. As we will see, only a modest version of this account proves plausible. What Kant writes in *The Doctrine of Virtue* has the merit however of locating the differences with illuminating starkness:

> It is contradictory to say that I make another person's *perfection* my end and consider myself obligated to promote this. For the *perfection* of another man, as a person, consists precisely in *his own* power to adopt his end in accordance with his own concept of duty; and it is self-contradictory to demand that I do (make it my duty to do) what only the other person can do.[125]

Notice that the focus is on "can" and not on "ought."[126] I think that Kant reasons as follows. We are not required to maintain and promote happiness and perfection in ourselves and others in the same way. To do so is impossible. Instead, I have a duty to develop my own natural and moral perfection, but my happiness cannot be a duty since I naturally desire it. I have a duty to promote the happiness of others, but not their perfection. I contradict myself if I say that it is my duty to promote the perfection of others, because each agent's perfection is, again naturally, the work of his or her own freedom. So in my own case, "another person can indeed compel me to perform actions which are means to his end, but he cannot compel me *to have an end*; only I can make something my end."[127]

To maintain that I naturally desire my own happiness is similar to holding that self-love needs no encouragement. Both estimates agree that it is *redundant* to command me to seek my own happiness.

Yet Kant refuses also to say that it is *corrupt* or at least always potentially corrupting to seek my own happiness.[128] Such seeking is a morally permissible end and even an indirect obligation.[129] Partiality to self he condemns whenever it involves making an arbitrary exception on one's own behalf. But partiality to self is not his concern in the statements just cited. Another sort of asymmetry is reflected in these statements. Structural differences in my relation to myself and to others exist, and exist unavoidably, even when I am not problematically partial to myself. Such differences pass the universalizability test because they display relevant dissimilarities which obtain for *any* agent and *any* recipient.[130] No charge of arbitrariness therefore applies.

The claim about structural differences thus concerns sheer capabilities. What we can *effect* in others is more restricted than what we can effect in ourselves. And some things we can only do for ourselves, if they are to be done at all. It is crucial to distinguish this claim from our more commonplace evaluative assumptions about what protection and promotion encompass respectively, in the case of every human being. These assumptions focus on "ought" rather than "can." Protection involves negative restraints on doing harm, and harm is understood as reducing someone to a mere means or instrument. Each person should be viewed as possessing a sphere of inviolability. A direct and independent limit is set on what one person ought to do to another. Each recipient should retain a kind of veto power. Promotion involves positive cultivation of each person's well-being. Traditionally the principle—one should not do evil that good may come—restricts such cultivation to morally permissible actions. Apart from this restriction, help extends to what happens to a person as well as what he or she does. These commonplace assumptions all remain within the circle of the realizable. To insist that a direct and independent limit should be set on what one person may do to another assumes that the limit *can* be crossed. To commend positive cultivation assumes that a recipient *can* be benefited.

The claim about structural differences, on the other hand, concerns what is ineluctable. At Kant's hands this claim reflects his view that each human being possesses the capacity for free action, and that free action is the indispensable condition for one's moral good. To put it differently, the capacity to be an agent is descriptively fundamental to our concept of the person. Otherwise we are not fit subjects for praise and blame: the capacity is a necessary condition for either assessment. Now it follows that I cannot attain *another's* moral good by the exercise of *my* freedom. So I can have no duty (at least no "perfect" or "narrow" duty) to bring about another's moral good because I cannnot actually *adopt* another's ends for him or her or actually *achieve* another's moral good. An inescapable limit is thereby fixed respecting what I can do for another. Alternatively, I and I alone can adopt my own ends and attain my moral good by the exercise of my freedom.

It is important to notice that to accept this claim we do not have to distinguish as sharply as Kant does between one's own perfection and another's happiness. Indeed, one of Kant's most sympathetic interpreters, Allen W. Wood, criticizes the distinction as overly neat and incompatible with what Kant himself says elsewhere. Wood shows that Kant generally believes we can help others in their *moral* development and therefore that we can properly concern ourselves with their moral perfection. The ways we can influence the moral character of someone else are rich and varied; Wood's list includes advice, encouragement, example, discipline, education, and social improvement.[131] He acknowledges however that these exceedingly important kinds of influence do not invalidate the inescapable limit. The limit must remain, however suitably modified, if sense is to be made of the capacity for free action and of judgments of praise and blame. For where there is no limit, a person is not a subject whose actions may be imputed to him or her.

6.2. A theocentric assessment. Let us ask once more: how is the claim about structural differences viewed within a theocentric frame of explanation and evaluation? No simple answer will do, for distinctive theological considerations impinge here as well to establish an agenda of their own. The focus shifts irreversibly from moral perfection to redemption. That which waits on God and on God's prevenience is now the starting point. And it is clear at once that I emphatically cannot, by my own efforts, redeem either myself or my neighbor. This inability relativizes severely the importance that we ascribe to the asymmetry. Moreover, to say that each agent's perfection is necessarily the work of his or her own freedom is too susceptible to Pelagian readings to survive intact in most theological schemes. Thus, we confront limits of a far deeper kind than the inescapable one which is our immediate concern. The deeper limits under which the entire Christian community lives are indicated plainly by Barth:

> The Christian community cannot redeem the world. It cannot redeem even a single individual from any one of his enslavements by sin and its consequences, just as within the community itself no one brother can redeem another. . . . What men require is the freedom of the Spirit. This the community cannot give them. This they can only declare to them in the hope that their testimony will not be in vain, that God will use it to cause that which it attests to be revealed to them and effective for them.[132]

Yet the community also lives by the testimony it is commissioned to give, "to see to it that the comfort and exhortation of the divine Yes are declared."[133] We are to attest and conform on our own level and with our own capacities to this divine Yes. The "we" is crucial. That Christians characteristically stress community should never be ignored. The commission itself after all is in the first instance communal: two or three at least, who gather together in the Lord's name. We accordingly have good reason to make strong sociality claims and to resist any ghostly individualism which many take Kant's distinction to assume. At a minimum, we should recognize that we never create from scratch the beliefs and convictions that we employ to form and explain our behavior. We inherit, willy-nilly, a language and a tradition. Philosophically we should follow the familiar route charted by the later Wittgenstein, namely, that the conditions for understanding any given concept necessarily presuppose a public, social context, and so by extension that self-awareness cannot occur without some initial contact with others. My relations to others are necessary to my knowledge of myself.[134] We are not self-contained atoms, each complete in itself, impervious to companions and surroundings. In short, we influence one another, render mutual assistance, and prize personal and social relations more pervasively than Kant's distinction, with its high doctrine of autonomy, suggests.

We also noticed, however, that Wood modifies Kant's high doctrine but does not thereby abandon the claim about an inescapable limit. Is this claim affirmed in any similar ongoing way within the Christian tradition? I think that in major historical segments of the tradition we find a paradoxical attitude. On the one side, we find the limit *relativized* in two ways I have considered here. Any difference between myself and my neighbor is relativized in importance as we focus not on perfection but on redemption. And the stress on community aids and abets this relativization. On the other side, we find the limit *intensified* wherever each self's relation to God is affirmed as distinctive and the final end of the self's pilgrimage. To say the self is more than merely the product of social forces now does not go far enough. We must also say that the self's relation to God is incommensurable with social forces of every kind. To say as many followers of Kant do—that the self-contradiction in compelling an agent to have an end is a logical or conceptual matter only—likewise does not go far enough. We must also say in a religious or theological account that each person *is* a qualitatively unique entity. This says a good deal more than what a formal elucidation of the concepts requires in order to make sense of the capacity for free action and of judgments of praise and blame.

The religious or theological account will then intensify the asymmetry we have examined along the following lines. One's love for God does not occur by passive necessity, even through the working of grace or at the hands of another person. There is something each person must do, for it to be done at all. So another person can witness to me and endeavor to influence me in all the ways Wood mentions, for instance. Witnessing, mutual support and care, admonition, counsel, etc. are certainly integral to the life of the Christian community. But another person cannot transmit to me, exhaustively and without remainder, whatever faith he or she has. If such transmission were possible, we would have to abandon the teaching that religious faith to be genuine must be uncoerced. And this teaching has a long and central place in the Christian tradition. Thus Luther writes: "As nobody else can go to heaven or hell for me, so nobody else can believe or disbelieve for me; as nobody else can open or close heaven or hell to me, so nobody else can drive me to belief or unbelief."[135] If one truly loves God, God cannot be lost against one's will. I do not possess the power to take my neighbor with me all the way to perdition without the other's complaisance, or vice versa. Persons are separate in their identity and, if we believe perdition has duration, in their final destiny. However the matter stands with perdition, each person in this intensification process has a destiny superior to time, and so a noninterchangeable pilgrimage.

6.3. Two effects: to cleave and to commend, and the pocket of agency. An ongoing task in interpreting the law of love is to specify effects this asymmetry has but not to inflate the role it plays. This task proves difficult, especially if I am right to find a paradoxical attitude within the Christian tradition. Here I want to specify two effects and expose two inflationary moves. I shall compare relevant senses of impartiality as I go along.

The first effect concerns love for God. Each agent's own love for God differs from the agent's role in helping his or her neighbor to love God. Augustine (according to Oliver O'Donovan) identifies the difference in this way:

> ... [T]he love which this man bears his neighbor is not the same love that he bears himself, for the end of action is cleaving to the supreme good, and that is something one can do only on one's own behalf. There is an imbalance between the "cleaving" which he does for himself and the "commending" which he does for the neighbor. Loving his neighbor "as himself" can mean only that he seeks to instill in the neighbor a self-love similar to his own.[136]

To speak of an imbalance does not mean that objectively I matter more than others. It means rather that a doctrine of the *imago Dei* will have to accommodate a combination of elements: the dignity of every person consists in features we share in common, one of which is a difference between loving God oneself and commending love for God to others.

Moreover, we should view this imbalance in light of two beliefs. (a) The first is that in our respective prospects for loving God, my neighbor and I cannot be rivals. No situation of scarcity or other reason for conflict arises. One has rather to do with God whose love is inexhaustible. The supreme good is not a finite resource subject to competing claims of which only some can be satisfied. So for example, if I fail to cleave to the supreme good (when to cleave means to love God with heart, soul, and mind), I sacrifice no advantage that my neighbor can *thereby* (and not otherwise) possibly acquire. (b) The second belief is that one's love for God is relational rather than reciprocal. That is, one depends on and communes with God at the deepest level imaginable (and a further belief in petitionary prayer assumes that genuine interaction is possible). But there is no reciprocity in that no *mutual* needs are met, assistance rendered, or enrichment provided.[137] One depends on redemption which, as I noted earlier, relativizes totally the asymmetry that concerns us here. Redemption comes by God's grace, the grace that Christians confess is fully disclosed in Jesus Christ. It is pernicious folly if either my neighbor or I suppose we can in our interactions each redeem the other. Our interactions are more limited, yet within these limits more reciprocal and interdependent. And often we do confront finite resources, conditions of scarcity, competing claims, and gains and losses at one another's expense.

Such interdependence is pervasive. Before I mention aspects of it which one inflationary move I shall consider disregards, I want to identify a second effect of the asymmetry. This effect concerns the second love command: sometimes here as well I cannot do as much for my neighbor as I can do for myself, despite the conditions of reciprocity that characterize our historical existence.

There are certain religious actions, for example, that I perform for myself in a way I cannot fittingly perform for my neighbor. Repentance before God is one such action I undertake for myself. I can exhort my neighbor to repent, but if I try to repent on his or her behalf I transgress a boundary that renders me culpably arrogant and demeans my neighbor.[138] Forgiveness may be another such action. For me to forgive someone who has wronged me is appropriate; for me to forgive (rather than to pardon, or rather than as a priest or pastor to declare God's forgiveness) someone who has wronged another person is presumptuous.

Certain other actions the agent can perform fully on the neighbor's behalf and, moreover, can envisage complete reciprocity as their possible result. Yet these actions remain in two senses unilateral. I referred to the actions in subsection 1 as I described *agape's* efforts to found and enhance personal relations marked by closeness and social relations marked by concord. The agent refuses to make a demand for reciprocity a condition for care about another's well-being. Though one does not await, anticipate, or demand a response in kind, one nevertheless desires and hopes for such a response, and takes actual attainment as both a genuine possibility and as the fruition one seeks. How do they remain unilateral? First, they require my own initiative. It is plausible to claim that I can bind or commit only myself. Or at least I can commit myself in a way I cannot commit others.[139] I must set in motion an offer of love to another and so establish the conditions within which a response takes place. Second, the actions cannot coerce the desired response in kind. When I attempt to force the desired response to occur, I violate the conditions of another's consent and so I invariably fail, whether or not I ostensibly achieve my aim because I can bring some type of superior power. I must learn to allow for the possibility that the response may never occur, and discipline my desire accordingly. I can continue nonetheless to commit myself to my neighbor in independence from the response for which I hope. Yet I must be prepared to modify the expression my commitment takes. And certain modifications I deem appropriate but do not welcome.

Actions like these suggest that the second effect of the asymmetry provides another reason to ask how far it is possible to identify with others. It seems that I *cannot* just go into the hopper with everyone else—whether or not it is *undesirable* to do so. I cannot, not because I lack the requisite disinterestedness when my own interests are at stake. I cannot, because the asymmetry points, as remarked before, to sheer capabilities. To be one finite agent among others means that what I can effect in others is more restricted than what I can effect in myself. To be in community with others involves a distinction as well as a relation, a distinction that includes conditions of agency on each side of the relation.

But must proponents of impartiality deny that each of us is a finite creature subject to such agential conditions? We noticed earlier that Kant does not think the structural differences in question require us to make an arbitrary exception on our own behalf or to be otherwise culpably partial to ourselves. Such differences do not then undermine the perpetual campaign against inordinate self-assertion which enlists arguments from impartiality as it proceeds. The differences pass the universalizability test because they display relevant dissimilarities that obtain for any agent and any recipient. They are thus compatible with the affirmation that objectively no one matters more than anyone else.

What the asymmetry does call into question are versions of impartiality that take the possibility of identifying with others to the point where no distinction remains between self-other and other-other relations. Let me give one example.

Hare, in an interesting passage, acknowledges that one may fail, even with the best will in the world, to benefit others as readily as one benefits oneself.

> ... [S]ometimes, when I do things for myself, I know that I benefit, but when I do or try to do things for other people, they may not be the right things, or, even if they are, may be ineffective without their cooperation. I have myself during the course of my life been much more successful in doing good for myself than in trying, with the same or greater expenditure of effort, to do good for other people, because often they do not have the same notion of their good as I have.[140]

The context for this statement however is that "prima facie principles requiring partiality have a high acceptance-utility even when judged by an impartial critical standpoint."[141] One *may* thus be partial to oneself. Yet Hare justifies this partiality under a general heading of "prudent investment" in reference to which he also justifies loyalties to certain other people to whom we stand in a special relation. So children in general are more likely to benefit if I as a parent (and every other person *qua* parent) devote the greater part of my time to raising my own. And similarly, I (and every other person *qua* agent) am more likely to benefit myself than others—because I have privileged access to my own notion of good and can more effectively carry it out—and so I may do more things for myself than for others. Yet the limit we are attempting to understand shows a relevant dissimilarity between these two cases as well. The dissimilarity recalls in part our previous discussion of how self-other and other-other relations differ. Suppose we agree that the prospects that children will flourish are enhanced immeasurably when they receive painstaking care and affection; and that the most adequate way to provide this is concentrated, ongoing, stable parenting (and of course much else besides that lacks this element of calculation, however benevolent the calculating is). I determine that I promote the good of *others* impartially when I focus my parental energies on the well-being of my own children, and commend that other parents follow the same course with their children. But in the second case when I consider why others are unlikely to benefit from my actions as much as I do, I confront the greater room for maneuver over my own actions that my agency affords. The asymmetry, in short, intrudes. Hare himself seems, perhaps unwittingly, to approach the limit in question when he admits that one's other-regarding efforts may prove ineffective because others refuse to cooperate. We can take his admission to witness to this: one simply controls others' actions less (including the actions of one's own children) than one's own. Therefore, however we decide to employ arguments based on impartiality, we should not ignore the pocket of agency that remains. We ignore it in this case when we try to assimilate it altogether to calculations that suit other-other relations.

Now that I have attempted to specify two effects that the asymmetry has, I want to locate two inflationary moves that we should avoid. These moves are not ones to which proponents of impartiality are especially liable, but they deserve to be identified to prevent misunderstandings of the asymmetry itself.

6.4. *First inflation: the self preferred.* One such move is to transmute a recognition that sometimes I can most effectively benefit myself into a policy that in general I should prefer myself. This move is illicit on three counts.

First, it fails to notice that the point about effectiveness is part of a larger recognition about comparative control. This larger recognition also includes a point about degrees of responsibility. Insofar as I enjoy greater control over my own actions, I am more responsible for them. And this is one of the reasons I should worry first about my own contributions to evil. My worry gives no support to a policy of preferring whatever benefits me. It disposes me instead to bring my own actions under particularly critical scrutiny.

Second, another point in the larger recognition is that I transgress the freedom of others when I equate what I can do for them with what I can do for myself. What is at stake then is the honoring of appropriate capabilities. And such honoring is as other-regarding as it is self-regarding. It does not authorize me to commend avoidable preference for myself.

Third, the weight of the Christian tradition stands predominantly against the policy that, in general, I should prefer myself. My love for God is tied to my love of the neighbor in so necessary and straightforward a way that such a policy is not to be seriously entertained. ("If any one says, 'I love God,' and hates his brother, he is a liar; for he who does not love his brother whom he has seen, cannot love God whom he has not seen. And this commandment we have from him, that he who loves God should love his brother also." [I John 4:20-21]) The policy is also too nearly akin to inordinate self-assertion, distracted self-preoccupation, etc., to be condoned. My resourcefulness at sinning I find appalling enough without the fresh opportunities this policy licenses. But, to find that these considerations in the Christian tradition are decisive for rejecting the policy does not require us to deny the asymmetry.

6.5. Second inflation: isolationist self-sufficiency. Another inflationary move proceeds from the belief that genuine love for God is uncoerced by other human beings—whether as attained or as lost—to a normative depiction of the individual as self-contained and autonomous *vis-à-vis* other human beings.

This move raises general questions about how to get the interplay right between agency and sociality, questions that take us beyond the present inquiry. I want, however, to give examples of interdependence to support my earlier insistence that we must resist any ghostly individualism. I shall do so by sampling possibilities that build again illicitly from the actions I introduced to illustrate how sometimes I cannot do as much for my neighbor as I can do for myself.

Consider first the claim that I can repent before God for myself in a way that I cannot repent before God for my neighbor. The asymmetry helps to make this claim intelligible. Yet I inflate this claim if I suppose it requires me to view myself as self-sufficient and isolated so that (a) I determine apart from community and tradition which actions call for repentance, and (b) I deliberate alone and struggle alone in coming to see that I should repent.

In the case of (a), the asymmetry in itself does not demand that I violate or otherwise except myself from intersubjective agreements that identify which actions are loving or unloving in general, actions that obtain for any agent and any recipient. It does not forbid me from holding that religious and moral values are inexpugnably social in that I cannot know what they are without learning about them within the communities of which I am a part. And their authority for me does not have to rest solely on my decision to give them authority. I need not then be self-sufficient in the sense that I decide which actions do and which do not count as having religious and moral significance. In the case of (b), the asymmetry does not consign me to practical solitude. I am at liberty to acknowledge unashamedly that I cannot acquire clarity about the evil I do apart from deliberation with others; and that I cannot summon the strength to repent of the evil I do apart from the encouragement of others. The asymmetry points only to this: deliberation and encouragement may well be essential and still may not, by themselves, *ensure* that repentance actually occurs.

I also inflate the role of the agent in repentance if I suppose that the evil I do concerns myself alone. On the contrary, the wrong that occasions repentance often consists in my harming my neighbor by what I do or fail to do. It includes culpable carelessness. It may require direct restitution. I must not assume that my responsibility in corrupting someone else is less than genuine because I cannot take the neighbor all the way to perdition without his or her complaisance.[142] That there must be final complaisance does not mean that I lack the power to make matters for someone else far harder than might otherwise be the case. And I must consider the effects of my failures not only on other individuals, but on the practices and values of the communities of which I am a part. Nothing about the asymmetry prevents my acknowledging these wider effects of my actions. Indeed, if what I said to counter the first sort of inflation is correct (see 6.4), the asymmetry should sensitize me to such effects.

Consider next the claim that *agape* includes a unilateral effort to found and enhance personal relations marked by closeness and social relations marked by concord. I inflate this claim when I attribute virtually exclusive attention to autonomy as defining the work of love in the case of both agents and recipients. On the one side, the attribution makes so basic my relative ability as an agent to initiate movements of love toward others that it obscures my total situation. Often I am also a recipient. We are reminded again of the point that moral principles not only tell agents what they may and should do and not do, but also what they may and should resist, object to, and demand. I offered suggestions in subsection 3 about how we may interpret the law of love to incorporate this point. Often too, both my initiatives and responses are constrained and otherwise affected by interactions with others. In fact, our lives are suffused with impure cases: unwanted decisions such as acceding to "coercive offers" in corporate business transactions, firing incompetent employees in need, giving money under threat to drug addicts, plotting to bring down tyrannical governments, etc. Neither my situation as a recipient nor the complexity of these cases receive their due when we focus single-mindedly on autonomous initiatives. We need not interpret the asymmetry we are considering as a transhistorical capacity to engage in absolute beginnings.[143]

On the other side, among the features of the neighbor's well-being that I am to protect and promote the attribution elevates the other's autonomous choices. This elevation easily leads to two mistakes. First, it can result in a tacit equation of dignity and autonomy. And this equation conflicts with a traditional understanding of neighbor-love in which what happens to a person and not only what he or she decides should elicit one's care and concern.[144] Autonomy is integral to the neighbor's dignity, but not exhaustive of it. Once again, the asymmetry does not require us to make this tacit equation. Second, and less obviously, the elevation can result in a selective focus on the measure of accountable control those who are wronged retain over their own responses. I shall cite one example.

Augustine discusses in *The City of God* the case of the noble Roman matron Lucretia. She was sexually violated and proceeded to kill herself to show others by her self-inflicted punishment that she was not complicit in the evil that was done. Augustine contrasts her death with the response of Christian women similarly violated.

> They declined to avenge upon themselves the guilt of others, and so add crimes of their own to those crimes in which they had no share. For this they would have done had their shame driven them to homicide, as the lust of their enemies had driven them to adultery. Within their own souls, in the witness of their own conscience, they enjoy the glory of chastity. In the sight of God, too, they are esteemed pure, and this contents them; they ask no more: it suffices them to have opportunity of doing good, and they decline to evade the distress of human suspicion, lest they thereby deviate from the divine law.[145]

The Christian women cannot share the culpability of their violators. They retain a measure of accountable control only over whether they add to the evil inflicted on them.

The asymmetry supports to this extent the points Augustine emphasizes: certain actions are chiefly responses to the initiatives of others, especially their transgressions; and sometimes we can retain accountability for our responses that we cannot extend to the initiating actions of others. Yet the asymmetry allows us as well to stress critical points about social reform. For instance, the evil that was done to Lucretia and the Christian women reflects deformed views of women resident in the society at large. It is surely not enough to dwell on what the individual recipients do. We should oppose the deformed views themselves and labor to change the character of the society so that men are less apt to treat women in this way.

Identifying this second inflation shows that the asymmetry need not support the doctrine that William Galston calls *hyperindividualism*. Such a doctrine "overemphasizes the separateness of individuals, focusing on the claims or 'rights' they can assert without considering their effects on other individuals or on the nature and very possibility of the political community."[146] These effects and the nature of the political community are proper concerns of *agape*, which the asymmetry does not undermine.

My primary aim in this subsection, however, is to trace the asymmetry's own importance for an account of *agape*. Although the asymmetry is distinct from hyperindividualism, it also more obviously is distinct from a doctrine at the other extreme, *hyperorganicism*, which "devalues individual subjectivity and particularity, hypostatizing the community as a unified entity."[147] The lengths to which this doctrine goes is brought out in the following story by Simone de Beauvoir:

> Toward the end of the afternoon, sitting on the grass next to Queneau, I had a discussion with him about the "end of history." It was a frequent subject of conversation at the time. We had discovered the reality and weight of history, now we were wondering about its meaning. Queneau ... thought that one day all individuals would be reconciled in the triumphant unity of Spirit. "But what if I have a pain in my foot?" I said. "*We* shall have a pain in your foot," Queneau replied.[148]

A less amusing variant to the exchange is: "But what if I die?" "*We* shall die." Because the exchange moves attention from agency to consciousness, it leads beyond the present discussion. Still, the asymmetry helps indirectly to consign Queneau's reply to the category of wishful thoughts.

It is easier to repudiate both extremes than it is to bring agency and sociality viably together. Christianity has had its radically individualist and collectivist moments, movements, and defenders. Again, I cannot attempt here to propose a viable mixture. I argue only that ineluctable agency does not make each one of us self-contained, but it enters nonetheless into our efforts to depict one's fundamental situation before God and neighbors.

Section Three
The Case Reviewed

I took as my point of departure a traditional conviction about fitting differences and essential connections between love for God, neighbor-love, and self-love. According to the conviction, God demands absolute attachment and devotion, adoration of a kind that we transfer to our neighbors or to ourselves on pain of idolatry. The great and first commandment—to love God with all your heart, soul, and mind—retains a necessary discreteness, generating attitudes and actions for which it alone supplies the final rationale. Love for God also remains the most basic and comprehensive human love of all; it subtends the others. The second commandment—to love your neighbor as yourself—also retains a discreteness, in that such love is more than a mere means through which we love God. Each of us constitutes a terminal point for another's attitudes and actions, an irreducibly valuable end. The conviction emphasizes essential connections as well as fitting differences between the three loves. While we must never reverse the order of the commandments, the second is "like" the first. Those who love God supremely may rightly love their neighbors and themselves. The connections among the three loves are neither accidental nor capricious.

In this inquiry I concentrated on questions of right neighbor-love and self-love. As I explored these questions, I sought to pay homage to the priority of love for God in two chief ways. First, I placed the discussion of neighbor-love and self-love within a theocentric frame of explanation and evaluation. I thereby treated the second commandment and not only the first as part of a determinately religious and theological body of belief and practice. Second, I took a particular meaning of love for God to authorize a case for universal love. Love for God includes fidelity to God in loving whom God loves. Such fidelity leads us to attest, on our own level and with our own capacities, to the conviction that all people are created, sustained, and redeemed by God.

The case for universal love I pursued in three stages. We noted first that a serious commitment to inclusiveness leads us to focus on the enemy. How the enemy is treated is the key test of whether we love our neighbor. The enemy's claim on our attention and care is linked to the human countenance he or she bears, and to beliefs about creation and redemption. I observed that these same links make the self a proper object of attention and care. A case for universal love then plausibly extends to neighbor and self. I took this conclusion as axiomatic for the remainder of the inquiry. But how are we to intepret this extension? At the second stage I introduced what appeared to be the most straightforward interpretation. Inclusiveness demands that we appraise impartially the claims of neighbor and self. To say there can be proper neighbor-love and self-love is to say that we *require* no disparity in either direction. But this interpretation fails to confront various kinds of unease with impartiality. Thus, at the third stage I identified and discussed four of the most important challenges to impartiality. I located the challenges in the asymmetries between one's relation to one's neighbor and one's relation to oneself. The asymmetries help to shape a full account of neighbor-love and self-love.

I believe the truth of the matter lies in combining considerations introduced at the second and third stages. Universal love should reckon with both similarities and differences between neighbor-love and self-love. Christians need not in this case abjure efforts to acknowledge complexities and to strive for a judicious resolution.

My task now is to review the second and third stages a final time, and offer general conclusions about the similarities and differences with which universal love should reckon. Let us start with similarities, in subsection 7, and turn to differences, in subsection 8. I shall conclude by identifying two important subjects, in subsection 9, that I must leave for discussion elsewhere.

7. WHAT SIMILARITIES BETWEEN NEIGHBOR AND SELF DOES UNIVERSAL LOVE LEGITIMATE?

That universal love extends to neighbor and self means at a minimum that both are to be serious subjects of attention and care. To mark such seriousness, I presented at the beginning of the second subsection a series of claims that went from excluding no one to considering neighbor and self alike. Although I shall refer to earlier claims in the series when I review the asymmetries, I focused then and focus now on the last claim: we should appraise impartially the neighbor's well-being and the self's well-being. I noted that in modern discussions impartiality is not one determinate view, but a class of views. What unites them as a class is that they commonly stress interpersonal consistency, and invoke a role-reversal test exemplified in the golden rule. Before I considered the more specialized meanings that impartiality acquires in positive ethical theories, I called attention to an informal alliance between appeals to consistency and the law of love. Our subsequent discussion reinforces the importance of this alliance. Indeed, I think we should conclude that universal love legitimates such appeals as practically indispensable, whatever we say about other senses of impartiality, and whatever modifications the asymmetries bring. Let me elaborate.

7.1. Interpersonal consistency, and the role-reversal test. We saw that general appeals on behalf of interpersonal consistency, or universalizability, encompass also, and often interchangeably, justice and even-handedness. Double standards of varying kinds represent the common foe. Self-partiality in particular comes under critical scrutiny. Within and not simply outside the Christian tradition, appeals to impartiality as interpersonal consistency oppose, above all, one's unrelenting tendency to make an arbitrary exception in one's own favor.

We took similar note of the role-reversal test. Some critics of impartiality, e.g., Williams, refer favorably to it. This test is often interpreted as an extension of the demand for interpersonal consistency. Yet the test carries independent weight. Gewirth usefully distinguishes between interpersonal consistency as embodying a kind of judicial impartiality, and the role-reversal test as embodying as well a kind of legislative impartiality.[149] The test combats disparity between neighbor and self by asking me to put myself in the other person's place. I must be prepared to test judgments I make by asking if I find them acceptable irrespective of whether I am on the giving or receiving end. ("You wouldn't like it if your sister did that to you, would you?" "No." "Well, then, don't do it to her.") The most minimal version of the test asks me to imagine myself in my neighbor's place, but leaves intact my own beliefs, values, and preferences (although only those I find acceptable whether I am on the giving or receiving end).

Both interpersonal consistency and the role-reversal test suffer from widely canvassed difficulties. Do they recognize sufficiently that what an agent wants *qua* recipient may not accord with what the neighbor wants? Do they allow the wants on which a particular agent and recipient happen to agree to be immoral ones? And even if such difficulties can be met, the appeals cannot be sufficient criteria for an account of universal love that forms part of a determinately Christian ethic.[150]

Still, they can be necessary criteria. It is wrong to suppose that they are either platitudes for which we need not regularly speak up, or themselves legitimate targets for dismissal. We should strive to adhere to the requirements of interpersonal consistency and to accept the constraints that the role-reversal test imposes. For both do significant normative work. They provide continuously summonable points of reference in deliberation and debate and they reduce the range of morally permitted disagreements. They alert us to the myriad forms that partiality takes: our readiness to criticize and our bristling at criticism, our harshness with groups we oppose and our indulgence of groups we support, our indifference to those we victimize and our pleas for understanding and forbearance when we are tried for our crimes. In short, we are sensitized above all to our partiality to ourselves, but also more generally to the double standards that others employ, sometimes against our own legitimate claims. To love our neighbors and ourselves similarly means here fairly or even-handedly, in the sense that we refrain from making arbitrary exceptions in either direction.

The war against arbitrariness that love must continually wage then legitimates general appeals to impartiality as consistency and reciprocal acceptability. Such appeals occur too frequently in the Bible and elsewhere to support an unqualified contrast between impartiality and justice that we find in a number of writings nowadays. For example, Alan Verhey draws such a contrast in his study of ethics and the New Testament. Verhey assumes that impartiality is invariably associated with a perspectiveless view of things, one which ignores or disowns "the identity and integrity of moral agents."[151] I discussed and rejected such a perspectiveless view, especially in connection with the third asymmetry. But we neglect important complexities when we attend only to this view. We then fail to credit the normative work that everyday appeals to interpersonal consistency and the role-reversal test perform, work that often coincides with justice and with universal love, and that need not disown the identity and integrity of moral agents. This failure is important to remedy, given current widespread and sometimes indiscriminate theological and philosophical attacks on impartiality.

7.2. Impartiality in positive ethical theories. I turned next to more specialized meanings impartiality acquires in modern moral philosophy, rehearsing standard utilitarian and neo-Kantian accounts. We found that impartiality is nuanced in accordance with particular ethical theories. Utilitarians and neo-Kantians may be impartial, in that they avoid interpersonal inconsistency and pass the role-reversal test, and yet may disagree among themselves.

To examine these disagreements shifts attention away from the general war on arbitrariness that love must continually wage. We descend here to a level where particular interpretations of impartiality, and not self-evident ones, make their appearance. No longer can we ask straightforwardly which interpretations universal love legitimates. We cannot do so because at this level especially universal love is also not self-interpreting. How we construe it depends on a range of specific considerations. I shall confine myself to two disagreements and hope to illustrate the following. (a) Christians confront as well the tensions these disagreements reflect. (b) The disagreements themselves do not turn on an unwillingness by the disputants to treat neighbor and self alike. By assuming similarities between neighbor and self, the disagreements point to other considerations that a comprehensive account of the law of love must weigh.

The first disagreement centers on how we should honor the very inclusiveness that universal love mandates. To affirm that we should protect and promote the dignity of every person leaves open how *actively* we should try to take *every* person into account. That is, should we view all of humankind as the recipients of our actions? Or should we focus on particular recipients with whom we have directly to do? To say that the neighbor is anyone affected by one's actions proves ambiguous in this respect. How many neighbors one affects depends partly on how many one strives to affect.[152] The utilitarian enjoins us to maximize the most desirable state of affairs overall, and this includes viewing all of humankind as the recipients of our actions. Gewirth, as one neo-Kantian, here opposes utilitarianism expressly; he enjoins us to concentrate on specific duties that one owes to one's particular recipients.[153]

The second disagreement centers on the trade-offs we permit among the persons whose dignity we should protect and promote. We saw that as utilitarians focus on the state of the total causal nexus, they propose an ideally complete form of imaginative identification with others, a doctrine of negative responsibility, and a determination to an indefinite degree of decisions that any given agent makes by the decisions of others. We also saw that neo-Kantians hold that such a focus on the state of the total causal nexus allows too many sacrifices of certain persons' claims in order to advance a greater number of other persons' claims. They seek to build in limits to permissible trade-offs by considering at a basic level actions and policies, and not only overall outcomes.

Christians confront tensions that correspond in part to those we encounter among utilitarians and neo-Kantians.[154] Consider the first disagreement. On the one side, the focus on the enemy carries by itself expansionist pressures. And Christians often interpret inclusiveness radically to foster particular concern for the poor and oppressed.[155] One thinks, for example, of Jacques Ellul's injunction to care about the "uninteresting poor" around the world, i.e., those whose plight it is unfashionable to mention, who risk being forgotten altogether.[156] On the other side, some Christians claim that I should distinguish between near and distant neighbors and concentrate on those nearest, i.e., those with whom I have to do directly and distinctively. Near and distant neighbors do not make up a single class whose members all have claims I am positively obliged to consider on an equal footing. I do not then commend generalized benevolence as utilitarianism does.

Instead I am prepared to allow the claims of my actual neighbors to take precedence over the claims of "humanity at large." The distinction remains inclusive in two senses. First, to say that I am not positively obliged to consider everyone's good on an equal footing still allows me to say that each person's good is equally worthy of consideration. Second, *anyone* can become an actual neighbor. No special conditions are attached in advance. So the Good Samaritan transcends religious and ethnic barriers when he aids the definite man he does. The distinction does not therefore eliminate a place for stringent demands on agents actively to promote good. But it also provides no warrant for adding "overall."

Consider the second disagreement. Many Christians confront similar tensions again. They have reasons of their own to treat "ethical maximalism" seriously, and show some affinity with utilitarians in this respect. At least they go beyond minimal, non-risky duties to avoid harm as they seek positively to promote good. Yet utilitarian maximization is another matter, when it abandons independent moral constraints on total gains and losses. Traditionally Christians stand closer to neo-Kantians in seeking to limit permissible trade-offs. One rationale for setting limits goes back to a point I introduced in the second subsection. I said then that to regard each person as irreducibly valuable appears vacuous apart from particular estimates of what we should always or never do to people when we believe they have worth. The estimates center on noncomparative attention to what treatments every person's dignity requires and prohibits.

Such estimates establish restrictions on what we may do to promote good overall. The sole normative word does not rest in the outcome itself. The estimates are sometimes marshalled to support the traditional Christian claim that one may not do evil to achieve good.[157] As previously noted, Christian writers may differ strenuously among themselves about which actions qualify as "doing evil." Some, for example, eschew violence altogether. Others forbid only direct and intentional taking of innocent life. Certain actions are nonetheless forbidden absolutely, no matter how beneficial the overall effects of these actions might be.

The estimates of what we should always or never do to people when we believe they have worth may also support a focus on individual persons considered as inviolable in themselves. Each person's well-being is to constitute a terminal point for another's attitudes and actions. This focus generates resistance to practices that threaten to make any person merely part of, or systematically subservient to, the larger society. To take a contemporary example from biomedical ethics, experiments on individual patients are justified only when the patients themselves stand to benefit, and not when the benefits go solely to third parties, even the entire human race.[158]

It is crucial to realize that in both areas of disagreement, we may feel the tensions in question without ceasing to honor similarities between neighbor and self. Consider again the first disagreement. On the one side, radical interpretations of inclusiveness can encompass concern for the self as one of the poor and oppressed. On the other side, the distinction between near and distant neighbors does not on its own signal a disparity between neighbor and self, since I am at least as close to myself as I am to my near neighbors. Consider too the second disagreement. On the one side, many proponents of ethical maximalism are uniformly stringent, even disallowing, as I indicated, an impartialist case for supererogation. On the other side, we can interpret as universal in scope the claim that one may not do evil to achieve good. Whatever forbidden actions we take it to include, the claim is no "respecter of persons".[159] Its binding force applies to all: extending to those outside the particular groups of which we are a part, attesting to the dignity of every person by erecting at least uniformly stringent negative safeguards. These safeguards have been taken to apply to neighbor and self alike. Moreover, resistance to practices that threaten to make any person merely part of, or systematically subservient to, the larger society can apply to one's neighbor or oneself.

Christians should keep their own counsels and wrestle with their own legacies in attempting to resolve such disagreements. Yet we should not expect perfect unanimity. The currents that pull us back and forth are too strong and the difficulty of the questions too substantial to foreclose reasonable debate. In any case, although I have offered suggestions, this is not the place to propose my own resolutions. I shall content myself with having shown respects in which judgments diverge about how to honor universal love, and that many such judgments remain compatible with treating neighbor and self similarly.

8. WHAT DIFFERENCES BETWEEN NEIGHBOR AND SELF DOES UNIVERSAL LOVE ACCOMMODATE?

Since I assessed each asymmetry in its own right, I concentrate here on determining more precisely in what respects each is compatible with universal love. I shall try to show that universal love is a more adequate final point of reference than impartiality. While universal love allies itself with impartiality at certain junctures, it represents an advance over impartiality because it more readily accommodates differences between neighbor-love and self-love. It is less liable to the impersonalizing pressures that certain versions of impartiality exert. The advance is considerable, if I am right to claim that an understanding of what proper neighbor-love and self-love include turns on both similarities and differences. Let us review then differences between neighbor and self to which the asymmetries call attention. I hope thereby to answer a question I mentioned at the outset: we can affirm the asymmetries as marking suitably different ways to love God, and our neighbors and ourselves in God.

8.1. A practical swerve. The first asymmetry challenges impartiality on the neighbor's behalf. Proponents focus on radically other-regarding elements in *agape* and defend a strategy of altruistic dedication to the good of others. Here impartial protection and promotion of the self's good and the neighbor's good represents a gain over egoism and yet remains normatively flawed by New Testament lights.

To assess this challenge, I had first to show that the initial contrast between impartiality and altruism was overdrawn. First, we found in nuanced accounts of impartiality wider room for normative maneuver than a simple refusal to permit any disparity between self and others suggests. Impartiality in these accounts does not reduce to a comprehensive tit-for-tat. And it does allow for dissimilar treatment on the neighbor's behalf even when such treatment involves disproportionate inconvenience to oneself. The accent falls, to be sure, on allowance: the disparity between self and others is neither required nor forbidden. It rests on agent-consent. Still, such allowance supplies one reason to distinguish between self-other and other-other relations, and to make a place for supererogation.

Second, we found that within the Christian tradition, some do not stress altruism as such. Their concern is with the convictions that bind all those within the church. They rule out violence, for example, as a response to evil for anyone in the community, self and neighbor alike. Impartiality of a sort is then upheld, at least in this area.

Third, we found that Christian altruists occupy a complicated position in relation both to secular impartialists and to those in the peace churches. Altruists distinguish between self-other and other-other relations, though not for the reason that secular impartialists do. Altruists insist in turn on a distinction between the shedding of blood and the shedding of innocent blood in other-other situations, but not in self-other ones. They may agree in part with secular impartialists in the former situation, and agree with those in the peace churches in the latter situation.

These qualifications of the initial contrast between impartiality and altruism led me next to distinguish, in effect, two questions. First, does love ever warrant resistance, and if so, what kinds? Second, do loving attitudes and actions differ in other-other relations and self-other relations, and if so, in what respects? Our answers to each question sometimes overlap, yet we achieve greater clarity when we refuse to collapse them.

Answers to the first question depend on what we find a Christian ethic substantively to require and permit. How uniformly binding we take nonviolence to be, for instance, reflects our exegetical verdicts on various Biblical passages, our moral judgments and empirical estimates about the importance and possibility of justice-oriented power within and between societies, etc. This was not the place to pursue such matters, although I acknowledged that I find myself a realist in the tradition of Augustine. What I argued here was that in the midst of countless nonviolent interactions, when a person is reduced to a wholly menial status, in assaults on the human countenance that both neighbor and self bear, resistance in the name of love is sometimes justified.

Answers to the second question depend on how we finally bring together the complex considerations associated with universal love, altruism, and impartiality that we canvassed under the first asymmetry. Again, I propose to make universal love the final point of normative reference. This move, as I interpret it, will prove here to give qualified comfort to altruists and impartialists, but will satisfy neither entirely.

On the one side, universal love establishes limits in relation to the first asymmetry. I argued that we should not endorse altruism in principle, if such endorsement means that the self does not matter. Universal love must safeguard the conviction that in a theocentric frame the self matters as well as the neighbor, in a way that altruism fails to do. This inclusiveness allies universal love with impartiality in part, whatever specific judgments we give on issues of resistance and the like. The most effective strategy that altruists can pursue is to abandon any focus on a purely private self-other situation. To think of an isolated self meeting an isolated neighbor is too abstract. Our meetings always occur within an array of social relations. I am a husband, a father, a teacher, someone responsible for the well-being of others, and not simply my own. To neglect my own well-being altogether could betray them unjustly. If I think in this way, I may reach verdicts frequently similar to impartialist ones. The normative difference between altruism and impartiality may produce little concrete difference. Universal love is closer to such a strategy, when we recall the case I made earlier for keeping self-regarding reasons not to issue a blank check as congruent as possible with other-regarding reasons. Yet my case still referred to the self's well-being directly, and not wholly derivatively from other-regard, as the altruist does. This case remains preferable to altruism because it registers more decisively the implications of universal love, and authorizes us more directly to attend to the temptations of sloth as well as pride. It frees us in general to ask what self-regarding considerations may carry legitimate normative and descriptive force.

On the other side, universal love also permits us to commend an ongoing practical *swerve* away from concentrating on what one owes oneself toward what one may do for others. To disallow altruism in principle does not require us to set aside all of the concerns we connect with the first asymmetry. The swerve has attitudinal and behavioral effects at the level of directing our attention and enlisting our energies. James M. Gustafson writes of the fundamental moral outlook nourished and sustained in Judaism and Christianity that we are "to be for others" and not just ourselves. This outlook "shapes a bias, gives a weight, toward the well-being of the other against inconvenience or cost to oneself."[160] Many versions of impartiality neglect at two points to support this swerve adequately. They sometimes sound a slightly grudging or strained note when they commend works of supererogation. And they insist, as we have seen, on making disproportionate concern for others a matter of strict consent by individual agents. The swerve, however, is more naturally incumbent on Christians. They are enjoined to display a certain heedlessness with respect to the self's claims—to care about and for others and not simply to take them into account. Because universal love underscores inclusiveness more than comparative measurement, it accommodates this swerve more easily.

8.2. Ineradicable unease. The second, predominantly descriptive asymmetry also challenges impartiality on the neighbor's behalf. Impartiality fails to take seriously enough the power of self-preoccupation, and so neglects an ameliorative strategy required to offset such power. Excessive attention to one's own wants and ambitions constitutes, *de facto*, a permanent temptation to which we regularly succumb. This self-preoccupation shows itself as a basic unease we seem unable to eradicate altogether. I as an agent find myself unable to achieve "mutual disinterest" when my own interests are directly at issue. Something deeper, and more somber, is also at stake. I am tempted incurably to make myself the center of existence, presuming to ignore or flout God, and doing injustice to my neighbors. This temptation is more than a weakness, susceptible to correction by human effort and learning. It is rather always potentially pernicious, giving no final peace in this life.

Proponents of this asymmetry dwell on failures in love that this unease promotes. The more one's own plans and projects are centrally challenged, the greater one's unease becomes. I find it harder to judge fairly a rival for a position we both seek than to aid a person who needs shelter and poses no threat to my career, who displays only gratitude for my largess. And La Rochefoucauld is often right: "The most trifling disloyalty to ourselves does people far more harm in our eyes than the greatest they commit to others."[161] A doctrine of sin that encompasses inordinate self-assertion is confirmed in ordinary places.

How far can universal love accommodate the second asymmetry? Such love must continually reckon with the forces of self-aggrandizement that jeopardize our love for our neighbor. Proponents of the second asymmetry call attention to these forces with exceptional candor. Certainly we should try to appropriate their descriptive insights. Inordinate self-assertion does pose the preeminent threat to the law of love. When Christians confess in public worship that we have not loved God with our whole heart and have not loved our neighbors as ourselves, we generally do not mean that we have loved our neighbors too much. This confession supports the practical remedy that I find the first normative asymmetry promotes, namely, an ongoing swerve away from what one owes to oneself toward what one may do for others.

Though the second asymmetry describes forces with which universal love must contend, it does not exhaust all the factors we must consider. Two factors warrant special mention.

First, when we take this asymmetry solely to heart, we are apt to view universal love as significant largely because it includes our neighbors and not just ourselves. How seriously I love my neighbors is then tested by my readiness to take the measure of my self-partiality and to compensate for its excesses. And such a test *is* important in any Christian ethic. Yet it generates by itself only one sort of criticism of impartiality. Defenders of impartiality underestimate the difficulties in attaining the measure of self-transcendence that their standard requires. "Not other-regarding enough" means complacency respecting such difficulties, abstraction from the unpleasant truth that the self, given half a chance to exercise self-partiality, will take it. But this allegation, whatever palpable descriptive hits it scores, has a slightly paradoxical consequence. As it sensitizes us to our failures to attain even-handedness, it supports even-handedness as our normative aim.

It thereby sustains and deepens a theoretically unambitious normative alliance between impartiality and universal love already noticed. I defended such an alliance, though I claimed that it makes self-partiality the main but not the exclusive matter for criticism. I also argued that the alliance neglects certain factors (discussed primarily in relation to the third and fourth asymmetries) that universal love accommodates more than impartiality. This is because universal love underscores inclusiveness more than comparative measurement.

Second, it is possible to identify too much as well as too little with others. To insist that inordinate self-assertion generally tempts us more need not deny that to identify too much with others is a bona fide temptation. Sloth and not only pride reveals faithlessness. To succumb to either temptation can put one's own life of obedient willing at risk. The second asymmetry guards against arrogant soaring, but not against indolent inertia.

8.3. Obedient willing. The third asymmetry challenges impartiality on behalf of legitimate, normative, self-regarding considerations. I tied this asymmetry to a strand in the Christian tradition where the sins of sloth as well as pride receive serious attention. Even so, the effort to identify a positive sense of self-love within Christianity is fraught with genuine difficulties. The sense I identified was under theocentric control. I distinguished it from a number of other senses I either bracketed or rejected. And it was continuous with the wider case for universal love under such control—the case to which this entire inquiry is devoted. Self-love specifically is not then a self-referring obligation independent of love for God. Josiah Royce expresses the dependence I wish to affirm: "the God who loves me demands not that I should be nothing, but that I should be his own."[162]

To mark this continuity with universal love, I argued on two fronts. On the one side, I am not to regard my life as having greater value than other lives, or suppose that objectively I matter more than others. On the other side, I am not to regard my life as interchangeable with others. The temptations on each side are distinct, although to succumb in either direction is a form of faithlessness, a failure in one's love for God.

The case against interchangeability was linked to a case for obedient willing. It is in terms of the latter that a positive sense of self-love was developed under theocentric control. A case for obedient willing has two controversial implications. First, it allows certain self-regarding considerations to carry legitimate normative force. We can specify what it means to be self-regarding in the right way. To grant this possibility goes against some weighty theological and philosophical opinion. For we, in effect, contend that it is *not redun-*

dant to enjoin me to value my particular life. We can even say that a command to love ourselves plays a role alongside a command to love our neighbors. We must say this with extreme care. One's life of obedient willing is not tantamount, for example, to one's pursuit of happiness or to independently derived duties to oneself. Yet we do then provide essential support for saying that the sins of sloth are serious in their own right. Second, a case for obedient willing constitutes a normative claim in every time and place. It is more than a temporary corrective suited, for instance, to Miss Birdseye in the context of nineteenth century feminism. Of course we must attend to specific circumstances and opportunities. Yet we do then insist that the case be part of ongoing efforts to interpret the law of love.

To make the case led us to resist impersonalizing pressures found in many developed versions of impartiality. It led us likewise to construe universal love as resistant to such pressures. Inclusiveness must permit room for seeing the self as an independent center of activity, valuable on that account, to be taken up in the depiction of obedient willing. It must bring us together without levelling out all particularities.

8.4. Ineliminable imbalance. The last asymmetry challenged impartiality on behalf of legitimate, descriptive, self-regarding considerations. It provided a basis for saying that we cannot always protect and promote our neighbor's good and our good in exactly the same way. The "cannot" is fixed. Structural differences exist *unavoidably* between my relation to my neighbor and my relation to myself. They point to an element of subjectivity we cannot eradicate, from any agent's perspective. Indeed, they appear to be part of the conditions of finitude.

These differences serve to show that the basic unease to which I referred in reviewing the second asymmetry has more than one source and promotes more than failures in love. We find another kind of descriptive doubt about whether the self *can* go into the hopper with everyone else. The fourth asymmetry complicates an account of why I find it easier to be impartial in other-other than in self-other relations. I must do justice not only to the temptation to inordinate self-assertion, but also to the greater control I normally retain over my actions and refusals than I do over others'. To acknowledge that regions of responsibility accordingly differ is anything but an exercise in self-assertion. Rather, it supports the exhortation to look first at the evil within oneself.

The asymmetry drew our attention to respects in which an ineliminable imbalance remains between loving God ourselves and commending love for God to others. What the asymmetry then implies is that a doctrine of the *imago Dei* will have to incorporate a combination of elements. Among the features we share in common is this ineliminable imbalance. We can do something *more* for ourselves because what we can *effect* in others is more restricted than what we can effect in ourselves. We have comparatively greater control and responsibility in the case of our own love for God. We can also do something *different* because, according to a widely held traditional belief, if we truly love God, God cannot be lost against our will. We do not possess the power to take from our neighbors their love for God without their complaisance, in the same way that we do possess the power to lose our own.[163] This traditional belief views the asymmetry against a larger providential and eschatological landscape. It takes the integrity of each person with a religious and moral seriousness that forbids interchangeability, now and later.

Universal love represents an advance over impartiality because once again it accommodates these structural differences more easily. We must, however, take pains not only to give these differences their due, but to avoid either misconceiving or exaggerating their place in an overall account of the law of love. Three areas call for particular comment.

First, I argued in subsection 6 that the asymmetry does not imply either that in general I should prefer myself, or that I should see myself as self-contained and autonomous *vis-à-vis* other human beings. I tried to show how these inflations are both illicit. To oppose the first inflation we must simply stress again that according to the asymmetry, structural differences exist unavoidably between my relation to my neighbor and my relation to myself. To suspect that the asymmetry discloses egoism in some form misses the meaning we take such differences to have. The suspicion makes sense only when we deny that structural differences actually exist. What accepting their existence implies is that whether or not I honor agency remains distinct from whether or not I am problematically partial to myself.

Second, I also argued against a doctrine of isolationist self-sufficiency. To oppose this second inflation requires us to distinguish the traditional belief that God's love is shed among all persons from a sense of love that includes all individuals, but takes them to be essentially unrelated. In my arguments against the latter sense, I attempted to do some justice to our mutual interdependence. I contended in the case of repentance that we do not determine apart from community and tradition which actions call for repentance; and that in coming to repent we do not deliberate or struggle alone. I similarly maintained that the evil we do does not concern ourselves alone. Our power to corrupt others is genuine. We retain responsibility for the effects of our actions on the practices and values of the communites of which we are a part. I held too that we should not give exclusive attention to autonomy in defining the work of love in the case of both agents and recipients. To honor dignity includes much more than protecting and promoting autonomous choices. All our initiatives and responses are constrained and otherwise affected by our interactions with others. Universal love must integrate an account of the asymmetry into the vast and pervasive world of human interaction.

Third, we should not exaggerate the contrast between universal love and impartiality that accepting this asymmetry requires. Recall that the structural differences in question pass the universalizability test, in the sense that they display relevant dissimilarities which obtain for any agent and any recipient. How more precisely universal love and impartiality overlap and diverge in the case of the fourth asymmetry I can make clearer if I review a final time the series of claims I introduced at the beginning of subsection 2, going from universal scope to impartial appraisal.

One claim is that in the judgments we formulate to protect and promote the dignity of each person, we should endeavor to include fully both neighbor and self. Because both neighbor and self bear the human countenance, neither must cease to matter, or be made a mere means or instrument. This claim we can certainly take universal love to legitimate and the asymmetry to allow.

A further claim—that full inclusion leads to equal inclusion—our later discussion leads us to endorse in terms of the following formulations: one person's well-being is as valuable as another's; no one of us objectively matters more than anyone else; the neighbor's well-being and the self's well-being are equally worthy of protection and promotion. These formulations we can take universal love to accommodate, and the asymmetry to allow. What the asymmetry disallows is one sense of equal inclusion, namely, that we can invariably protect and promote the neighbor's well-being and the self's well-being in exactly the same way. If I am right about the asymmetry, then full inclusion can always mean *genuine* inclusion, but not always equal inclusion in this latter sense.[164] The asymmetry challenges versions of impartiality that require the latter sense of equal inclusion. We confront a pocket of agency in our own case that we cannot assimilate altogether to calculations that suit other-other relations. This agency confounds impartialist pressures that advance the cause of total assimilation. While universal love also accommodates such agency, it retains in so doing an alliance with weaker forms of impartiality in the following sense. The crucial claim on which the fourth asymmetry sheds light is that we should honor appropriate capabilities. Such honoring is as other-regarding as it is self-regarding.

9. WHAT FUNDAMENTAL SUBJECTS REMAIN UNADDRESSED?

Finally, I want to mention two subjects, not as mere afterthoughts, but as matters that should be addressed in their own right, certainly at a length that exceeds this inquiry in its entirety. They are unavoidable in a comprehensive account of the law of love. I shall suggest briefly how the positions I have taken here could be incorporated and refined when one turns to the two subjects.

9.1. *Communion as the fulfillment of love.* Aquinas writes: "Charity signifies not only the love of God, but also a certain friendship with Him; which implies, besides love, a certain mutual return of love, together with mutual communion. . . ."[165] At its highest reaches, love is about communion, between God and ourselves, and between each other. This inquiry did not approach such heights, where communion as the fulfillment of love receives full attention. My concentration here should not be taken to imply, however, that what I discussed is at odds with the subject of love as communion, or an alternative to it. I intend this inquiry to be wholly compatible with the affirmation that communion *is* the fulfillment of love. I hope too that my concentration may enhance an understanding of conditions and possibilities that serious accounts of the final good of communion are bound to consider. We cannot separate our account of the communion we deem suitable from our judgments about essential connections and fitting differences among the three loves. And a portion of these judgments I did attempt to trace here.

The judgments about fitting differences, for example, may serve to give nuance to a standard insistence that communion precludes undifferentiated unity. We noted two distinct respects in which this is so.

First, our love for God is relational rather than reciprocal. That is, there is genuine interaction between God and ourselves, "a certain friendship," but not reciprocity in the sense that mutual needs are met, assistance rendered, or enrichment provided. From God's side, Christians believe, the will to communion is irrevocable, and the grace it reveals prevenient. God establishes covenant; God brings redemption. Our love for God remains dependent and responsive in a manner that God's love never is.

Second, our love for one another is reciprocal precisely in the sense that mutual needs are met, assistance rendered, and enrichment provided. While communion is again the fulfillment of our love for one another, it is subject to creaturely conditions parts of which I identified when I described similarities and differences between neighbor-love and self-love. I also stressed that love for God involves fidelity to God in loving whom God loves and that this warrants a case for our love being universal in scope. And like God's love for us, our genuine love for one another stops short of final coercion. To be in community with others involves a distinction as well as a relation, a distinction that includes equivalent conditions of agency on each side of the relation. One's love of others remains unilateral in that one does not await, anticipate, or demand a response in kind as a requirement for one's attention and care. (The text does not tell us whether a friendship arose between the Good Samaritan and the man he helped, yet the Samaritan proved to be a neighbor to the man.) In loving, one nonetheless desires and hopes for a response, and takes actual attainment as both a genuine possibility and as the fruition it seeks. We should say then that mutuality is the internal, ideal fruition of *agape*.[166] As we say this, we likewise acknowledge that the works of love encompass more than such fruition.

9.2. Particular roles and practices. A further large subject is how to do justice both to the recurrent insistence we find in the Christian tradition that "every human being is my neighbor" and the large and positive place for special covenants and particular commitments and obligations that many writers in the Christian tradition also take pains to secure. The latter include particular social structures and roles, or what Alasdair MacIntyre calls practices.[167] Should we accept intractable tensions between a love that is discernibly universal in scope and the special bonds between, e.g., friends, lovers, spouses, parents and children, coreligionists, members of a given class, party, tribe, or society? This question is unavoidable for a comprehensive account of the law of love. Although it remains distinct from the question of whether and how universal love includes neighbor and self, the answers in one area will surely have implications for those in the other.

Let me offer the following observations that indicate briefly the directions in which this subject might be pursued in another time and place.

First, my interest in the present inquiry is to explore what sense of universal love follows from the beliefs, commitments, and manner of life shared by those within the church. We must be careful not to conflate the account of universal love given here with a range of other meanings that "universalism" carries and the assocations it elicits. It is a mistake to assume in advance, for example, that to affirm a love discernibly universal in scope commits us either to trying to dissolve all tensions with particular roles and practices or to resolve them in only one way.

Second, it is crucial to recognize that particular roles and practices differ among themselves. Personal preference may be essential to friendship, for example, but it is not similarly constitutive of the bond that matters especially in Christian ethics, again, the beliefs, commitments, and manner of life shared by those within the church. We oversimplify matters if we suppose that tensions between universal love and particular roles and practices are all of one kind, or if we fail to examine particular roles and practices in their various historical and social settings.

Third, a love can be discernibly universal in scope in two respects at least: it can set boundaries within which particular roles and practices come into their own and it can go beyond the limits these roles and practices may impose. To set boundaries includes the minimal moral prohibitions against our doing anything whatever to those outside the personal relations and social groups with which we identify for the sake of those inside. In the case of friendship, Gilbert Meilaender defends a promising approach by urging us "to prefer some to others, but to remain open to those others and refuse to harm them for the sake of those we prefer. . . ."[168] I would also stress that we should guard against any sanguine assumption that minimal moral prohibitions against harming others hold as a matter of course.[169] Why they hold, which of them hold, and how absolutely they hold, are controversial issues that show the importance of giving independent attention and weight to universal love. To go beyond the limits particular roles and practices may impose is illustrated quintessentially in the parable of the Good Samaritan, and in injunctions such as Ellul's to care about the uninteresting poor around the world.

Fourth, the two respects I have just mentioned still allow particular roles and practices to come into their own. We need not construe such love as itself the sole originating source of all other religious and moral claims. Such love is not then "universal" in the sense that all other claims stand in a strictly deductive order of dependence upon it. Indeed, we can insist that particular roles and practices possess their own life. This is not to say that particular roles and practices generate demands that universal love may never override. However, it is to say that particular roles and practices furnish their own substantive considerations on the basis of which we often justifiably act.

We should beware of a simplified egalitarianism that ignores or denigrates these considerations. Our special bonds and affections—ecclesiastical, familial, societal, etc.—shape by necessity rather than by accident our religious and moral identities. And we can love more complexly in these special relations (in the manner of *eros* and *philia* as well as *agape*). Alas, we can also hate more intensely. The possibility of injustice increases with the closeness of our relations. For such closeness makes us at once more vulnerable and heightens and orders our expectations. In short, our capacity for reciprocal help and harm is deeper and more varied with those closely related to us.[170]

If the observations offered so far are correct, we are left with permanent tensions. We misrepresent our situation when we seek to evade them. To accept them we need not abandon the claim that objectively no one matters more than anyone else. We need, however, not to interpret that claim as requiring us to be equally concerned to promote everyone's good on every occasion. The tensions call for perpetual vigilance on two fronts. Universal love sensitizes us to needs, rights, and preferences that people have not all of which are refracted through special covenants or claims connected to stations and roles. It disposes us to review critically the roles bequeathed to us, and not to assume that they are all compatible with universal love. It prompts us sometimes to oppose forms of tribalism and hierarchy. Particular roles and practices sensitize us to the importance of communal and role-related demands, including the large extent to which roles effectively determine the distribution of our moral attention and energy. They dispose us to recognize how pervasively our religious and moral lives are tied to certain traditions, communities, and institutional arrangements. They define claims of justice of their own, that are internal to the goals and requirements they establish.[171]

Detailed discussion of these two subjects I leave to the future. Here I pay different, but I hope no less suitable, homage to the law of love as a practical doctrine to which Christians are necessarily committed.

ACKNOWLEDGMENTS

Those who read earlier versions of this inquiry include Robert Adams, Steven Dalle Mura, Richard Fern, Hans Frei, Timothy Jackson, Cathleen Kaveny, George Lindbeck, Ping-cheung Lo, Alasdair MacIntyre, Robert McKim, Gordon Marino, Gilbert Meilaender, Cyril O'Regan, Paul Outka, John Reeder, and Philip Turner. They offered valuable criticisms and suggestions many of which I tried to address and incorporate. And I am grateful to my colleagues in New Testament, Richard Hays, Leander Keck, Abraham Malherbe, and Wayne Meeks. They spent time helping me with questions of biblical exegesis on which the inquiry touches. I am also grateful to Arthur Dyck who responded to one subsection that I presented at the annual meeting of the Society of Christian Ethics in January 1988. Finally, I acknowledge special indebtedness to Susan Owen and Russell Reno, who gave extensive and acute counsel on matters of substance, organization, and style, and persevered with me through various drafts.

NOTES

1. George A. Lindbeck, *The Nature of Doctrine: Religion and Theology in a Postliberal Age* (Philadelphia: Westminster Press, 1984), p. 85.

2. James M. Gustafson emphasizes the importance of a theocentric frame of explanation and evaluation in his monumental two volume work, *Ethics from a Theocentric Perspective* (Chicago: University of Chicago Press, 1981 and 1984). My beliefs about God and God's relation to the world reflected in this inquiry differ, however, from his at certain crucial points. For indications, see Gene Outka, "Remarks on a Theological Program Instructed by Science," *The Thomist* 47/4 (October, 1983), pp. 572-91.

3. Gene Outka, *Agape: An Ethical Analysis* (New Haven: Yale University Press, 1972).

4. Hans W. Frei, *The Identity of Jesus Christ: The Hermeneutical Bases of Dogmatic Theology* (Philadelphia: Fortress Press, 1975), p. 162.

5. National Conference of Catholic Bishops, *The Challenge of Peace: God's Promise and Our Response* (Washington, D.C.: United States Catholic Conference, 1983), p. 6. See also *Gaudium et Spes* (Pastoral Constitution on the Church in the Modern World: Second Vatican Council, December 7, 1965) in *The Gospel of Peace and Justice*, Joseph Gremillion, ed. (Maryknoll, N.Y.: Orbis, 1980), pp. 264-66. For another affirmation that all persons, Christians and non-Christians alike, are "temples of God," see Gustavo Gutiérrez, *A Theology of Liberation*, Sister Caridad Inda and John Eagleson, trans. (Maryknoll, N.Y.: Orbis, 1973), p. 193. On the Protestant side, see for example Nicholas Wolterstorff's claim in discussing Calvin that "every human being is . . . my neighbor," in *Until Justice and Peace Embrace* (Grand Rapids, Mich.: Eerdmans, 1983), p. 78. See also the account of how the sixth commandment of the Decalogue against killing is widened to include all human beings and not only members of a particular community in James Wm. McClendon, Jr., *Systematic Theology: Ethics* (Nashville: Abingdon Press, 1988), pp. 181, 311-12. Cf. as well Benjamin Nelson, *The Idea of Usury: From Tribal Brotherhood to Universal Otherhood*, 2nd ed. (Chicago: University of Chicago Press, 1969).

6. *The Challenge of Peace*, p. 26.

7. See also the Joint Pastoral Letter of the West German Bishops, *Out of Justice, Peace* and the Joint Pastoral Letter of the French Bishops, *Winning*

the Peace, James V. Schall, S.J., ed. (San Francisco: Ignatius, 1984). For a searching case on behalf of nonviolence, see John Howard Yoder, *The Politics of Jesus* (Grand Rapids, Mich.: Eerdmans, 1983). For criticism of Yoder and a defense of an alternative to pacifism, see Joseph L. Allen, *Love and Conflict: A Covenantal Model Of Christian Ethics* (Nashville: Abingdon Press, 1984), especially pp. 181-217. For exegetical treatments of relevant New Testament passages, see for example Victor Paul Furnish, *The Love Command in the New Testament* (Nashville: Abingdon Press, 1972), especially pp. 45-59; Luise Schottroff, "Non-Violence and the Love of One's Enemies," in *Essays on the Love Commandment*, Reginald H. and Ilse Fuller, trans. (Philadelphia: Fortress Press, 1978), pp. 9-39; Pheme Perkins, *Love Commands in the New Testament* (New York: Paulist Press, 1982), especially pp. 27-41, 89-103.

8. Oliver O'Donovan, *The Problem of Self-Love in St. Augustine* (New Haven: Yale University Press, 1980), pp. 121-22.

9. Jonathan Edwards, *The Nature of True Virtue* (Ann Arbor: University of Michigan Press, 1960), p. 23; *The Works of Jonathan Edwards: Ethical Writings*, Vol. 8, Paul Ramsey, ed. (New Haven: Yale University Press, 1989), p. 557. See also Stephen G. Post, *Christian Love and Self-Denial: An Historical and Normative Study of Jonathan Edwards, Samuel Hopkins, and American Theological Ethics* (Lanham, Md.: University Press of America, 1987).

10. I owe the first example in this paragraph to Joel Feinberg, *Social Philosophy* (Englewood Cliffs, N.J.: Prentice-Hall, 1973), p. 98; the second example to John Martin Fischer in an unpublished paper.

11. R. M. Hare, *Moral Thinking: Its Levels, Method and Point* (Oxford: Clarendon Press, 1981), p. 129.

12. Alan Gewirth, *Reason and Morality* (Chicago: University of Chicago Press, 1978), p. 140. On general differences between Hare and Gewirth, see, e.g., R. M. Hare, "Do Agents Have to be Moralists?" and Alan Gewirth, "Replies to My Critics," in *Gewirth's Ethical Rationalism*, Edward Regis, Jr., ed. (Chicago: University of Chicago Press, 1984), pp. 52-58, 205-15, 219-22.

13. Bernard Williams, *Ethics and the Limits of Philosophy* (Cambridge, Mass.: Harvard University Press, 1985), p. 82. This test, however, can be variously interpreted. J. L. Mackie usefully identifies some of the possibilities in *Ethics: Inventing Right and Wrong* (Harmondsworth: Penguin, 1977), pp. 83-102.

14. For a comparative study of divine impartiality in the Old Testament, Rabbinic literature, Philo, and Paul, see Jouette M. Bassler, *Divine Impartiality: Paul and a Theological Axiom* (Chico, Calif.: Scholars Press, 1982).

15. H. Richard Niebuhr, "Introduction to Biblical Ethics," in *Christian Ethics*, 2nd ed., Waldo Beach and H. Richard Niebuhr, eds. (New York: Ronald Press, 1973), p. 23.

16. Thomas Nagel, *Mortal Questions* (Cambridge: Cambridge University Press, 1979), p. 126.

17. Williams, *Ethics and the Limits of Philosophy*, p. 83.

18. Derek Parfit, *Reasons and Persons* (Oxford: Clarendon Press, 1984), p. 331.

19. Bernard Williams, "A Critique of Utilitarianism," in *Utilitarianism For and Against*, J. J. C. Smart and Bernard Williams, (Cambridge: Cambridge University Press, 1973), p. 95.

20. *Ibid.*, p. 96.

21. *Ibid.*, pp. 116-17.

22. T. M. Scanlon, "Contractualism and Utilitarianism," in *Utilitarianism and Beyond*, Amartya Sen and Bernard Williams, eds. (New York: Cambridge University Press, 1982), p. 110.

23. John Rawls, *A Theory of Justice* (Cambridge, Mass.: Harvard University Press, 1971), pp. 148-49.

24. Bernard Williams, *Moral Luck* (Cambridge: Cambridge University Press, 1981), pp. 3-4.

25. David A. J. Richards, *A Theory of Reasons for Action* (Oxford: Clarendon Press, 1971), p. 87.

26. Paul Ramsey, *Basic Christian Ethics* (New York: Charles Scribner's Sons, 1950), p. 243.

27. Alan Donagan, *The Theory of Morality* (Chicago: University of Chicago Press, 1977), p. 86.

28. Ambrose, *The Duties of the Clergy*, III, iv, 27, in *Nicene and Post-Nicene Fathers of the Christian Church*, Philip Schaff, ed. (New York: Charles Scribner's, 1887), cited in Paul Ramsey, *War and the Christian Conscience* (Durham: Duke University Press, 1961), p. 37. For Ambrose, "to love the neighbor" in this passage is to imitate Christ, and Christ does not defend himself against the persecutor who seeks to kill him. Ramsey stresses that both Ambrose and Augustine agree in renouncing self-defense in the private realm. Yet Augustine, in the passage Ramsey cites, offers a line of argument that at least goes beyond the simple appeal to imitate Christ. Augustine contends that we ought not to love those things we can lose against our will. God and our neighbor in God cannot be so lost. But creaturely goods such as our physical life and possessions can be so lost. This argument seems to include the thought that to turn the other cheek is not contrary to self-love. Indeed, one can jeopardize one's life in God by attempting to save it; one should not lose oneself by attaching inordinate importance to this life. See Augustine, *On Free Will*, Book I, C. 5, in *Augustine: Earlier Writings*, J. H. S. Burleigh, trans. (Philadelphia: Westminster, 1953), pp. 118-20.

29. Ramsey, *War and the Christian Conscience*, pp. 39-46.

30. Gewirth, *Reason and Morality*, pp. 188-89.

31. John G. Simon, Charles W. Powers, and Jon P. Gunnemann, *The Ethical Investor* (New Haven: Yale University Press, 1972), pp. 22-26.

32. Thomas Nagel, *The View from Nowhere* (New York: Oxford University Press, 1986), pp. 200-204.

33. Hare, *Moral Thinking*, pp. 198-201.

34. David Heyd, *Supererogation: Its Status in Ethical Theory* (Cambridge: Cambridge University Press, 1982), p. 23.

35. *Ibid.*, p. 5.

36. *Ibid.*

37. This sense seems linked to the structure of the Protestant conscience and arguably finds a modern secular home in the phenomenon of "liberal guilt." Conversation with George Lindbeck helped me to recognize such connections. See Gene Outka, "The Protestant Tradition and Exceptionless Moral Norms," in *Moral Theology Today: Certitudes and Doubts*, Donald G. McCarthy, ed (St. Louis: The Pope John Center, 1984), pp. 158-59.

38. Heyd, *Supererogation*, p. 15.

39. Thomas Aquinas, *Summa Theologica*, I-II, q. 108, a. 4; from *Summa Theologica of St. Thomas Aquinas*, I, Fathers of the English Dominican Province, trans. (New York: Benziger, 1947), p. 1118.

40. *Ibid.*

41. Heyd, *Supererogation*, p. 21.

42. Aquinas, *Summa Theologica*, I-II, q. 108, a. 4, ad 1; from *Summa Theologica of St. Thomas Aquinas*, p. 1119.

43. John Calvin, *Institutes of the Christian Religion*, I, Ford Lewis Battles, trans. (Philadelphia: Westminster, 1960), pp. 672-73. Calvin's objections here are Christological; he rejects any claim that merit might be transferred from one person to another through a surplus entrusted to the church.

44. Article XIV; from *The Principles of Theology: An Introduction to the Thirty-Nine Articles*, W. H. Griffith Thomas, ed. (London: Church Book Room Press, 1945), p. 215.

45. Ramsey, *Basic Christian Ethics*, p. 188.

46. For more on this distinction, see Gene Outka, "Following at a Distance: Ethics and the Identity of Jesus," in *Scriptural Authority and Narrative Interpretation*, Garrett Green, ed. (Philadelphia: Fortress Press, 1987), pp. 144-60.

47. Nagel, *The View from Nowhere*, p. 184.

48. Gewirth, *Reason and Morality*, p. 213.

49. *Ibid.*

50. *The Challenge of Peace*, p. 24.

51. Ramsey, *Basic Christian Ethics*, p. 168.

52. *Ibid.*, p. 243.

53. *Ibid.*, p. 172.

54. *Ibid.*, p. 175.

55. *Ibid.*, p. 171.

56. See e.g., R. B. Brandt, "Utilitarianism and the Rules of War," and R. M. Hare, "Rules of War and Moral Reasoning," *Philosophy and Public Affairs* 1/2 (Winter, 1972), pp. 145-81.

57. Yoder, *The Politics of Jesus*; Stanley Hauerwas, *The Peaceable Kingdom: A Primer in Christian Ethics* (Notre Dame: University of Notre Dame Press, 1983).

58. John Howard Yoder, *The Original Revolution: Essays on Christian Pacifism* (Scottdale, Pa.: Herald Press, 1977), p. 72.

59. John Howard Yoder, *The Priestly Kingdom: Social Ethics as Gospel* (Notre Dame: University of Notre Dame Press, 1984), p. 27.

60. Yoder, *The Original Revolution*, p. 78.

61. *Ibid.*, pp. 76-77.

62. For another view, which appears to regard the teachings of the Sermon on the Mount as counsels rather than precepts, see G. E. M. Anscombe, *Ethics, Religion and Politics* (Minneapolis: University of Minnesota Press, 1981), especially pp. 55-58.

63. Roland H. Bainton, *Christian Attitudes Toward War and Peace* (Nashville: Abingdon Press, 1960), pp. 156-57.

64. Yoder, *The Original Revolution*, p. 79.

65. Basil Mitchell, *Morality: Religious and Secular* (Oxford: Clarendon Press, 1980), p. 144.

66. *Ibid.*, pp. 47-63.

67. Paul Ramsey, *The Patient as Person* (New Haven: Yale University Press, 1970), pp. 185-86. The line between gifts and rights is sometimes difficult to draw of course. For a discussion of the difficulties in one case of a bone marrow transplant, see James F. Childress, *Who Should Decide? Paternalism in Health Care* (New York: Oxford University Press, 1982), especially pp. 29-32.

68. Heyd, *Supererogation*, p. 31.

69. For a statement of the more traditional view, see Henry Davis, S.J., *Moral and Pastoral Theology*, I (London: Sheed and Ward, 1959), pp. 196-200. According to one reappraisal, biblical teaching does not inspire any neat distinction between precept and counsel, and all Christians are called to perfection. See Charles Curran, *Catholic Moral Theology in Dialogue* (Notre Dame: University of Notre Dame Press, 1976), especially pp. 33-34.

70. Bernard Häring, *The Law of Christ*, I, Edwin G. Kaiser, trans. (Westminster, Md.: The Newman Press, 1961), pp. 305-6.

71. Aquinas however distinguishes the precept that anyone must "be prepared to do good to his enemies, and other similar actions, where there is need," from the counsel that "anyone should actually and promptly behave thus towards an enemy when there is no special need." See *Summa Theologica*, I-II, q. 108, a. 4, a 4, in *Summa Theologica of St. Thomas Aquinas*, p. 1119.

72. Charlotte Brontë, *Jane Eyre* (New York: Washington Square Press, 1982), p. 62.

73. *Ibid.*

74. James F. Childress, "Resistance," in *The Westminster Dictionary of Christian Ethics*, James F. Childress and John Macquarrie, eds. (Philadelphia: Westminster Press, 1986), pp. 539-41.

75. An unpublished paper by Albert J. Raboteau has helped my understanding of King.

76. Outka, *Agape: An Ethical Analysis*, p. 21.

77. Yoder, *The Original Revolution*, p. 48.

78. T. S. K. Scott-Craig, *Christian Attitudes to War and Peace*, (New York: Charles Scribner's Sons, 1938), p. 43.

79. Outka, *Agape: An Ethical Analysis*, pp. 21-24.

80. W. G. Maclagan, "Self and Others: A Defence of Altruism," *Philosophical Quarterly* 4 (April, 1954), pp. 118-19.

81. The statement is found in his Nobel Prize Lecture quoted by John Finnis, *Fundamentals of Ethics* (Washington, D.C.: Georgetown University Press, 1983), p. 117.

82. Robert Nozick, *Anarchy, State, and Utopia* (New York: Basic Books, 1974), pp. 30-32. This example in particular requires nuancing. We should not generalize from it to disallow the narcotics agent to infiltrate a dope ring, though members of the ring would be prepared to do more than decline to interact with the agent if they knew the use to which he or she intends to put the interaction. Personal relations like friendship and love demand the trust and openness that the example I cite is designed to illuminate.

83. Immanuel Kant, *Groundwork of the Metaphysic of Morals*, H. J. Paton, trans. (New York: Harper, 1964), p. 96. This wide appeal includes attempts by Christian writers to appropriate the formulation. Here are two examples. "St. Thomas' philosophy of human nature, confirmed and enriched by his theology, led him to conclude that each man has a unique, sovereign value and a unique, sovereign destiny or end which cannot be subordinated to any other purpose on earth. He would have been delighted, one feels, with Kant's principle, 'Always treat men as ends, never simply as means.' This is the controlling principle, the absolute to which all lesser proposals must be referred, and in whose light they must be judged." Eric D'Arcy, *Conscience and Its Right to Freedom* (New York: Sheed and Ward, 1961), p. 198. "The idea that God affirms each person as an end and not only a means is not merely a Kantian idea grafted onto theological ethics. (Historically it may have been the reverse—a Christianly derived idea that Kant separated from its theological roots to be the central principle of his moral philosophy.) The idea is so important to Christian ethics that to overlook it today would be to misread the spirit of God's covenanting." Allen, *Love and Conflict*, p. 63.

84. These problems are examined by Ping-cheung Lo, *Treating Persons as Ends: An Essay on Kant's Moral Philosophy* (Lanham, Md.: University Press of America, 1987); See also T. E. Hill, Jr., "Humanity as an End in Itself," *Ethics* (1980), pp. 84-99; John E. Atwell, "Kant's Notion of Respect for Persons," in *Respect for Persons*, O. H. Green, ed. (New Orleans: Tulane Studies in Philosophy, Vol. XXXI, 1982), pp. 17-30; Atwell, *Ends and Principles in Kant's Moral Thought* (Dordrecht: Martinus Nijhoff, 1986).

85. Paul Ramsey, *Christian Ethics and the Sit-In*, (New York: Association Press, 1961), pp. 120-21.

86. John Locke, *Two Treatises of Government* (New York: Mentor Books, 1965), p. 316.

87. In the case of Freud, see Ernest Wallwork, "'Thou Shalt Love Thy Neighbor as Thyself': The Freudian Critique," *The Journal of Religious Ethics* (Fall, 1982), pp. 264-319.

88. Martin Luther, *Lectures on Romans*, Wilhelm Pauck, trans. and ed. (Philadelphia: Westminster Press, 1961), p. 366.

89. *Ibid.*, p. 367.

90. Reinhold Niebuhr, *Moral Man and Immoral Society* (New York: Charles Scribner's Sons, 1960), p. 271.

91. Hare, *Moral Thinking*, p. 46.
92. Niebuhr, *Moral Man and Immoral Society*, p. 28.
93. *Ibid.*, p. 44.
94. Marilyn McCord Adams, "Redemptive Suffering: A Christian Solution to the Problem of Evil," in *Rationality, Religious Belief, and Moral Commitment*, Robert Audi and William J. Wainwright, eds. (Ithaca: Cornell University Press, 1986), pp. 252-53.
95. Henry James, *The Bostonians* (Oxford: Oxford University Press, 1984), p. 23.
96. Williams, *Moral Luck* , p. 12.
97. *Ibid.*, p. 14.
98. Susan Wolf, "Moral Saints," *The Journal of Philosophy* , 8 (August, 1982), p. 422.
99. *Ibid.*, p. 438.
100. *Ibid.*, p. 437.
101. See also Nagel, *The View from Nowhere*, pp. 195-200.
102. Wolf, "Moral Saints," p. 438.
103. Karl Barth, *Church Dogmatics*, III/4, A. T. MacKay, et al., trans. (Edinburgh: T. & T. Clark, 1961), p. 385.
104. *Ibid.*
105. *Ibid.*, p. 386.
106. *Ibid.*
107. *Ibid.* Barth attacks natural self-assertion in this passage; but he affirms elsewhere a natural self-positing, a sense of "myself as this being in the cosmos; myself in all the freedom and necessity of my being; myself in the totality of the movement of my distinctions and connexions in relation to what is for me the outside world; myself in my desire and ability to project myself into this world." See Barth, *Church Dogmatics*, III/2, Harold Knight, *et al.*, trans. (Edinburgh: T. & T. Clark, 1960, p. 245. We avoid incompatibility if we see his attack as part of his general denial that I can or should try to live in self-sufficient isolation from God and other persons. The basic form of humanity, he insists repeatedly, is co-humanity. And when he depicts such co-humanity, he affirms self-positing once more, now in a deepened sense: "We cannot replace one another. . . . I cannot accept thy responsibility, nor Thou mine. For I and Thou are not inter-changeable. I and Thou are ultimate creaturely reality in their distinction as well as their relationship." *Ibid.*, p. 261.
108. Barth, *Church Dogmatics*, III/4, p. 388. One can appropriate Barth's distinction between indolent inertia and arrogant soaring without having to appropriate his account earlier in the same volume of male and female as ordered inescapably to a sequence in which the man precedes and the woman follows (*ibid.*, pp. 168-181). For theologically conservative criticism of the latter, see Paul K. Jewett, *Man as Male and Female* (Grand Rapids, Mich.: Eerdmans, 1975). For feminist criticism, see e.g., Elizabeth Clark and Herbert Richardson, eds., *Women and Religion* (New York: Harper, 1977), pp. 239-244.
109. Valerie Saiving, "The Human Situation: A Feminine View," in *Womanspirit Rising: A Feminist Reader in Religion*, Carol P. Christ and Judith

Plaskow, eds. (San Francisco: Harper, 1979), p. 37. See also Barbara Hilkert Andolsen, "*Agape* in Feminist Ethics," *The Journal of Religious Ethics*, 9/1 (Spring, 1981), pp. 69-83; Christine E. Gudorf, "Parenting, Mutual Love, and Sacrifice," in *Women's Consciousness, Women's Conscience: A Reader in Feminist Ethics*, Barbara Hilkert Andolsen, Christine E. Gudorf, and Mary D. Pellauer, eds. (Minneapolis: Winston, 1982), pp. 175-191; Judith Plaskow, *Sex, Sin and Grace: Women's Experience and the Theologies of Reinhold Niebuhr and Paul Tillich* (Lanham, Md.: University Press of America, 1980).

110. Susan Nelson Dunfee, "The Sin of Hiding: A Feminist Critique of Reinhold Niebuhr's Account of the Sin of Pride, " *Soundings*, 65/3 (Fall, 1982), p. 324.

111. *Ibid.*, pp. 318-19.

112. That distinct temptations (and hence failures) can have a common source in faithlessness is a possibility David Kelsey suggested to me in conversation. The particular failures he and I discussed differ from those I consider here; and he should not be held accountable in any case for the way I develop the suggestion. I owe him a debt nonetheless.

113. For example, see Henry Sidgwick, *The Methods of Ethics* (London: Macmillan, 1963), pp. 379-80; Marcus G. Singer, *Generalization in Ethics* (New York: Knopf, 1961), e.g., pp. 15-17; Singer, "The Golden Rule," *Philosophy* 38 (October, 1963), pp. 293-314; Singer, "Golden Rule," in *The Encyclopedia of Philosophy*, vol. 3, Paul Edwards, ed. (New York: Macmillan, 1967), pp. 365-67; R. M. Hare, *Freedom and Reason* (New York: Oxford University Press, 1965), pp. 85-125, 155-85; Hare, "Abortion and the Golden Rule," *Philosophy and Public Affairs* 4 (1975), pp. 201-22; Hare, *Essays in Ethical Theory* (Oxford: Clarendon Press, 1989), e.g., pp. 144, 191-211, 248; J. L. Mackie, *Ethics: Inventing Right and Wrong*, pp. 83-102; Alan Gewirth, *Reason and Morality*, pp. 169-71; Gewirth, "The Golden Rule Rationalized," in *Human Rights: Essays on Justification and Applications* (Chicago: University of Chicago Press, 1982), pp. 128-42; Alan Donagan, *The Theory of Morality*, pp. 58-59; Alasdair MacIntyre, *Against the Self-Images of the Age* (Notre Dame: University of Notre Dame Press, 1978), pp. 96-108; Nelson T. Potter and Mark Timmons, eds., *Morality and Universality: Essays on Ethical Universalizability* (Dordrecht: Reidel, 1985).

114. The metaphor is Thomas Nagel's in *Mortal Questions*, p. 126.

115. My awareness of such difficulties was heightened in discussions with Richard Fern.

116. Robert Merrihew Adams, *The Virtue of Faith and Other Essays in Philosophical Theology* (New York: Oxford University Press, 1987), pp. 170, 172.

117. This point is persuasively demonstrated by James M. Gustafson, "Religion and Morality from the Perspective of Theology," in *Religion and Morality*, Gene Outka and John P. Reeder, Jr., eds. (Garden City, N.Y.: Doubleday Anchor, 1973), pp. 125-154.

118. See the depiction of Jesus' humility by H. Richard Niebuhr in *Christ and Culture* (New York: Harper, 1956), pp. 25-27.

119. Williams, "A Critique of Utilitarianism," p. 117.

120. Adams, *The Virtue of Faith*, p. 172.

121. Mitchell, *Morality: Religious and Secular*, p. 161.
122. Adams, *The Virtue of Faith*, p. 169.
123. Ibid.
124. My comments in this paragraph are indebted to discussions with Cyril O'Regan.
125. Immanuel Kant, *The Doctrine of Virtue* (Part II of *The Metaphysic of Morals*), Mary J. Gregor, trans. (New York: Harper, 1964), pp. 44-45.
126. I did not heed this distinction sufficiently when I referred to Kant's statement in *Agape: An Ethical Analysis*, p. 305, an oversight Ping-cheung Lo first pointed out to me.
127. Kant, *The Doctrine of Virtue*, p. 38.
128. Allen W. Wood, *Kant's Moral Religion* (Ithaca: Cornell University Press, 1970), p. 56.
129. Mary J. Gregor, *Laws of Freedom* (New York: Barnes & Noble, 1963), pp. 90, 176-79.
130. Outka, *Agape: An Ethical Analysis*, p. 302.
131. Wood, *Kant's Moral Religion*, p. 76.
132. Barth, *Church Dogmatics*, III/4, pp. 502-3.
133. Ibid., p. 508.
134. See also Gene Outka, "Character, Vision, and Narrative," *Religious Studies Review* (April, 1980), especially pp. 111-12.
135. Martin Luther, "Temporal Authority: To What Extent It Should Be Obeyed," in *Luther: Selected Political Writings*, J. M. Porter, ed. and J. J. Schindel, trans. (Philadelphia: Fortress Press, 1974), p. 61.
136. O'Donovan, *The Problem of Self-Love in St. Augustine*, p. 116.
137. For elaboration of the difference between relationality and reciprocity, see Outka, "Following at a Distance," pp. 152-53, 157-58.
138. Cf. the discussion of how a son may repent of his father's faults, but not for his father's sake, in Gene Outka, "Equality and Individuality: Thoughts on Two Themes in Kierkegaard," *The Journal of Religious Ethics*, 10/2 (Fall, 1982), pp. 195-96.
139. On this general subject, see Margaret A. Farley, *Personal Commitments: Making, Keeping, Breaking* (San Francisco: Harper, 1986).
140. Hare, *Moral Thinking*, pp. 202-3.
141. Ibid., p. 202.
142. For more on such dual responsibility, see Gene Outka, "On Harming Others," *Interpretation*, 34/4 (October, 1980), pp. 381-93.
143. This way of putting the matter I owe to Philip Turner.
144. Outka, "Following at a Distance," pp. 148, 156-57; Edmund N. Santurri and William Werpehowski, "Substituted Judgment and the Terminally-Ill Incompetent," *Thought*, 57/227 (December, 1982), pp. 484-501.
145. Augustine, *The City of God*, Marcus Dods, trans. (New York: Modern Library, 1950), Book I, C. 19, p. 25.
146. William A. Galston, *Justice and the Human Good* (Chicago: University of Chicago Press, 1980), p. 3.
147. Ibid., pp. 2-3.

148. Simone de Beauvoir, *Force of Circumstance*, Richard Howard, trans. (New York: Putnam, 1965), pp. 34-35.

149. Gewirth, *Reason and Morality*, p. 164.

150. For an interpretation of appeals to the golden rule within a Christian ethic, see my essay, "Augustinianism and Common Morality," in *Prospects for a Common Morality*, Gene Outka and John P. Reeder, Jr., eds. (Princeton: Princeton University Press, 1992), pp. 114-48.

151. Allen Verhey, *The Great Reversal: Ethics and the New Testament* (Grand Rapids. Mich.: Eerdmans, 1984), p. 178.

152. I did not come sufficiently to grips with this ambiguity in *Agape: An Ethical Analysis*, e.g., pp. 12-13.

153. Gewirth, *Reason and Morality*, p. 201.

154. Though writers in Christian ethics may not routinely offer detailed assessments of how their views relate to utilitarian and neo-Kantian theories, notable discussions do exist. Joseph Fletcher equates *agape* and utilitarianism in "What's in a Rule?: A Situationist's View," *Norm and Context in Christian Ethics*, Gene Outka and Paul Ramsey, eds. (New York: Charles Scribner's Sons, 1968), p. 332. See also his *Situation Ethics* (Philadelphia: Westminster, 1966). James M. Gustafson provides a full examination of utilitarianism, including comparisons with Protestant ethics in particular, in *Ethics from a Theocentric Perspective*, vol. 2, pp. 100-16. Harlan R. Beckley traces affinities between Rawls's theory of justice and *agape* as "equal regard" in "A Christian Affirmation of Rawls's Idea of Justice as Fairness: Part I and Part II," in *The Journal of Religious Ethics*, 13/2 (Fall, 1985), pp. 210-42; 14/2 (Fall, 1986), pp. 229-46. For general assessments of Rawls's theory, see e.g., William Werpehowski, *Social Justice, Social Selves: John Rawls's A Theory of Justice and Christian Ethics* (Ph. D. Dissertation, Yale University, 1981); Richard L. Fern, "Religious Belief in a Rawlsian Society," *The Journal of Religious Ethics* 15/1 (Spring, 1987), pp. 33-58.

155. Alasdair MacIntyre contrasts, for example, what Stoic and Augustinian accounts of universality require, in *Whose Justice? Which Rationality?* (Notre Dame: University of Notre Dame Press, 1988), especially p. 153.

156. Jacques Ellul, *Violence: Reflections from a Christian Perspective*, Cecelia Gaul Kings, trans. (New York: Seabury, 1969), e.g., p. 67. For further discussion, see Gene Outka, "Discontinuity in the Ethics of Jacques Ellul," in *Jacques Ellul: Interpretive Essays*, Clifford G. Christians and Jay M. Van Hook, eds. (Urbana: University of Illinois Press, 1981), pp. 202-3.

157. See Richard McCormick and Paul Ramsey, eds., *Doing Evil to Achieve Good* (Chicago: Loyola University Press, 1978).

158. Cf. for example the rival verdicts of Paul Ramsey, *Fabricated Man: The Ethics of Genetic Control* (New Haven: Yale University Press, 1970) and Joseph Fletcher, *The Ethics of Genetic Control: Ending Reproductive Roulette* (Garden City, N.Y,: Doubleday Anchor, 1974).

159. To be no respecter of persons is to judge fairly, giving no undue weight to considerations of privilege and station. The sense here differs from the philosophical tradition of "respect for persons." For an account of the

latter, see e.g., Gene Outka, "Respect for Persons," in *The Westminster Dictionary of Christian Ethics*, pp. 541-45.

160. James M. Gustafson, "Mongolism, Parental Desires, and the Right to Life," in *On Moral Medicine: Theological Perspectives in Medical Ethics*, Stephen E. Lammers and Allen Verhey, eds. (Grand Rapids: Eerdmans, 1987), p. 488. See also Garth L. Hallett, *Christian Neighbor-Love: An Assessment of Six Rival Versions* (Washington, D.C.: Georgetown University Press, 1989).

161. La Rochefoucauld, *Maxims*, Lenonard Tancock, trans. (Harmondsworth: Penguin, 1986), p. 83.

162. Josiah Royce, *The Problem of Christianity* (Chicago: University of Chicago Press, 1984), p. 88.

163. Conversations with Gordon Marino helped me to trace these implications.

164. P. T. Geach made me aware of the distinction between genuine and equal, though he employs it to defend the view that all persons have a genuine but not an equal chance of attaining God's grace and glory. See his *Providence and Evil* (Cambridge: Cambridge University Press, 1977), especially pp. 112, 120-22.

165. Aquinas, *Summa Theologica*, I-II, q. 65, a. 5; from *Summa Theologica of St. Thomas Aquinas*, p. 865.

166. On mutuality as the ideal fruition of neighbor-regard, see also Outka, *Agape: An Ethical Analysis*, p. 37. My remarks in the inquiry here should allay some of the worries about my views Stephen Post registers in "Communion and True Self-Love," *The Journal of Religious Ethics* (Fall, 1988), pp. 345-62. I have never held that "selfless love" is "ethically superior to communion" (p. 345). Communion is precisely the fulfillment that love seeks. And Post acknowledges that giving and unrequited love have their place (pp. 354-55). His discussion is marred when he oscillates between saying that love is sometimes unrequited but always seeks communion as ideal fruition, and saying that we must define love as either unilateral or mutual. I want to adhere consistently to the former option.

167. Alasdair MacIntyre, *After Virtue* (Notre Dame: University of Notre Dame Press, 1981), pp. 175-89.

168. Gilbert Meilaender, *Friendship: A Study in Theological Ethics* (Notre Dame: University of Notre Dame Press, 1981), p. 31.

169. Williams is unduly sanguine when he dismisses as absurd that one must prefer any possible demand of friendship "over other, impartial, moral demands." Such a friendship would be pathological, "since both parties exist in the world and it is part of the sense of their friendship that it exists in the world." See *Moral Luck*, p. 17. Existence in the world does not constitute an argument for impartial moral demands. Lawrence A. Blum similarly needs to work harder to justify his claim that considerations of an impartial kind should be taken into account, and one should not act until one has done so. See his *Friendship, Altruism, and Morality* (London: Routledge & Kegan Paul, 1980), p. 62.

170. For introductory discussion, see Outka, *Agape: An Ethical Analysis*, pp. 268-74. I take matters further when I compare claims about *agape* with

Aristotle's claims about *philia* in my "Love," in *Encyclopedia of Ethics*, II, Lawrence C. Becker and Charlotte B. Becker, eds. (New York: Garland, 1992), pp. 742-51.

    171. Alasdair MacIntyre rightly insists that marriage, for example, "as traditionally understood in our culture, is the institution central to the practice of family life. And that practice cannot flourish without justice in the relationship of the persons inhabiting the various roles, a justice that requires a particular kind of caring, on occasion highly self-sacrificial caring between husband and wife." See his "The Magic in the Pronoun 'My'," *Ethics* 94 (October, 1983), p. 123. He defends a kind of impartiality as morally required in certain types of relationship.

Edmund N. Santurri

Who Is My Neighbor?
Love, Equality, and
Profoundly Retarded Humans*

INTRODUCTION

On behalf of mentally retarded humans in our society, advocates frequently lay moral claim to a wide assortment of communal protections and services, and it is not uncharacteristic for the claimants to justify their demands with egalitarian arguments—that is, with appeals to principles stating or clearly implying that all retarded humans, simply because they are human, have a moral standing equal to that of any human being. Thus, we hear it said that retarded individuals, despite their disabilities, are full-fledged *persons* or *citizens*, that they are bearers of the highest moral worth, possessors of equal human dignity, and that they retain their place in the moral community irrespective of social recognition through custom or law.[1] To deny these humans equal standing, the advocates typically assert, is arbitrary and unjustly discriminatory, reflective of an attitude morally akin to racism or sexism, and acknowledging the retarded's equal worth is quite naturally said to carry important implications for the determination of specific moral rights. In particular, it is insisted that any right attributed to nonretarded humans should be attributed

---

*Versions of this paper have been presented as part of the Villanova University Summer Lecture Series, the Society of Christian Ethics national meeting, and the St. Olaf College Summer Theological Conference. Thanks to the participants in those convocations. Thanks also to John Barbour, Stanley Hauerwas, Robert Jenson, Bruce Marshall, Gilbert Meilaender, Edward Langerak, Gene Outka, Douglas Schuurman, Joseph Shaw, Gary Stansell, William Werpehowski, and Charles Wilson for helpful comments. My research in this general area was made possible by a NEH College Teachers Fellowship and a St. Olaf College sabbatical grant.

likewise to retarded humans—at least, that is, where such makes practical sense given the capacities required for exercising the right in question.

Accordingly, advocates have tended to speak of retarded individuals as beings who possess, in principle at any rate, all of the fundamental "human" rights that have been or might be ascribed to nonretarded human beings, including the oft-mentioned rights to life, liberty, and welfare. In turn, this commitment to equal human rights has informed a variety of social policy recommendations. Thus, there is considerable talk among the advocates about rights to such things as "normalization" and "habilitation", talk which funds specific moral claims to a number of communal arrangements—deinstitutionalization, mainstreamed education, marriage and family life, sexual expression, meaningful work in the community, and other social goods traditionally restricted to nonretarded human beings. Not surprisingly, the particular arrangements proposed vary from list to list. Indeed, advocates will often disagree strenuously about preferred social strategies for securing, enhancing, or promoting conditions of equality for retarded human beings. Witness, for example, controversies regarding mainstreaming or deinstitutionalization. At the same time, most of the advocates do appear to share the assumption that the best social arrangements will be exactly those warranted by egalitarian considerations. And this assumption typically reflects the deep normative view already identified, namely, that mentally retarded humans have equal standing in the moral community, a standing legitimated precisely by their membership in the human community. For the sake of subsequent discussion, it will be useful to designate this account of equality's moral foundation as the *humanist* view of equal worth.

Undoubtedly, most in our culture would assess this view of equality as perfectly unexceptionable. After all, it will be asked, what could be more reasonable or more just than to claim that all humans, including retarded humans, have equal moral standing simply because they are human? Indeed, what could be more unreasonable or more unjust than to deny same? Yet, as obvious as the answers to such questions might appear to be for most and as credible as this account of equality may be for our culture at large, the humanist view of equal worth has had its critics, especially in certain philosophical circles. What the philosophical critics have argued specifically is that a range of theoretical considerations bearing on the nature of moral worth poses enormous difficulties for any attempt to attribute equal standing to some retarded human beings.[2] As we shall see, the particular considerations in question vary from critic to critic. At the same time, there are features common to the arguments, and it is useful to describe in general terms a standard account, which takes as its point of departure a distinctive notion of personhood.

This account has it that morality is concerned preeminently with respect for persons and that persons are beings who possess a certain rational capacity, variously described, but typically related in an assortment of ways to powers of desire, choice, evaluation, or moral discernment. According to this view, morality requires above all else that beings with this rational capacity be respected. These are the beings presumably who are the bearers of the highest moral worth; these are the beings—and not *human* beings per se—who are, properly speaking, the bearers of equal moral rights. Of course, adult humans do meet the stipulated requirements of personhood in the normal cases, and human children typically are on the way, but the mere fact of membership in the human species, according to this position, is simply irrelevant to the determination of moral standing.[3] Indeed, arguments that ground egalitarian claims in species membership are regarded in the present account as deeply flawed morally— arbitrary and unjustly discriminatory. To offer such arguments, some will contend, is to adopt the so-called "speciesist" point of view, a perspective often presented itself as the moral equivalent of racism or sexism.[4] Morality, by contrast, is said to require strict impartiality, and this means that persons are to be accorded equal worth irrespective of species considerations *inter alia*. Once again, *persons* here are to be understood as beings in possession of the prized rational capacity; and from here on, accordingly, I shall refer to this account of equality's moral foundation as the *rationalist* view of equal worth.

I have mentioned already that the crucial implication of this view for present purposes is that it renders problematical the moral standing of certain mentally retarded human beings. More specifically, if the rationalist view turned out to be correct, retarded individuals lacking the appropriate rational capacities could not be judged *persons* in the required sense and therefore could not in any straightforward manner be characterized as bearers of equal worth. The consequence is that, if these individuals were to be accorded the moral status of persons, the ascriptions would require special justification, and that justification, given the terms of the argument, could have no better than a secondary, extrinsic, or derivative character. Thus, one might contend that retarded humans lacking the requisite capacities still should be accorded equal moral standing in practice because doing so is called for *indirectly* by the principle of respect for *genuine* persons. It might be suggested, for example, that while these retarded individuals have no moral right to life intrinsically, still, as a matter of social convention, we ought to assign such a right because the assignment accords with the wishes of parents who are genuine persons or because it will cultivate life-affirming social dispositions and habits that work ultimately to the benefit of real persons, who do possess an intrinsic moral right to life. Details aside, the essential point here is that given the rationalist view, some such argument is called for if the claim to equal standing of all retarded humans is to be made in any way morally intelligible. Again, in this view the mere fact of their humanity is insufficient to warrant the claim. Moreover, it is important to stress, the best one could hope for here is the fictional imputation of equal status. To repeat, retarded humans bereft of the appropriate capacities could not count as persons intrinsically in the rationalist account, despite the fact that personhood status might be accorded conventionally on extrinsic grounds. Of course, these individuals still could be said to have an intrinsic moral value of a certain sort. One might maintain, for instance, that they are in their own right the proper objects of our compassion. Yet the same could also be said about a range of nonhuman animals, and a morally proper object of compassion is not necessarily a being of moral standing commensurate with the standing of persons.

Needless to say, this rationalist account is unlikely to satisfy advocates of the retarded, who naturally will worry that extrinsic justifications of equal standing and collapsed moral distinctions between certain retarded humans and nonhuman animals could, over time, cultivate social attitudes and practices that threaten the welfare of retarded humans. Indeed, it is not outlandish to suppose that a society in which certain retarded humans were regarded as persons by convention only would be a society unable to sustain the political commitments and energies necessary to maximize the quality of these individuals' lives. Yet it would be mistaken to reduce the advocates' potential concerns about the rationalist view of equal worth to worries about anticipated social consequences, as significant as these may be. On the contrary, a principal objection most assuredly would be that denying genuine equal standing to some retarded humans, quite apart from any consequences of the denial, is morally offensive in itself, and this judgment would follow from a vision of the moral community radically at odds with positions that tie moral standing to a being's rational capacity. Again, advocates of the mentally retarded typically hold to the *humanist* view of equality; for these advocates the highest moral worth attaches to retarded individuals simply because they are human.

I want to consider here what stake Christian ethics has in this debate between the humanist and rationalist views of equal worth, particularly as the controversy bears on the moral assessment of profoundly retarded humans. Note that, in this essay, I use the term "profoundly retarded" interchangeably with "severely retarded" to denote the class of developmentally disabled individuals who fail to meet standards of equality prized by various rationalist accounts. Thus, my usage departs from that of mental retardation professionals, who employ the terms "mild," "moderate," "severe," and "profound" to designate classes of individuals suffering from increasing levels of developmental disability (where the levels are specified in terms of IQ scores *inter alia*). Note also that individuals who fall short of rationalist standards of equality will represent a fairly small percentage of the retarded population, the exact percentage varying, of course, depending on what sort of rational capacity is singled out.

In essence, I am reconsidering, with an eye to profoundly retarded humans, a classic theological question: If Christianity enjoins love of neighbor, just who is the neighbor to be loved? Of course, within contemporary Christian ethics a standard response to this question embraces the humanist view of equal worth in no uncertain terms:

> Jesus' great account of the active love which breaks out of in-group limits is the story of the Good Samaritan (Luke: 10.29- 37). The parable is told in response to the question "Who is my neighbor?" (v. 29). The astonishing answer is that the neighbor is the one least likely to be so considered: a Samaritan; or if you are a Samaritan, a Jew. Your neighbors include the "neighbor" who would seem to be excluded by definition: the enemy, the opposing ethnic, religious or economic group. It is any person in need whom one encounters. . . .
> People are candidates for our love because they are our fellow *human beings*, not because they are members of the same community or have some other special characteristic beyond being human.[5]

In this rendering, Christian love requires equal consideration of all *humans*, and thus features serving to differentiate human beings from one another—e.g., race, gender, ethnicity, class, intellectual or physical endowment—are simply irrelevant to determining who counts as neighbor.[6] Hence, even profoundly disabled humans fall within the scope of the love command:

> We need only ask what fidelity to another human life, perhaps lacking any further potential and lacking reciprocity, requires of an agent. Persons are not reducible to their potential. Patients are to be loved and cared for no matter what their potential for

higher values is, and certainly not on account of their responsiveness. Who they are, in Christian ethical perspective, is our neighbors. They do not become nearer neighbors because of any capacity they own, nor lesser neighbors because they lack some ability to prevail in their struggle for human fulfillment.[7]

Yet this view of the matter has not gone unchallenged in Christian theological circles. While a good number of theological accounts advocate, either explicitly or implicitly, the humanist view of equal worth, others propose variations on the rationalist view.[8] Still others embrace what appears to be a *tertium quid*.[9]

Without question a principal difficulty here is that scripture, the primary normative resource for Christian ethical reflection, affords anything but a straightforward resolution of our problem; that is, the Bible is especially ambiguous about the place held by retarded human beings in the moral community. Indeed, as Robert Veatch has recently noted, despite a tendency of certain historical accounts to attribute to the biblical tradition a deep appreciation of the worth of retarded humans, that tradition in fact says "virtually nothing" about the matter.[10] If the Bible does evince a noteworthy concern for certain vulnerable human beings, such concern is explicitly for the poor, the politically powerless, the physically handicapped, the demonically possessed, and so forth—i.e., not for the retarded per se. Of course, in an important sense this omission ought not to surprise since, as Veatch has also pointed out, the concept of mental retardation is a relatively modern notion, particularly as it is explicated in current genetic, psychological, or sociological terms, and it would be unreasonable naturally to expect to find such terms displayed in an ancient text. At the same time, we might reasonably hope to discover in the biblical text plausible phenomenological analogues to humans now designated mentally retarded. Yet, interestingly enough, even such biblical references are difficult to find, though, to be sure, historians of mental retardation occasionally claim to have found them. Thus some scholars have attributed to Paul in 1 Thessalonians 5:14 an injunction to "comfort the feebleminded," an injunction whose presence in the biblical text is taken to indicate Christianity's deep moral concern for retarded human beings. Unfortunately, that attribution to Paul appears to be based on the King James rendering of the text and rests on a poor translation of the Greek word *oligopsychos*, which current authoritative versions translate as "the fainthearted" (RSV, NEB) or the "apprehensive" (JB), i.e., those who are griefstricken, fearful, or anxious about persecution or the delayed Parousia or the deaths of community members prior to the Parousia.[11]

Apart from the Thessalonian text, of course, there is a good deal in the Bible about human beings who are simple, foolish, etc., and one might be tempted to identify such individuals as those sought for analogues, but, as is well known, biblical characterizations of simplicity and foolishness are typically offered as contrasts to what the Bible calls wisdom, which generally denotes right knowledge of God and the associated proper conduct, not intellectual capacity per se. To lack wisdom in the biblical sense, then, is not necessarily to lack rudimentary intellectual capacity; indeed, that is an improbable interpretation. Beyond such texts there are, as suggested already, the stories of Jesus's healing of the demonically possessed, who may reasonably be taken as analogues to humans now described as mentally ill, so a certain kind of intellectual incapacity seems to be within the biblical purview. As far as I can gather, however, one simply cannot find in Christian scripture what one seems to be able to find, for example, in Islamic scripture, namely, some expression of the view that certain vulnerable humans, at least plausibly interpreted as retarded human beings, fall fully within the scope of moral concern.[12]

Confronted with the Bible's silence on mental retardation, some Christian ethicists, including Robert Veatch, have tried to reconstruct from the *general* biblical concern for the vulnerable a Christian egalitarianism inclusive of all retarded human beings. The suggestion is that this general concern for vulnerability *entails* the humanist view of equality and that the Bible, therefore, affirms by implication the equal worth of all retarded humans even if it does not mention the retarded explicitly. All things considered, I think that such a line of approach is a fruitful one. Yet it must also be noted that this reconstruction from the biblical evidence will be taken by certain Christian ethicists simply to beg the question we are raising here, since it will be argued that a normative concern for the most vulnerable members of the moral community is perfectly consistent with the rationalist account of equal worth as the position that sets the limits of full and equal citzenship in that community. After all, human beings can be competent or potentially competent in the rationalist's sense and still be subject to the sorts of vulnerabilities that seem generally to command the Bible's moral attention (i.e., they can be poor, physically disabled, politically powerless, indeed, even mentally ill). So a concern for the kinds of vulnerable humans typically identified in the Bible does not entail without further argument a concern for humans who are vulnerable in that they lack the capacities prized by the rationalist account. Indeed, we shall see that some contemporary Christian ethicists argue precisely that when the Bible appears to enjoin moral consideration of *human* vulnerability, it has principally in mind vulnerable *persons,* and the class of persons envisaged is the class of all beings in possession of certain rational capacities. Given this rendering, profoundly retarded humans, at least as implied by the biblical account, simply fail to meet the conditions requisite for intrinsically equal moral standing. It will sometimes be added that this dismissal of the profoundly retarded's equal worth derives independent support from philosophical argument.

The point here is not to suggest that the rationalist reading of the biblical evidence carries the day. On the contrary, in my judgment, the rationalist view of equal worth, despite the counterclaims of certain Christian ethicists, is finally unsubstantiated by the biblical and theological evidence typically introduced in support of the position, and a portion of what follows will bear the burden of establishing that claim. In addition, I shall argue that distinctively *philosophical* (as opposed to theological) defenses of the rationalist view of equality are inconclusive in the final analysis.

THEOLOGICAL CONSIDERATIONS

In surveying the theological issues generated by our topic, it is useful to begin with an interpretation of Christian love recently proposed by theological ethicist Joseph Allen.[13] At a certain level Allen clearly intends to offer an account of love that affirms, among other things, the humanist view of equal worth. Yet on precisely this point his theory is marked by a fundamental ambiguity, which illustrates with considerable force some of the difficulties confronting Christian ethical attempts to resolve the problem we have identified.

The point of departure in Allen's account is the divine love for humanity, a love he characterizes as *covenantal* in the sense displayed by the biblical portrayal of God's dealings with humankind. In that portrayal God's love expresses itself by establishing and sustaining a variety of covenants with assorted individuals and peoples (Noah and subsequent humankind, Abraham and his seed, Moses and the Israelites, David, the Christian community, etc.). Given the covenantal character of this divine love, we may determine, according to Allen, the essential normative elements in Christian love by attending to the salient features of God's covenantal commitments. Now in Allen's view a principal feature of those commitments is precisely their gracious or unconditional quality. God's covenantal activity, in other words, embraces those it embraces irrespective of individual talent, merit, utility, capacity, etc., and thus even human beings who are the "least in the eyes of the world" fall within the scope of divine covenantal concern.[14] Christian love, then, qua *covenant* love, is likewise to be construed in unconditional terms: "To have covenant love is to affirm the worth of each covenant member, to regard each as someone who matters individually, irreplaceably, and equally. It is to recognize each one's humanity under God, each one's sacred worth. A test of love is whether we ultimately affirm alike as human beings the outcasts and failures of society along with its contributors and achievers—the heroin addicts, the Willy Lomans, the retarded children, the senile, along with the Mozarts and Lincolns and Einsteins."[15] In sum, what Allen advocates here is a variation on the humanist view of equal worth, including its associated affirmation of equal human rights, grounded distinctively in a Christian theology of covenantal love.[16]

I have mentioned already that, given scripture's silence on the subject of mental retardation, interpretive questions are posed by any attempt to deduce the equal standing of all retarded humans from the general biblical concern for human vulnerability. Thus, Allen needs to say more than he does about the hermeneutical strategies that support inclusion of "retarded children" *sans phrase* in a biblically based egalitarian theory. At present, however, I want to focus on a rather different problem, which arises when one attempts to reconcile Allen's general claims about love's unconditional character vis-à-vis humans with other claims he makes about the moral standing of nonhuman animals. While nonhuman animals presumably fall within the scope of God's concern, they are not, as Allen sees it, objects of God's *covenantal* love; they are not objects of God's covenantal love simply because that love is channeled toward "creatures capable of covenant, that is, toward human beings."[17] Indeed, for Allen it is precisely this capacity for covenant that marks human beings as created in the image of God and thus grounds their claim to equal moral consideration. "The capacity for covenant is then an essential feature, created by God, through which each person individually, irreplaceably, and equally has worth as an end, and not only as a means."[18] Since nonhuman animals lack the *imago dei*, since they lack, that is, the capacity for covenant, they lack equal standing with beings who possess that capacity, though presumably nonhuman animals do maintain some moral standing in virtue of the fact that they fall within the scope of a noncovenantal divine love distributed generally throughout creation.[19]

The question we must ask here is whether a denial of equal standing to animals for the reasons cited is entirely consistent with an apparently unqualified affirmation of such standing for *all* mentally retarded human beings, some of whom, one might surmise, also lack the covenantal characteristics said to be constitutive of the *imago dei*. Much depends, of course, on what is meant finally by *covenantal capacity*, and despite some equivocation on this point, most of what Allen says implies that certain retarded humans will fail to meet the relevant standards:

> The self [created in the image of God] is not only rational and not only transcends itself, but as one who must choose its own total end in a community of others who do likewise, it has *the capacity to enter into covenant with God and with other human selves.* The capacity for self-transcendence provides not only the possibility for gaining perspective upon one's life, but also for committing oneself steadfastly to others. The apex of the *imago dei* is then the capacity for covenant, a capacity that is possible because the self also has the capacity for rationality and for self-transcendence.[20]

In short, bearers of the divine image are presumed to be self-conscious as well as socially and morally capacious, and such implies (though Allen never says so directly) that human beings lacking these capacities are not, properly speaking, bearers of the image of God. Admittedly matters are clouded somewhat by Allen's ad hoc suggestion that a human child can exist in covenantal relationship prereflectively, i.e., through subconscious entrustment of herself to others (e.g., parents), even though she cannot form the appropriate cognitive intentions to forge the relation.[21] Naturally, if the capacity for prereflective entrustment is all that is necessary to bear the image of God, then there is room for arguing that even profoundly retarded humans are image bearers. Yet similar things could be said on behalf of nonhuman animals, at least some of whom, it would appear, are capable of prereflective social relations (e.g., domesticated dogs and cats). All in all, then, it seems clear that one cannot cast the doctrine of *imago dei* in diminished terms of covenantal capacity so as to ensure the equal standing of children and at the same time appeal to the doctrine as a way of legitimating a sharp moral distinction between human beings and nonhuman animals. If the equality of children is to be affirmed within the confines of the general theory, such will probably have to be justified on the grounds that children normally have the potential for developing covenantal capacity in the unattenuated sense of the term. It hardly needs saying, of course, that this argumentative strategy leaves out precisely those beings, human or otherwise, who lack the requisite potential.

In order to avoid the full force of this conclusion, contemporary Christian ethicists have offered a variety of proposals, all of which are ultimately question-begging in significant ways. Thus, Gene Outka has intimated that refusing to count certain mentally retarded humans as full-fledged neighbors to be loved simply because they lack rational potential would seem to presume a God-like certainty about our moral assessments. From our limited perspectives, it is utterly hubristic to think we can know what sort of worth these lives might have, and thus epistemic, if not theological, humility supports counting them as neighbors to be loved, especially given the belief that retarded humans are in some sense "related to God."[22] Yet a central difficulty with this argument in the present context is that whether and how these humans might be related to God despite their covenantal incapacities is precisely one of the issues at stake. Thus, appealing to divine relationality as a way of settling the matter of moral status simply begs the question. Beyond this difficulty, the argument from epistemic humility proves too much; for if we cannot be certain that human lives without rational potential lack significant worth, neither, it might be argued, can we be certain that nonhuman beings lack such worth. Unless one is prepared, then, to grant equal standing to these other beings, one will need a principle of differentiation, a principle naturally that focuses on something other than covenantal capacity in the full-blown sense of the term.

Similarly problematic is a theological maneuver that tries to preserve the equal standing of profoundly retarded humans by appealing to the utterly gracious character of God's love. This maneuver is suggested both by Outka and Allen, who underscore particularly the anti-utilitarian element in divine grace as a justification for egalitarian commitments. Again, just as God loves graciously or unconditionally, i.e., without regard for an individual's social utility, productivity, talent, or merit, so Christian love should abstract from such considerations, and thus Christian believers ought to regard all humans, whatever their "disutility value," as full-fledged neighbors to be loved.[23] But the problem with this argument is its failure to recognize that cast in a certain way anti-utilitarian principles are fully compatible with an unqualified rationalism, which can acknowledge that God's love is unconditionally gracious and that equal consideration of *persons* ought not to be affected by individual utilities but which at the same time defines persons or neighbors to be loved precisely as beings with certain rational or covenantal endowments. The general point is that if there is good theological reason for tying equal standing to covenantal capacity, as Allen and others suggest, then anti-utilitarian principles *simpliciter* can afford no justification for exceptions that would be required by an egalitarianism fully inclusive of retarded humans.

As a final example of question-begging theological maneuvers designed to preserve the retarded's claim to equality, we may consider Robert Veatch's argument, which draws on H. Richard Niebuhr's claims about the relativizing character of God's radical sovereignty.[24] According to Veatch, exclusion of the retarded from equal membership in the moral community collides with the Christian belief that all human beings are equally finite creations of an utterly sovereign God, who alone retains infinite value. Relative to this infinite value, all differences among finite existents are inconsequential, and thus fundamental normative discriminations among humans not only lack theological warrant but also fly in the face of the "radical monotheism" that constitutes the Christian construction of reality. Needless to say, on the *assumption* that humanity sets the boundaries of moral community, the appeal to common finitude can serve as a powerful support for the humanist view of equality. Yet a moment's reflection also reveals that as a strategy designed to counter rationalist construals of equal worth, Veatch's argument from "radical monotheism" proves, again, either too much or nothing at all. If, on the one hand, finite creation *simpliciter* is the ultimate moral leveler, then equality will have to encompass *all* finite existents, including nonhuman animals, inanimate lives, and, it would seem, inorganic objects. If, on the other hand, some or all of these nonhuman finite existents are to be excluded from full equality, then one needs a principle of differentiation, and that need signifies a return to the original question. Interestingly enough, at one point Veatch seems to recognize the problem and argues, albeit tentatively, for discriminating principles reminiscent of Allen's covenantal criteria. ". . . The capacity for experience and social interaction is sufficient and necessary for humans to have moral claims including the claims of justice." He adds that "if other species show similar capacities for social interaction as well as experience, then they would have to be included among those who bear claims to equality, but . . . the likelihood of finding such species on this earth is remote."[25] Yet, *pace* Veatch, if the capacity for experience and social interaction is complex enough to exclude from equal consideration all known nonhuman species (even highly sophisticated species such as dolphins and chimps), it would also seem to be complex enough to exclude certain human beings. To avoid this implication, it needs to be shown why these incapacitated humans should be exempted from fulfilling requirements generally held as necessary and sufficient conditions of equal claims to justice. But that question is passed over in silence by Veatch.

Enough has been said to establish the principal point of the moment that if covenantal capacity in anything like Allen's sense is given privileged theoretical standing, then profoundly retarded humans will be threatened with diminished moral status. Much rides, then, on the justifications given for privileging covenantal capacity in this way, and the standard theological rationales, I want to argue, are anything but conclusive. Consider Allen's claim that covenantal criteria for equality follow naturally from a theological understanding of moral community as covenantal community. Covenantal relationships, not unlike contractual relationships, presumably require what might be called interchange capacities. Hence, God *can* covenant, in this account, only with beings capable of reciprocal commitment and entrustment. Yet whatever one might say about contractual relations as they are understood ordinarily, it is implausible to suggest that covenantal relations understood biblically always require the participants' interchange capacities. For one thing, as Allen himself affirms and as Christian proponents of animal liberation are fond of reminding us, the Noachic account in Genesis 9 depicts a divine covenant (the covenant of the rainbow) that extends not simply to humans but to all living creatures, many of whom clearly lack skills for reciprocal commitment and entrustment.[26] To be sure, one might try to distinguish different sorts of biblical covenants and related moral communities based on the presence or absence of the capacities in question, but the important point here is that the warrant for those distinctions could not derive without additional premises from the conditions of covenantal association understood simply as covenantal in the biblical sense.

Indeed, these conclusions about the relatively inclusive character of covenantal association gain considerable support from the biblical account of circumcision, a rite remembered by the Israelite community both as a sign of the Abrahamic covenant and as a mark of entry into the covenantal community. That this rite is legislated for male infants on the eighth day after birth suggests that covenantal association per se does not depend on the presence of interchange capacities (Genesis 17:12, Leviticus, 12:3, Luke 1:59, 2:21, Philippians 3:5). Of course, one might contend that these infants typically had the potential to develop the capacities in question and that the potential is what is prized overall in the biblical view. Yet, again, none of this follows simply from the idea of covenant. The general point is that rationalist theological construals of moral community require argument independent of the observation that biblical morality is in some significant way covenantal morality.

Now, according to some Christian ethicists, the independent argument necessary for establishing the rationalist view can be reconstructed, more directly than is done so by Allen, from the doctrine of the *imago dei*, particularly as that doctrine is displayed in certain biblical texts.[27] Thus Bouma, Langerak, Verhey, et al., who are largely sympathetic with Allen's covenantal account of equal worth, contend that the account derives direct support in particular from two biblical characterizations of the divine image. First, as evidenced forcefully in the Noachic prohibition of murder (Genesis 9:6), scripture attributes significant moral value to beings created in the image of God. Persons, that is, have a moral claim not to be murdered or wronged in various other ways precisely because they are image bearers. Second, as witnessed presumably in the creation account of Genesis 1:26, scripture connects the image of God *essentially* with the capacity for stewardly responsibility ("Let us make humanity in our image, after our likeness; and let them have dominion over the fish of the sea, and over the birds of the air, and over the cattle, and over all the earth, and over every creeping thing that creeps upon the earth"). Because the exercise of dominion requires an array of rational capacities, these same capacities must be taken as constitutive of the divine image.[28] From such observations it is concluded that "fetuses, newborn infants and those human beings with profound mental retardation are not persons."[29] In other words, they lack intrinsically the moral standing borne by genuine image bearers, although there might be justification for imputing equal standing in the problematic cases given the possibly beneficial effects of so doing on real persons. Of course, such imputation is fictional, even if warranted on pragmatic grounds.

There are, in my view, at least two difficulties with this line of argument. First, understanding the biblical *imago dei* both as rational capacity and as foundation for the Bible's prohibition of murder bears a special burden of explanation given what appears to be a deep biblical polemic against the killing of children (as evidenced in Isaiah 57:5, Jeremiah 7:31, Leviticus 18:21, Exodus 13:1-2, 11-16, 22:29, 34:20). If one can reasonably assume that this polemic includes strictures on the killing of infants (and the aforementioned practice of infant circumcision makes this assumption reasonable), then there are grounds for thinking of infants as image bearers despite their stewardly incapacities. Of course, the rationalist could counter, once again, with the argument that strictures against the killing of infants are justifiable given their potential rationality or given pragmatic considerations bearing on the well-being of real persons.[30] Understood in this fashion, the prohibitions are wholly consistent with rationalist renderings of the biblical *imago*. Yet the problem here is that arguments from potentiality or pragmatics supporting strictures against the killing of children are not clearly articulated in the Bible itself. At best, then, such arguments would have to be ascribed to the biblical texts hypothetically in the way of offering plausible interpretive reconstructions *given* the supposition that rationalist construals of the *imago dei* are sound.

And this brings us to the second difficulty with the line of argument under consideration. In short, as most biblical scholars and theologians know, rationalist renderings of the biblical *imago dei* are exceedingly controversial. While a significant tradition of interpretation, of course, does link the divine image to intellectual endowments of various sorts, other traditions propose different meanings, with different textual justifications, and there seems to be no consensus emerging from the interpretive debate.[31] Thus, Karl Barth, drawing partially on Genesis 1:27 ("So God created humanity in his own image, in the image of God he created him; male and female he created them.") proposes that the divine image be understood essentially as social or relational being, a mode of existence presumably reflective of God's intrarelational nature.[32] Indeed, something like Barth's rendering of the *imago* would seem to lie behind Stanley Hauerwas's recent proclamation that "God's face is the face of the retarded; God's body is the body of the retarded; God's being is the being of the retarded," by which he means, I take it, that the deep need for others displayed acutely in retarded human beings but present essentially in all human beings reflects a relational neediness internal to God's trinitarian nature.[33] Of course, relational readings of the *imago* are themselves controversial, but even if one thinks that such interpretations pay insufficient attention to the dominion theme in Genesis 1:26, it is not at all clear that this favored text of the rationalists actually *defines* the image of God in terms of stewardly capacity ("Let us create humanity in our image . . . *and* let them have dominion"). Thus, Claus Westermann proposes in his landmark commentary that "dominion over other creatures is not an explanation, but a consequence of creation in the image of God. . . . Gen, 1:26f. is not making a general and universally valid statement about the nature of humankind; if it were, then the Old Testament would have much more to say about this image and likeness. The fact is that it does not. . . ."[34] In this rendering of Genesis 1:26, then, only image bearers rule, but the capacity for rule does not define image bearing.

That reading, of course, leaves open the question of what constitutes image bearing precisely, and, as I have suggested, the scholarly answers to this question have been numerous and varied. It is perhaps useful to note here that many biblical scholars interpret the attribution of the *imago* in Genesis 1:26 as signifying, at least partially, the sharing of a physical likeness with God (an interpretation that gains some support, it would seem, from Genesis 5:3, which characterizes

Seth as the image [*selem*] of his father Adam), and while one might be tempted to dismiss such a correspondence between the human and divine as a crude anthropomorphism of the ancient world, one might also surmise that the priestly writer was trying to convey something about the moral significance of the human form, quite apart from any connections that might be drawn between that form and rational endowment.

More generally, I want to suggest that what emerges from the biblical narrative overall is a picture of moral worth and moral community at odds with exclusively rationalist depictions of same. In this larger biblical narrative, *all beings born of humankind* are created in God's image and thus all of this lineage are bearers of the associated moral worth. That interpretation, I believe, explains most economically the biblical assessments of circumcision and child sacrifice and accords well with Genesis 5:1-3, which, through an apparent play on the word *likeness* (*dîmut*), suggests the intergenerational transmission of the image from Adam to Seth.[35] But if all humans bear the divine image, what precisely is the image's content? I suspect that no simple answer to that question is forthcoming and that the writers of the relevant texts probably meant to gather under *imago* constructs a variety of disparate properties and relations—again, human visage and general physical comportment, but also distinctively human gestures and emotional capacities (e.g., to laugh and cry), infant-parent relational attributes, moral capacities, and rational endowments—in short, all those properties and connections we tend to associate with the human way of life. This collection of attributes undoubtedly defies easy systematic elaboration, and I sense that in the biblical understanding no single property serves as a necessary condition of image bearing (i.e., an image bearer might lack human visage or rational endowment). The important point is that all who are born into this human way of life *thickly described* carry the divine image in a sense crucial for moral assessments.

If this rendering is correct, then profoundly retarded humans would count as image bearers in the biblical view, and the central question before us is whether this biblical account of moral status can withstand the philosophical objections likely to be brought against it. To put the matter straightforwardly, are philosophical defenses of the rationalist view of equality impressive enough to justify rejecting what I take to be the biblical view? While I can hardly cover the whole terrain of relevant argumentation here, I hope that I can say enough to suggest the deficiencies of philosophically inspired rationalist proposals. Accomplishing that task is important for two reasons at least: First, theological versions of the rationalist view sometimes appear convinced, if not primarily driven, by philosophical defenses of the position.[36] Second, some theologians who want to grant significant moral standing to retarded humans seem to accept the validity of much of the rationalist philosophical argument. Thus, Stanley Hauerwas affirms unequivocally the full moral standing of retarded humans but suggests at various points that such affirmation requires the abandonment of rights-based, egalitarian discourse.[37] That is, his proposal intimates that the philosophical rationalists have won the argument about equality. Yet this concession, I want to suggest, is premature.

PHILOSOPHICAL CONSIDERATIONS

An especially straightforward philosophical account of the rationalist view has been given recently by John Harris, who begins his discussion with the following reflections:

> In identifying the things that make human life valuable we will be pointing to the features that would make the existence of any being who possessed them valuable. It is important to have a word for such beings which is not simply anthropocentric or species specific. I shall use the term *person* to stand for any being who has what it takes to be valuable in the sense described, whatever they are otherwise like. Although in normal use 'person' is just another (and usefully gender-neutral) term for 'human being,' as I shall use it from now on it will also be species-neutral. This does not put as great a strain on our normal understanding of the word as may be imagined. For example, the question of whether or not there are people on other planets is a real one. If there are, we need not expect them to be human people (it would be bizarre if they were!), nor need we expect them to look or sound or smell (or anything else) like us. They might not even be organic, but might perhaps reproduce by mechanical construction rather than by genetic reproduction. But if we are able to answer the question in the affirmative, we will be distinguishing between people on other worlds and animals, plants or machines on those worlds. We will be deciding whether an appropriate response to them would be to have them for dinner in one sense or in the other. And if the people who we find (or who find us) turn out to be technologically very much our superiors, we may hope to persuade them that we are also people, not just like them maybe, but enough like them to be valuable, and to warrant being accorded the same concern, respect and protection as they would show to each other. And, if

> the boot is on the other foot, to warrant our according to them the same concern, respect and protection as we accord to one another. But in what respects must we be like them and they like us?[38]

As Harris sees it, the answer to this last question is that individual members of our respective species must each have the capacity for valuing her, his, or its own existence. It is the possession of this capacity that warrants putatively an individual's claim to the highest worth and therefore to equal "concern, respect and protection." Since that capacity requires in turn the *cognitive* capacity for entertaining *inter alia* the concept of one's own existence as an entity separate from others, the concept of that existence extended into the future as well as the concept of possible nonexistence, it is clear that a range of profoundly retarded humans could never become genuine persons intrinsically commanding the highest moral consideration. At least, such is the implication of Harris's theory.[39]

But why should we accept this account of persons as beings who can value their own existences? Harris's discussion suggests at least two rationales for so doing. First, the account would appear to explain deep intuitions we have about the ultimate reasons for attributing the highest moral worth to human life, intuitions presumably uncovered in reflection on examples such as those involving hypothetical worlds of nonhuman rational beings. In other words, our inclination to assign the highest moral worth to nonhumans evincing the appropriate rational capacity would seem to reflect our deep intuition that the possession of this capacity is precisely what grounds our ascription of such worth to human life.[40] Second, the account in question is said to have the advantage of explaining moral standing in terms that are "value- and species-neutral."[41] Characterizing personhood in the manner described, that is, presumably allows us to identify persons without begging controversial questions about which "mode of existence" is greatest in worth and without favoring arbitrarily one species (our own) over another. In this view, all that matters for the determination of personhood is the being's capacity for valuing its own existence. Whether the being is of this or that species *kind*, according to Harris, is simply immaterial.

Both of these rationales, in my view, are exceedingly problematic. In the first place it seems doubtful that the account in question does explain fully our deep intuitions about the ultimate reasons for attributing the highest moral worth to human life—at least if this is taken to mean explaining intuitions connected with *ordinary* ways of thinking about these matters. After all, typically we accord such worth to beings who fail to meet the standards implied by the account, and this fact suggests that our basic convictions about moral worth are *not* captured by a theory that links equal standing without exception to possession of the rational capacity described. Most important, there is little reason to believe that simple reflection on hypothetical examples of nonhuman, rational, alien worlds should result in normative conclusions compelling us to modify these ordinary convictions.

As an illustration, consider an extension of the hypothetical case suggested by Harris. Imagine that we encounter beings from another world, beings who in their outward appearance and physical structure differ markedly from us. We discover that, despite the radical dissimilarities, these beings do have a system of communication analogous to ours, and we hit upon a translation scheme. From a study of their communicative practices we learn among other things that individuals of the alien "species" distinguish themselves from other individuals, have a sense of themselves as mortal, generally value their own existences, and prefer to go on living. How would we assess the moral standing of these beings? Barring some further explanation, it seems that we would accord them a standing roughly commensurate with the standing of adult humans, at least in the sense of according them an equal right to continued existence. But all this would show is that a being's capacity for valuing its own existence is *sufficient* for the ascription of equal worth to that being. We cannot go on to infer that the capacity is also *necessary* for the ascription of such worth. Indeed, further extension of the hypothetical example would appear to lead us to precisely the opposite conclusion, namely, that there exist reasons sufficient for assigning equal worth that have nothing at all to do with the capacity in question.

Imagine that the community of aliens exhibited a certain social organization informed by a distinctively moral discourse. These beings, in other words, regulate mutual behavior by adhering to widely recognized prescriptions taken with utmost seriousness. Imagine also that the contents of the prescriptions as well as their explicit justifications reflect the aliens' regard for each other as beings of equal worth. However, in addition to ascribing such worth to fellow beings who can value their own existences, the rational aliens also count as full-fledged, equal members of the moral community a number of beings who lack the conceptual skills required for such valuing. When we inquire about the justification for including these other beings along with the most advanced, we are given various explanations. Most of the nonrational beings, we are told, eventually will develop the conceptual skills they presently lack, and partly in virtue of that potential equal worth is attributed. At the same time, it is also admitted that some of the nonrational beings will never develop these skills. We are told, nonetheless, that these beings too are judged to have equal worth. When we ask further why they are given this exalted status, we are treated to a complex description of genesis and social interaction. "These beings," it is said, "are born of our own kind. They are generated by our acts of creation. They look like us. They are nurtured by us. They participate with us in a variety of practices that constitute the shared meaning of our communal existence. In all of these senses, they belong to us. And since they do, we recognize their equal value even if they are limited in capacity. We acknowledge, in other words, that they have fundamental interests which are always to be given consideration equal to that given the fundamental interests of the most conceptually advanced among us. Thus, despite their disabilities, these fellow beings bear a value for us that is not borne by other nonrational beings of our world (the alien analogues to nonhuman animals) who neither share our origins nor participate in our most significant communal practices."

Now there can be little doubt that this normative view would accord quite well with our own moral sensibilities. That is, we would regard neither as unreasonable nor as unfair the alien practice of attributing equal worth to their disabled beings. Indeed, we would find the practice and its associated discourse quite familiar since they both come very close to matching the patterns of our own culture. After all, we do tend to think of retarded humans, among others, as intrinsic bearers of equal worth even if they are unable to conceptualize in the sense relevant to the present discussion. For example, we typically regard it a violation of their intrinsic moral rights to kill them in order to promote the fundamental interests of conceptually sophisticated nonhuman animals such as dolphins and chimpanzees. Moreover, we would account for our attitudes with reasons roughly analogous to those given by the hypothetical aliens. Still, the rationalist might ask, how would *we, humans*, regard the disabled beings *of the alien world*? Wouldn't we tend to think of them much in the same way as we regarded the nonhuman animals of our own world? Suppose we encountered an alien world populated *only* by beings lacking the capacity to value their own existences. Wouldn't we be reluctant to accord the inhabitants of that world a moral standing equal to our own? And wouldn't this reluctance betray our deep conviction that the possession of some rational capacity is after all a necessary condition of equal worth?

The trouble with this line of questioning is its apparent assumption that in sorting out our most fundamental convictions about moral standing we are to abstract entirely from considerations of various historical and social connections embedded in species life. Yet it is not at all clear why we ought to do so, and our intuitions about these matters suggest that such connections are indeed morally significant. To be sure, we might hesitate to grant equal standing to the inhabitants of an alien world populated exclusively by beings lacking the capacity to value their own lives. But it is much less clear that we would be reluctant to grant such standing to the disabled beings connected with the rational aliens. After all, we could appreciate the normative force of their historical and social relations by analogy with our own. We might, for example, recognize their disabled beings as their *children* and as such attribute equal standing to them just as we grant equal standing to our own children whatever their conceptual capacities or potentials. Moreover, such attribution on our part need not be taken as morally reducible to *respect for the preferences of the rational aliens themselves*, just as we do not regard the attribution of equal standing to human children as morally reducible to respect for the preferences of rational human parents. Indeed, typically we think of human children as equal bearers of fundamental moral rights whether their parents agree or not![42] But even if it is conceded that such reasoning by analogy is strained and that *humans* could have no justification for regarding the disabled alien beings as intrinsically equal members of the moral community, this is not to imply that the *rational aliens* themselves would lack justification for so doing. On the contrary, it appears they would have all sorts of identifiably good reasons deeply rooted in their histories and social relations. And similar things can be said, of course, about our own attitudes toward profoundly retarded humans. Despite their disabilities, we do tend to recognize these beings as "belonging to us"—as fellow members of the *human* community, beings who are born of us, look like us, partake in our human history and share in our human practices—and this recognition does seem to provide *us* with good reason for regarding them as beings of equal worth, though naturally such a justification could have normative force solely within the human community.[43]

My principal contention here is simply that our deepest intuitions about how equal worth is determined are more complex than Harris's account (and others like it) would lead one to believe. In other words, while we might be comfortable with his notion of personhood as one affording a sufficient condition for ascribing equal worth, we would be less than comfortable with that notion as one affording a necessary condition. At best, then, a theory like Harris's would have to be taken as a recommendation to *reject* basic convictions about moral standing as such are reflected in our ordinary judgments, and the recommendation would have to be grounded in something other than simple reflection on hypothetical examples of nonhuman rational worlds.

Of course, an oft-stated purpose of the rationalist view is precisely to challenge our ordinary judgments on these matters, and the challenge is typically grounded in an indictment of those judgments for singling out *species membership* as a characteristic morally relevant to the ascription of equal standing. This point, of course, brings us to the second reason suggested by Harris for adopting his theory, namely, that it affords a "value- and species-neutral" criterion of personhood. We have seen that Harris prizes this theoretical feature partly because it enables him to account for our intuitions affirming the equal standing of hypothetical rational beings outside the human community. At the same time, we have also seen that appeals to membership in this community appear necessary to account for other intuitions we have about the intrinsic equal worth of some human beings, including the profoundly retarded. So why, we may ask, should appeals of this sort be excluded *categorically* by our theories of personhood and equality?

As I have suggested already, a standard rationalist response to this question is that such appeals are unfairly prejudicial and consequently repugnant from the moral point of view.[44] In this account, judgments based on humanist principles are no better, morally speaking, than judgments based on racist or sexist principles. Just as it is morally pernicious to give special consideration to members of one's own race or sex, so presumably it is morally wrong to give such consideration to members of one's own species. What racist, sexist, and speciesist attitudes supposedly have in common is an unjustified *partiality* in outlook, and morality, it is proposed, requires strict *impartiality*. So to say that all severely retarded humans are bearers of the highest moral worth simply because they are human is putatively like saying that all caucasians are bearers of such worth simply because they are caucasian or that all males are bearers of such worth simply because they are male.

Of course, as proponents of this argument would have to concede, the mere fact of partiality in an outlook is probably insufficient to render it morally unacceptable. Indeed, under certain circumstances partiality seems called for as a matter of moral obligation. For example, we typically regard as obligatory a parent's showing special interest in her or his child's welfare or taking special intiatives to promote that welfare, and it is doubtful that our judgments in favor of such partiality could be explained entirely in terms of more general duties and obligations owed to all persons.[45] Moreover, it is not obviously mistaken to regard the humanistic partiality reflected in prizing the severely retarded as much closer in moral kind to familial preferentiality than to racial or sexual prejudice.[46] But even if the comparison between familial and humanistic partiality turned out to be imperfect, more would have to be said to sustain the humanist/racist/sexist analogy, a fact rationalists and others have appreciated. For certainly the humanist will argue that racism and sexism are objectionably partial because they discriminate in unwarranted ways among members of the *human* community, all of whom are bearers of equal worth by reason of such membership, and clearly the same charge cannot be leveled against humanism itself.[47] To defeat the humanist's argument and avoid begging the question, the rationalist needs to establish on independent grounds that rational capacity rather than membership in the human community legitimates the ascription of equal worth or at least that human membership is irrelevant to determinations of equal standing.

Given these sorts of considerations, rationalists have responded with the argument that the humanist/racist/sexist connection is based precisely on the moral irrelevance of the property each attitude singles out for special consideration. Just as racial and sexual characteristics are morally insignificant, so presumably are species characteristics. What, after all, could be morally noteworthy about a being's *biological* constitution, the rationalist typically will ask?

Such a response, admittedly, is forceful as far as it goes. Yet it also assumes that the moral significance of membership in the human community could have no explanation other than one cast in purely biological terms, and, as I have intimated already, matters seem to be more complicated than this view implies. Indeed, the conclusions of our thought experiment involving the hypothetical alien world suggested that the moral significance of such membership has more to do with social history and social relations than with biology *simpliciter*. In this view, we value severely retarded humans not primarily because they have, say, a distinctive genetic code but rather because they have a certain history, a certain visage, a certain location in various practices that constitute our human way of life. Again, despite their disabilities, the retarded are born of us, look like us, and interact with us in a wide assortment of highly distinctive communal settings. They are beings with whom we have deeply significant historical and social relations. Certainly it is artificial to assess the value they bear for us apart from a consideration of such connections. And if these connections are taken as central to membership in the human community, then rationalist claims about the moral irrelevance of such membership begin to look abstract, unreal, the product of philosophers held in the grip of a theory.[48]

Neither is our sense of abstraction relieved by the now familiar argument that grounds the claims of rationalists in purported conceptual connections among desires, interests, and rights.[49] This argument begins with an intuitively plausible assumption, namely, that persons, however else they might be characterized, are beings who have a moral right to continued existence. Given this assumption, it is concluded that one could not classify as persons those beings who lacked the capacity to value their own existences since one could not intelligibly ascribe to such beings a moral right to continued existence. The reasons lying behind this last judgment are as follows: For a being to have a *right* to x, the being must be capable of having an *interest* in x. But to have an interest in x, a being must be capable of *desiring* x. Now, at least some desires involve what philosophers call "propositional attitudes." That is, one cannot have the desires without conceputalizing certain states of affairs expressible in propositional form, states of affairs constituting the objects of the desires in question. I could not, for instance, desire a world free of nuclear weapons unless, indeed, I could conceptualize such a world. Certain desires, then, require for their formation a degree of conceptual capacity; and this is certainly true of the desire to have one's existence continued. One could not have this desire unless one could comprehend, among other things, the idea of one's own existence extended in time. Granted this fact, as well as the aforementioned connections among desires, interests, and rights, a being could not have a moral right to continued existence without also having the ability to conceptualize the object of that right. And if *per definitionem* persons are minimally the bearers of this right, one could not count as persons those beings who lacked the conceptual capacities required to form the corresponding desire.

Needless to say, a crucial feature of this argument is the stipulated connection between rights and desires, a connection which may seem plausible enough if we focus on certain moral conventions (e.g., the practice of an agent's waiving a right). Still, as one proponent of the rights-desires connection has acknowledged, the position that a right *always* presupposes a desire in the relevant sense is obviously vulnerable to counterexample.[50] Thus, we would judge that painlessly castrating an infant to prepare it for a soprano's career would violate the rights of the infant even though it was incapable of forming a desire not to have the operation performed. Similarly, we would regard as a violation of her rights a woman's conditioning from early childhood to accept a life of domination by others even though she could not, by the very nature of the conditioning, form a desire that things were otherwise. Counterexamples such as these have prompted various adjustments and qualifications of the rights-desires theory. Thus,

Michael Tooley has argued that the connection between rights and desires does not hold without exception but does obtain in certain cases, including those involving the right to continued existence.[51] Given the validity of the connection in these contexts, neither infants nor certain retarded humans could have this right since neither could form the appropriate desire.

Now, the problem with modifying the theory in this way is twofold. In the first place, the more one qualifies the connection between rights and desires, the more one attenuates any argument relying on the *general* claim that the connection holds. In the second place, exactly how one qualifies the connection will depend upon which instances are allowed as morally relevant counterexamples, and on this score it is difficult to see how a position such as Tooley's could avoid the charge of begging the question. If an infant's right not to be castrated and a woman's right not to be brainwashed count as exceptions to the rule linking rights and desires, why not also count an infant's right to continued existence? After all, in ordinary circumstances at least, we do regard the killing of an infant as an attack on its interests and a violation of its intrinsic right to life even though infants cannot form the corresponding desires. This conviction of ours, moreover, appears to be as deeply entrenched as any moral beliefs we have about infant castration and the brainwashing of women. So why should we not account for that conviction by qualifying further the theoretical connection between rights and desires? Of course, analogous things could be said about rights to continued existence had by profoundly retarded human beings. If it is true that we typically recognize such rights, one would think that this fact should be incorporated in any theory of the relation between rights and desires. A decision not to incorporate simply begs the principal normative question and abstracts without obvious warrant from the historical connections and social relations reflected in our ordinary moral convictions.[52]

Finally we must consider the rationalist view that identifies a being's *moral* capacity as a condition of equal worth. In this account, any proper understanding of the moral community or the circumstances of its origination should lead one to conclude that qualification for full membership in that community is a certain power of moral discrimination or judgment. Attainment of equal worth, then, is a function of coming to possess this moral power, which is beyond the reach of some retarded humans. Among the most important contemprary defenses of this position is that offered by Tristram Engelhardt, whose arguments I shall focus on here.

At the center of Engelhardt's account is a particular understanding of the nature and foundation of ethics in a secular society. "Ethics is at the very least a means for resolving controversies regarding proper conduct on bases other than direct or indirect appeals to force as the fundamental basis for a resolution."[53] The controversies in question are endemic to pluralistic societies marked by competing understandings of the good life. Thus, it might be debated in these societies whether suicide ought to be available as an option for an individual who has judged that her life is no longer worth living. Prospects are dim for adjudicating such controversies by appealing to overarching substantive principles, and therefore one is left with the alternatives of resolution by brute force or mutually agreed upon accommodation. Since, according to Engelhardt, ethics is a rational enterprise *per definitionem* and since employing force without justification is intrinsicially irrational, seeking an *ethical* resolution of moral controversy involves seeking an agreement by way of "peaceful negotiation."[54] Such negotiation requires no commitment to specific understandings of the good life, but does presume allegiance to certain procedural principles reflecting a core morality of mutual respect. In other words, if the goal of ethics is resolution of controversy by way of peaceable agreement, then no settlement will be binding ethically *unless* it is acceptable to all the parties involved. Hence, respecting the autonomy of moral disputants is a rational requirement of participation in the ethical enterprise, and this general account of ethics is said to support a particular depiction of moral community. "Since moral controversies can in principle encompass all moral agents (and . . . *only* moral agents), one has the means of characterizing the moral community as the possible intellectual standpoint of persons interested in resolving moral controversies in ways not fundamentally based on force."[55]

What is crucial for present purposes is Engelhardt's opinion that this vision of moral community has implications for the determination of equal worth. In brief, "not all humans are equal."[56] On the contrary, only those beings, human or otherwise, who can participate in the deliberations of the moral community have genuinely equal standing in that community. A condition of such participation naturally is possession of a range of rational capacities, including self-consciousness, autonomy and the power of moral discrimination. If beings with these capacities did not exist, there could be no moral community—at least in the sense described—and thus, from the perspective of *ethical* assessments, morally rational beings have privileged standing. These beings are persons "in the strict sense," i.e., intrinsic bearers of equal worth, and are to be distinguished from persons "in the social sense," i.e., beings, human or otherwise, who lack the relevant moral capacities and therefore intrinsic equal standing but who are nonetheless *granted* personhood status on extrinsic grounds. Thus, the community of rational agents may reasonably choose to treat profoundly retarded humans *as though* they were genuine persons (contrary to fact) since the practice of so doing will cultivate "important virtues such as sympathy and care for human life," virtues which contribute in various ways to the well-being of persons in the strict sense.[57] Still, given the nature of the moral community, persons in the strict sense retain a higher intrinsic moral standing than persons in the social sense.

As we have seen, for Engelhardt this account of equal worth follows naturally from a view of *ethics* as a deliberative mode of conflict resolution among rational agents in a secular society. If the point of ethics is to settle such conflict through peaceable negotiation and agreement and if a condition of such agreement is a certain mutual respect constituted by the participants' recognition that no resolution will be adopted unless it is acceptable to all, then ethics *qua* ethics provides a justification for respecting the autonomy of rational agents and thus affords at least implicitly a criterion (moral competency) for determining equal standing. In sum, the conditions of peaceable arbitration set the limits for the conception of moral community. But why, we might ask, should these conditions particularly constitute our point of departure for envisioning moral community?

Perhaps it will be thought that what makes this point of departure reasonable is precisely the *pragmatic* requirement of living in a pluralistic society. In this understanding, citizens of a pluralistic society are inexorably faced with competing interests and conflicting views of the good life. If, in such circumstances, it is reasonable to shun brute force and seek peaceful accommodation, it is also reasonable to assume a point of view that recognizes at the outset the equal standing of participants in the deliberative process. Without such recognition, naturally, peaceable agreement would be impossible in practice. The main point is that given the de facto constraints of life in a pluralistic society, there is, in the present account, pragmatic justification for regarding all rational deliberators as free and equal members of the moral community *ab initio*. At the same time, there is no similarly pragmatic warrant for regarding infants or severely retarded humans as having equal moral standing *ab initio*, although such standing might be (albeit need not be) conferred by the rational deliberators as the outcome of peaceable negotiation. Thus pragmatic considerations compel us presumably to envisage moral community and attendant notions of equal worth in *essentially* rationalist terms.

As forceful as this line of argument may appear to be, there are at least two problems with it. First, what counts as a pragmatic consideration in any given instance will depend on the character of the interests at stake, and a rational deliberator with a severely retarded child is likely to deem as imprudent the acceptance of any agreement that denies the child full personhood status *ab initio*, even if the alternative is a breakdown in peaceable negotiation. Pragmatic justification, then, can cut either way. Second, a rational deliberator might harbor a conception of the good life such that pragmatic considerations are overridden by perceived moral ones. Thus, a Christian might reason that the intrinsic equality of infants, profoundly retarded humans, or Alzheimer's patients must be preserved in the larger society's conception of moral community, even if pressing this claim jeopardizes peaceful deliberations. In other words, depending on what is at stake and depending on one's vision of the good, *ethics* might reasonably advise against peaceful accommodation in a pluralistic society. To assume that ethics always favors such accommodation or that accommodation is always reasonable is to assume a highly controversial—indeed, question-begging—notion of ethics or reasonableness. All in all, then, pragmatic considerations *simpliciter* provide no clear warrant for rationalist construals of moral community even in the pluralistic society.

Neither is the warrant provided by "transcendental" arguments unearthing conditions for the possibility of ethics as such.[58] Arguments of this type characteristically take the following form: Any enterprise reasonably construed as ethics presupposes a community of moral deliberators and agents. After all, ethics as a practice could not exist apart from the existence of such deliberators and agents. Thus, beings who can reflect and act on the advice ethics gives must be regarded as the moral community's principal members, having privileged standing in the order of *ethical* assessments. Yet the problem with this argument is that it confuses two separate points. It is one thing to say that ethics as a practice would not be possible without the existence of morally rational deliberators and agents. It is another thing entirely to say that in order to be the fully proper recipient of moral attention and consideration one must be capable oneself of giving moral attention and consideration. Establishing the second claim requires argument beyond establishing the first. Now it might be proposed that the additional argument follows from a normative principle of fairness or reciprocity: "Those who can give justice are owed justice. . . . By giving justice to those who can give justice in return, the principle of reciprocity is fulfilled at the highest level."[59] Yet it is unlikely that any plausible notion of reciprocity could be marshalled finally in support of the rationalist view of equal worth. It is one thing, and unquestionably true, to say that fairness requires the reciprocation of just behavior by those having the capacity for such. It is another thing, and highly doubtful, to claim that fairness requires all recipients of justice to have this capacity.[60] On the contrary, one determines quite reasonably that it would be *unfair* and *unjust—exploitative—*to exclude certain humans from the scope of equal consideration simply because they lacked the capacity for moral reciprocation. Indeed, that such exclusion would be unfair *is*, I submit, the judgment of the common moral consciousness.

It is also the judgment, if I am correct, of the biblical tradition and Christian love properly understood. In this vision, all humans count as neighbors to be loved, whatever their characteristics or circumstances, not because they do or can respond in kind but simply because they are members of the human community.[61] Exactly what implications such an egalitarianism will have for social policies affecting the lives of retarded humans is, of course, an enormously complicated matter. If all human beings, including the profoundly disabled, are genuine bearers of equal worth, how are we to resolve current controversies surrounding calls for normalization, deinstitutionalization, mainstreaming, and the like?[62] Discussion of these and related matters understandably must be left for another time. Here I propose simply that nothing we have considered in the rationalist account compels us to abandon the humanist view of equality as the starting point for all such policy deliberations.

NOTES

1. For representative statements see Lawrence A. Kane, Jr., et al., eds., *The Legal Rights of Citizens with Mental Retardation* (Lanham, Md., New York and London: University Press of America, 1988); Stanley S. Herr, *Rights and Advocacy for Retarded People* (Lexington, Mass.: D. C. Heath and Company, 1983), pp. 37-41; David S. and Victoria S. Allen, *Ethical Issues in Mental Retardation* (Nashville: Abingdon, 1979), pp. 139-41; Michael Kindred, et al., eds., *The Mentally Retarded Citizen and the Law* (New York and London: Macmillan, 1976); Robert M. Segal, ed., *Advocacy for the Legal and Human Rights of the Mentally Retarded: The Proceedings of the Advocacy Conference of the Institute for the Study of Mental Retardation and Related Disabilities* (Ann Arbor: The University of Michigan Publications Distribution Service, 1973); Mental Health Law Project, *Basic Rights of the Mentally Handicapped* (Washington, D.C.: Mental Health Law Project, 1973); Paul R. Friedman, *The Rights of Mentally Retarded Persons* (New York: Avon Books, 1976). The last reprints as appendices two important declarations: (1) The United Nations' *Declaration on the Rights of Mentally Retarded Persons* (pp. 175-77) and (2) *Rights of Mentally Retarded*

Persons: An Official Statement of the American Association on Mental Deficiency (pp. 179-86).

2. For a brief statement of this position as well as a general survey of other ethical issues related to mentally retarded humans see Susan Rose-Ackerman, "Mental Retardation and Society: The Ethics and Politics of Normalization," *Ethics*, Vol. 93, (October, 1982): 81-101.

3. Representative philosophical statements of the general position described here include: H. Tristram Engelhardt, Jr., *The Foundations of Bioethics* (New York and Oxford: Oxford University Press, 1986), pp. 39-56, 104-21; Joseph Fletcher, *Humanhood: Essays in Biomedical Ethics* (Buffalo, N.Y.: Prometheus Books, 1979), pp. 7-19; John Harris, *The Value of Life: An Introduction to Medical Ethics* (London, Boston, Melbourne and Henley: Routledge & Kegan Paul), pp. 7-28; Helga Kuhse and Peter Singer, *Should the Baby Live: The Problem of Handicapped Infants* (Oxford, New York, Melbourne: Oxford University Press, 1985), pp. 118-39; Earl Shelp, *Born to Die: The Fate of Critically Ill Newborns* (New York: The Free Press, 1986), pp. 107-40; Peter Singer, *Practical Ethics* (Cambridge: Cambridge University Press, 1979), pp. 48-157; Michael Tooley, *Abortion and Infanticide* (Oxford: The Clarendon Press, 1983), pp. 50-164.

4. See Harris, pp. 23-24; Kuhse and Singer, pp. 121-23; Rose-Ackerman, p. 89; Shelp, pp. 117-18; Singer, pp. 48-54.

5. Stephen Charles Mott, *Biblical Ethics and Social Change* (New York and Oxford: Oxford University Press, 1982), pp. 45-46.

6. "Agape is a regard for the neighbor which in crucial respects is independent and unalterable. To these features there is a corollary: the regard is for every person qua human existent, to be distinguished from those special traits, actions, etc., which distinguish particular personalities from each other.... This typically means that (1) [the neighbor] is valued as, or in that he is, a person qua human existent and not because he is such-and-such a kind of person distinguishing him from others; and (2) a basic equality obtains whereby one neighbor's well-being is as valuable as another's." Gene Outka, *Agape: An Ethical Analysis* (New Haven and London: Yale University Press, 1972), pp. 9, 12.

7. Paul Ramsey, *Ethics at the Edges of Life: Medical and Legal Intersections* (New Haven and London: Yale University Press, 1978), p. 227.

8. Paul D. Simmons, *Birth and Death: Bioethical Decision-Making* (Philadelphia: Westminster, 1983), pp. 85-89, 126-28; Hessel Bouma, Douglas Diekema, Edward Langerak, Theodore Rottman, Allen Verhey, *Christian Faith, Health, and Medical Practice* (Grand Rapids, Mich.: Eerdman's, 1989), pp. 27-66; Robert Wennberg, *Life in the Balance: Exploring the Abortion Controversy* (Grand Rapids, Mich: Eerdmans, 1985).

9. Thus Stanley Hauerwas boldly affirms the full moral standing of all retarded human beings, yet remains skeptical of the humanist account of equality: "But as I have tried to suggest, being morally a member of the human community, even with a dime, will not buy you a cup of coffee. The recognition and respect due infants and children are not insured by posing their 'rights' as members of the human community, but by their existence in

the kind of community that has learned to value children as members of that community." (*Suffering Presence: Theological Reflections on Medicine, the Mentally Handicapped, and the Church* [Notre Dame, Ind.: University of Notre Dame Press, 1986], p. 139.)

10. Robert Veatch, *The Foundations of Justice: Why the Retarded and the Rest of Us Have Claims to Equality* (New York: Oxford University Press, 1986), p. 22.

11. J. Terence Forestell, C.S.B., "The Letters to the Thessalonians," in *The Jerome Biblical Commentary*, Raymond E. Brown, S.S., Joseph A. Fitzmeyer, S.J., and Roland E. Murphy, eds. (Englewood, Cliffs, N.J.: Prentice-Hall, 1968), II, p. 233. For examples of the mistaken attribution to Paul see R. C. Scheerenberger, *A History of Mental Retardation* (Baltimore, Md.: Paul H. Brookes, 1983), p. 22, and Marvin Rosen, Gerald R. Clark, and Marvin Kivitz, eds., *The History of Mental Retardation: Collected Papers* (Baltimore, London, Tokyo: University Park Press, 1976), p. xiii.

12. The *Qur'an* passage is from Surah, IV, verse 5: "Give not unto those weak of understanding (what is in) your (keeping of their) wealth, which Allah hath given you to maintain; but feed and clothe them from it, and speak kindly unto them." Cited in Scheerenberger, *A History of Mental Retardation*, p. 22.

13. Joseph Allen, *Love and Conflict: A Covenantal Model of Christian Ethics* (Nashville: Abingdon Press, 1984), pp. 15-81.

14. Ibid., p. 64.

15. Ibid., p. 78.

16. For the connection between covenantal love and universal human rights see Allen, pp. 156-59. Allen's description of Christian love echoes earlier accounts. See Outka, *Agape: An Ethical Analysis*, pp. 1-24, 75-92, 257-312, and Mott, *Biblical Ethics and Social Change*, pp. 39-58.

17. Allen, p. 69.

18. Ibid., p. 68.

19. One wonders whether even this concession to nonhuman animals is warranted in Allen's case since he states explicitly in the remark just quoted that any intrinsic moral value depends upon the presence of covenantal capacity.

20. Allen, pp. 67-68.

21. Ibid., p. 40.

22. Outka, p. 268.

23. Outka, p. 268. Allen, pp. 62-68.

24. Veatch, pp. 65-70.

25. Ibid., p. 115.

26. Allen, p. 39. See also Andrew Linzey, *Christianity and the Rights of Animals* (New York: Crossroad, 1987), pp. 29-36.

27. Simmons, *Birth and Death: Bioethical Decision-Making* pp. 85-89, 126-128; Bouma, et al., *Christian Faith, Health, and Medical Practice* (Grand Rapids, Mich.: Eerdman's, 1989), pp. 27-66; Wennberg, *Life in the Balance*, pp. 36-43.

28. Bouma, et al., pp. 30-33.

29. Bouma, et al., p. 36.
30. Cf. Wennberg, *Life in the Balance*, pp. 88, 94.
31. See J. Robert Nelson, *Human Life: A Biblical Perspective for Bioethics* (Philadelphia: Fortress Press, 1984), pp. 75-77.
32. Karl Barth, *Church Dogmatics* (Edinburgh: Clark, 1961), III, iv, pp. 116-17.
33. Hauerwas, *Suffering Presence: Theological Reflections on Medicine, the Mentally Handicapped, and the Church*, pp. 178-79. Hauerwas draws explicitly on the trinitarian formulations of Arthur McGill in *Suffering: A Test Case of Theological Method* (Philadelphia: Westminster Press), p. 78.
34. Claus Westermann, *Genesis 1-11: A Commentary*, John J. Scullion S.J., trans. (Minneapolis: Augsburg Publishing House, 1984), p. 155. For a criticism of Westermann's reading, see Cornelius Plantinga, Jr., "Images of God," in *Christian Faith and Practice in the Modern World*, Mark A. Noll and David F. Wells, eds. (Grand Rapids, Mich.: Eerdman's, 1988), p. 54.
35. This emphasis on the intergenerational transmission of the *image* corresponds to the traditional rabbinic reading. See Daniel F. Polish, "Judaism and Human Rights," in *Human Rights in Religious Traditions*, Arlene Swidler, ed. (New York: The Pilgrim Press, 1982), pp. 41-42.
36. See, for example, Bouma, et al., pp. 34-35.
37. See Hauerwas, pp. 130-31, 161-62, 207-8, 213-14.
38. Harris, pp. 9-10.
39. Ibid., pp. 14-21.
40. Ibid., pp. 14-15.
41. Ibid., p. 18.
42. On the moral significance of children *qua* children see Hauerwas, pp. 125-141. The position suggested here is to be distinguished from one offered by philosopher Loren Lomasky, who argues that children are to be given equal standing because they are potential rational agents ("project pursuers") and that all retarded humans are to be accorded equal standing because they are "permanently childlike." Lomasky's argument is clearly invalid since some retarded humans, in his own account, can only be "childlike" in ways irrelevant to the conditions generally warranting childrens' equal standing. That is, some retarded humans are not potential rational agents. In any event, Lomasky's position is *at bottom* an expression of the rationalist view. See *Persons, Rights, and the Moral Community* (New York and Oxford: Oxford University Press, 1987), p. 203.
43. Cf. Robert Nozick, "About Mammals and People," *The New York Times Book Review*, (November 27, 1983), p. 29: "But perhaps it will turn out that the bare species characteristic of simply being human, as the most severely retarded people are, will command special respect only from other humans—this is an instance of the general principle that the members of any species may legitimately give their fellows more weight than they give members of other species (or at least more weight than a neutral view would grant them). Lions too, if they were moral agents, could not then be criticized for putting the interests of other lions first." Cf. also Richard Rorty, *Philosophy and the Mirror of Nature* (Princeton, N.J.: Princeton University Press,

1979), pp. 190-91, 382 n. 22. Cited in Stephen Macedo, *Liberal Virtues* (Oxford: Clarendon Press, 1990), p. 34. On this matter I think that Rorty's intuitions are correct, but I also have reservations about the metaphilosophical account he gives of those intuitions. For my views on "Rortyian pragmatism" and related issues see my "Nihilism Revisited," *Journal of Religion*, 71 (January 1991), pp. 67-78.

44. See, for example, Harris, pp. 23-24; Kuhse and Singer, pp. 121- 23; Rose-Ackerman, p. 89; Shelp, pp. 117-18; Singer, pp. 48-54.

45. See Outka, pp. 268-74. For a different view see Robert E. Goodin, *Protecting the Vulnerable: A Reanalysis of Our Social Responsibilities* (Chicago and London: The University of Chicago Press, 1985).

46. Cf. Mary Midgley, *Animals and Why They Matter* (Athens: The University of Georgia Press, 1983), pp. 22-23.

47. C. A. J. Coady, "Defending Human Chauvinism," *Philosophy and Public Policy*, VI, 4, p. 12.

48. As Leon Kass says: "All of the people with retardation, however, are related to us in another sense: as parents, as siblings, as neighbors, and as friends. Our humanity consists of these bonds and relations. Human warmth, mutual affection, shared joys and sorrows are the emotional ties of all close human relations. . . . Much of the current writing by professors and policy makers treats the retarded abstractly and impersonally, outside of their concrete, humanly connected contexts. Discussion focuses on degrees of ability and disability, inherent worth, and legal rights of the individual human being, with virtually no awareness that it is primarily the bonds and relations between human beings that are both central to human self-definition and worth, and also the source of our moral relations and duties." ("Citizens with Mental Retardation and the Good Community," in Kane, *et al.*, ed., *The Legal Rights of Retarded Citizens*, p. 13.)

49. See Tooley, pp. 50-164. Cf. Singer, pp. 72-92.

50. See Tooley, pp. 110-11. The counterexamples that follow are his. See also David B. Wong, *Moral Relativity* (Berkeley: University of California Press, 1984), pp. 190-91.

51. Tooley, pp. 118-21.

52. Cf. Bernard Williams, *Ethics and the Limits of Philosophy* (Cambridge: Harvard University Press, 1985), pp. 114-15.

53. Engelhardt, p. 39.

54. Ibid., p. 41.

55. Ibid., p. 42.

56. Ibid., p. 104.

57. Ibid., p. 117.

58. It should be noted that Engelhardt presents his argument as resting on "transcendental" rather than pragmatic foundations: "This view of ethics should not be seen as grounded on a conditional concern for peaceableness. It is not simply based on an interest in establishing the peaceable community. It should, instead, be recognized as a disclosure, to borrow a Kantian metaphor, of a transcendental condition, a necessary condition for

the possibility of a general domain of human life and of the life of persons generally." (Engelhardt, p. 42)

59. John Rawls, *A Theory of Justice* (Cambridge: Harvard University Press, 1971), pp. 510-11. Unlike Engelhardt, Rawls allows that the *potential* for "moral personality" is sufficient for a being's claim to "equal justice." Thus, normal infants and children, who are on the way to acquiring moral capacity, have genuine equal standing in this account. (Rawls, p. 509) Rawls's assessment of profoundly retarded humans is less clear. On the one hand, what he says about the moral standing of nonhuman animals suggests that he regards the potential for moral personality as a requirement all subjects of justice must satisfy. While we have certain moral obligations to animals, we cannot, he claims, owe them "strict justice" precisely because they cannot develop the requisite moral capacities. (Rawls, p. 512) On the other hand, in considering the scope of justice with respect to humans, Rawls leaves open "whether moral personality is also a necessary condition" of entitlement to equal justice. (Rawls, p. 506; also p. 512) Additionally, he argues that even if moral personality were a necessary condition of equality in theory, "it would be unwise in practice to withhold justice on this ground" since "the risk to just institutions would be too great." (Rawls, p. 506; cf. Donald Van De Veer, "Of Beasts, Persons and the Original Position," *The Monist* Vol. 62, no. 3, pp. 369-70; also Veatch, p. 114)

60. Cf. Singer, *Practical Ethics*, pp. 16-17, 68-71.

61. On Christian love as independent of reciprocity, see Outka, pp. 17-18, 27, 34-42, 209-210, 280-81.

62. See Rose-Ackerman, "Mental Retardation and Society: The Ethics and Politics of Normalization". See also Stanley Hauerwas, ed., *Responsibility for Devalued Persons: Ethical Interactions Between Society, the Family, and the Retarded* (Springfield, Illinois: Charles E. Thomas, 1982).

WILLIAM WERPEHOWSKI

"Agape" and Special Relations

I: INTRODUCTION

An important area of inquiry in Christian ethics involves the critical redescription of how a norm of love of neighbor is related to more particular human bonds. Attention can be directed especially to the fruitful connections and inescapable tensions associated with a Christian moral conception that contains commendations both to love human creatures "universally" and to meet one's responsibilities in "special" roles and relationships. In recent discussions of this topic, these questions are often asked: How is allegiance to a norm that is nonpreferential and unlimited in scope regarding the object of love related to forms of moral regard in which the good of some persons is pursued at the expense of failing to advance the good of others? Does *agape*, in setting aside human differences in merit, personal interests, and attractiveness as fundamental bases of moral concern, essentially conflict with relations that are at least partially constituted by a preference for the beloved in light of such differences (e.g., friendship, erotic love)?[1] Does adherence to a principle of universal love tend, in a modern cultural environment, to abstract from and thus corrupt the situated moral realities of tradition and historical social practice?[2]

In this essay, I consider two specific questions that bear on those just noted in important ways. First, ought the basic relation between universal love and particular attachments be conceived in terms of a requirement that the latter be morally *justified* by the former? Are we bound to *derive* one from the other, as the particular from the general? Second, what internal connections obtain between *agape*'s demands and the demands of certain particular bonds? Is there a defensible and nonredundant way to speak of my spouse or friend or colleague as also my *neighbor*? If so, what moral wisdom can be gathered from the designation?

In response to the initial question, I argue that derivation of special relations from a principle of universal love tends to be theologically unhelpful in disclosing the nature of the Christian moral life; other factors pertaining to the good of creaturely attachments, the vocation of the Christian, and the role of moral discernment need to be introduced to account for them adequately. My answer to the second question is that adherence to a norm of *agape* involves a disposition to view all of our fellow human beings as "creatures," as "sisters and brothers for whom Christ died," and as "possible companions in beatitude." They are neighbors in this threefold sense. Seeing them in these ways may illumine, invigorate, and transform special relations.

These conclusions, perhaps, are commonplace. Working out their details, however, is not. I hope that I help to show how special relations cohere and conflict with the requirement to love the neighbor. In addition, my consideration of contemporary philosophical materials may indicate the relative usefulness of some lines of conversation between Christian ethics and moral philosophy.

II: A THEOLOGICAL CONSENSUS

James Gustafson believes that the idea of deriving special relations exclusively from a norm of universal love rests on a peculiar conception of the character of Christian love and ethics:

> "Special relations" such as the love of marriage, the intensity of love between parents and children, and friendship do not require the kind of distinctive justification from my perspective that they do for those Christian theologians and ethicians for whom *agape*, or Christian love, becomes virtually synonymous with Kant's principle of respect for persons. It is the case that in the Bible and throughout much of the history of Christian thought Christian love is deemed to require that the particular characteristics of individuals be transcended in love, that love be nonpreferential. One is to love another person even though he or she is one's enemy; one is to love another person regardless of their particular features and accomplishments. If this becomes *the* principle of Christian ethics, and if Christian ethics is understood to be exclusively the application of moral principles and the maxims that they support to individual cases, then the justification of special relations is a problem. If, however, the "natural" ordering of life has theological and moral dignity, i.e., if God is ordering the world through special relations between persons, they are not morally problematic in the same way. Part of the problem in Christian ethics that centers on love exclusively is that the term either has to have a univocal meaning which creates the difficulties with special relations, or it becomes an

umbrella term under which are put all sorts of relationships that can and ought to be distinguished.³

Stephen Post has recently argued that Gene Outka's writings on Christian love are liable to Gustafson's criticism regarding the overly narrow grounds for conceiving a "problem" about justification in Christian ethics.⁴ Post's argument fails simply because Outka has consistently denied the need and even the possibility of exhaustively grounding special bonds in *agape*. His view of the matter is that

> [a]gape is the guardian in rather than the direct inspiration of every special relation. It sets the boundaries within which the power of romantic eros, for example, may be allowed distinctive expression. Insofar as many such particular obligations and bonds legitimately involve preference and the like, their respective urgencies cannot all, exhaustively and without remainder, be simply derived from or founded directly upon *agape*.⁵

In his most recent writing on the subject, Outka reaffirms this position, underscoring how the work of *agape* gives room for other bonds "to come into their own."⁶ Implicitly, honor is paid to God's ordering work in creation, distinct from what is uniquely enabled through neighbor love.

Following this line of reflection, Gilbert Meilaender has shown how friendship, a preferential and reciprocal interpersonal love graciously provided by God's creative work, need not be derived from *agape*, a nonpreferential love that may persist in the absence of reciprocation.⁷ For example, both he and Outka entertain and reject attempts at derivation that invoke a premise about the inevitably and properly *finite* character of creaturely love. "Our finite condition may explain why we cannot love everyone; it will give no justification for preferential (as opposed to random) choice of those whom we do love."⁸ They also suspect efforts to base limited bonds on "an estimation of the comparative efficiency and long-term importance of various kinds of service open to the agent";⁹ Meilaender in particular sees such an instrumental appeal, offered in the name of a universal benevolence, to lead "to grudging concessions made to the constraints of time, space, and particular bonds of affection rather than glad affirmation of these as essential for human existence."¹⁰

I would be content at this point merely to join the consensus that is in fact shared by Gustafson, Outka, and Meilaender, were it not for an impressive recent attempt to set out the very sort of derivation that they think is unnecessary and perhaps impossible. It is an argument of analytic moral philosophy rather than theological ethics, but it is noteworthy for my purposes because it explicitly addresses the problem of the "fit" between preferential and nonpreferential forms of moral regard. In the next three sections, I proceed to analyze and evaluate this more recent account.

III: CONSENSUS CHALLENGED

"My aim," says Alan Gewirth, "is to show that ethical universalism can justify certain kinds of ethical particularism." He defines ethical universalism "as the doctrine that all persons ought to be treated with equal and impartial positive consideration for their respective goods and interests." The doctrine appears basically to conflict with particularism because the latter requires that one give preferential consideration to the interests of some persons as against others, such as family members or friends or fellow citizens of some community. So to try to prove that universalism can justify this stance in some cases may "seem like trying to square the circle, for it involves showing that impartiality toward all persons can justify partiality toward some persons, that equality of consideration can sanction inequality of consideration." Thus, the issue is drawn in a manner congenial to our reflections here.[11]

Gewirth's universalist norm, the Principle of Generic Consistency (PGC), holds that all persons have equal rights to freedom and well-being, where these are understood, respectively, as the procedural and substantive neccessary conditions of agency. The PGC may justify not only individual actions that fulfill individual duties correlating with these rights, but also certain roles and institutions. The second, indirect application of the PGC imposes its requirements on the rules of these roles and institutions; the rules then apply directly to constrain the actions of individuals. Gewirth relies on these indirect applications of PGC to justify certain sorts of ethical particularism. "The general point of the justification is that the social groups and institutions justified by the PGC involve differentiations of roles and status which require certain preferential differences of treatment. If impartiality of consideration and equality of rights meant that no such differentiations were permitted, then not only would the right to freedom in the formation of voluntary associations be severely limited, but such an institution as the criminal law would also be illegitimate."[12]

Consider the typical preferences of family members for one another's well-being over, say, the well-being of strangers. According to Gewirth, these can be justified indirectly by the PGC in the following way.

First, the universalist principle of moral regard guarantees, in its respect for freedom, a right to form voluntary associations, "whereby persons freely band together for various purposes, so that all their members voluntarily consent to belong to the respective groups and to obey their rules." These groups are at least morally *permitted* as long as they do not involve the violation of other persons' human rights by adversely affecting their freedom and well-being in ways not derived from the rights themselves.[13] The proviso allows us to distinguish the morally relevant difference between, say, a gang of robbers and a university.

Second, a subprinciple permitting the formation of voluntary associations justifies the formation of families "with their special purposes."

> A marital coupling is a kind of voluntary association or grouping that, like other voluntary associations, is justified by the universal right to freedom. But, unlike baseball teams and other voluntary associations, it is formed for purposes of deeply intimate union and extensive mutual concern and support for the participants, purposes which enhance the partners' general abilities of agency. Such couples are families, and with their children they are simply larger families which are also characterized by the parents' special concern and support for their children.[14]

Within the "rules" of the familial institution, there may be certain *infringements* on a member's rights to freedom, such as are associated, for example, with the requirement to give up a unilateral luxury (Mom's coveted new set of golf clubs) for the "common good" (put the cash toward the family vacation instead). But these are not *violations* of a universalist right to freedom, since they follow from rules that are justified by that right, given the moral legitimacy of the voluntary association of the family itself.

Third, the particularist purposes for which families are formed justify the particularist and preferential concern that family members have for one another's interests.[15] Gewirth concludes that preference is both morally required and intrinsically valuable. He stresses the second point. The claim is not that the practice of preference advances some universalist end, such as the well-being of persons generally (although that may also be true); rather, it is that the practice of preference is constitutive of certain purposes (the purposes for which families are formed) that are good in themselves.[16]

I think that a parallel argument is available in a Christian theological context. One can say that personal freedom is among the "generic characteristics" to which universal love attends in advancing the well-being of the neighbor.[17] To respect freedom includes respecting the formation of voluntary associations suitably constrained, and these will include persons who voluntarily consent to marry for the intrinsically valuable purposes marriages realize. But marriage and family commitments require partiality and preference. A norm of *agape* justifies these requirements by indirectly justifying the institution of which they are a part.

IV: TWO OBJECTIONS

What are we to make of this argument? A standard objection would be that it distorts the particular character of the preferential relation by subsuming it under general principle and impersonal value. Gewirth may be liable to this criticism. One might try to trace a "voluntarist" strain in the reasoning from general respect for freedom to respect generally for groupings of mutual consent, and from the latter to honoring the consensual relation of marriage with its preferential character. Recall that in fact Gewirth commends marriage for the way in which it enhances "the partners' general abilities of agency." The criticism would claim, then, that the focus on free choice and consent corrupts the account of marriage and family by interpreting it merely in contractual terms, rather than through categories that capture features of covenantal fidelity and gracious response to need not covered by a contract model.[18]

As popular as this sort of move is these days, I do not believe that it succeeds in the way suggested as a refutation of Gewirth. To believe that it would seems to require unfair interpretation, in part because Gewirth's "general abilities of agency" include multiple categories of well-being in addition to freedom.[19] The critic would also appear to refuse to take seriously Gewirth's insistence that the justification of preference *through* (not *by*)[20] ethical universalism is both *indirect* and *intrinsic*. Presumably there is room for building fidelity and graciousness into a case for the purposes of marriage. These aspects need not be compromised by a mode of justification that authorizes, with reference to the value of freedom, the *roles and institutions* in which they fit. Of course the warrants for the institution underdetermine its depiction; but what exactly is wrong with that? In any case, the projected criticism charges an overdetermination of the special relation by the universal norm.

Closer to the mark, perhaps, is Bernard Williams's objection that the very project of justifying particularism through universalism misrepresents the role of deep attachments in the moral life, both by having them bear some special burden of proof with respect to impartiality, and by forcing an incongruous dissociation "between the theorist in oneself and the self whose dispositions are being theorized."[21] Deep loyalties need not carry any such burden, and the separation in the moral self that such theorizing involves (between, say, the universalist reason-giver and the husband and father) may blind us to some inevitable and important features of practical life. Here the issue is not so much a matter of the *substantive corruption* of particular bonds by universalist justification; rather, it is that their fundamentally self-legitimating *place* in moral existence is not given its due. As a consequence, one tends to miss the fact that at some point "such things as deep attachments to other persons will express themselves in the world in ways that cannot at the same time embody the impartial view, and that they also run the risk of offending against it."[22] The father and husband, for example, should recognize how his love for his children and wife will be motivated and expressed in ways that "cannot at the same time embody" universalist justification.

Gewirth's initial response to this sort of criticism is that "it seems to confuse logical structure with psychological episode." Whatever one might *actually* think in a particular moral situation, universalist justification displays how one *ought* to think "when the full structure of justification is involved."[23] At first glance, the response appears simply to miss the point of Williams's concern—that this very distinction is suspect, since it would dispose us to fail to see how deep attachments do in fact, in the living of them, *resist* universalist warrants. The challenge to Gewirth is to show how his theoretical reflections, which presumably illuminate moral practice, are not undermined by the way they deform it.

Gewirth could begin to answer the challenge by defusing the claim about deformation. After all, his is an *indirect* strategy of justification, and the specific (and intrinsically valuable) purposes of marriage and family may provide enough justification for much of what properly goes on in these institutions in practice. Given these relatively independent and intrinsic legitimations, the universalist appeal need seldom, if ever, come into play "at the same time" as these more narrowly based warrants to deform or distort anything at all of the moral life. The success of this answer, however, is limited, because Gewirth takes the universalist case to be decisive for rationally accrediting the moral status of the deep attachments. So, as Williams says, if we need to live the moral life both during and after our "rational" reflection about it, our simultaneous existence as "rational" agents and as husbands, wives, etc., will reflect distortion in some way. To adapt Williams's famous example, the moral agent who would be motivated to choose to save his drowning wife over a stranger not simply because she is his wife, but also because that preference is part of an institution that is warranted by the Principle of Generic Consistency, is still having "one thought too many."[24]

Gewirth's final response to Williams, accordingly, must be to question whether his critic has offered up a tendentious analysis of the stance of the moral agent, the one practically concerned both about the specific purposes of deep attachments and about their full rational justification. If such justification is successful from a universalist premise that is itself rationally warranted, as Gewirth contends, this result, he would claim, is a very good thing; it offers a non-arbitrary basis for the attachments and imparts a real (if complex) unity to the moral life.[25] And if there also remains room aplenty in the structure of justification for the specific purposes underlying the attachments, why speak of any deformation at all? Why not say instead that Williams begs the question of what sorts of justification satisfactorily explain moral behavior "in real life"?

On the basis of the preceding critical discussion, I conclude that these two criticisms of Gewirth do not clearly defeat his argument justifying particularism through universalism in the case of marriage and family relations. The conclusion applies also to an analogous argument that indirectly justifies such relationships (and others like them, such as friendship) through a norm of *agape*. At the very least the strategy of indirect justification takes the sting out of criticisms which hold that a universalist grounding leads either to a certain substantive corruption of special relations or to a misrepresentation of their constitutive place in the moral life.

V: THE PROBLEM WITH UNIVERSALIST DERIVATION

Nevertheless, an argument like Gewirth's that is applied to Christian ethics seems to me to illuminate very little about the Christian moral life. Issues emerging in the discussion of each of the criticisms detailed above suggest why this so. Recall, first, that a universalist principle in the argument appears to underdetermine the description of the institutions of marriage and family it is warranting. Perhaps from the standpoint of an interest in demonstrating a sort of unity to the moral life there is nothing fatal about this; but it also seems true that in such a case the universal principle bears only the most slender relationship to the special relations themselves. It does not appear integral to them, but rather hovers outside rationally to authorize them. There is room in theological ethics for a more substantive connection. *Agape* may preserve, transform, and perfect special relations in a fashion that is not captured by the pattern of indirect justification.

Second, note that universalist justification is rationally decisive for Gewirth. In the theological case, this type of position directs attention to *agape* as the ultimate source of justification. It would correspondingly subordinate the importance of more specific and detailed descriptions of the purposes that inform special relations. But these purposes may attain a non-arbitrary character insofar as they are explained by sources other than *agape simpliciter*. The sources may include, as Meilaender has insisted, the purposes of the Creator for the human creature with regard to bonds such as friendship and marriage. As for the "rationality" of these and other bonds, what is centrally at issue in Christian ethics is not so much derivation from universal principle as it is conformity or consent to the will or ordering efficacy of God. That will or ordering efficacy may be understood in ways that include, but are not limited to, conformation to the character of God's universal love for human beings in Jesus Christ. To say this is not to deny that *agape* remains in a real way the sum of all Christian virtue, but rather just to question one way of expressing *agape's* ascendency.

Whatever its strengths, then, the argument we have considered tends to place special relations far removed from *agape* and from other theologically relevant purposes that *agape* need not directly encompass. This double distancing is unhelpful because it hampers an important activity of Christian ethics—to depict the work of love in preserving and transforming relationships provided by God's good governance.

Gewirth's model of justification and others like it may impede this activity in another way. The model reflects what Amelie Rorty has labeled "justificatory judicialism," or the view that

> locates the focus of moral theory and moral action in the processes and rules for justification, as if the primary problem of an agent is that of resolving uncertainty about what to do, and her primary task is that of forming a judgment about what is best to do. Even when the focus is on the first-person singular, as an agent, the focus is epistemological: What should I do? is interpreted as What alternative have I most reason to follow? Which is most justified?[26]

Yet "even if the reasons that prompt an action are appropriately justified, they usually underdescribe and underdetermine the detailed thoughtfulness required for appropriate action. The manner in which actions are performed is often as essential to acting well as the selection of the appropriate action."[27] Rorty's point is that often the required "detailed thoughtfulness" involves processes of moral discernment that lead to actions which concretely embody and modify the values, principles, and purposes contained in our "good reasons." The processes of formulating an intention in the moral situation often specify our more general ends and principles; the latter "are crystallized, further determined, by the ways we imagine or envisage the details of what we do." Hence, to rely just on the general principle of universal love to render action rationally intelligible can distract one from the need to perceive possibilities for action that genuinely illuminate the work of love with regard to special relations, and that specify in new and nuanced ways the purposes of the relations themselves.[28]

Judicialism should be reformed and complemented[29] with an account of how discernment enables fitting judgment and action in light of the character, habits, and aptitude of the moral agent in a particular social and temporal context. In the Christian tradition, an expanded conception of the *vocation* of the Christian can be of use in providing such an account—vocation here understood as "the whole of the particularity, limitation and restriction in which every man meets the divine call and command . . . and to which above all wholeness and therefore total differentiation and specification are intrinsically proper."[30] Consideration of this situated intrapersonal and interpersonal "place of responsibility" can deepen an understanding of good action in the Christian life. In the case of special relations, the necessarily limited ways in which love of neighbor may be realized both within and outside of them can be carefully exposed. Thus, justification of special relations and actions constitutive of them becomes more a matter of aligning and integrating them with a surrounding context of character, social situation, and normative ideals—including the ideal of *agape*.[31]

Christian moral discernment, or the exercise of the virtue of prudence, gives a reading of the moral situation sensitive to the subtle ways in which *agape* may affect various special relations. It gives a reading of the situation that would disclose the purposes of God in special relations, purposes that have their own gravity distinct from the weight of neighbor love. And, to return to Meilaender's concerns, it gives a reading that acknowledges in fitting ways the co-present claims of norms that *prefer* others for their attractiveness and excellence, and a norm that significantly *does not*.

Yet *agape* may still be characterized as the sum of Christian virtue. This claim does not require reliance on a scheme of justification such as Gewirth's, but only a commitment to the rule that all human relationships are for the Christian to be tested and transformed by the love of neighbor. How this may be so in the case of special bonds is the topic of the next section.

VI: THE NEIGHBOR TO BE LOVED

In sketching a few positive connections between Christian *agape* and certain special relations, I rely on Jonathan Edwards:

> And all things which are loved with a truly holy love are loved from some respect to God. Love to God is the foundation of a gracious love to men. Men are loved either because they are in some respect like God, either they have the nature or spiritual image of God; *or because of their relation to God as his children, as his creatures, as those who are beloved of God, or those to whom divine mercy is offered, or in some other way from regard to God.*[32]

Thus I will try to describe how the neighbor may be loved in virtue of his or her relation to God as a creature, as a sister or brother for whom Christ died, and as a possible companion in beatitude. To love the neighbor in these ways confirms, I believe, the sense it makes to speak of one's child or one's spouse or one's friend, as also one's neighbor.[33]

1. The neighbor is, like oneself, a creature of God, a finite being in the world whose being originates with and is owed to God. He or she does not ultimately belong to oneself, or to any other creature. Not self-sufficient, the human creature calls and claims the assistance of fellows who may be assisted in turn. Creatures have needs that make them vulnerable to our actions, as well as needs (e.g., for free self-expression or self-respect) that make us vulnerable to them. Like all of creation, the fellow is a gift, unreckoned and unexacted, and our opportunity to pursue his or her good with a view to a mutuality of assistance should be taken gladly and gratefully.

To love the neighbor as a creature includes, then, a stance of respectful reverence toward the other in the ways the other is independent of us, and a posture of "attention" or loving clear-sightedness regarding the other in his or her call to us. These two, respect and attention, are interrelated in that the latter "lets difference emerge without searching for comforting commonalities, dwells upon the other, and lets otherness be."[34] But attention is not so much the acknowledgment of human inviolability as it is the truthful apprehension of the other in his or her need. Attending to the creature in his or her basic reality of otherness and dependence "teaches us how real things can be looked at and loved without being seized and used, without being appropriated into the greedy expansion of the self."[35] Finally, both reverence and attention are framed by serenity, a sense of the limits of our moral regard. The neighbor is a creature of God, with a destiny appropriate to that reality that is not and cannot be ours to give.

Russell Baker has written of how he had once responded to the ills and despondency of his mother of seventy-eight.

> [I] had written her with some banal advice to look for the silver lining, to count her blessings instead of burdening others with her miseries. I suppose what it really amounted to was a threat that if she was not more cheerful during my visits I would not come to see her very often. Sons are capable of such letters. This one was written out of a childish faith in the eternal strength of parents, a naive belief that age and wear could be overcome by an effort of will, that all she needed was a good pep talk to recharge a flagging spirit. It was such a foolish, innocent idea, but one thinks of parents differently from other people. Other people can become frail and break, but not parents.[36]

I want to say that Baker discerns here something of a failure on his part of clear-sighted attentive love. It is a failure to which sons, and children generally, may be especially prone given the nature of their connections to their parents. Loving mom in this case means seeing the depth of her need, just like "other people." Mom writes back, half defiantly, "If I seemed unhappy to you at times, I am, but there's really nothing anyone can do about it, because I'm just so very tired and lonely that I'll just go to sleep and forget it." Here a son's response that acknowledges (sadly but serenely) the separateness of her life, and that relinquishes fantasies of controlling outcomes may be most fitting. It would be a loving response, and one that may be inspired by apprehending that mother is a creature of God.

2. The neighbor is a "sister or brother for whom Christ died." Where creatureliness denotes a common status stressing both finitude and otherness, this description points to a common status of kinship. "Kinship" refers both to solidarity in sin and solidarity in the promise of redemption. It indicates, furthermore, that all are bound to each

other as each is bound to Christ, in whom we may become adopted children of God.

That the neighbor shares with us a solidarity in sin means that we live together as doers and sufferers of acts that alienate us from ourselves, one another, and God. We are suffering, dying creatures made vulnerable by the evil in our midst. And we are defensive creatures, disposed to policies of manipulation and evasion in the quest to secure for ourselves safe harbor apart from God. But a solidarity in promise is also shared. This means that suffering which alienates is not the last word in life. Those who suffer are liable to words that comfort and reconcile. Defensiveness may be measured and challenged and overcome in these words, by which creatures may live a life bearing promise of wholeness and peace.

To love the neighbor as a kind of sibling in these ways would be to encounter him or her in a humble spirit, and to witness to common kinship through fidelity to his or her well-being along the manner of God in Jesus Christ. Fidelity may call for mercy and long-suffering, but also for the willingness to criticize and correct hostility, injustice, and passivity. Above all, such a love holds fast the beloved as a sufferer in need and as a recipient of unconditional grace.

Often people see their special relations as isolated things. They may be special in their splendor, or in their resistance to the wear of time, or in their comfortable inevitability. One's stance toward the beloved can correlate with setting the relationships apart in such fashion. Thus, the beloved becomes for us an utterly splendid being, or one who is not or ought never be made anxious by many concerns, or a being who is merely "always there" or "old reliable." Yet the beloved is a sister or brother for whom Christ died. She or he is one who is, among other things, suffering with us in "the whole ocean of human meanness and painfulness."[37] Special bonds, too, flounder in this ocean. Nevertheless, they may be sustained by the humility which does not assume too much or seek self-justification, by the faithfulness that forgives and waits patiently, and by the sense of righteousness that may correct and resist. For example, the spousal vow of marriage represents a remarkable and unlikely wager against the erosions of time and the prospects for little and bigger betrayals. And why may we still promise in Christian faith? Paul Ramsey had it right.

> Because, just as we know the heart and needs of a stranger from God's care for us while we were yet strangers, we also know the heart and the need of a dying one from God's care for us who live always in the midst of death. This means that the perfection of love is a working knowledge of another as a creature of flesh

and blood whose fate it is to live always in the valley of the shadow of death. The essence of a care-full love is respect for the shadow of death upon another human countenance, a sense of the griefs and grievances they bear because of the power of death that is in them, an awareness of the temptations to despair and estrangement because we and our loved ones exist from day to day in the shadow of some shared, ambiguous destiny that Christ took on himself when for our sakes he became mortal man. This is why the marriage vow proposes provisionally to take hold of the shadow of death upon the human countenance and promises permanence "till death us do part."[38]

3. The neighbor would be a companion in beatitude.[39] His or her life and relations may possess in themselves an eternal validity. There is cause, then, to appreciate that possibility by persevering in one's regard across the lifetime of a relationship, watchful of the manifold ways in which the neighbor may manifest such validity. The prospect can also provoke a vigilant interest in the beloved's virtue and self-responsibility as they bear on the love of God in its various dimensions. To love the neighbor in this way, above all, is hopefully to seek, recognize, and elicit in the present the beloved's essential beauty in the world—a beauty finally authorized by its life in God.[40]

This third perspective works to intensify and recast the first two, as the second intensifies and recasts sensitivity to creaturely vulnerability. Both hopeful, present wonder and a noninstrumental persistence seem to mark it. It enables the "sense of an ending" of which Meilaender speaks in his recollection of Sally, a foster child raised for eight months in his home:

> She came to us at a very busy time, when I was already burdened with too much work. Even so, I noticed how careful I was not to ignore her, to pay attention to her no matter how busy I might be. Far more careful, I am afraid, than I have sometimes been with my own children. Not fair to them? Perhaps. But I know why. They—their future joined with mine—can all too easily be taken for granted, as if stories never ended. She came on a day's notice and would leave with little more, as if in the middle of a chapter. We always knew that, and so each day had to be savored, for we lived constantly with the sense of an ending near at hand.
>
> Such a little teacher, but she made it clear that all our days and hours are equidistant from eternity; none is merely preparatory for some future that may never come.[41]

Loving the neighbor with this sense of equidistance can work to enrich and perfect human bonds across time.

Before concluding this section, I want to make two points that are implicit in the preceding. The first (and here again I follow Edwards) is that the basis for neighbor-love is the love of God. Reverence and attention for the creature derive from a respect shown to the ultimate source of sacredness and the ground of reality. Humility and fidelity stem from a love that apprehends true loveliness and follows true righteousness in Jesus Christ. The hope for eternal validity with and for the neighbor is a reflection of the creaturely desire to see its origin in God. To love the neighbor is to love what God loves, out of love for the one who graciously creates, redeems, and completes.

The second point is that the account given here is an attempt to follow the lines of my discussion of moral discernment. I have tried to present a theocentric interpretation of the reality and situation of the neighbor that frames normative behavior in special relationships. The interpretation and accompanying conceptions of virtue help to specify more general notions about the meaning of *agape* for these bonds. They permit more nuanced discriminations between, for example, respect for a parent's separate life that acquiesces in reality and a cheerful, relieved abandonment; or between "care-full" love for a spouse and constancy that borders on cynicism or despair; or, finally, between cherishing the other with a "sense of an ending" and a cautious love that hedges its bets.[42] My reflections may also enable more vivid disclosure of the work of love in transforming and perfecting special relations. Thus, they could go some way toward depicting how the relations and their purposes may be aligned or integrated, and in that sense "justified," in connection with neighbor-love.

VII: CONCLUSION

Recently Christian ethicists have challenged the view that there is a tension between neighbor-love and special relations like friendship that are, in contrast, preferential and reciprocal. Stephen Post says right out that "the tension between philia and *agape* is ... a false one."[43] Stanley Hauerwas has held that the alleged difference depends on a model of *agape* that owes more to Kant than to Christianity.[44] Both scholars also suspect that *agape*, as a mode of universal love that is independent and unalterable, is too often depicted as a principle of the Enlightenment, a principle that commends merely notional respect for abstract "human existents" stripped of the ties and stories that truly identify them and their well-being.[45]

The preceding section of this essay is a response to these questions and suspicions. I have pointed to three theological descriptions of the neighbor that have universal scope, that would apply to all fellow humans, but that are based on theological traditions and Christian "stories." No determining appeal to the Enlightenment appears necessary or desirable. Models of kinship and friendship do emerge to enrich these descriptions, but they do not compromise their basic universal thrust.

It follows that *agape*, as founded on these descriptions, can stand in tension with various special relations. Its governance in the Christian life includes forging the positive connections discussed above; but neighbor-love also judges and overturns "the tendency to apathy about the fate of those beyond the range" of special responsibility.[46] How these tensions are confronted is, as I said at the outset, an important question for Christian ethics.[47] I hope to turn to it at another time.

NOTES

1. Gene Outka, *Agape: An Ethical Analysis* (New Haven and London: Yale University Press, 1972), pp. 268-70; Gilbert Meilaender, *Friendship: An Essay in Theological Ethics* (Notre Dame and London: University of Notre Dame Press, 1981), pp. 6-35.
2. Stephen G. Post, *A Theory of Agape: On the Meaning of Christian Love* (London and Toronto: Associated University Presses, 1990), pp. 79-90. On this issue Post is indebted generally to the work of Stanley Hauerwas.
3. James M. Gustafson, *Ethics from a Theocentric Perspective. Volume Two: Ethics and Theology* (Chicago and London: University of Chicago Press, 1984), p. 164, n. 3. For a pertinent study of Thomas Aquinas and "natural ordering," see Stephen J. Pope, "The Moral Centrality of Natural Priorities: A Thomistic Alternative to 'Equal Regard,'" *The Annual of the Society of Christian Ethics*, 1990 (Washington, D.C.: Georgetown University Press, 1990), pp. 109-29. Cf. Christina Hoff Sommers, "Filial Morality," in *Woman and Moral Theory*, Eva Feder Kittay and Diana T. Meyers, eds. (Totowa, N.J.: Rowman and Littlefield, 1987), pp. 69-84.
4. Post, pp. 31ff.
5. Outka, *Agape*, p. 274.
6. "Universal Love and Impartiality," in this volume.
7. Meilaender, *Friendship*, p. 32.
8. *Ibid.*, p. 28. Cf. Outka, *Agape*, p. 270.
9. Outka, *Agape*, p. 273.
10. Meilaender, *Friendship*, p. 30.

11. Alan Gewirth, "Ethical Universalism and Particularism," *The Journal of Philosophy*, Volume LXXXV, No. 6 (June 1988): p. 283. Because of limitations of space, my discussion addresses but one of Gewirth's two examples showing the justificatory relation between particularism and universalism; moreover, it does not detail the substance and theoretical background of Gewirth's universalist "Principle of Generic Consistency." Finally, I will not dwell on the question of how Gewirth's notion of "impartiality" does and does not conform to Christian *agape*. See Outka's essay in this volume, *passim*. I assume only the obvious point that the sort of impartiality that Gewirth has in mind includes a nonpreferential element.

12. Gewirth, p. 292.
13. Ibid.
14. Ibid., p. 294.
15. Gewirth's account of the preferential regard of children is interesting but undeveloped; although they "have not themselves voluntarily participated in setting up the family, their special concern for their parents and siblings is appropriately viewed as derivative, both morally and psychologically, from the parents' special concern both for one another and for each of their children and, in this way, for the family as a whole." *Ibid*. I do not take up whether this "derivative" status undermines the coherence of the position's general reliance on "voluntariness."
16. *Ibid.*, pp. 288-89, 294-95. It appears also that Gewirth would reject a deontological extrinsic basis for preference, such as a general requirement to honor agreements or answer to *de facto* institutional expectations.
17. Outka, *Agape*, pp. 266-67.
18. An important and influential example of this sort of challenge in the literature of Christian theological ethics can be found in William F. May, *The Physician's Covenant: Images of the Healer in Medical Ethics* (Philadelphia: Westminster Press, 1983). See also Paul Ramsey, *Ethics at the Edges of Life: Medical and Legal Intersections* (New Haven and London: Yale University Press, 1978), pp. 9-18. Cf. Christina Sommers, "Philosophers Against the Family, " in Christina Sommers and Fred Sommers, eds., *Vice and Virtue in Everyday Life*, 2d ed. (New York: Harcourt Brace Jovanovich, 1989), pp. 728-53.
19. Gewirth, p. 290.
20. *Ibid*, p. 294.
21. Bernard Williams, *Ethics and the Limits of Philosophy* (Cambridge: Harvard University Press, 1985), p. 110.
22. Bernard Williams, *Moral Luck*, (Cambridge: Cambridge University Press, 1981), p. 18. Cf. *Ethics*, p. 116: "The only serious enterprise is living, and we have to live after the reflection; moreover (though the distinction between theory and practice encourages us to forget it), we have to live during it as well."
23. Gewirth, p. 297.
24. Williams, *Moral Luck*, p. 18.
25. Gewirth, pp. 284-85, 302.

26. Amelie Oksenberg Rorty, *Mind in Action: Essays in the Philosophy of Mind* (Boston: Beacon Press, 1988), p. 283.

27. *Ibid.*

28. Rorty's case for the significance of *phronesis* may be instructively compared with James M. Gustafson, "Moral Discernment in the Christian Life," in *Norm and Context in Christian Ethics*, Gene H. Outka and Paul Ramsey, eds. (New York: Charles Scribner's Sons, 1968), pp. 17-36.

29. Reformed and complemented, not replaced. Cf. Gustafson on rules and justification, *Ibid.*, pp. 32-34. See also Rorty, pp. 287-88.

30. Karl Barth, *Church Dogmatics*, III/4. A. T. McKay, T. H. L. Parker et al., trans. (Edinburgh: T. and T. Clark, 1961), pp. 599-600. See also Robert Merrihew Adams, "Vocation," *Faith and Philosophy* 4/4 (October 1987): pp. 448-62; and William Werpehowski, "The Professions: Vocations to Justice and Love," in *The Professions in Ethical Context*, Francis A. Eigo, O.S.A., ed. (Villanova: Villanova University Press, 1986), pp. 1-24.

31. "This conception of *justification* brings it closer to its use in printing and carpentry: to justify a page is to align its margins; to justify a wall is to assure its stability by integrating it with its surrounding corners." Rorty, p. 287.

32. Jonathan Edwards, *Ethical Writings*, Paul Ramsey, ed. (New Haven and London: Yale University Press, 1989), pp. 133-34, my emphasis.

33. See Sören Kierkegaard, *Works of Love* (New York: Harper & Row, 1962), p. 142. For an alternative recent approach to this issue, see Margaret A. Farley, *Personal Commitments: Beginning, Keeping, Changing* (San Francisco: Harper & Row, 1986).

34. Sara Ruddick, *Maternal Thinking: Towards a Politics of Peace* (Boston: Beacon Press, 1989), p. 122.

35. *Ibid.*, p. 121. Ruddick makes this claim about the attentive love of children. I see no problem in applying this description generally to creaturely love. Perhaps I would if I believed that children were the only or exclusive objects of attentive love, or that the particularity of that form of love somehow calls the universal requirement to love human creatures in this way into question, or that the very notion of universal love of neighbor is necessarily tied to bad Enlightenment ideas about "abstract selves" and the like. But I do not believe any of this. I do agree with Meilaender that aspects of particular loves may instruct us in how neighbors generally are to be loved; but it should be clear from this discussion that I would also hold out for the reverse relation, i.e., where love for the "stranger" instructs us in our more particular loves. See *Friendship*, pp. 20-21.

36. Russell Baker, *Growing Up* (New York: Congdon & Weed, 1982), pp. 4-5. Deborah Roberts first pointed out the importance of this passage to me.

37. Karl Barth, *Church Dogmatics*, III/2, Harold Knight et al., trans. (Edinburgh: T. and T. Clark, 1960), p. 241.

38. Paul Ramsey, "The Biblical Norm of Righteousness," *Interpretation* 24/4 (October 1970): p. 429.

39. Josef Pieper, *About Love*, Richard and Clara Winston, trans. (Chicago: Franciscan Herald Press, 1974), p. 120.

40. Cf. L. A. Kosman, "Platonic Love," in *Facets of Plato's Philosophy*, W. H. Werkmeister, ed. (Amsterdam: Van Gorcum, 1976), p. 67.

41. Gilbert Meilaender, *The Limits of Love: Some Theological Explorations* (University Park and London: Pennsylvania State University Press, 1987), p. 16.

42. Cf. Rorty's discussion of "the delicate tonality of *petites actions*," pp. 284-87.

43. Post, p. 33.

44. Stanley Hauerwas, "Happiness, the Life of Virtue and Friendship: Theological Reflections on Aristotelian Themes," *The Asbury Theological Journal* 45/1 (Spring 1990): p. 46, n. 1.

45. Post, pp. 30-31; Stanley Hauerwas, *Truthfulness and Tragedy. Further Investigations into Christian Ethics* (Notre Dame and London: University of Notre Dame Press, 1977), pp. 127-31. Also see Pope's criticism in "The Moral Centrality of Natural Priorities," p. 110: " . . . proponents of 'equal regard' do not sufficiently appreciate the kind of love that is part of ordinary human life and that, in particular, is marked by special degrees of affection, loyalty, and moral obligation." This is because these proponents accord "ultimate significance to disinterested modes of regarding others." Needless to say, I think that the criticism rests on an unduly narrow vision of "equal regard."

46. Outka, *Agape*, p. 273.

47. An important philosophical resource for this project is Robert E. Goodin, *Protecting the Vulnerable: A Reanalysis of Our Social Responsibilities* (Chicago and London: University of Chicago Press, 1985).

DAVID LITTLE*

The Law of Supererogation

INTRODUCTION

Toward the end of *Agape*, Outka mentions and briefly discusses a distinction between "rock-bottom duties" and "works of supererogation,"[1] a subject that is of the greatest importance in the history of the ethical understanding of Christian love. His comments, although undeveloped by his own admission, serve as an interesting backdrop for recent controversies surrounding that distinction. This essay is offered as a partial response to those controversies in hopes of further clarifying the notion of supererogation and its relevance to Christian ethics.

Outka remarks:

> [T]he concept of supererogation can allow for certain complexities in the moral life which the typical notion of duty fails to include. For a variety of laudable attitudes and actions seem not strictly to be duties, i.e., are not what is normally involved when one adheres to contracts, complies with job-specifications and role-definitions, and fulfills special promises. Sometimes one may wish to say that a given action is permitted rather than required. One regards a rebuke for its non-performance as inappropriate. Yet its performance is far from being morally indiffer-

---

*The author wishes to express his thanks to a number of people who have in some cases taken considerable trouble to respond thoughtfully and challengingly to this essay in an earlier and considerably shorter version: William DeVries, James Childress, John Whittaker, Paul Lauritzen, Robert McKim, Stanley Hauerwas and Michael Duffy. I am also grateful to John Reeder, Jr., Gene Outka, Edmund Santurri, and William Werpehowski for stimulating responses to a discussion of the early version in a seminar at Yale some years ago. Of course, the author bears full responsibility for the use made of the responses.

ent when it enhances significantly the welfare of others. Such an action may be spontaneous and uncoerced; it goes beyond or is simply other than behavior dictated by obligatory formulas and authoritative sanctions (p. 297).

In other words, "typical" duties, like fulfilling contracts, promises, and role-responsibilities, as well as telling the truth, and repaying debts, are "duties for all and from every point of view, and to which anyone may call attention."[2] They are, that is, fully universalizable. As such, they are claimable and, upon default, blameworthy and sanctionable or enforceable by one human being against another. While non-performance is blameworthy, performance is not particularly praiseworthy, since behavior of that sort is simply expected.

By contrast, supererogatory acts are, as Outka suggests, considered to be "permitted rather than required"—they are usually voluntary or "spontaneous and uncoerced." A supererogatory deed constitutes, it appears, a special gift or benefice or "act of grace" that intentionally bestows a significant benefit upon some individual or group of individuals. And just as true gifts cannot by definition be demanded or coerced, but only praised and admired when they occur, so supererogatory acts cannot, it seems, be compelled, nor non-performance criticized or rebuked, while the proper response to such acts is praise and esteem. As such, supererogatory acts appear to be "agent-specific," or thoroughly optional for each person, and may not, like duties of justice, be prescribed universally.

In the most recent comprehensive treatment of supererogation, David Heyd[3] calls attention to the significance of the subject in moral theory and practice, and laments "how little [systematic] attention has been paid to it in past and current ethical doctrines" (p. 10). In analysing the history of the concept, he properly admits that the distinction between what is strictly required and what is virtuous and partly optional in the moral life has in one way or another been of strong interest in the Graeco-Roman tradition, even more intensely in Christian teaching, and then also among Western moral philosophers like Kant and Mill. Still, Heyd remains dissatisfied in varying degrees with the different accounts he uncovers in these traditions, as well as in more contemporary reflections. He therefore sets out afresh "to define the concept of supererogation, to study its relation to other moral concepts, and to justify its special status."[4]

Heyd's proposed definition appears to capture parsimoniously some of the central features of supererogation we have already informally identified:

An act is supererogatory if and only if
1. It is neither obligatory nor forbidden [permissibility].
2. Its omission is not wrong, and does not deserve sanction or criticism—either formal or informal [immunity from critical reaction].
3. It is morally good, both by virtue of its (intended) consequences and by virtue of its intrinsic value (being beyond duty) [moral value].
4. It is done voluntarily for the sake of someone else's good, and is thus meritorious [altruistic intention and personal merit] (p. 115).

Still, Heyd interprets and applies this definition in some rather controversial ways. For our purposes, this is particularly true of his brief discussion of the Christian backgrounds of the notion. In contrasting the scholastic Roman Catholic teachings of Thomas Aquinas with the Reformation doctrine of Luther and Calvin, Heyd avers that, despite certain liabilities the Catholic tradition actively supports and provides for an adequate doctrine of supererogation whereas the Reformation, to its discredit, does not (p. 29).

He naturally calls attention to the Reformers' vigorous attack on Catholic teaching which he thinks rules out in no uncertain terms any doctrine of supererogation whatsoever. For example, in Calvin's words:

> To boast [as the 'Papists' do] about works of supererogation—how does this square with the injunction laid upon us that, when we have done whatever is commanded us, we call ourselves 'unworthy servants,' and say that 'we have done no more than we ought to have done'? (Luke 17:10) . . . Therefore, the Lord bids us sincerely perceive and consider within ourselves that we perform no unrequired duties for him but render him our due service. . . . This fact we must accept completely: that there is nothing that can come to mind which contributes to the honoring of God or the love of neighbor *that is not comprised within God's law. But if it is a part of the law, let us not boast of voluntary liberality when we are constrained by necessity.*[5]

The commandments—'Do not take vengeance; love your enemies,' which were once delivered to all Jews and then to all Christians in common—have been turned by the Schoolmen into 'counsels,' which we are free either to obey or not to obey. What pestilential ignorance or malice is this! Moreover, they have saddled the requirement to obey these 'counsels' upon the monks, even more righteous in this one respect than simple Christians because they voluntarily bound themselves to keep these 'counsels,' and the reason they assign for not receiving them as laws is that they seem too burdensome and heavy, especially for Christians who are under the law of grace. Do they dare thus to abolish God's eternal law that we are to love our neighbor? Does such a distinction appear on any page of the law?[6]

According to Heyd, this sort of argument results in a strict anti-supererogationism. To subsume all conceivable Christian prescriptions under the one law of God appears to efface any distinction between "counsels" and "commandments." By implication, each of Heyd's defining characteristics of supererogation would seem to be excluded: All acts are either obligatory or forbidden ("required"), contrary to the permissibility condition; to omit living by all of the commandments is wrong and susceptible to censure, contrary to the condition concerning immunity from critical reaction; no acts are morally valuable in being beyond duty, contrary to the condition regarding moral value; and no act is meritorious, at least in the sense of earning any special praise or esteem, contrary to the condition concerning altruistic intention and personal merit.

Although there can be no doubt that Calvin is inalterably opposed to certain aspects of medieval teaching concerning supererogation, Heyd's references to Calvin's thought are, in fact, singularly insensitive to the room Calvin makes for what might be called a reconstructed view of supererogation. To be exact, Calvin's whole idea of "Christian freedom," which occupies so central a place in his theology, simply amalgamates in a rather innovative way some of the main indicia of Heyd's concept of supererogation.

For example, Calvin contends that in genuine Christian freedom

> consciences observe the law, not as if constrained by the necessity of the law, but that freed from the law's yoke, they willingly obey God's will. For since they dwell in perpetual dread so long as they remain under the sway of the law, they will never be disposed with eager readiness to obey God unless they have already been given this sort of freedom ... (p. III, xix, 4).

> Not that the law no longer enjoins believers to do what is right, but only that it is not for them what it formerly was; it may no longer condemn and destroy their consciences by frightening and confounding them ... (p. II, vii, 14).

And in identifying the essential content of the law of God, Calvin writes:

> [S]ince God wills that our whole soul be possessed with a disposition to love, we must banish from our hearts all desire contrary to love. To sum up, then: no thought should steal upon us to move our hearts to a harmful covetousness that tends to our neighbor's loss. To this corresponds the opposite precept: whatever we conceive, deliberate, will, or attempt is to be linked to our neighbor's good and advantage.... The Lord has previously commanded that the rule of love govern our wills, our endeavors, our actions. Now he enjoins that the thoughts of our mind be so controlled to the same end that none of them may become depraved or twisted and thus drive the mind in the opposite direction (p. II, viii, 49).

In other words, for Calvin the unmistakable ideal is that all Christian action be, finally, undertaken as something permissive, as something freely chosen, rather than being undertaken "as if constrained by the necessity of the law." Properly understood, the law is not imposed from without, but imposed from within, by a "deliberate consent of will." Moreover, while failure to live by the commands of God clearly remains "wrong" for Calvin, such failure, when correctly interpreted, is now "liberated" (in Calvin's word) from sanctions and from judgment. Non-performance becomes, in Heyd's terms, immune from critical reaction. Such immunity is the intended result of God's grace and mercy.

Next, genuine conformity to the law of God, which Calvin repeatedly summarizes as the "rule of love," involves above all a benevolent spirit, a "good will," again, freely elected, rather than determined "under the sway of the law." Accordingly, acts motivated by that sort of attitude have, in Heyd's words, intrinsic moral value precisely because they are not externally sanctioned and enforced, and are in that sense "beyond duty."

Finally, as we have just mentioned, deeds that conform to the law of God are defined, for Calvin, by an altruistic intention. The whole point of such deeds is that they are "done voluntarily for the sake of someone else's good." At the same time, whether deeds of this sort are "meritorious" for Calvin is a more complicated question. On the one hand, Calvin's fundamental objection to the Catholic doctrine of supererogation was the idea that performance of the "counsels," regarded as optional, could earn one special merit, and thereby make one extraordinarily "acceptable and pleasing to God." The belief that certain people on their own and without any supernatural assistance might make themselves meritorious contradicted Calvin's deep conviction that apart from God's grace and assistance all human beings are finally "unworthy servants." In this respect, proper behavior is *not* meritorious from Calvin's point of view.

However, in another sense, action that is inspired and enabled by divine grace and assistance to accomplish the ideals of Christian moral practice is decidedly meritorious. Calvin leaves no doubt that for him action that conforms to the standards of the "rule of love," that freely and deliberately intends someone else's good, has merit in that it is intrinsically valuable and worthy of the highest praise and esteem. The mistake is believing that such meritorious action can be performed without divine assistance, or that it is optional for Christians.

We have surely said enough to show that although Calvin rejected a certain version of the doctrine of supererogation, he by no means rejected the essential considerations involved in the concept of supererogation. In fact, Calvin's ethics can be seen as developed around those essential considerations. This is not to suggest that Calvin produced a thoroughly clear or persuasive doctrine of his own. Indeed, Calvin struggled without total success throughout his mature life to clarify the boundary lines between the sphere of "free righteousness" and the sphere of "constrained and forced righteousness" that, to his mind, remained necessary so long as human beings, in their recalcitrant state, were not "disposed with eager readiness to obey God." Still, Heyd's overall assessment of the approach of the Reformation to the subject of supererogation is inadequate and needs correction.

But there are some larger flaws in Heyd's general treatment of supererogation that his lack of acuteness in dealing with the Reformation also reveals. I wish to suggest that whatever shortcomings may exist in Calvin's account, he does succeed in identifying something that seems deeply embedded in our commonly accepted understanding of supererogation, even though Heyd as well as numerous other contemporary commentators have overlooked it.

It is that despite appearances, our idea of supererogation is, after all, closely tied to the notion of "law" in two senses. First, without ignoring the distinction between what is required and what is permitted that is clearly so central to the idea of supererogation, it is nevertheless appropriate to speak of supererogatory acts as in some sense universalizable according to a set of rules that governs the application of the term. Second, again without ignoring the distinction between what is required and what is permitted, it is appropriate to associate the idea of "duty," albeit a "permissive" or "subjective" duty, with supererogation. I suggest, in other words, that when Calvin used the word "law" to describe the standards of ideal action, he was retaining these two senses in combination—law as universally binding, although he meant to retain them in a way that respected the distinguishing features of supererogation.

As I say, this suggestion is at odds with Heyd's treatment as well as with the treatment of some other contemporary philosophers. In the first place, Heyd contends that acts of supererogation "are characterized as purely voluntary, optional, and *in a sense arbitrary, that is, not determined by universal standards and rules.*"[7] In the second place, although admitting that supererogatory acts are typically regarded as obligatory in some sense, Heyd proceeds to explain away such reports either as examples of "moral modesty" or as based on a misunderstanding.

> '[M]oral modesty' can be interpreted in two ways: the agent knows that he acted supererogatorily but does not say so (being shy, he wished to avoid being praised or publicly rewarded); or the agent sincerely believes that he was only doing his duty. The second interpretation is problematic, because it may mean either that the agent mistakenly takes a supererogatory act to be obligatory (and, accordingly, expects others to do so as well), or he takes a supererogatory action to be personally binding, that is a subjective duty (and does not consider others bound by it as well). Only the latter is a case of moral modesty, but in a different way from the modesty of the agent who knows that he acts beyond the call of duty but does not say so. For believing that a certain action is one's 'subjective duty' means rejecting the universalizability of that requirement. 'I feel I ought to do it', uttered sincerely, means that the agent does not regard his act as meritorious, although he does not expect others to do the same. Strictly speaking, this attitude is inconsistent, and the subjective binding force cannot be identified with duty (*Heyd*, p. 138).

In what follows, I shall dissent from Heyd and others by trying to defend the relevance of the two aspects of law to the idea of supererogation.

PERMISSIVE ACTS, UNIVERSALIZABILITY, AND 'SUBJECTIVE DUTY'

In *Freedom and Reason*, R. M. Hare remarks:

> Offences against the thesis of universalizability are logical, not moral. If a person says, 'I ought to act in a certain way, but

> nobody else ought to act in that way in relevantly similar circumstances,' then, on my thesis, he is abusing the word 'ought'; he is implicitly contradicting himself.[8]

On the face of it, this seems an undiscriminating statement. Are there not some perfectly common uses of "ought" that are restricted to a given agent's own conduct, but are, at the same time, both at home in a moral context, and also quite intelligible (non-contradictory)?

Alasdaire MacIntyre, for one, believes that works of supererogation provide such an example:

> A work of supererogation is by definition not numbered among the normal duties of life. Those duties—such things as keeping one's promises and paying one's debts—are partly characterized by the fact that the maxims which enjoin them are universalizable. But there are a great many acts of moral worth which do not come within their scope. . . . A moral hero, such as Captain Oates, is one who does more than duty demands. In the universalizable sense of 'ought' it does not therefore make sense to assert that Captain Oates did what he ought to have done. To say of a man that he did his duty in performing a work of supererogation is to contradict oneself. Yet a man may set himself the task of performing a work of supererogation and commit himself to it so that he will blame himself if he fails without finding such failure in the case of others blameworthy. Such a man might legitimately say, 'I have taken so-and-so as what I ought to do.' And here his valuation cannot, logically cannot, be universalized.[9]

This helps to prove, according to MacIntyre, that the U-thesis cannot be as central a feature of moral reasoning as Hare and others believe.

W. D. Hudson has attempted to defend Hare's version of the U-thesis against MacIntyre's challenge. Since Hudson's comments on MacIntyre's claims, and particularly concerning the Captain Oates case, both fill in some useful details, and require critical scrutiny, I hope I may be forgiven for quoting his comments at length.

> [MacIntyre] evidently thinks that the language which saints and heroes use about themselves, or which we use about them, is inconsistent with the U-thesis. The story of Captain Oates is often told to exemplify heroism. He was a member of Scott's ill-fated expedition to the Antarctic. Being disabled to a degree which was delaying his companions' return to safety, Oates, having said simply, 'I am going outside for a moment,' left the tent and

walked away into the blizzard to a certain death. On the U-thesis, if Captain Oates had said to himself, 'I ought to walk away,' or if we said of him that he did what he ought to have done, he would have meant, and we would mean, that anyone else so placed also ought to have done it. There are two questions: a) would Oates naturally have spoken, or would we naturally speak, in terms of 'ought' about this case? and b) if he, or we, would do so, what would he have meant, or we mean? We have already noted the distinction which Hare draws between 'ought' and 'good': 'ought' commits to the view that no similar person in a similar situation ought to fail to do the same thing; 'good' only to the view that whatever is the same in relevant respects is good. Now, we should certainly say that what Oates did was good. But should we say that he *ought* to have done it? Prima facie it seems clear that we would not. We should not have blamed Oates, or anyone else in his position, if they had failed to walk away. That is what is meant by calling this heroic act supererogatory. By the U-thesis, this commits him to the view that no one else similarly placed ought to fail to do so. Would Oates have rejected this implication? I doubt it. Surely a man in his position, acting as he did, we presume from a sense of duty, would think that anyone in the same position who failed so to act would be blameworthy. Admittedly, we can conceive of him imagining some acquaintance, X, in his position, and saying to himself, 'If X were in my shoes, I wouldn't think less of him if he didn't do what I'm doing.' But, if he asked himself why, the answer would reveal some relevant respects—e.g., 'I have a duty to set others an example,' 'I've had a good life,' 'I shouldn't be able to live with myself afterward if I didn't'—in which he took his own situation to *differ* from X's. There may even be, as I think Hare suggests, a sense in which, not only Oates himself, but we also are perfectly entitled to say that he ought to have done what he did. We would naturally say that a man ought to live up to his own ideals, even though we were not prepared to say that everyone ought to have the same ideals.[10]

Hudson's general interpretation of the Oates affair is, in certain respects, I believe, misleading, and, furthermore, at odds with Hare's own discussion. According to Hudson, if Oates says to himself that he *ought* to take a walk under the stated conditions, then, by the U-thesis, Oates is committed to the view that anyone similarly placed ought to do the same, and would be blameworthy if that did not occur. "Surely," says Hudson, "a man in [Oates's] position, acting as he did, we presume from a sense of duty, would think that anyone in the same position who failed so to act would be blameworthy."

But would we really? It seems more natural to assume that what Oates felt bound to do governed only his own action, that whatever other people might believe they ought to do, his decision committed him alone. In short, it seems more natural to assume that Oates would have regarded his as essentially a *permissive act*, and that onlookers would so regard it, as well. That means that it would not be appropriate for Oates to tell others what they ought to do under such circumstances, nor for others to tell him what he ought to do. It also means that Oates would ascribe to others in similar circumstances an equivalent degree of permissiveness.

Given what we normally understand in respect to heroic acts of beneficence, Hudson's subsequent comments about the special circumstances under which Oates might not have blamed someone else in a similar predicament would appear to be beside the point. Hudson's suggestion seems to be that having committed himself to an act of heroic self-sacrifice, Oates would have assumed that anyone else similarly situated ought to do the same (and be blamable for non-performance), *unless* some special circumstance could be adduced to differentiate his case from others. The presumption would thus be in favor of heroism and deviations would have to be specially justified.

But if an act of extreme beneficence, such as giving one's life for others, is *conceived*, as I am suggesting, as a permissive, rather than a mandatory, act, then it is not because Oates believed he, in distinction from others, had had a good life, or owed others a good example, or some such, that it would be inappropriate for him to blame people in similar circumstances for not sacrificing themselves. It would be inappropriate to blame them because acts of extreme beneficence are understood, by definition, not to be determined or sanctionable by other people. They are, in the deepest sense, *gifts of self-sacrifice*, and, like all true gifts, must (logically) be left up to the agent to give or withhold. It would simply make no sense to demand that someone else give a gift or to censure another person for not offering one.

Thus, Hudson's initial attempt to protect the relevance of the U-thesis to supererogatory acts fails. By trying to force heroic acts into conformity with his understanding of the U-thesis, he distorts our common understanding of such acts. So far, MacIntyre would seem to have the upper hand.

Nor is Hudson's next move much more successful, for he appears to confuse Hare's position. He takes a cue from some comments by Hare in *Freedom and Reason* and suggests that onlookers might properly hold Oates responsible for taking a walk if he held ideals which included, presumably, principles of self-sacrifice. Since he held such ideals, he "ought" to act consistently with those ideals, and could be criticized for not so doing.

The reference is curious because as Hare discusses it, this "ought of consistency" has little to do with his arguments concerning the U-thesis, at least in its principal sense.

> There is also another use of 'ought', in connexion with ideals, which may seem more harmless. A man who has adopted the ideal of physical fitness, which requires him to run before breakfast, may say of himself that he ought to get out of bed now—or even, if he is weakwilled, that he ought to have got out of bed half an hour ago. But this may be only a hypothetical 'ought'; he may mean that if he wants to live up to his ideal, he ought. . . . This would not commit him to any moral judgment on those who do not have such an ideal (p. 154).

To Hare's mind, using an "ought" in this way is not to employ it in his principal, or "golden-rule," sense, according to which everyone similarly situated ought to do what is prescribed. On the contrary, it is a "hypothetical ought," which is to say logically marginal, from Hare's point of view. For that reason, the use does not involve a moral judgment on others at all. In fact, "oughts" of consistency, like the one mentioned in his example, are, for Hare, more on the order of aesthetic judgments—that is, judgments of "goodness," rather than of "rightness." Goodness judgments are, according to Hare, universalizable in one sense: If one calls something good in one context one is committed to applying the same judgment to any object similar in the relevant respects. But judgments of goodness are not universally prescriptive in respect to action. Insofar as they bear on action, they admit of a wide range of discretion among actors.

> It follows from these logical properties of the words and from the universalizability of all value-judgments, that, whereas the judgment that I ought in a certain situation to do a certain thing commits me to the view that no similar person in a precisely similar situation ought to fail to do the same thing, this is not the case with a judgment framed in terms of 'good.' For it is perfectly possible for a person to say, consistently, that he is acting well in going for a run before breakfast, but that his neighbor is not acting ill in staying in bed and closely studying the *Financial Times* (p. 153).

In other words, Hare's view, which Hudson is supposed to be defending, inclines to put supererogatory acts altogether beyond the reach of the U-thesis in its principal and moral sense. Such acts are matters of personal preference, rather than matters of duty or rightness. In fact, in his brief discussion of J. O. Urmson's famous essay, "Saints and Heroes," Hare underlines this point: "if a soldier, in order to save his fellows, sacrifices his life by throwing himself on an exploding grenade, he does something 'good', but not something which anybody in that situation ought to do" (pp. 154-55).

There is, it is true, one way in which heroic acts might, on Hare's view, be subject to the U-thesis. If a person embraced an ascetic ideal specifically intended for everyone, that person would then (but only then) "express himself in terms of 'ought,' and thus commit himself to adverse judgments" regarding those who did not live up to the ideal (p. 154). Only if the heroic soldier, mentioned above, or if Captain Oates, had embraced that sort of view, which would by their own intention make their ideal of self-sacrifice binding upon everyone, could we properly speak of the soldier or Captain Oates having done what they "ought" to have done.

It is clear, then, that Hudson and Hare are at cross purposes when it comes to applying the U-thesis to works of supererogation. Hudson seems to suggest that onlookers might blame and hold someone accountable for not living up to that person's ideals, even though the onlookers did not share those ideals. But Hare does not say that, and it would be a peculiar application of the U-thesis, if he did. On the contrary, Hare's view is that unless a person means to legislate for all similarly situated people, that person is not using "ought" in its principal prescriptive or moral sense at all.

It begins to look as though Hare and MacIntyre are joining hands behind Hudson's back. Both wish to distinguish between standard moral duties and works of supererogation. Both wish to restrict the U-thesis in its prescriptive use to the first class of actions, where it makes sense to require that everyone similarly situated conform to a standard act.

But are MacIntyre and Hare in basic agreement? I do not think so. Although the similarities are interesting and need to be attended to, perhaps more than they have been, the remaining difference is plain. For MacIntyre, it is perfectly intelligible (and non-contradictory) to use the word "ought" in relation to deeds like Captain Oates's, and to consider such usage to be of thorough-going moral significance, without needing to universalize such "oughts." Indeed, MacIntyre's position is that the attempt to universalize such oughts destroys their point.

Hare, on the other hand, holds to the view that "ought" is not properly applied to Oates's decision to take a walk, unless, of course, Oates is willing, because of a particular ideal he has adopted, to prescribe his act for everyone similarly situated, and blame them on default. Naturally, if Oates were willing to do that, he would, in effect, have turned his act from a work of supererogation (one "above and beyond the call of duty') into a normal moral act. Whichever way one slices it, supererogatory acts do not, for Hare, have a logically independent status as fully prescriptive moral "oughts." Either the supererogatory ought is hypothetical, as Hare puts its, or supererogatory acts lose their permissive status by being subsumed under the requirements for standard universal prescriptions.

By way of resolving the difference here, I propose we attempt to squeeze in between MacIntyre and Hare, and combine certain features from the positions of both men. I suggest that there is a distinction of the greatest importance for reflecting on the logic of supererogation between what we may call "mandatory oughts" and "permissive oughts." That means, against Hare, that there are legitimate (non-contradictory) uses of "ought" in relation to supererogatory acts, though their operation is different from the operation of "mandatory oughts" in what MacIntyre calls "normal" contexts. I do not believe Hare (along with others) has grasped the nature of "permissive oughts." Whether or not one elects to perform acts of supererogation may depend on happening to prefer ideals of self-sacrifice or some such, as Hare suggests. However, that may not be the whole story. Finally, I suggest, against Hare and with MacIntyre, that these permissive oughts are not marginal with respect to moral reasoning. They occupy an important, if distinctive, place.

On the other hand, against MacIntyre, I contend that these oughts can readily be understood as prescriptively universalizable—that is, as binding in some important sense upon the action of others similarly situated. The *way* they are binding is different in some respects from Hare's account of universalizability.

We need first to clarify further the distinction between mandatory oughts and permissive oughts by focusing on the nature of permissiveness that is involved in the second group. We suggested earlier that acts of extreme beneficence, like Captain Oates's decision to take a walk or the soldier's decision to hurl himself on the exploding grenade to save his fellows, are permissive in the following way: Decisions of that sort are not appropriately determined or sanctioned by any but the actor, nor will the actor normally incline to hold others accountable for failing to follow suit in similar circumstances.

But are all acts of beneficence understood to be permissive in that sense? In order to explore this question, we may quote an example and some commentary from Joel Feinberg's interesting essay, "Supererogation and Rules":

Suppose a stranger approaches me on a street corner and politely asks me for a match. Ought I give him one? I think most people would agree that I should, and that any reasonable man of good will would offer the stranger a match. Perhaps a truly virtuous man would do more than that. He would be friendly, reply with a cheerful smile, and might even volunteer to light the stranger's cigarette.

Now suppose Jones is on the street corner and another stranger politely requests a light from him. Jones is in a sour mood this morning, and even normally he does not enjoy encounters with strangers. He brusquely refuses to give the stranger a match. I think we can agree that Jones's behavior on the street corner does not constitute an ideal for human conduct under such circumstances; that it is not what a perfectly virtuous man would have done; that it is not what Jones ought to have done.

If we reproach Jones, however, for his uncivil treatment of the stranger, he may present us with a vigorous self-defense. 'Perhaps I was not civil,' he might admit. 'But I was under no *obligation* to give a match to that man. Who is he to me? He had no claim on me; he has no authority to *command* any performance from me. I don't *owe* him anything. It may be nice to do favors for people; but a favor, by definition, is nothing that we are legally or morally *required* to do...

Jones's defense makes me think no better of him. Still, from a certain legal-like point of view, it appears perfectly cogent. Everything Jones said in his defense was true. The moral I draw from this tale is that there are some actions which it would be desirable for a person to do, and which, indeed, they *ought* to do, even though they are actions he is under no obligation and has no duty to do.[11]

(In the light of recent reflections on the dangers of smoking, the example of the match introduces extraneous moral complications. Is it in fact a favor to give a match to a smoker? To avoid missing the deeper point of the example, therefore, we would do well simply to substitute more innocuous examples, such as a stranger's request for a scrap of paper or for the time or for directions—all for benign purposes.)

To begin with, Feinberg's observations appear to point to the distinction we are after between mandatory oughts and permissive oughts. The statement, "Jones ought to provide a scrap of paper under these circumstances," is *not* reducible to standard mandatory oughts, such as "Jones ought to repay his debt or keep his promise." The stranger does not have a normal claim on Jones. It would be logically as well as socially inappropriate if instead of making a request for a piece of paper, the stranger strode up to Jones and declared: "Gimme some paper," or "Where's my piece of paper?" (By contrast, similar utterances would not be inappropriate if the stranger were instead Jones's creditor, who was seeking repayment of a debt or fulfillment of a contract.) In other words, even so trivial and (we might say) "low-grade" an act of beneficence as this is clearly marked off from other "oughts"—it is neither imposable by others nor enforceable in the way more standard oughts are. There remains something permissive about it.

If permissiveness in this connection means "granting liberty," then even requests for trivial favors, which are nothing more than requests for gifts of a sort, implicitly acknowledge "the privilege of benefaction." As we have already established, giving gifts is of a different order from fulfilling "duties of justice," and accordingly entails an opportunity for self-initiation or "freedom" on the part of the benefactor that appears to be respected by the common linguistic and social conventions that Feinberg refers to.

Moreover, Feinberg's remarks about the "ideal of human conduct" associated with doing even trivial favors for others—ideally, displaying "good will," or benevolence, "being friendly," replying "with a cheerful smile," and perhaps undertaking other small forms of assistance—points to a related feature of the privilege of benefaction. It is that if gifts, even minor ones, are given at all, they are suitably accompanied by a certain form of "self-giving" that involves an inner disposition toward the well-being of the beneficiary. Such an "altruistic intention," properly understood, must be "freely given." Like the gift to which it is attached, it cannot be compelled or demanded. To try to compel benevolence is to misunderstand it. In these senses, then, doing even trivial favors falls under the rubric of permissive acts.[12]

But now the plot thickens. Feinberg's discussion makes clear that although we do ordinarily respect the permissiveness of performing minor favors, we appear then to turn right around and severely restrict the range of permissiveness that we ascribe to acts of this sort. If individuals behave as Jones does in Feinberg's example; if, that is, they grumpily refuse, with no apparent excuse, to supply a scrap of paper to give someone directions, particularly when it is at minimum inconvenience to themselves, we would obviously feel inclined, as Feinberg does in his example, to criticize such individuals rather harshly. With Feinberg, we want to say much more than simply that "it would be good," or even "very good" if Jones performed the favor. We want to tell Jones in no uncertain terms what he "ought" to do, and to sanction him should he default, by saying something derogatory like, "What a creep that Jones is" (which is roughly Feinberg's assessment). On inspection, we seem now to be moving very close to prescribing universally (in the mandatory sense) a piece of conduct.

We seem to have discovered, then, certain acts, like trivial favors, that are in some respects permissive acts, and yet are very close in our moral experience to being controlled by something like Hare's understanding of the U-thesis. "Jones ought to provide a scrap of paper to the stranger" is, on the one hand, up to Jones and his benevolent instincts, but, on the other, it is the sort of thing that anyone in a similar situation ought to do, or face strong censure.

What is the difference between low-grade acts of beneficence, like the stranger's request to Jones, and "high-grade" or extreme acts of beneficence, like Captain Oates's taking a walk or the soldier's throwing himself on the exploding grenade? The key difference, I propose, is the degree of permissiveness that we assign, respectively, to the different sorts of beneficent act. Low-grade acts have low permissiveness (though they do have some, as we saw). High-grade acts have high permissiveness. That means we are less inclined to honor and respect or "live with" a non-beneficent decision in a low-grade context than we are in a high-grade one. If Jones refuses to provide the scrap of paper, we are disposed to blame him unless he can provide some very effective excuse. We do not readily "understand" his action. On the other hand, if Oates, after all, decides against taking a walk, we are much readier to "understand" rather than to blame him. It would seem that Oates's sacrifice, as a gift of the highest cost, is not something that is fitting for us to determine for him.

These variations do not appear to be random or optional. In fact, they appear to work according to identifiable, commonly assumed rules, which rules are at the same time our clue to ascertaining the special way that universalization works in connection with acts of beneficence. "Oughts" of beneficence appear to function according to a law of their own.

It looks as though we grade acts of beneficence according to five variables as proposed in a somewhat different form by Eric D'Arcy.[13] These are 1) the *benefit* for the potential beneficiary, 2) the *cost* (or risk) to the potential benefactor, 3) the benefactor's *capacity*, 4) the benefactor's *availability* for providing the benefit, and 5) the *probable effectiveness* of the projected act in providing the benefit.[14] Thus, a model of high-grade beneficence, as, for example, Captain Oates's walk, consists of strong weights for all the variables: 1) high benefit for the beneficiary, 2) high cost or risk to the benefactor, 3) ample capacity, 4) ready availability, and 5) high probable effectiveness.

In contrast, a model of low-grade beneficence, as, for example, giving a stranger a scrap of paper, consists of relatively weak weights for the first two variables, and relatively strong ones for the last three: 1) minor benefit to the stranger, 2) negligible cost to Jones, 3) ample capacity, 4) ready availability, and 5) high probable effectiveness.

At this point, we need to take note of some interesting and revealing complexities in the logic of beneficent acts. If it is true, as we have suggested, that low-grade beneficent acts come close to being like mandatory duties in that they are externally sanctionable, this is even truer of those beneficent acts in which the first variable—benefit to the beneficiary—is increased in weight, while the other variables remain as they were in the case of Jones and the stranger: Along with high benefit, there is 2) low cost to the benefactor, 3) ample capacity, 4) ready availability, and 5) high probable effectiveness.

The following case makes this clear: A small child is obviously drowning in a shallow pond that is located in a remote area. The child's only hope is a robust young hiker, dressed in a bathing suit, who happens, at that very moment, to pass by, not four feet from the struggling child. If anything, the hiker's "duty" to rescue the child would appear to be more binding, and on default more severely sanctionable by imagined onlookers, than Jones's "duty" to provide a scrap of paper to the stranger.

On the one hand, the act still retains, in certain interesting respects, a quality of permissiveness. The locutions normally associated with communicating a mandatory duty do not seem appropriate, even in this extreme case. The child, or, let us say, the child's representative—perhaps a distraught but suddenly incapacitated grandmother sprawled nearby—might not appropriately *demand* help from the hiker in the way a creditor might demand repayment from a debtor, or a promisee might demand satisfaction from a promisor. That is because there exists between the child and the hiker no specific role-relation, no institutionalized context within which demands of the mandatory kind make sense. Rather than demand, the appropriate form of communication in this case would appear to be an urgent appeal, an appeal, that is, to provide a critical benefit to the child. Accordingly, that sort of language implicitly acknowledges the hiker's privilege of benefaction, as we called it.

On the other hand, the circumstances of this case would no doubt dispose the grandmother, as well as all imagined onlookers, to conclude that saving the child's life at such minor inconvenience is in some sense *required* of the hiker, on pain of the strongest forms of censure and blame, should the hiker ignore the child rather than interrupt his accustomed pace. If this is an example of a permissive act, it is permissive in only the most minimal sense.

Incidentally, John Locke, no doubt trading on a venerable medieval tradition, refers to certain basic duties of charity, in discussing the response to a starving person expected of the well-to-do, that appears to manifest the same combination of permissiveness and requiredness as in the case of the drowning child. "*Charity* gives every Man a Title to so much out of another's Plenty, as will keep him from extream want, where he has no means to subsist otherwise"[15]; And this conviction is related to Locke's assertion of a duty of limited charity or beneficence in *The Second Treatise of Government*. He claims that along with other basic moral requirements, "Everyone ... when his own preservation comes not in competition, ought ..., as much as he can, to preserve the rest of mankind" (p. II, 6, 311). Insofar as the concept "charity" denotes benevolent concern for the welfare of others, it presupposes the quality of permissiveness that we have seen is associated with all beneficent, or "gift-giving" acts. On the other hand, as Locke states, in extreme circumstances charity is required ("gives every Man a Title"). In those circumstances, one is, so to speak, bound to give gifts, bound to be benevolent, a condition that puts an obvious strain on the normal conceptual boundaries between justice and charity.

We may conclude that if we are to describe beneficent acts as lying on a spectrum from low-grade to high-grade, and if we mean by low-grade "barely permissive," and by high-grade "highly permissive," then instances with the critical features of the case of the drowning child, or Locke's case of the desperately needy, should be classed as the *lowest grade* of all (that is, as allowing the benefactor the most minimal degree of permissiveness).

Assuming that capacity, availability, and effectiveness remain relatively high across the board, then the crucial variables for determining the grade of a beneficent act would appear to be the first two—benefit to the beneficiary and cost to the benefactor. The following rough calculus suggests itself. (Opposite page.)

It will be noted that, as between the two extremes, the determining variable is 2), cost to the benefactor. Given that the other variables are fixed at high levels, the range of the benefactor's permissiveness increases as the cost of beneficence increases. As we saw, if it is a question of whether Captain Oates or the heroic soldier will pay the "supreme price," that is something that they, in the deepest sense, must be permitted to decide for themselves, and their decision—either way—ought to be morally respected by everyone.

BENEFICENT ACTS COMPARED

	Drowning Boy; Needy Person	Jones and the Stranger	Captain Oates; Heroic Soldier
Grade of Beneficence	Lowest	Less Low	High
Degree of Permissiveness	Minimal	Less Minimal	Maximal
Benefit to Beneficiary	High	Low	High
Cost to Benefactor	Low	Low	High
Capacity	High	High	High
Availability	High	High	High
Effectiveness	High	High	High

These two cases optimally satisfy Heyd's defining characteristics of supererogation. Any decision either by Oates or the soldier to sacrifice oneself could not be regarded as required. Under the circumstances, both would be fully immune from sanction or blame, should they have reneged. But their supererogatory action would normally be regarded as having moral value by virtue of the beneficial consequences intended and achieved, quite above and beyond the call of duty. Finally, theirs would constitute paradigm examples of action moved by an altruistic intention ("done voluntarily for the sake of someone else's good"), and such action would be considered to be consummately meritorious and praiseworthy.

If, by contrast, the cost to the benefactor is low (and the other variables remain the same), the "permissiveness quotient" declines sharply. Correspondingly, the applicability of Heyd's defining characteristics of supererogation is also altered substantially, so that we would not be inclined, contrary to Heyd, to describe low-grade beneficent acts as supererogatory at all. In fact, by the terms of Heyd's own definition, we would more naturally reserve the category of supererogation for higher-grade beneficent acts.[16]

Consider: Beneficent action in the case of the drowning child or the starving person is in some important sense required; censure and blame are thoroughly appropriate if the action is not done. The action is certainly morally valuable, although since it is in some sense expected and easy to perform, it does not generate great credit or merit for the person rendering assistance; and while altruistic intention no doubt normally accompanies such an action, such cases are hardly the most exemplary illustrations of voluntary self-sacrifice for someone else's good. It is apparent that such action does not qualify in major respects as supererogation.

Now, the main point of all this is that these variables and the patterns in which they appear to operate constitute a *set of rules* that governs the use of "oughts" in connection with beneficent acts. It is this set of rules that determines the way universalizability works in relation to beneficent acts.

Thus, in respect to high-grade beneficent, or genuinely supererogatory acts, if Captain Oates (under the familiar circumstances) says to himself, "I ought to take a walk", he will be implying the following, assuming he has assessed the act in high-grade terms: Any person similarly situated (situated, that is, such that the weights, from Oates's point of view, are similarly high in all respects), is (logically) to be permitted to decide, free of any external prompting, whether or not to perform an act of extreme self-sacrifice. Put negatively, no one in a situation of this sort has warrant to require or impose a decision upon the agent, or to "react critically" (with censure or blame), once the agent's decision has been made. In short, if Captain Oates (or the heroic soldier) uses the word "ought" in relation to his action in high-grade beneficent cases, it can only (logically) be an "agent-specific" or "self-imposed" or permissive ought. It (logically) cannot be a mandatory ought. That sort of ought would make no sense. It is, we are suggesting, these maximally permissive oughts that properly fall under the rubric of supererogation.

Contrastingly, if the hiker says to himself, "I ought to save the child"—assuming he has assessed the act in low-grade terms, he will be implying that anyone similarly situated (weights for benefit, capacity, availability, probable effectiveness, very high; cost to himself, very low) ought to do likewise. And, indeed, in doing so, the hiker ought to "give himself" freely and eagerly—ought, that is, to manifest the attributes of benevolence in moving to the aid of the child. While something permissive remains in even low-grade beneficent oughts, the range is drastically restricted. (The same goes, as we have argued, for the "lower-grade" beneficent acts—the case of Jones and the stranger.) Because of that restriction, the characteristics of supererogation either no longer apply, or apply in a much-modified way. Accordingly, low-grade acts are much closer to mandatory duties, and therefore predictably universalize in related ways.

We are now in a position to begin to see the way the "law" of supererogation works. In the first place, we have discovered that it is misleading to suggest, as Heyd does, that acts of supererogation are "characterized as . . . in a sense arbitrary, that is, not determined by universal standards or rules." If our analysis is correct, a definite set of rules, applicable in their own way as universally as the rules of mandatory actions, governs decisions concerning works of supererogation. Although supererogatory oughts are most assuredly permissive oughts, and therefore allow room for personal determination, they are operable only when a specific set and weighting of conditions (the five variables, fixed at high levels) exist. If those conditions do exist, then one is bound both to exercise the privilege of benefaction—one way or the other, and to ascribe that same privilege to all other people who find themselves controlled by those particular conditions.

Moreover, the range of permission is, apparently, determined to a large degree by "objective conditions." As our examination of all the cases made clear, widely shared notions of significant cost and benefit, as well as of what counts as capacity, availability, and effectiveness in carrying out an action, naturally prompt us to make transsubjective judgments concerning the sort of ought that is warranted in a given set of circumstances. We would not ordinarily find it compelling if the hiker told us that he ought not be blamed or criticized for failing to rescue the child since keeping a set walking pace is more important than anything else in the world, and therefore to sacrifice his pace even to save a child is to pay too high a price. Nor would we likely be convinced if he asserted that, after all, four feet is too far to travel, even to assist a child, and that, therefore, he was not really "available" to do the job.

In short, it seems obvious that individuals are not at liberty to interpret and apply the five variables in just any way they please. For example, they appear to be "bound" by certain conventional interpretations of the "weightiness" of human life, either as benefit or as cost, and of what does and does not serve basic human welfare. Furthermore, even if there are disagreements in particular cases over what counts as cost, benefit, capacity, etc., the disputes must be argued before the bar of the five variables. Withal, they provide the framework for identifying works of supererogation.

In addition, the relationship between the low-grade and the high-grade beneficent acts reveals another way in which some aspects of the law of supererogation bind. We suggested that low-grade beneficent acts fall squarely in neither the supererogatory nor the mandatory class. They are a kind of hybrid in that they combine elements of permissiveness and elements of requiredness. Nevertheless, that supererogatory and low-grade beneficent acts do share the quality of permissiveness, particularly in respect to the elements of "self-giving" and benevolence, or "good will," indicates that these crucial features of supererogation are, at low and relatively undemanding levels, required or "binding." As we saw in the case of Jones and the stranger, small favors (or trivial gifts) performed with fitting tokens of friendliness and readiness to help are socially expected and enforced, by means of applying criticism and censure to non-performance. Locke's suggestion of a moral requirement of "limited beneficence" ("when his own preservation comes not in competition, ought he, as much as he can, to preserve the rest of mankind") that is comparable to other basic moral requirements, underscores this somewhat paradoxical, but no less real, characteristic of "required liberality" in low-grade contexts.

In the second place, Heyd's inclination to reduce expressions of duty in connection with acts of supererogation either to "moral modesty" (the agent's shyness in wishing to avoid praise or public reward) or to a mistake in comprehending what supererogation amounts to, is unpersuasive. While moral modesty may account for some of the many instances in which people declare that they were "duty-bound" to perform a substantial sacrifice for the good of someone else, there are other perfectly intelligible (and I believe more plausible) ways to interpret such expressions.

One way that is no doubt widely influential in our culture emerges from the Christian tradition. Accordingly, a Christian might personally feel "bound in gratitude" to return the benevolence manifested in Christ's life and death by undertaking to display benevolence, in turn, to God and fellow human beings. And one might also feel, as, for example, Calvin did, that "the rule of love" universally governs human life. Consequently, acting voluntarily for the sake of someone else's good constitutes the highest fulfillment of the "law " of human nature. On this view, one is bound to permissive action.

On the one hand, one quite consistently feels a deep and unavoidable requirement to act in charitable ways, and, in the light of Christ's "supreme sacrifice," even to be prepared to pay one's own high price in appropriate situations. Moreover, a sense of guilt or personal self-criticism may naturally attend non-performance.

On the other hand, it is in the nature of the required action (and dispositions) that it be "permissive," that it come freely from the heart as a true gift should, that it be delivered, as Calvin said, "with eager readiness," and "not as if constrained by the necessity of the law." Action of that sort is clearly not truly performed as long as it is regarded as heteronomous, as being motivated by the "outside" demands or reactions of others. It is, therefore, action that does not properly belong in the strictly mandatory class.

These standard features of a Christian understanding of love, as we say, make perfectly intelligible and natural the association of an idea of "subjective duty" with works of supererogation. So construed, that idea is not best comprehended as an example of "moral modesty," nor is it correctly described as some kind of conceptual mistake.

I do not argue that all expressions of subjective duty in connection with supererogation reflect this Christian understanding. Determining whether that is true is in part an empirical task. I do propose, though, that it is highly probable, given the cultural influence of Christianity, that the sort of understanding embedded in that tradition has profoundly affected the rules according to which the concept of supererogation appears to operate.

It does seem clear that an examination of Christian backgrounds begins to clarify and make comprehensible the otherwise apparently paradoxical notion of a "law" of supererogation.

NOTES

1. Gene Outka, *Agape: An Ethical Analysis* (New Haven: Yale University Press, 1972), pp. 293ff.

2. Cited by Outka, p. 297, from J. O. Urmson, "Saints and Heroes," in *Essays in Moral Philosophy*, A.I. Melden, ed. (Seattle: University of Washington Press, 1958), p. 204. Following philosophical convention, by "typical duties" I mean essentially role or institutional duties (including the institutions of promise-keeping and truth-telling) which, it seems clear, rest on a consensual (explicit or implicit) basis. This does not include "duties of non-maleficence," which, while normally universalizable in the same way as the "typical duties," are, I suspect, of a different genre from the institutional duties. In fact, there may well be an important logical relation between duties of non-maleficence and "duties of beneficence," which has just begun to occur to me as I have been preparing this paper. However, I do not now have any very clear thoughts on this "deep" subject.

3. David Heyd, *Supererogation* (Cambridge: Cambridge University Press, 1982).

4. Heyd, p. 10. Though I am critical of aspects of Heyd's book, it is generally an illuminating and careful study. In this paper I devote attention to examining the concept of supererogation, along, to some degree, with its relation to other moral concepts. I do not spend time on Heyd's interesting attempt "to justify its special status," though that needs to be done.

5. John Calvin, *Institutes of the Christian Religion* (Philadelphia: Westminster Press, 1960), p. III, xiv, 14; emphasis added.

6. Calvin, p. II, viii, 56; cf. *Calvin's Commentaries: First Epistle of Paul the Apostle to the Corinthians* (Grand Rapids: Eerdmans, 1960), pp. 193-95.

7. Heyd, p. 9; emphasis added; cf. 7. While I shall not argue that works of supererogation are, as such, determined by universal standards and rules, I shall argue that they are determined *in reference to* universal standards and rules. This is in some ways an indirect criticism of Heyd, but it is an important one, I believe, and one that he very much overlooks.

8. R. M. Hare, *Freedom and Reason* (New York: Oxford University Press, 1965), p. 32.

9. Alisdaire MacIntyre, "What Morality Is Not," in *Definition of Morality*, G. Wallace and A. D. M. Walker, eds. (London: Methuen, 1970) p. 30. In a stimulating discussion of these matters, my son, Jonathan Little, pointed out that the Captain Oates example, which plays an important part in this discussion as a "case" of supererogation, might not be as clear an example of sheer high-cost beneficence as one could think of since the code of expeditions (like that of dangerous military missions) might raise expectations concerning sacrificial acts in extreme circumstances. The same is true, incidentally, of another example that will come up later—the soldier who throws himself on a live grenade to save a buddy. I think this is a tricky matter; we would, after all, still likely refer to Oates's or the soldier's action as "above and beyond the call of duty," and no doubt heap posthumous praise on such actions as "highly meritorious." Still, however this matter stands, we should not be distracted by these complexities. We can easily think of purer examples of sheer high-cost beneficence, if we so desire. The reader is advised to do that if my son's point seems convincing.

10. W. D. Hudson, *Contemporary Moral Philosophy* (Garden City, N.Y.: Doubleday & Co., 1970), pp. 220-22.

11. Joel Feinberg, "Supererogation and Rules," in *Ethics*, Judith J. Thomson and Gerald Dworkin, eds. (New York: Harper & Row, 1968), pp. 392-93; original emphasis.

12. Feinberg's passing discussion of the "ideal of conduct" pertinent to Jones and the stranger is rather ambiguous. On the one hand, he mentions that behaving in a friendly, kindly way is what a "perfectly virtuous man" would do, as though such behavior were quite extraordinary. But he also appears to criticize Jones for not living up to such virtuous ideals. My own impression is that it is perfectly normal to expect some modest degree of friendliness and responsiveness in relation to trivial favors, and that, for example, directions to a passer-by that are delivered in a grudging or stingy way are ordinarily regarded as legitimately liable to censure.

13. Eric D'Arcy, *Human Acts* (Oxford: Clarendon Press, 1966), pp. 56-57.

14. I am indebted to my former colleague, James Childress, for suggesting some changes in my earlier version of these variables. I still admit that much needs to be done by way of clarifying and operationalizing these variables. I do believe they are suggestive and have some intuitive power to them, and I think I say enough about them to make them useful for my limited purposes here.

15. John Locke, *Two Treatises of Government* (New York: New American Library, 1960), p. I, 42 (206).

16. As Heyd remarks: "[T]here are those acts of kindness and consideration. These . . . are borderline cases of supererogation. Still, they ought to be discussed under that title as they meet—in most cases—the conditions of supererogatory acts mentioned above. Helping a stranger to find his way in town, or assisting an old woman to cross the road cannot be considered as saintly or heroic, nor as generous and beneficent. Yet they are supererogatory" (p. 2). This is a confusing statement. If acts of this sort are "borderline," then they are marginal in respect to the defining characteristics of supererogation, and it is important to sort out why and in what way. Heyd does not do that, but, in the last sentence, rather gives the impression that minor favors are very similar to other purer examples of supererogation. This is surely mistaken.

TIMOTHY P. JACKSON*

Christian Love and Political Violence

INTRODUCTION

Essays on love and violence often become disquisitions on the ethical uses of adversity. How can love respond effectively to a violent world? How, more specifically, can we translate our charitable motives into the prevention of conflict and the avoidance of coercive force altogether? These questions are important, but one liability of approaching matters via such violence-centered "Hows" is that it may lead us to assume that we understand what love is, and that it is morally unproblematic. I believe such an assumption is unwarranted; both love and violence must be interrogated, both independently and in their interrelation. One should not doubt the value of techniques whereby love avoids or, if it must, manages social strife. But the more fundamental (and antecedent) questions are: Why are we moved to violence in the first place? and, What is the nature of love that it should even be concerned with violence?

In answer to "Why violence?," Christians traditionally refer to the fear and mistrust endemic to fallen humanity, pointing ultimately to personal sin. In reply to "What's love?," Christians speak initially and above all else of the self-sacrificial example of Jesus of Nazareth. Although there is some warrant in common speech for defining all violence pejoratively, as the *unjust* use of force, such usage is not universal. Moreover, it would largely beg the key normative question of what Christian love demands in the political sphere. For my purposes, therefore, political violence will mean force deliberately employed between two or more individuals so as to cause psychological or bodily injury, or death. Christian love will be treated as synony-

---

*I thank Richard Hays, Janna Jackson, Gene Outka, Paul Ramsey (RIP), Cornel West, and the Editors of this volume for helpful responses to an earlier version of this essay.

mous with the Biblical term "*agape*." *Agape* may be defined interpersonally as the active promotion of the good of others (neighbor love), but its meaning is communicated most adequately via narrative accounts of the life of Christ. I ask the standard question: (1) How, if at all, may *agape* combat unjustifiable forms of violence?; but I also address a second major issue: (2) Does love itself ever act violently?

First, I examine consecutively the relevant views of an in-principle pacifist, a Christian "realist," a just war theorist, and a liberationist: Stanley Hauerwas, Reinhold Niebuhr, Paul Ramsey, and Juan Segundo, respectively. The stage thus being set, I briefly discuss the age-old tension between religious Separatism and Apology. I then offer a more constructive analysis of moral conflict and how this relates to the Christian commitment to putting charity first among the virtues. A third question, at best only implicit in (2) above, looms large at this point: (3) To what extent may love be the *cause* rather than the remedy of *culpable* political violence? This query cuts to the very heart of Christian social ethics, for while violence is stereotypically seen as the crudest response to the frustration of desires themselves rather crude, it appears upon reflection that even our (putatively) best moral aspirations may lead us, at times, into elaborate forms of aggression. Violence, we commonly presume, is a cheap consolation; but, in fact, we seem led to cruelty and intolerance by such "worthy" motives as pursuit of the common good and cultivation of individual righteousness. That *agape* may be a vice is a rather disconsoling thought for believers.

In concluding, I defend a species of just war theory inspired by Christian charity. The key to this defense comes in locating a host of traditional contrasts (e.g., judgment/mercy, defense of the innocent/embodiment of forgiveness) *within* love itself, rather than identifying love with one or the other pole exclusively. Such a view of love is not new, but it provides a helpful approach to the specific debate over *agape* and political violence.

I. STANLEY HAUERWAS AND THE PEACEABLE KINGDOM

Stanley Hauerwas is an indefatigable exponent of visionary ethics, in the best sense. He is rightly admired for helping to restore the centrality of virtue and imagination in Christian moral reflection: of primary import is who we are and what we can see, rather than which rules to follow or what results to generate. Somewhat more controversial is his commitment to pacifism. This commitment springs from an inspiration (Judeo-Christian Scripture) and from an exasperation (modern secular society). Because the first is by far the more basic, however, his position represents a eucharistic rather than a tactical nonviolence. It looks first to Christ, only secondarily to consequences.

The redemptive self-sacrifice of Jesus on the cross frees his disciples from the need to use coercion to protect or further their interests, according to Hauerwas. The world at large knows not the reality of God's grace and therefore believes it must employ violence to survive; Christians trust otherwise. Knowing themselves to be creatures of the Most High, in need of and granted forgiveness, Christians are able to relinquish control of their lives and of history for a more "adventurous" vocation, love of God and neighbor.

> Jesus proclaims peace as a real alternative, because he has made it possible to rest—to have the confidence that our lives are in God's hands. . . . We can rest in God because we are no longer driven by the assumption that we must be in control of history, that it is up to us to make things come out right.[1]

At the center of Christian ethics is the imitation of Christ, which is facilitated by the Biblical stories of his life, death, and resurrection. Appropriation of these narratives—recognizing them to be true and forming our lives by them—develops personal virtues and communal traditions which, in turn, allow the church to be a peaceable witness to the world. The church is able to welcome the stranger and generally to live without fear because it has glimpsed the justice and mercy of God's kingdom. Conversely, because they belong to the heavenly city, Christians can never be at home in any earthly state. All states, especially modern secular ones, are founded on powers and resentments foreign to a covenant community, thus the church "stands as a political alternative to every nation, witnessing to the kind of social life possible for those who have been formed by the story of Christ."[2] Christians are "resident aliens,"[3] in whatever culture they live.

Although he speaks of the faith community's necessary "separation" from the world, Hauerwas insists that he is not offering an ethic of withdrawal. "I have no interest in legitimating and/or recommending a withdrawal of Christians or the church from social or political affairs. I simply want them to be there as Christians and as church."[4] Such disclaimers repeatedly make the point that although the Christian's first institutional loyalty is to the church, he or she nonetheless constructively engages the temporal powers. In fact, it is exactly in living faithfully to God and the confessing community that individual Christians best serve their respective states: they inspire by example of their extraordinary love. "[The confessing] church knows that its most credible form of witness (and the most 'effective' thing it can do for the world) is the actual creation of a living, breathing, visible community of faith."[5] This much is clear and cogent.

Less clear, however, is how these claims relate to the evaluation of concrete social institutions designed to restrain violence, such as armies, police forces, law courts, and prisons. With respect to liberal institutions in particular, Hauerwas displays two tendencies that are not always distinguished. At times his insistence that the church remain true to its traditions and to the example of Jesus serves to distance liberalism by distancing *all* (secular) political arrangements. The message here is a bracingly prophetic one: all temporal structures and ideologies are of relative and secondary importance, and only if Christians keep this in mind may they contribute significantly to "the nations."[6] Sometimes the best way to realize an end is not to aim at it directly or to value it too highly, and Hauerwas reminds us that this applies to federal government as well as to personal friendship. At other times, however, he brings liberal institutions under specific and sustained attack, as though he has something better in mind *qua political economy*. Not only is liberalism and its distinctive way of coping with conflict not to be identified with the kingdom, for Hauerwas it is not even compatible with striving for the kingdom. Pluralism and the balance of power are not, even now, the norms of a good polity.[7] This is troubling because by jumping back and forth between the general and the particular thesis, between prophesy and partisan politics, he appears to hit and run without accountability. Thus, one finds Hauerwas saying simultaneously that the church *is* a social ethic, but that it must also *have* a social ethic; that it *does not need* a particular theory of government, but that it also *has a stake in* a limited state.[8] This leaves the political implications of Christian pacifism unclear and as such is frustrating for sympathizer and critic alike.

The problem, as Hauerwas realizes, is that responsible political engagement that wishes to avoid withdrawal cannot be purely negative or anachronistic: it must have a consistent vision of what it is for as well as what it is against, including how to govern a modern society in which everyone is sinful but not everyone is of the same race, creed, party, or sex. If Hauerwas's point is that the church ought not to subordinate itself to or to pattern itself after a violent secular polis, the proper response is to note that this is precisely what liberalism at its best is designed to allow groups to do.[9] If, in contrast, Hauerwas's point is that liberal democracy is unacceptable even *qua* theory of statecraft, then he owes it to his readers to elaborate and defend a viable alternative to its various institutions, especially those designed to cope with conflict. In fact, Hauerwas must offer alternatives to *all* political structures (liberal or otherwise) which depend on force to govern.

Hauerwas's response here, as indicated, is that "[t]he most creative social strategy we [Christians] have to offer is the church. Here we show the world a manner of life the world can never achieve through social coercion or governmental action."[10] But this suggests, after all, a rather decisive "either/or" between church and state. Hauerwas does not advocate political withdrawal for its own sake, but what he does advocate partially entails it. Not all politics is based on state killing or coercion, as he notes, so a commitment to nonviolence does not dictate complete abstention from political involvement. Yet by the same token nonviolence alone is not an adequate philosophy of government.[11] We may say "Amen" to the desire to preserve religious integrity against the hegemony of worldly politics. But we still need to know a good deal about concrete means and ends. Who should hold public office and on what basis; who may own what and how much or how little; with whom may we associate and under what conditions? More important for present purposes: Who should be imprisoned and for what reasons; how is civic order to be maintained against domestic and foreign threats; etc.? These are not the only questions facing modern society; but if Christians are not responsible for any of this, then in effect we do have an ethic of withdrawal.

Hauerwas rightly wants to avoid what he calls "the false Niebuhrian dilemma of whether to be in or out of the world, politically responsible or introspectively irresponsible,"[12] but to note that "[t]he church's only concern is *how* to be in the world, in what form, for what purpose" is but to ask the crucial question not yet to answer it.[13] It is best, I believe, just to acknowledge that an implication of Christian pacifism is that believers must refrain from participating in the army, police forces, and probably much of electoral politics. Admittedly, this only amounts to a charge of "impracticality" if one already assumes that practicality is measured largely in secular terms: e.g., preservation of life, liberty, and property. But there are a number of important challenges facing eucharistic pacifism, even on its own terms.

As I have indicated, Hauerwas's version does not look first to consequences, so it is not to be confused with utilitarianism. But talk of rights and duties is also alien to its interpretation of the Bible, so deontology is not its mode either. Though it has medieval antecedents, the language of natural rights is a modern development, first coming into its own only with the Enlightenment. Hauerwas largely cuts himself off from such developments in political philosophy, but this is a mixed blessing. It allows him to escape critiques of in-principle pacifism as a misconstrual of the logic of rights, for example, but it also rules out enlisting contemporary analyses of rights as support for Christian social reform. Certainly no appeal to the right of self-defense or to the duty to defend others against unjust attack can have a decisive place for Hauerwas, but neither can most claims to liberty or equal justice, since these presuppose the calculation of countervailing interests. Moreover, if Jesus's injunction to "resist not evil" (Mt. 5:39) is taken nonliterally, so as to permit *nonviolent* resistance, then already a strict obedience to Christ is itself compromised. As Paul Ramsey emphasized, a Biblical pacifist must explain, without primary reference to rights or duties, why the line is drawn at nonviolence and not at nonresistance.[14]

Such explanation has been attempted, of course. Some Christian pacifists aver that certain forms of coercion (e.g., economic boycotts) are compatible with respect for other people as free agents and thus with the heart of Jesus's teaching. These forms are thought not to include violence, however, because this (especially when lethal) inevitably treats others as objects only.[15] Apart from the rather odd elevation of autonomy, here the debatable assumption by pacifists is that it is impossible to distinguish between justifying violent resistance to evil and justifying hatred of one's enemies. Love never hates or objectifies, seeking always the good of the other, but this leaves open the question of whether even lethal force might not sometimes be loving. Hauerwas's own defense of pacifism is often deft, particularly when it seeks to unmask various forms of political idolatry. But the basic issue remains: Does the logic of Christlike love itself dictate refusal of all resort to violence? We may begin to answer this question by turning to the work of Reinhold Niebuhr.

II. REINHOLD NIEBUHR AND PROPHETIC CHRISTIANITY

In Reinhold Niebuhr's view, "prophetic Christianity" is distinctive for maintaining a tension between immanence and transcendence, between a genuine concern for history and the natural order and a recognition that full redemption of that order comes from God and only at the end of history. If we lose sight of the fact that God is creator of the world, we tend to deny the meaningfulness and (original) goodness of temporal reality; if we forget that God is also the world's judge and redeemer, we tend to a pantheistic complacency. Truly prophetic faith, in contrast, recognizes that ultimate meaning can be exclusively identified with neither temporality nor eternity. The kingdom is "both here and not yet."

This attempt to live between the extremes of naturalism and otherworldliness defines Niebuhr's genius, but it moves him to say some quite paradoxical things, especially about Jesus Christ:

> [Jesus's] Kingdom of God is always a possibility in history, because its heights of pure love are organically related to the experience of love in all human life, but it is also an impossibility in history and always beyond every historical achievement. Men living in nature and in the body will never be capable of the sublimation of egoism and the attainment of the sacrificial passion, the complete disinterestedness which the ethic of Jesus demands. The social justice which Amos demanded represented a possible ideal for society.[16]

Interpretation of these words is subject to the very same problems and temptations faced by prophetic religion itself: we want to eliminate the paradox by ignoring one or the other pole of opposition. Thus, some commentators (e.g., Hauerwas[17]) accent the "impossibility" of Christian love, at least on the group level, and construe Niebuhr as saying that we must simply leave *agape* behind as a political ideal, favoring justice instead. Yet this misses his exquisite, sometimes tortured ambivalence. Also simplistic is any move which so accents the "possibility" of Christian love that politics is believed compatible with nonviolence and pacifism. The second reading is not very tempting as Niebuhr-exegesis, but the first is not altogether implausible. Niebuhr himself is not always consistent here. He too lapses occasionally into a philosophical contrast of the horns of the dilemma (suggesting an either/or), when faith demands accepting the contradiction as such (affirming both/and). In *Moral Man and Immoral Society*, for example, he writes:

> A rational ethic aims at justice, and a religious ethic makes love the ideal. A rational ethic seeks to bring the needs of others into equal consideration with those of the self. The religious ethic ... insists that the needs of the neighbor shall be met, without a careful computation of relative needs.[18]

Given his frequent claims that *agape* is nonresisting while politics is built on the balance of power of resisting forces, it is tempting indeed to ascribe to Niebuhr a sharp (almost cynical) discontinuity between love and justice, Christianity and politics. But this too easily resolves the central paradox of prophetic morality. In spite of himself, Niebuhr forgets at times that Christian ethics must combine both horizontal and vertical referents, as when he asserts that "neither natural impulses nor social consequences are taken into consideration" by

Jesus and that we are to love all our neighbors "not because they are equally divine, but because God loves them equally."[19] This is contrary to his own best insights concerning God as both creator and redeemer. To contend that moral universalism is based *solely* on our reflection of or obligation to "the loving will of God,"[20] rather than also on the nature and excellences of our fellow creatures, is to do violence to the Biblical doctrine of creation in which a loving Deity makes human beings in His own Image, and calls them "good."

Reminiscent of Kierkegaard, Niebuhr's characteristic trope is to resist all reductive gambits and to depict Christianity paradoxically. The law of love, for example, is both a cogent norm and an impractical ideal; it is neither simply possible nor simply impossible, but rather an "impossible possibility."[21] Those with a philosophical turn of mind will immediately pounce on this as contradictory, and so it is on one level. Niebuhr's point, however, is that prophetic religion avails itself of myths and mysteries which transcend philosophical reason. Any rationalistic attempt to dismiss the love command as impractical and therefore irrelevant, and any romantic attempt to preach it as fully realizable and therefore straightforwardly binding, evacuates Christian piety of its distinctive tension. Faith believes in a higher unity, a transcendent Personality, who, despite current appearances will ultimately reconcile the contradictions of our moral lives. Because complete reconciliation takes place only at the end of time, all political utopias are relativized; but because the stage is decisively set within time, political engagement is ethically essential. "Prophetic Christianity . . . demands the impossible," and yet "the prophetic tradition in Christianity must insist on the relevance of the ideal of love to the moral experience of mankind *on every conceivable level*."[22] Anything else encourages a less than mature faith and is founded on a less than adequate anthropology.

Niebuhr's depiction of prophetic religion is deeply informed by his Augustinian-Kierkegaardian conception of human nature. The various forms of theological liberalism, naturalism, and idealism all fail to understand "that though man always stands under infinite possibilities and is potentially related to the whole of existence, he is, nevertheless, and will remain, a creature of finiteness."[23] Man himself is a paradox, a tense unity of opposites which might be called "an impersonal personality." Men and women are compounded of body and soul so as to be free yet determined by physical and biological circumstances, invariably sinful yet capable of a degree of self-transcendence and reformation. Both horns of the dilemma of selfhood must be grasped simultaneously, thus a qualitatively similar dynamic appears on the individual as on the collective level. Earthly moral perfection is out of reach, but rigorous moral responsibility is unavoidable because fallen humanity is still made in the Image of God. No creature is capable of the righteousness of Christ, but anticipation of adoption as Son or Daughter compels upon every individual the *Imitatio Christi*, the absolute rule of *agape*.

What may be said by way of criticism of Niebuhr's position? In a phrase, I think that he is less sensitive than he ought to be to the fact that he seeks to "eff" the ineffable. (S.K. was more self-conscious about the limits of his "irrationalism"; Christianity appeared absurd to his pseudonyms, but not to the believer himself.) One must distinguish, for example, between an ideal itself being contradictory or counter-productive and our pursuit of it being flawed, even inevitably flawed. If, though our moral efforts are halting, the ideal itself is theoretically and practically appropriate, then it still makes sense to *try* to realize that ideal. If, on the other hand, it is unintelligible or destructive even to strive for the ideal, then in what sense is it still a valid measure of success or failure? Niebuhr's use of the language of paradox fails adequately to distinguish between these two scenarios. He does speak in places of the eschatological overcoming of the oppositions of human existence; but he does not discriminate rigorously enough between an apparent or temporary contradiction and a real and enduring one, thus inviting the charge of irrationalism or various reductionist readings designed to avoid this very charge. Niebuhr's own retreats from the prophetic, mentioned earlier, are due to the failure to make clear that ultimately faith does not oppose, but rather completes, reason, and love does not contradict, but rather fulfills, justice.

Is it possible to formulate Niebuhr's insights into Christian ethics so as to avoid the problems just described? I believe so, and the cue may be taken from Niebuhr himself. At his most lucid, Niebuhr acknowledges that love and justice, Christianity and politics, are not in their natures opposed. In these contexts he supplements (or replaces) the language of "paradox" with that of "approximation." "[A] religion which holds love to be the final law of life stultifies itself if it does not support equal justice as a political and economic approximation of the ideal of love."[24] The key word in this sentence is "final." Love and justice may *seem within history* to be contradictory, due to human ignorance; they may temporarily *be* so, due to human sin. But if they are forever and irremediably at odds, even *beyond history* and *independently of sin*, then a stark dualism prevails in which it is absurd to affirm both love and justice and in which eternity breaks covenant with time. Such Manichaeanism cannot be Niebuhr's considered opinion any more than it could be Augustine's.

Just as faith may appear *contra rationem* while actually being *supra rationem*, so love may appear *contra justitiam* while actually being *supra justitiam*. The essential distinction is between a truth which cannot be fully rationalised (and thus calls for myths) and a garden variety absurdity which is against reason (and thus necessarily false). Niebuhr never backs away from the claim:

> Love is both the fulfillment and the negation of all achievements of justice in history. . . . the achievements of justice in history may rise in indeterminate degrees to find their fulfillment in a more perfect love and brotherhood; but each new level of fulfillment also contains elements which stand in contradiction of perfect love.[25]

But the hard edge of this paradox is softened when we note that the qualifying phrase "in history" is repeated twice. If these phrases do not mitigate the contradiction of love's being both fulfillment and negation, justice's being both approximation and contradiction, then Niebuhr is simply a misologist. I urge the more charitable reading.

Niebuhr is neither misologist nor relativist. Such charges fail to grasp that, for him, Christian belief is finally beyond paradox, even as Christian ethics is beyond tragedy.[26] On the latter score, though he claims to reject "absolute standards," Niebuhr does not merely leave love behind for the sake of political expediency. Indeed, love itself tends to become an absolute, however much it may elude discursive articulation:

> For the Christian the love commandment must be made relevant to the relativities of the social struggle, even to hazardous and dubious relativities.[27]

and

> [Man's] freedom consists in a capacity for self-transcendence in infinite regression. There is therefore no limit in reason for either his creativity or his sin. There is no possibility of giving a rational definition of a just relation between man and man or nation and nation short of a complete love in which each life affirms the interests of the other. . . . *Love is the only final structure of freedom.*[28]

The problem here is not with irrationalism or nihilism, but with a potentially too easy consequentialism in which love, claiming to transcend justice, actually falls below it in embracing too violent means to political ends. Enter Paul Ramsey.

III. PAUL RAMSEY AND LOVE TRANSFORMING JUSTICE

Paul Ramsey is the worthy inheritor of Reinhold Niebuhr's prophetic legacy, as well as a faithful steward working interest on the principal. Ramsey's signal contribution is to retrieve Augustine's view of charity and in its light to elaborate the love/justice relation so as to avoid both Niebuhr's hard paradoxes and his tendency to soft consequentialism. At the heart of Ramsey's view of Christian politics is a principled love which seeks innovatively to restrain evil.

> [S]ometimes love does what justice requires and assumes its rules as norms, sometimes love does more than justice requires but never less, and sometimes love acts in a quite different way from what justice alone can enable us to discern to be right. When one's own interests alone are at stake, the Christian governs himself by love and resists not one who is evil. When his neighbor's need and the just order of society are at stake, the Christian still governs himself by love and suffers no injustice to be done nor the order necessary to earthly life to be injured.[29]

An adequate account of love avoids contradictions, for these may contribute to an unduly pessimistic view of human nature and thus to an impoverished view of moral responsibility. Love is not left behind on the political plane in favor of natural justice, nor does it stand in an irrational tension with it. Love may sometimes assert its autonomy and transcend (but not violate) natural categories, but it characteristically both informs and transforms justice by simultaneously altering its motive and placing limits on its means. With respect to motive, we are to will the good for all creatures for whom Christ died—friend and foe, guilty and innocent, alike—thus vengeance and the unchecked will to power are ruled out. The desire to protect the innocent from unjust attack *is* a part of love's inspiration, however. Thus, at least on the corporate level, impassivity and nonresistance are also ruled out. With respect to means, because effectively willing the good for the innocent neighbor may sometimes require the use of violent force, just wars are a possibility, according to Ramsey. But because unbridled lethal means would themselves contradict the end of love, poisoning wells and obliteration bombing (all forms of direct attack on the innocent) are *not* a possibility. This last insight accounts for the centrality and inviolability of the principle of discrimination (noncombatant immunity) in Ramsey's account of *jus in bello*, and it represents a corrective to Niebuhr's occasional readiness to embrace a too purely utilitarian approach to political means.[30]

Behind Ramsey's axiology lies his eschatology. Just as the belief that temporal life is not the greatest good leads some Christians to in-principle pacifism (out of a denial of self), so this same belief leads Ramsey to the just use of force to restrain evil (out of love of neighbor). Although it is hard to settle this dispute on purely theological grounds, I believe that Ramsey has a powerful case. On the face of it, it is logically odd to derive an in-principle prohibition on killing from a denial of the absolute value of living. To admit that some things are in themselves more important than temporal existence suggests that both living and dying (one's own and others') may be means to a greater good. Short of doing something evil in itself (*malum in se*), even killing may be a proportionate means precisely because death is not the worst calamity. Taking the life of an aggressor to defend the innocent may serve both parties, even as God destroyed Sodom to deliver it from itself. Though a "hard saying," it may sometimes be better/juster to be killed than be permitted to become a successful murderer, and better/juster forcefully to restrain evil than to allow the political triumph of the murderous. Because I can and should forgive him, I may be called not to defend *myself* by taking another's life; but I cannot forgive *for others* who may come under his unjust attack. With fear and trembling, I may repeat Saint Augustine: "as it is not benevolent to give a man help at the expense of some greater benefit he might receive, so it is not innocent to spare a man at the risk of his falling into graver sin."[31]

Ramsey teaches us to avoid the assumption that all war is unmitigated moral failure, at most a prudent second-best that we engage in because we are incapable of doing what love demands on the political level. The belief that all war results either because we try and fail to avoid it or because we fail even to try, is inadequate. All war is evil in the sense of being destructive and in itself undesirable, but not all war (much less all politics) is wicked or to be avoided. Reinhold Niebuhr's comments on love and justice can contribute to misunderstanding here. To the extent that he *seems* on occasion to say that on the group level we must leave behind the ideal of selfless love (*agape*) and settle for justice (*suum cuique*), he invites a romantic response. "Let us not compromise with the world but cling to what we know is right, no matter how difficult or costly" is the call of some Christian pacifists. If, as evident in Ramsey, love and justice are not finally in opposition, however—conceding that love itself may demand different things in different circumstances—then any necessary link between Christian virtue and political nonviolence is far less plausible. In fact, the issue then becomes whether, by failing to protect innocents from unjust attack, pacifism represents not admirable perfectionism but dereliction of duty.

Ramsey has sought to distance the phrase "love monism" as a characterization of his position,[32] but whatever the terminology, he improves on Niebuhr by avoiding the latter's occasional drift into dualism. Ramsey's insistence on "love-informed justice" and on justifying actions "in terms of countervailing requirements of *agape*" locates the standard Niebuhrian tensions between self/others and conscience/ power within love itself.[33] *Love does not choose between justice and mercy, for these two goods are internal to agape.* Though substantive tensions may remain, this means we should not flinch from calling Ramsey's corpus a defense of the "loving war tradition." (Just war is an "alien work," but still a work, of love.) It also suggests, somewhat ironically, that he shares to a degree Joseph Fletcher's conviction that justice is "love distributed." It may be that on the interpersonal level a loving distribution is often all one way, thus talk of justice tends not to arise; but this is still a limiting case of justice, at least not an injustice. In Ramsey's view, the in-principle pacifist is not holding out for the moral ideal (much less for supererogation) and merely disagreeing with the just war theorist over what is feasible in a fallen world; rather, he or she is disagreeing on the ideal itself.

We are no doubt imperfect and incapable of acting always in love. But to say with Niebuhr that "the world is only partially amenable to the strategy of the cross," is not to say (rightly) that we are only partially capable of realizing love's strategy, but rather to say (relevantly) that love's strategy is not always noncoercive. *It is not that in the political sphere we leave love behind, but rather that here love leaves (or may leave) nonviolence behind.* For a proponent of *bellum justum*, the question is not whether love sometimes permits violent restraint of evil (it does), but whether it ever categorically demands it. In the latter case, in-principle pacifism must seem less than fully responsible; but to the extent that mercy is an ineliminable aspect of love, it is hard to defend an *imperative* to violence as an outgrowth of Christian charity (even in the direst situation).

A further clarification of the responsiblity of and to love may be had by reviewing the work of Juan Segundo.

IV. JUAN SEGUNDO AND LIBERATED ETHICS

Juan Segundo's thoughts on "Christian love" and "political violence" may first be approached via the adjectives rather than the nouns in those two phrases. What Segundo thinks about love and violence is more deeply and self-consciously conditioned by his account of Christianity, politics, and their interrelation than is the case with the other theologians I have discussed, with the possible exception of Niebuhr. This is not an unforseen implication of his work but part of its basic intent. Segundo's conception of and commitment to human liberation, especially as these are worked out in *The Liberation of Theology*, prevent him from giving *a priori* accounts of love and violence which might then "prove" that they exclude one another on purely logical grounds. In his view, there is no ahistorical essence of love which might entail nonviolence, just as there is no ahistorical essence of violence which might entail nonlove. In any concrete context, the theological meaning of love and violence will depend on our understanding of a host of contingent facts, including the nature of the church, the state, the economy, and theology itself.

Let me begin, therefore, by briefly describing Segundo's views on theology and liberation. My chief concern is to ask whether his work represents an advance over—a liberation of—that of Hauerwas, Niebuhr, or Ramsey. My answer will be that, for the most part, the later Segundo (i.e., the author of *The Liberation of Theology*) falls short of the insights of these other writers as well as those of his own former self (i.e., the author of *A Theology for Artisans of a New Humanity*).

Early in *The Liberation of Theology*, Segundo advances a recurrent thesis: "We must realize that there is no such thing as an autonomous, impartial, academic theology floating free above the realm of human options and biases."[34] This means that any belief system which claims universal validity or unmediated access to atemporal reality is false and an obstacle to solving real problems: it encourages an empty, and inherently conservative, spirituality. Human life is characterized by such complexity and ambiguity that choices must be made without benefit of neutral perspectives or absolute rules. Not even Holy Scripture can escape being conditioned by time and place.

> [T]he Bible is not the discourse of a universal God to a universal man. Partiality is justified because we must find, and designate as the word of God, that *part* of divine revelation which *today*, in the light of our concrete historical situation, is most useful for the liberation to which God summons us.[35]

Because our social situation is constantly changing and presenting us with new challenges, our theology (exegesis, sacraments, ecclesiology, etc.) must also change and adapt, or else die. To the extent that classical theology pictures an immutable and impassive God and fixed and incorrigible dogmas, it denies the need for openness to history and thus frustrates the liberation of actual human beings. It contributes often to an otherworldliness leading to political quietism and moral insensitivity. But, the later Segundo contends, "There is no doubt that the picture of God in the Bible is a very different one, presenting us with a passionate God who suffers along with his people. . . ."[36] In this age in which "politics is the fundamental human dimension," theology is deeply implicated in every critical social choice, either for good or for ill. If it would be liberating, Christian theology must come to grips with the social sciences (especially sociology and economics) and realize that to preach an apolitical love is a "distortion" of the gospel message itself. Partially correcting the Medellin documents of the Latin American bishops, Segundo suggests that political commitment to the oppressed and appropriation of the gospel message go hand in hand, each supporting the other, although the hearing of the gospel usually comes first temporally.[37]

As we have seen, Paul Ramsey places primary emphasis on the nature of Christian love, allowing it to define political ends (justice) and limit political means (discrimination and proportionality). Some forms of liberation theology (e.g., Hugo Assmann's) simply reverse this ordering, making political praxis prior to and interpretive of the content of faith, but the later Segundo rejects such a move. He says explicitly that "no one can enter into the revolutionary process without forming some idea for himself of the goal of the process and the proper means to be used to achieve it."[38] For Segundo, priority cannot be given to political commitment; but it is also clear that no single religious creed can be the immutable touchstone of all action. Creed and commitment are related dialectically, such that political ends (liberation) and means (revolution and violence) do *help* to define and limit the nature of love. Ramsey believes that love rules out some things categorically as *malum in se* (e.g., counter-population warfare), but in *The Liberation of Theology* Segundo commits himself to no such absolutes. Variables of time and place, theology and history, may prompt us to alter even our most fundamental beliefs and entrenched patterns of behavior.

The later Segundo's analysis of the relation between faith and ideologies brings many of the above themes to a head. He clearly wishes to distinguish the two notions. Faith "claims to possess an *objectively* absolute value," while ideologies have no such *"pretensions"*; faith embodies the "permanent and unique" content of divine revelation, while ideologies represent "changing" reflections on particular means and ends and are "bound up with different historical circumstances."[39] Yet in the end this looks to be a distinction without a difference. For him, no concrete content can be given to faith, not even *agape*. "If someone were to ask me what I have derived from my faith-inspired encounter as a clear-cut, absolute truth that can validly give orientation to my concrete life, then my honest response should be: nothing."[40]

Segundo (unlike Hauerwas) sees some forms of political violence as compatible with Biblical faith and the example of Christ. He (like Ramsey) construes Jesus's admonitions to "turn the other cheek," "resist not evil," and forswear the sword as tactical rather than in-principle, as historically conditioned expressions rather than the essence of love. While Ramsey thinks that some moral deeds and rules *are* essential to love, however, the later Segundo's contextualism leaves any enduring content to love extremely hard to specify. The difference between Ramsey's and Segundo's view occasionally resembles that between rule-agapism and act-agapism,[41] but it actually goes deeper. At times, *agape* itself seems for the later Segundo not to be permanently valid. He endorses the opinion that "The only perduring rule is that one should try to display the most effective and wide-ranging love possible in a given situation," but he also allows that "the concrete kind of love proclaimed by Jesus constitutes an *ideology*."[42] And this is the source of my primary criticism.

Especially in his later work, Segundo is so concerned not to give comfort to the forces of theological or political reaction that love and covenant fidelity become devoid of content. Violence is not ruled out by Christian faith, but we are hard pressed to know when, where, how, or why it might be ruled in. No action or instrument is evil in itself; thus "We cannot decide whether love or egotism is at work by examining the means employed."[43] But are there no limits then to what might be done in the name of God? May we lie, steal, torture, or murder even for temporal goals? These questions are especially urgent in light of the incipiently totalitarian claim noted above that "politics is the fundamental human dimension" and the related notion that "the only truth is liberation itself."[44] One does not have to be an advocate of the status quo or of otherworldliness to want more detailed criteria for moral judgment, criteria that are consistent and informed (however fallibly) by Scripture, reason, and tradition. The observation that God sides with the oppressed, though important, is not a sufficient basis for discriminating ethically between complex political means and ends. It suffers from the same moral ambiguity as the Marxist claim that history favors the proletariat: unqualified, it may give license to the oppressed to become oppressors.[45] One may adopt what the early Segundo calls "an evolutionary outlook"[46] and acknowledge the provisional character of all ideology, but to contend that no belief can apprehend a permanent truth is to assume either the unattainability of truth *per se* or the perpetual flux of all reality, including God. Both are substantive ideas and require argument; neither follows from human finitude or fallibility alone.

The later Segundo's emphasis on the importance and open-endedness of human choice flirts with an extreme form of moral voluntarism. With respect to the parable of the Good Samaritan, he writes:

> Jesus does not end up his parable saying that every human being *is* our neighbor. His point is that we can make any given human being our neighbor if we take advantage of the countless opportunities offered us in life. That is a very different point.[47]

But one must not confuse loving someone in a particular way because they are your *near* neighbor with their *becoming* your neighbor *simpliciter* only because you *choose* to love them. Segundo's exegesis of the Good Samaritan blurs the fact that I may recognize other human beings as creatures of God, all of *equal value*, and yet not take this as demanding for them *identical treatment*.[48] His discussion of "deutero-learning" (learning how to learn) is a welcome contribution to pedagogy; but in the absence of substantive things *to* learn, its final significance is ambiguous at best.

If, in effect, we must view the whole of faith as one more radically contingent ideology, then theology's liberation is virtually indistinguishable from its demise. *The Liberation of Theology* laudably deflates dogmatism and sectarianism, which is surely its main point. But to the extent that it embraces in the process an extreme consequentialism cum contextualism—the end justifies the means, and there are few, if any, permanently valid ends—it threatens to undermine both love and justice. Segundo is aware of the dangers associated with many of his remarks. But this does not alter the fact that even on a generous reading his position offers minimal support for the principles and institutions necessary for the survival of morality and politics themselves. It is hard not to conclude that in *The Liberation of Theology*, Segundo purchases political relevance at too high a price, fostering not liberation but a relativism in which love and justice may be left behind.[49] He is more clearly committed to the ineliminable centrality of love in his earlier work, *A Theology for Artisans of a New Humanity*:

> Christ used two different formulas to describe the road which leads to salvation. When he was referring in general to God's judgment on humanity, the thing required of man was simply real love. When he referred to the function of the Church and

spoke about it to the apostles, he tied in salvation with faith and the sacraments. . . . Christ was talking about the same thing in both texts: real love.[50]

"*Efficacious* love is the only demand imposed by Jesus for all time," Segundo writes in a subsequent volume of *A Theology for Artisans*; and although he repeatedly emphasizes there the evolutionary character of Christian morality, he also insists that the most adequate interpretation of the gospel is one in which both in-principle pacifism and a purely contentless or utilitarian love is overcome in favor of a "complex" view of how and why love may sometimes employ violent tactics.[51] Segundo nowhere provides the sort of helpful details that Ramsey does (e.g., on discrimination and proportionality), but the early Segundo's position is decidedly more nuanced (and defensible) than *The Liberation of Theology*.

What the later Segundo says about minorities and the Christian church is very difficult indeed to defend. A vanguard must "relieve the masses of the burden of relative options," he maintains;[52] and although the former are not to constitute an abusive "elite," for practical reasons they must liberate the many in ways beyond their capacity to effect or even appreciate. What are we to make of this? Christianity's aiming at the masses only seems *im*practical when its goal is considered to be most fundamentally political, which is debatable. But even more troubling is the analogy Segundo suggests between members of the religious vanguard and medical doctors.[53] With this, Christianity becomes a complex intellectual skill beyond the reach of most of us. A physician serves others by restoring health, not by imparting medical knowledge itself, thus a basic inequality perdures between doctor and patient. Christian faith, in contrast, serves others via self-communication. Grace leaves both speaker and hearer, agent and patient, in possession of the same end (Jesus Christ). If Segundo wishes to avoid elitism, different images are called for.[54]

V. SEPARATISM, APOLOGY, AND POLITICAL IDOLATRY

When the views of the four theologians just discussed are placed squarely within the long and pendulum-like debate between Christian Separatism and Christian Apology—arguably as old as Paul, fully underway by the time of Tertullian—we are in a position to appreciate their strengths and weaknesses. If it is hard to keep Apology from deteriorating into compromise with, or even complicity in, idolatry, it is equally hard to keep Separatism from collapsing into moral irrelevance or even immoral retreat. At his best, Hauerwas tries not to betray Christian virtue into an irresponsible ethic of withdrawal; but neither at their best do Niebuhr, Ramsey, and the early Segundo simply sell out to the secular interests of the state. Because Ramsey wishes the church to foster "the ethos out of which statesmanship may come," Hauerwas charges him with offering, finally, a kind of "cultural Christianity."[55] But this charge underestimates the prophetic dimension of Ramsey's work; more critically, it is hard to see how anything less than such ethos-building can fail to be hopelessly aloof and sectarian. Ramsey assumes, in Hauerwas's words, that "the first subject of Christian ethics is how to sustain the moral resources of American society."[56] The adjective "first" is unfair, however. As Ramsey says (appropriately, in his first book):

> while Christian love cannot get along without seeking to find from any source the best possible social ethic, such love remains *dominant* and *free* in any partnership it enters. . . . Christian love ought never to be identified with or permanently bound to any particular program or stipulation for action, however important.[57]

Just as Christian love is not to be directly equated with natural justice, the kingdom is not to be equated with the church, and the church is not to be equated with the state. But the first fruits of the kingdom must find expression in concrete ecclesiastical and political structures, even as *agape* often clothes itself in *justitia*. It is always possible to argue that God's will directs Christians away from *any* such expression, but in that case we should simply acknowledge that this implies sectarianism with a vengeance—the death of the prophetic tradition.

In his 1795 essay "Perpetual Peace," Immanuel Kant contends:

> The state of peace among men living side by side is not the natural state (*status naturalis*); the natural state is one of war. . . . A state of peace, therefore, must be *established*, for in order to be secured against hostility it is not sufficient that hostilities simply not be commited; and unless this security is pledged to each by his neighbor (*a thing that can occur only in a civil state*), each may treat his neighbor, from whom he demands this security, as an enemy.[58]

Peace must be established politically, according to Kant, and surely he is at least *partially* correct. Though it is often also the agent of injustice, the modern state is currently a necessary (though obviously not a sufficient) condition to *build* a tolerable peace on earth. The state and its institutions are not the only relevant agencies, nor the most important. For Christians, the community of the faithful is the primary vehicle of grace and thus the most salient social body. But a subscriber to just war theory believes that the political building of peace requires (or at least permits) various forms of state coercion: armies, national guards, police, prisons, etc. If, in contrast, pacifism means political separatism, this may itself breach the peace because absenting oneself from the social nexus inspires fear in others not similarly at liberty. As Augustine notes, "as long as the two cities [of God and earth] are commingled, [Christians] also enjoy the peace of Babylon."[59]

These facts seem to place the burden of proof on pacifists like Hauerwas. Hauerwas is not Rousseau, however, identifying peace with the state of nature, any more than Ramsey is Hobbes or Kant, embracing a similarly misleading equation for war. Both Christian theologians recognize that neither the longing for peace nor the avoidance of war may be our prime moral focus; fidelity to God is means and end. Both theologians eschew Enlightenment contract theory in favor of an evangelical vision of the church's responsibility in the larger human community; indeed, both share an eschatological faith that has recently united them against both secular ethical theory and their own Methodist Bishops' pastoral letter on nuclear war. Hauerwas observes: "it is Ramsey's and my common conviction that—contrary to the Bishops' claim [in "In Defense of Creation"]—the nuclear crisis has not posed questions of faith that point beyond just war or pacifism." He adds: "I (and Ramsey ...) urged the Bishops to avoid . . . 'survivalist' rhetoric, noting that what we must fear as Christians is not our deaths at the hands of an unjust aggressor but how as Christians we might serve the neighbor without resorting to unjust means."[60]

In any event, two complementary vices are possible here: (1) an inadequate appreciation of the rights and responsibilities of governments such that nearly all political activity is seen as profane and so legitimate means and ends of state are ruled out, and (2) an inadequate circumscription of these same rights and responsibilities such that nearly all political activity is baptized and so illegitimate means and ends are ruled in. Seldom is either error found in pure form, but (1) is sometimes approximated by Hauerwas, in spite of himself. In seeking to avoid secular chauvinism, he may discourage good and faithful people from entering politics, thus abandoning it to the barbarians. Though well aware of the dangers of idolatry and what he earlier called "the Christendom mentality,"[61] a Marxist version of error (2) haunts Juan Segundo's later work. The error is perhaps most visible, however, in the writing of the secular philosopher Michael Walzer. Walzer contends that when faced with an unjust threat to its survival—a "supreme emergency" that is both "close" and "serious"—a nation may "override" the normal rules of war and torture or directly kill the innocent in its own defense.[62] Such actions "dirty one's hands" morally, but they are politically necessary. These comments encourage unscrupulous people to stay in politics thus securing it for the barbarians.

With respect to *jus in bello*, Hauerwas and Walzer (and arguably the later Segundo) provide a graphic illustration of how right Ramsey has been all these years to insist on the ordered pairing of discrimination (noncombatant immunity) and proportionality (a positive cost-benefit analysis). These men miss the Ramseyan mean, which, in emphasizing the governance of love, is Niebuhr's prophetic faith rendered consistent and free of moral dilemmas.[63] Hauerwas expands discrimination so as to undo the combatant/noncombatant distinction and thereby radically contracts the proportionate activity of the state; Walzer allows *jus ad bellum* considerations to override discrimination and thereby permits murder in the name of national interest. Ramsey, in contrast, insists that discrimination and proportionality form both an ordered *pair* and an *ordered* pair in the economy of *agape*: neither one alone is sufficient and, though both are necessary, one does not even consider proportionality if discrimination cannot be satisfied.[64] One may not directly take innocent life even to ensure national survival, but one may restrain political aggression in a just cause. In short, *agape* is politically active but morally self-limiting.

Absence of violence is always an end, but proximately it is to be insisted upon *only as long as nothing of superior moral import (e.g., justice) is sacrificed*. We must distinguish carefully between a prideful or nationalistic self-assertion and love's defense of innocent others from unjust attack.[65] It may be that most wars do not accomplish the latter, but this is a factual question and thus cannot provide support for a categorical pacifism. Without a perfectly general principle, grounded in love, to settle disputes concerning whether and when to employ force, in-principle pacifism is by definition ruled out. Nonviolence can only be a rule of thumb for *agape*, what Ramsey calls a "summary rule" and others call a "prima facie duty."

This accent on context would not mean that *all* political judgments are relative or that there are no ethical absolutes, however. The principle of discrimination could still be viewed as absolute because in violating it one would be attacking that very value (love's defense of innocent life) seen to validate the use of the sword in the first place.

Just as it can never be correct to affirm a theoretical paradox, so it can never be correct to perform a practical perversity. Attempting to believe in a contradiction undermines all thought, just as attempting to act on a contradiction undermines all praxis. Segundo's work is troubling at times precisely because of its failure to appreciate the centrality of certain principles of justice—too much is put up for grabs at the same time.

Is there, in fact, anything about *agape* that rules out violence *a priori*, as a matter of consistency? This will depend in part upon how the term is translated, but the fact that *agape* is directed toward and received from both God and our neighbors makes uniform translation difficult. Between human beings, phrases such as "personal respect" and "equal regard" are plausible paraphrases.[66] Concerning God, these terms seem less appropriate—expressions such as "self-surrender" and "fidelity" being more so. In neither case, however, is it clear that all forms of violence are self-defeating or incompatible with love's ends. The shape of God's own justice and mercy, revealed in Scripture and in history, suggests that evil may sometimes be restrained by force. Violent love is not a contradiction in terms.

The difference between just war theory and pacifism is not adequately captured with reference to Apology vs. Separatism. Particularly in liberal democratic contexts, we do better to ask how to resolve (or at least understand) the tension, *internal to love itself*, between judgment and mercy. Consider, for example, the relation between killing a would-be murderer and allowing him or her to kill. The initial consequence in both cases is the same (a physical death), but the other moral factors (deontological and theological) are reckoned differently by the two traditions. Just war theory sees the murder of the innocent as an evil more to be prevented than the killing of a murderer (either subjectively or objectively "guilty") is an action to be avoided. Pacifism takes the opposite line, proposing that love tolerates a murder more readily than it kills anyone at all. Both agree that one may not murder to prevent deaths, even to prevent more murders, but this does not settle the basic dispute. My preference for the just war tradition must finally appeal to a preference for justice over peace in the narrow sense. The events associated with the war years 1940-45 imply that it is not always possible to achieve justice, or perhaps even to be fully loving, without the use of some violence. To make true peace we may sometimes have to unmake unjust war by main force, even while refusing to hate those who are our enemies and for whom Christ died. Put most pointedly, Christian violence may, *in extremis*, be the content of political love. (Just war may be an "alien work" of those "resident aliens" who call themselves Christians.) The key point, however, is that *the governing factor is love, not political violence per se—neither withdrawal from it nor participation in it.* If I cannot as a matter of fact employ violence, even in a just cause, without hating my neighbor (who though unjust continues to be God's creature), then pacifism is the only faithful alternative.

VI. MORAL CONFLICT AND PUTTING CHARITY FIRST

Let me intensify some of the problems discussed so far, in order finally to say something more positive about Biblical faith. In the Old Testament, *shalom* encompasses all those things that comprise right relation with God, our neighbors, and ourselves—including justice.[67] Most broadly, it implies full spiritual and bodily flourishing within community and as such is, for Christianity, both a Christological and an eschatological concept. Complete human wholeness, in which body and soul, desire and conscience, judgment and mercy, are at one, is both realized in Christ and generally awaits the end of history (cf. the images in Isaiah 2:1-4, 11:1-9). For those within time, there will be approximations and trade-offs; the lion does not yet eat straw like the ox. Not all of the components of *shalom* can be achieved simultaneously, though all are relevant. Duties to God may be in tension with commitments to others, and commitments to others may be at odds with duties to oneself. Genuine goods may sometimes come into conflict. One must sometimes sacrifice physical safety for moral integrity, for example, and ethical ambiguity, as well as weakness of will, is inseparable from historical existence.

As many have pointed out, then, the either/or represented by *shalom* and its opposite is not peace/war but faith/sin. "Shalomism" (faithful action in service to others) may often ally itself with nonviolence, but for their part the Old Testament prophets certainly did not understand war as categorically contrary to the will of God. Today the phrase "holy war" suggests a no-holds-barred fanaticism, a form of unbridled bellicism. But this is alien to the Biblical conception.[68] In fact, the prophetic understanding of holy war as a battle ordained, directed, *and limited* by God for His purposes stands in marked contrast to many of the "just" wars waged by nation states for political ends. God's own covenant fidelity (*hesed*) sets the standard here, and again such fidelity is a combination of judgment and mercy that is both active and self-limiting—both dynamic and kenotic.

The internal complexity of God's steadfast love, at least as we view it, makes a single, more specific criterion for the resolution of moral conflict impossible. Scripture allows that conflict situations (together with their attendant opportunities) will be with us until "justice and peace embrace" (cf. Psalm 85). But how dilemmatic may our social ethics be? In particular, may *agape* itself ever conflict with other basic moral obligations? On the possible competition between *agape* and other human potentials, Saint Paul articulates the normative Christian opinion:

> If I speak in the tongues of men and of angels, but have not love, I am a noisy gong or a clanging cymbal. And if I have prophetic powers, and understand all mysteries and all knowledge, and if I have all faith, so as to remove mountains, but have not love, I am nothing. If I give away all I have, and if I deliver my body to be burned, but have not love, I gain nothing. (I Corinthians 13:1-3)

Yet this passage asserts the deficiency of various goods *without agape*; it does not directly address the possible incompatibility of these goods *with agape*, the possible undermining of other values (moral and nonmoral) by love itself. If prophecy without love is nothing, prophecy *with* love may be worse than nothing, a cruel tyranny with totalitarian pretensions.

The extent to which *agape* may be incompatible with other values is worth exploring in some detail. Contemporary Christian ethicists rightly criticize the Enlightenment for too readily equating rationality with harmony, as though the disinterested calculation of social utility naturally leads to justice and general goodwill. But does *caritas* fare any better than *ratio* in this regard? Both pacifists and just war theorists may admit, *à la* Hume, that even extreme forms of violence need not be irrational. Instrumental reason often guided the perpetrators of the Nazi Holocaust, for example; and, partly in consequence, the cooly objective sadist is now a cultural stereotype. But it is not enough for Christian theologians to reply to what might loosely be called the "rationalism" common to Plato, Locke, and Bentham; for the pressing challenges to *agape* currently come from Nietzsche, Freud, and their heirs, as well as from elements of the liberal tradition stemming from Kant to John Rawls. For all their differences, these figures concur that certain forms of political violence—including some forms we would clearly want to oppose—have actually been prompted by the aspiration to universal benevolence. Love as motive for (public) immorality is much harder for Christians to take than malevolent reason.

There are three basic objections to Christian charity; at least two are ancient, but each has been elaborated with renewed vigor by postmodernist authors.

(1) *The Meritarian Objection*: If Nietzsche is correct, selfless love is little more than disguised or repressed hatred of the weak for the

strong. The desire to "edify" or "serve" or "commune with" the healthy is but the will to objectify them for one's own vengeful or anarchic purposes, while the will to "pity" the sick stunts one's own (and their) moral growth.[69] Christian charity thwarts the heroic virtues (e.g., courage in battle, contempt for weakness) in favor of a decadent egalitarianism, undercutting those hierarchies of power and authority that make for real cultural achievement. In *Civilization and Its Discontents*, Freud too doubts what Nietzsche calls "the value of the 'unegoistic'."[70] Freud argues that to love humanity in general is to slight those genuinely "worthy" or close to us (e.g., family and friends) who rightly claim our special loyalty in particular.[71]

(2) *The Naturalist Objection*: In addition to faulting *agape* as unjust, Freud also contends that it requires inordinate repression of natural needs and instincts and thus inevitably makes people petulant and unhappy. *Eros* and ego do not get their due when *agape* is extolled as the highest virtue, and this makes for malaise in a civilization and maladjustment in an individual. The attempt to be universally benevolent may seem to safeguard one against the loss of a particular loved object, but such "aim-inhibited" love finally calls for too massive a self-denial, if not self-delusion. The psychic toll is too high, and this leads in turn to social friction. More recently, Susan Wolf has expressed powerful naturalistic sentiments in maintaining that "moral perfection, in the sense of moral saintliness, does not constitute a model of personal well-being toward which it would be particularly rational or good or desirable for a human being to strive."[72] We wrongly impede the development of basic human potentials (e.g., the aesthetic), she believes, if we rigorously demand that love and/or justice overrule personal desire. Saintliness is personally and socially impoverishing.

(3) *The Liberal Objection*: We may once again look to Freud for a third criticism of *agape*: "When once the Apostle Paul had posited universal love between men as the foundation of his Christian community, extreme intolerance on the part of Christendom towards those who remained outside it became the inevitable consequence."[73] Quite generally, the secular liberal argues, Christian love generates a self-righteousness that encourages dogmatism and aggression. The theological virtues frequently move those who think they have them to extirpate those who supposedly do not have them. Though believers may feel commissioned to "save" others, the fact that this salvation may come in spite of the others' actual preferences means that agapists often end up "loving" those others to death (as in the Inquisition). Hence, it is no surprise that "bourgeois liberals" like Richard Rorty want to distance all talk of "true virtue" as inclining us to "bash

each others' heads in" for the sake of dominant goods (natural or supernatural) about which we can get no general agreement.[74]

However much they may differ among themselves, the meritarians, naturalists, and liberals I have referred to all agree that the world would be a more just or noble or at least satisfying place if we were to read Christian charity and universal benevolence off the list of virtues and to construct our moral selves around the notions of autonomy and self-fulfillment, if not robust self-assertion. In trying to love the neighbor with all our heart, mind, and strength—which may very well mean self-sacrificially, as in the case of Christ—we set an ideal either undesirable or impossible or both. It is better, the post modernist consensus runs, to cultivate a prudent attention to one's own wants and needs and to leave social ethics on a largely procedural basis, defining justice in contractual terms. This way we avoid both self-pity and overweening pride. Though the price is some personal alienation in the face of our radical freedom and a polite disinterest in the private fortunes of others, it is a price worth paying.

It is a troubling prospect that the connection between Christian love and human misery (including that associated with political violence) is *internal*—not an historical contingency that may be guarded against but a psychological and moral given that undermines both pacifism and just war theory to the extent that these appeal to *agape*. But what may the agapist say in response?

It is evident that the first and third objections lodged above tend to cancel each other out. Nietzsche's lament is that Christian charity is too inclusive and egalitarian—in a word, too liberal—to give free reign to the will to power and hence the rule of the dominant few. Rorty, on the other hand, fears that the theological virtues make one *il*liberal, disposed to squelch dissent and overly fond of moral hierarchies and priestcraft. Nietzsche considered Protestantism the worst form of Christianity, Roman Catholicism's decline into an even more decadent (because more Pauline) form of religiosity. Rorty, in contrast, takes Protestant anti-authoritarianism and antinomianism to the extreme. God is dead for Nietzsche and Rorty, as well as for Freud, but whereas Nietzsche would have the "overman" spurn Christian love in order to be pitiless and cruel,[75] Rorty (following Judith Shklar) would have the bourgeois democrat be *un*Christian precisely to avoid cruelty.[76]

Meritarian and liberal criticisms of Christian love work to negate each other, not by directly demonstrating each others' falsity but rather by highlighting the merely partial character of each others' truth. *Agape* can indeed slip into a consoling light-mindedness that shuns strong evaluations and the vulnerability of individual ties, especially sexual ones; *agape* may even degenerate into an intolerant hubris that draws invidious distinctions between "the saved" (us) and "the damned" (them). But these are vestigial forms of the virtue. "We have just enough religion to make us hate," wrote Swift, "but not enough to make us love one another."[77]

(1') *Response to the Meritarian Objection*: The meritarian indicts *agape* in part out of the false assumption that love is a limited resource—a fixed quantity of undifferentiated psychic energy, with family, friends, strangers, enemies, and finally one's self all competing to receive from one the largest portion. Saint Paul was acutely aware that personal loyalties can conflict, and Jesus himself counsels "hating" father, mother, sister, and brother as a precondition for following him. Yet the issue in both cases is not one of quantity of love but of priority among loves: if love of God and neighbor takes precedence, then the other relations may find their proper place. It is from the vantage of the cross, after all, that Christ endorses both maternal and filial affection: "Woman, behold, your son," he says to his mother (John 19:26), and "Behold, your mother," to the beloved disciple (19:27). Love is not a zero-sum game, with someone's gain inevitably entailing another's loss.

More specifically, there is nothing inherent in Christian love that rules out relations based on merit (e.g., friendship), even as there is nothing that requires intolerance of those who do not share a Christian worldview. Charity's point is rather that special relations are relativized: one loves friends, fellow-countrymen, etc. first of all as neighbors. In fact, as Kierkegaard emphasizes, *agape* makes special associations more stable, less subject to the vicissitudes of time, place, and personal preference because preceded by a commitment to God that transforms the associations into matters of conscience.[78] A conscientious commitment to the principle "Thou shalt love" can constitute, moreover, an exceptionally heroic morality, a saintliness equal in rigor to anything envisioned by Nietzsche.

Finally, and perhaps most importantly, meritarians such as Freud find Christian charity unjust or deluded only because they fail to recognize that love is both appreciative and productive of worth: it both "appraises" and "bestows" value, to use Irving Singer's terms. In *The Nature of Love*, Singer observes that "love creates a new value, one that is not reducible to the individual or objective value that something may also have. This further type of valuing [opposed to appraisal] I call bestowal.... Here it makes no sense to speak of verifiability.... For now it is the valuing alone that *makes* the value."[79] Singer sometimes overemphasizes the gratuitousness of love and underemphasizes the way in which being loved objectively improves the beloved. But bestowal is surely *part* of what all love (especially *agape*) entails. What to a strict meritarian looks unjust is in fact one of love's greatest mysteries: the gift of worthiness not based solely on another's utility. As Singer points out, "Freud . . . failed to understand how love exceeds appraisive modes of valuation."[80]

(2') *Response to the Naturalist Objection*: Against the naturalist, the agapist maintains that love of neighbor is never a sign of slavish weakness or world-hatred. Jesus repeatedly affirms the goodness of all facets of incarnate life; and only a gnostic Christ would long for death or the thwarting of natural abilities. The agapist simply believes that to live without *agape* is itself a frustration of our highest human potential. This priority may be interpreted in a weak and a strong sense.

"Weak agapism" holds that the value of charity always exceeds that of its competitors, so the duty to love always wins out in cases of conflict or trade-off. Charity remains one good among many, however; it is more urgent than, but still qualitatively similar to, other virtues and benefits. One can fully realize these other desiderata (e.g., courage, liberty), moreover, without being loving. "Strong agapism," on the other hand, defines *agape* as a (indeed, *the*) "metavalue"[81]: it both surpasses and grounds all other aspirations. For the "strong agapist," charity is first virtue—our finest habit as agents and our deepest need as patients—but it is also a necessary condition for the fulfillment of every other human excellence. Without *agape*, nothing of worth (moral or nonmoral) may be properly enjoyed. Thus it is neither right nor, in a sense, even possible to sacrifice love for some lesser good. There are goods other than charity, but the uncharitable person has no substantive access to them. In the absence of love, putative pleasures are hollow indulgences and supposed virtues are glittering vices. There is this much unity to the moral life, a unity that ramifies throughout personal experience.[82]

However *agape* is interpreted, it is crucial to distinguish between the ideal (strong or weak) and the unhappy consequences of trying yet failing to live up to it. Many naturalists, including Nietzsche at times, object not so much to genuine love of neighbor as to the mendacity and peevishness that result from half-hearted attempts to embody it. A certain hard-headedness about human limitations is surely appropriate, as Niebuhr illustrates. Yet even if neighbor love were humanly impossible—or, less dramatically, even if a few (but only a few) were able to realize it—the *ideal* of universal benevolence could still remain intact. Unless one embraces *a priori* a strong principle of "ought implies can," which begs the central question, there is no contradiction between the agapist's claim that we should love one another equally and the naturalist's claim that this is for most of us just too taxing to be practical.

Of course, not all naturalistic objections to *agape* can be reduced to the issue of practicality. Christianity assumes that everyone, with God's help, is capable of *agape*; but some "strong naturalists," including Susan Wolf and Nietzsche at other times, fault the ideal as such. They contend that *agape* is impoverishing and therefore undesirable, not merely that it is too tough. In this instance, perhaps the most telling rebuttal (applicable to both strong naturalists and many liberals) is to turn the tables and ask why we should imagine neighbor love to be such a threat to personal development and/or the public weal. We continue to find modern versions of individualism and contractarianism plausible, and thus to find *agape* worrisome, because our central values of autonomy and justice still largely presuppose a model of the self as detached will. Moral maturity is frequently defined in terms of objectivity toward others and the ability to keep contingent promises to them. And because we value self-determination (if not self-sufficiency) so highly, we find it hard to picture an active and engaged charity that does not render the giver unduly encumbered or the receiver unduly dependent. I do not wish to minimize the importance of personal freedom and social tolerance, but the defenders of a more relational view of the self—a view in which interpersonal care and mutual assistance are emphasized—have become increasingly persuasive.[83] The more that such defenders can harmonize the best of naturalism (and liberalism) with their own communitarian concerns, the more adequate will be our conception of private and public virtue. And the more adequate is our conception of such virtue, I believe, the more compelling will be Christian charity's accent on human *needs* as well as human rights.

Again, *agape* only (or at least particularly) seems a threat to peace of mind or political freedom when we embrace an overly atomistic anthropology. For its part, in contrast, the Christian church considers a relationship to God through Christ to make possible nonoppressive relationships to other people, as well as to oneself. If persons are thought of as essentially separate beings who are most fully human in making rational choices independently of social context, then being deeply committed to or influenced by others (much less the Holy Other) must seem suspiciously heteronomous, even inherently violating. Yet the church believes self-giving love is worth the effort, an indispensable good. As the early Segundo eloquently puts it:

> To love means to lose our autonomy and to become dependent on another. And this dependence may end up one day as disillu-

sionment and heartbreak, leaving us empty inside. All love is a gamble, wherein we risk the best and deepest part of ourself. There are no guarantees in this world to cover the gamble. We either accept or reject love. For this very reason every act of love is more than an act of good will; it is an act of trust, an act of faith. It is an act of faith launched into the air, without any precise name or clear content. It is a belief that love is worthwhile, which defies fate and blind indifference to the importance of self-giving. The point is that *we* [Christians] know that this trust is well placed. We know that it is placed in good hands: i.e., that there is Someone who has responded with a yes and that this gesture is not lost in a void. We are those who "have believed in love," as Saint John says, because we know the name of him who is the origin and object of all love.[84]

Though Saint Paul is the great champion of "Christian liberty," he enjoins above all else a love that "bears one another's burdens" (Gal. 6:2). The virtue of *agape* may not obviate all recourse to violence, as I have defined it, but it does avoid the twin vices of injustice and insensitivity. Most importantly, as what Charles Taylor calls a "moral source,"[85] *agape* is both self-empowering and self-limiting precisely because it forges and sustains personal relations. It empowers people to act (even in the political sphere) by evoking a commitment to serve and protect the neighbor, but this same commitment also limits individuals in the motives and means they may employ (especially in the political sphere). For instance, just war checks on violence, as explicated by Ramsey in terms of "love transforming justice," are an enduring Christian response to naturalists and liberals alike. They are checks that grow out of love itself and its rootedness in that human community that would be the kingdom of God.

(3') *Response to the Liberal Objection*: The secular liberal begins by equating *agape* with an overly Platonic vision of love, only then to fault it as impersonal and potentially abusive. *Agape* must indeed seem prone to oppression if understood as intense concern for an abstract ideal whose individual representatives are ultimately dispensable. In this case, respecting the particularity of finite people will matter far less than promoting the *summum bonum* (e.g., God's will) in which they participate. Individuals will be, at best, interchangeable, and anyone may be sacrificed for the greater good which is the true source of value. Admittedly, both Augustine and Aquinas seem to lend support to this view of charity—Augustine claiming that only God is to be "enjoyed" for His own sake, thus that human beings are to be "used" for the sake of something higher, and Aquinas contending that "God is the principal object of charity, while our neighbor is loved out of charity for God's sake."[86] But all such scenarios unnecessarily impoverish (or risk impoverishing) love of others. A plurality of ends is possible, even if one end has metapriority: to love another human being for his own sake need not be to elevate him (idolatrously) to the highest good, even as to love God as *summum bonum* need not be to reduce people (cruelly) to means only.

The genius of true love is its attention to personal detail; such love *is* a respecter of persons, in all their uniqueness. While Platonic love ignores or transcends the particular in order to love the pure form, thereby making more personal kinds of love impossible,[87] a*gape* attends to and even accents the particular, thereby enhancing individual commitments. The agapist is not unegoistic because she would lose all personal identity (including her own) in the white light of infinity, but rather because she judges all persons equally valuable and treats them accordingly. Love of neighbor is preceded by and grounded in, but not negated by, love of God. In response to secular liberals, then, the agapist notes that love honors the free consciences of others (within the widest possible limits) precisely because they are fellow creatures made in the Image of God, distinct beings worthy of respect yet marred by the same Fall that touches everyone.

Love's "unegotism" applies to both intellect and will. This much was evident to Saint Paul. If faith in God makes for confidence in the ability to love the neighbor—for "it is no longer I who live, but Christ who lives in me" (Gal. 2:20)—it also makes for humility in the face of personal ignorance and culpability. In spite of his comments on "election" and "predestination," Paul was a universalist with respect to human depravity: "all men, both Jews and Greeks, are under the power of sin" (Ibid. 3:9). As a result, restraint and mutual forbearance are crucial elements in his social ethics. "Repay no one evil for evil, but take thought for what is noble in the sight of all. If possible, so far as it depends on you, live peaceably with all. . . . never avenge yourselves, but leave it to the wrath of God . . ." (Ibid. 12:17-19). The paramount measure of charity was for Paul (imitating Jesus) the patient willingness to suffer for others, rather than the insistence on converting them to a particular creed or form of life.[88] This is far from the political arrogance feared by bourgeois liberals.

CONCLUSION

We are at last in a position to answer summarily the question: What must Christian love be like to hold together, *in a unity*, such opposing principles as violent defense of the innocent (just war) and nonviolent embodiment of forgiveness (pacifism)? I disclose my preference for strong agapism in contending that love must first of all be a metavalue, as described above. Such a value "trumps" all others in that it can never be correct to surrender it in favor of some other good; but, more to the point, it is not even *possible* fully to realize another good if charity is absent. Love always takes priority because it is held to be at the very core of the divine personality, in which human nature is realized rather than sacrificed. The priority of *agape* to political philosophy, for instance, means that no calculation of social utility (e.g., preservation of the nation) can outweigh the obligation to love the neighbor, including the aggressive stranger.

There are many human goods (both moral and nonmoral), and, as I have emphasized, love itself is internally complex; so there will be tensions and trade-offs in the exercise of virtue. But a hard moral dilemma, in which one obligation must be culpably violated in order to meet another, is ruled out because *agape* is a metavalue.[89] We should always try to love; any failure to love is our own fault, a lack of openness to grace; and to love is to fulfill the law, i.e., to meet all obligations. Because *agape* also supercedes all nonmoral goods, moreover, there can be no tragic choice between aesthetic fulfillment and ethical uprightness. Cultivation of musical talent, say, is good in itself and may even contribute to the exercise of moral virtue; but to love God, oneself, and others is to be well-realized as a human being, regardless of what one must sacrifice to do so and of whether such love brings eschatological "reward."

Agape is, and knows itself to be, of such surpassing worth that love itself is its primary object. Love wants to generate more love. This is not to say that the agapist is chiefly concerned with his or her own subjective feelings or dispositions. The experience of love is attended by intrinsically valuable internal states, but Christian love's central aim is obedience to God in promoting the well-being of others. And *love serves others most profoundly by making them loving in their turn. Agape's* "bestowal" of value—its treating human beings as if fully lovable—contributes to their actually becoming so. Again, a loving will is not the only good, as Jesus's reaction to the poor and afflicted suggests, but it is fundamental. In the Gospels, Jesus shows deep concern for others' physical and psychological health: he cares about the everyday interests of incarnate human beings. But he repeatedly respects wants and meets needs so as to bring people out of immediate absorption in them. He touches individuals not merely to calm their private fears or to heal their personal infirmities—as important as these deliverances are—but to make them publicly loving like himself. The graciousness of Jesus's actions astonishes others into a similar altruism because they are able (at least momentarily) to forget themselves and attend to the world and its suffering. In this sense, *agape* is performative: it does not merely apprehend the "lovable" qualities of particular persons, it empowers these persons to care in new and unexpected ways. As in the Beatitudes, Jesus's love *makes* people blessed.

Love's emphasis on self-communication helps to explain, then, why judgment and mercy are irreducible components or tendencies of *agape*. Both tend to multiply charity. On the one hand, *agape* may forcefully defend the innocent not simply to sustain their bodily life but to preserve and enhance their potential for willing the good. Such a defense clarifies for the innocent their worth, and it may even impress upon their attackers the fact that respect is due those under threat. On the other hand, *agape* may embody nonviolent forgiveness because this attitude, in turn, can also prick the consciences of the unjust and make them more empathetic. Nonviolent forgiveness can summon potential victims to moral heroism as well. *Agape* is often accompanied by suffering, not simply because of external contingencies (the object of love may die or depart) but because of love's own internal complexity (it seeks both justice and mercy). A suffering love imitates Christ even if it does not actually "take," but self-proliferation is nevertheless love's aim. Such an expansive view of Christian charity captures the spirit common to many pacifists and just war theorists alike.

NOTES

1. Stanley Hauerwas, *The Peaceable Kingdom* (Notre Dame: Notre Dame University Press, 1983), p. 87.
2. Stanley Hauerwas, *A Community of Character* (Notre Dame: Notre Dame University Press, 1981), p. 12.
3. Stanley Hauerwas, *Resident Aliens: Life in the Christian Colony*, coauthored with William Willimon (Nashville: Abingdon, 1989), p. 12.
4. Stanley Hauerwas, *Against the Nations* (Minneapolis: Winston Press, 1985), p. 1; see also *Ibid.*, pp. 7 and 117; *The Peaceable Kingdom*, p. 102; and *Resident Aliens*, pp. 42-43.
5. *Resident Aliens*, p. 47.
6. See *A Community of Character*, pp. 3, 83-84.
7. Cf. *The Peaceable Kingdom*, p. xxiii and *Resident Aliens*, pp. 41 and 50.
8. *The Peaceable Kingdom*, pp. 111-13. William Werpehowski has suggested to me that the ambivalence here reflects a theoretical confusion between a meta-ethical claim ("We don't need theories") and a more

straightforward normative claim ("The state is part of God's preserving work, so Christians have a stake in it").

9. Liberalism can degenerate on the side of theory into attempts to be morally empty and on the side of practice into efforts merely to maximize individual desires; but this is neither compatible with Christianity nor what the founding fathers, for all their indebtedness to the Enlightenment, had in mind. I discuss these issues in "To Bedlam and Part Way Back: John Rawls and Christian Justice," *Faith and Philosophy*, Vol. 8, No. 4 (October 1991), pp. 423-47.

10. *Resident Aliens*, p. 83.

11. Robert Nozick argues in *Anarchy, State, and Utopia* (New York: Basic Books, 1974) that a state inevitably arises from the need for reliable protection against force, fraud, theft, etc. And as a necessary condition of its existence, "A state claims a monopoly on deciding who may use force when; it says that only it may decide who may use force and under what conditions; it reserves to itself the sole right to pass on the legitimacy and permissibility of any use of force within its boundaries; furthermore it claims to punish all those who violate its claimed monopoly" (p. 23). If the quoted passage is correct, then pacifists (like anarchists) must judge the state to be intrinsically evil. But see John Howard Yoder's *Christian Witness to the State* (Newton, Kansas: Faith and Life, 1964).

12. *Resident Aliens*, p. 43. Whether H. Richard Niebuhr himself was as unnuanced as Hauerwas and Willimon suggest is highly debatable.

13. *Ibid.*

14. See Paul Ramsey, *Speak Up for Just War or Pacifism* (University Park: Penn State, 1987), pp. 73-75.

15. Ronald Sider, *Christ and Violence* (Scottdale, Pa.: Herald Press, 1979), p. 45. See also Ronald Sider and Richard Taylor, *Nuclear Holocaust & Christian Hope* (New York: Paulist Press, 1982), pp. 111-13; and John Howard Yoder, *The Politics of Jesus* (Grand Rapids, Mich.: Eerdmans, 1972).

16. Reinhold Niebuhr, *An Interpretation of Christian Ethics* (New York: Seabury, 1979), p. 19.

17. *Resident Aliens*, p. 76.

18. Reinhold Niebuhr, *Moral Man and Immoral Society* (New York: Charles Scribner's Sons, 1960), p. 57.

19. *An Interpretation of Christian Ethics*, pp. 28, 30; and cf. p. 131.

20. *Ibid.*, p. 69.

21. *Ibid.*, p. 37.

22. *Ibid.*, pp. 62, 63; emphasis added.

23. *Ibid.*, p. 72.

24. *An Interpretation of Christian Ethics*, p. 80.

25. Reinhold Niebuhr, *The Nature and Destiny of Man*, Vol. II, (New York: Charles Scribner's Sons, 1964), p. 246.

26. See Niebuhr's *Beyond Tragedy* (New York: Charles Scribner's Sons, 1938), especially the Preface and Chapter 1. In Volume I of *The Nature and Destiny of Man*, he writes: "Though the religious faith through which God is apprehended cannot be in contradiction to reason in the sense that the ulti-

mate principle of meaning cannot be in contradiction to the subordinate principle of meaning which is found in rational coherence yet, on the other hand the religious faith cannot be simply subordinated to reason or made to stand under its judgment" (New York: Charles Scribner's Sons, 1964), p. 165.

27. *An Interpretation of Christian Ethics*, p. 121.

28. Reinhold Niebuhr, "Christian Faith and Natural Law," in *Love and Justice: Selections from the Shorter Writings of Reinhold Niebuhr*, D. B. Robertson, ed. (Glouchester: Peter Smith, 1976), p. 50; emphasis added. See also, *The Nature and Destiny of Man*, Vol. I, pp. 285, 295-96. For more on Niebuhr on love and justice, see Gene Outka, *Agape: An Ethical Analysis* (New Haven and London: Yale University Press, 1972), Chapter 3.

29. Paul Ramsey, *War and the Christian Conscience* (Durham: Duke University Press, 1976), p. 178.

30. *Ibid.*, pp. 190-91, 269-70. In "Perpetual Peace," Immanuel Kant writes: "[A] war of extermination, in which the destruction of both parties and of all justice can result, would permit perpetual peace only in the vast burial ground of the human race. Therefore, such a war and the use of all means leading to it must be absolutely forbidden. . . . these infernal arts [assassination, poisoning, breach of capitulation, and incitement to treason], vile in themselves, when once used would not long be confined to the sphere of war."

Kant here does for proportionality what Paul Ramsey does for discrimination. Ramsey shows how violating discrimination is self-defeating: it is incompatible with the law of love and its work of protecting the innocent. Kant shows how violating proportionality is self-defeating: it leads to the "undoing of the very spirit of peace," to preserve which is one of the main moral reasons for going to war. [See Immanuel Kant, "Perpetual Peace," tr. by Lewis White Beck, in *The Enlightenment: A Comprehensive Anthology*, Peter Gay, ed. (New York: Simon and Schuster, 1973), pp. 789 and 788-89.]

31. Saint Augustine, *The City of God*, Bk. XIX, Ch. 16, in Vol. II of *The Nicene and Post-Nicene Fathers*, tr. by Marcus Dods (Grand Rapids: Eerdmans, 1983), p. 412. Cf. Reinhold Niebuhr's observation that "as soon as the life and interest of others than the agent are involved in an action or policy, the sacrifice of those interests ceases to be 'self-sacrifice.' It may actually become an unjust betrayal of their interests." [*The Nature and Destiny of Man*, Vol. II, op. cit., p. 88.]

32. Paul Ramsey, "A Letter to James Gustafson," in *The Journal of Religious Ethics*, Vol. 13, No. 1 (Spring 1985), pp. 74-75.

33. Paul Ramsey, *The Just War* (New York: Charles Scribner's Sons, 1968), pp. 247, 460.

34. Juan Segundo, S.J., *The Liberation of Theology*, tr. by John Drury (Maryknoll: Orbis, 1982), p. 13.

35. *Ibid.*, p. 33.

36. *Ibid.*, p. 46.

37. *Ibid.*, pp. 71, 84-85.

38. *Ibid.*, pp. 101-102.

39. *Ibid.*, pp. 106-107, 116. In his earlier work, "ideology" is a much more pejorative term. In fact, "the alienating sin of the world is 'ideology,'" Segundo writes in *Evolution and Guilt*, thus making the notion very close to the antonym of "liberation." [See Juan Segundo, S.J., *A Theology for Artisans of a New Humanity*, Vol. 5 (Maryknoll: Orbis, 1974), p. 52.]

40. *The Liberation of Theology*, p. 108.

41. For a discussion of this distinction, see Ramsey, *Deeds and Rules in Christian Ethics* (New York: Charles Scribner's Sons, 1967), especially pp. 104-22.

42. *The Liberation of Theology*, p. 155; see also p. 116.

43. *Ibid.*, p. 164. Segundo goes so far as to claim "that *violence is an intrinsic dimension of any and all concrete love* in history" (*Ibid.*, p. 161). For a criticism of this as "badly exaggerated," see Gene Outka, "Discontinuity in the Ethics of Jacques Ellul," in *Jacques Ellul: Interpretive Essays*, Christians and Van Hook, eds. (Urbana: University of Illinois Press, 1981), pp. 219-20.

44. *The Liberation of Theology*, p. 118.

45. The early Segundo himself warns against the mere reversal of tyranny. See *Evolution and Guilt*, p. 69.

46. *Ibid.*, pp. 47, 59, and passim.

47. *The Liberation of Theology*, p. 159.

48. For more on this general distinction, see Outka, *Agape: An Ethical Analysis*, pp. 19-20, 90-91.

49. An extended discussion of the relation between means/ends and faith/relativism appears in *The Liberation of Theology*, pp. 170-81. There are sections here in which both contextualism and consequentialism are considerably muted, and any defense of Segundo must rely on these and related passages as normative. The difficulty is in making him consistent, however. On page 215, for example, he condemns the "inhuman means" employed by the church to convert people, "mass means that are intrinsically opposed to liberation." Such language directly contradicts his earlier claim that "We cannot tell whether love or egotism is at work by examining the means employed" (p. 164). Apparently, certain sorts of violence and coercion may be "categorically" ruled out after all.

50. *A Theology for Artisans of a New Humanity*, Vol. 1, *The Community Called Church* (Maryknoll: Orbis, 1973), p. 52; see also p. 66.

51. *Evolution and Guilt*, pp. 120-21.

52. *The Liberation of Theology*, p. 209; and compare *Evolution and Guilt*, pp. 68-69.

53. *The Liberation of Theology*, pp. 210-211.

54. See *Evolution and Guilt*, p. 68 and *The Community Called Church*, p. 90. Christians are "the minority" but must steer between "mass mechanisms on the one hand or elitism on the other" (*Evolution*, p. 131).

55. *Against the Nations*, p. 11.

56. *Ibid.*, p. 36.

57. Paul Ramsey, *Basic Christian Ethics* (New York: Charles Scribner's Sons, 1950), p. 343.

58. "Perpetual Peace," pp. 789-90; second emphasis added.
59. *The City of God*, Bk. XIX, Ch. 26, op. cit., p. 419.
60. See his Epilogue to Ramsey's *Speak Up for Just War or Pacifism*, pp. 149-150.
61. *The Community Called Church*, p. 49. Though the early Segundo sees the church and the world as "two distinct aspects of an indivisible unity," he still contends that the Church "would appear to be faithful to her rationale and mission if she evinced a clear commitment to collaborate in the work of authentic human development, without getting mixed up in the political government of the state; or even if she reacted strongly against political regimes that violate man." (*Ibid.*, p. 97.)
62. Michael Walzer, *Just and Unjust Wars* (New York: Basic Books, 1977), pp. 251-68.
63. Gene Outka has maintained that, in fact, Niebuhr's remarks on *jus in bello* are rather thin, probably even incompatible with viewing noncombatant immunity as exceptionless. If so, this is a palpable difference from Ramsey. See Outka, "The Protestant Tradition and Exceptionless Moral Norms," in *Moral Theology Today: Certitudes and Doubts* (St. Louis: The Pope John Center, 1984), pp. 150-54.
64. Ramsey, *The Just War*, p. 431.
65. Hauerwas asks at one point, "what is war but the desire to be rid of God, to claim for ourselves the power to determine our meaning and destiny?" (*Against the Nations*, p. 196). In answer, he contends without qualification, that war is "but the manifestation of our hatred of God" (*Ibid.*). Is this an adequate account of the motives of those who took up the sword against Hitler—Dietrich Bonhoeffer, for instance?
66. Outka, *Agape: An Ethical Analysis*, passim.
67. On these topics, see E. M. Good, "Peace in the OT," *Interpreter's Dictionary of the Bible* (Nashville: Abingdon Press, 1962), Vol. 3, pp. 705-706; C. L. Mitton, "Peace in the NT," *IDB* (*Ibid.*), Vol. 3, p. 706; E. R. Achtemeier, "Righteousness in the OT," *IDB*, Vol. 4, pp. 80-85; P. J. Achtemeier's "Righteousness in the NT," *IDB*, Vol. 4, pp. 91-99; and John Donahue's "Biblical Perspectives on Justice," *The Faith that Does Justice*, John C. Haughey, ed. (New York: Paulist Press, 1977), pp. 68-112.
68. See James Turner Johnson's critique of Roland Bainton's account of holy war in *Just War Tradition and the Restraint of War* (Princeton: Princeton University Press, 1981), pp. 230-35.
69. See, e.g., Friedrich Nietzsche, "The AntiChrist" and "Thus Spoke Zarathustra," both in *The Portable Nietzsche*, Walter Kaufmann, tr. and ed. (New York: Viking, 1968).
70. Friedrich Nietzsche, *The Genealogy of Morals* in *Basic Writings of Nietzsche*, Walter Kaufmann, tr. and ed. (New York: Modern Library, 1968), Preface, Section 5, p. 455.
71. Sigmund Freud, *Civilization and Its Discontents*, James Strachey, tr. (New York: Norton, 1961), pp. 56-57. Juan Segundo discusses Freud's view of neighbor love in *Evolution and Guilt*, especially p. 18.

72. Susan Wolf, "Moral Saints," in *The Journal of Philosophy*, Vol. 89, No. 8 (August 1982), p. 419.

73. *Civilization and Its Discontents*, p. 61.

74. Richard Rorty, "Postmodernist Bourgeois Liberalism," *The Journal of Philosophy*, Vol. 80, No. 10 (October 1983), pp. 583-89.

75. On the importance of not allowing "morbid softening and moralization" to make one ashamed of cruelty, see *The Genealogy of Morals*, Second Essay, Section 7, p. 503.

76. See Judith Shklar, *Ordinary Vices* (Cambridge: Harvard University Press, 1984), and Richard Rorty, *Contingency, Irony, and Solidarity* (Cambridge: Cambridge University Press, 1989).

77. Quoted in Howard Mumford Jones, *Violence and Reason* (New York: Atheneum, 1969), p. 35.

78. Sören Kierkegaard, *Works of Love*, Howard and Edna Hong, tr. (New York: Harper & Row, 1964), pp. 140-45.

79. Irving Singer, *The Nature of Love*, Vol. 1, *Plato to Luther* (Chicago: University of Chicago Press, 1984), p. 5; and see also pp. 10-13.

80. *The Nature of Love*, Vol. 3, *The Modern World* (Chicago: University of Chicago Press, 1987), p. 157. Singer makes the salient point most explicitly: "Within itself, love includes appraisiveness as well as the bestowing of value. To neglect either is to misconstrue both" (p. 396). Singer also criticizes Freud for his assumption "that the quantity of love must be limited in accordance with his economic theory [of psychic energies]" (p. 153).

81. I take the term "metavalue," as well as aspects of its basic definition, from Gerald Doppelt, "Is Rawls's Kantian Liberalism Coherent and Defensible?," in *Ethics*, Vol. 99, No. 4 (July 1989), pp. 823-24.

82. Elements of this paragraph are incorporated from my "The Disconsolation of Theology: Irony, Cruelty, and Putting Charity First," in *The Journal of Religious Ethics*, Vol. 20, No. 1 (Spring 1992), pp. 12-13.

83. See, *inter alia*, the essays by Carol Gilligan and Martha Nussbaum in *Reconstructing Individualism: Autonomy, Individuality, and the Self in Western Thought*, Heller, Sosna, and Wellbery, eds. (Stanford: Stanford University Press, 1986); and Charles Taylor's *Sources of the Self: The Making of the Modern Identity* (Cambridge: Harvard University Press, 1989). I am particularly indebted to Gilligan in what I say here.

84. *The Community Called Church*, p. 57.

85. *Sources of the Self*, especially Chapter 4.

86. See Augustine, *On Christian Doctrine*, Bk. I, Ch. 22, and Aquinas, *Summa Theologiae*, II-II, Q. 23, art. 5, ad 1. Christian Platonism and Aristotelianism are not the only accounts of love that may invite injustice, however. Utilitarianism is a naturalized version of an essentially Platonic scheme, inasmuch as individuals are subordinated to an extremely generalized norm: producing the greatest happiness for the greatest number.

87. Cf. Singer, The *Nature of Love*, Vol. 1, p. 84.

88. In closing his first letter to the Corinthians, Paul does write: "If any one has no love for the Lord, let him be accursed" (I Cor. 16:22); but the

much more dominant theme is that of these famous lines: "Love does not insist on its own way; it is not irritable or resentful; . . . . Love bears all things, believes all things, hopes all things, endures all things" (*Ibid.* 13:5-7).

    89. On the subject of moral dilemmas, see Edmund Santurri, *Perplexity in the Moral Life* (Charlottesville: University of Virginia Press, 1987), and Christopher W. Gowans, ed., *Moral Dilemmas* (Oxford: Oxford University Press, 1988).

John H. Whittaker

"Agape" and Self-love

If the requirements of Christianity could be summarized, no better summary could be found than Jesus's own words, "Thou shalt love thy neighbor as thyself." This commandment gives the ideal of charity its distinctively Christian flavor, so much so that we use another word, *agape*, to describe it.

Since it is a burdensome commandment, many people have tried to soften it. They have asked, "Who is my neighbor," as if the complications introduced by this question would justify their noncompliance. They cannot so easily ask, however, *how* they are to love their neighbors; for the commandment makes that clear: we must love our neighbors *as ourselves*. These two words make the commandment stick, and stick hard. To struggle against them, as Sören Kierkegaard says, is to wrestle with God. For they wrap themselves around a person so tightly that one who wishes to fulfill the commandment while persisting in selfishness must always fail, and by so doing learn what proper self-love is.[1]

That is a deep thought, and I would like to pause over it. Indeed, it takes some time to realize how deep it is, since the point of the commandment seems fairly clear on the surface. We know, for example, that *agape* is a richer concept than benevolence. Loving one's neighbor must mean more than treating one's acquaintances in a spirit of generosity. Benevolent acts can be dispensed in a patronizing spirit, and one can selfishly enjoy the sense of superiority that comes with treating others kindly as inferiors. This is true no matter how benevolent a person might be: as long as one enjoys the feeling of superiority that goes with being generous, one's actions will perpetuate a distinction between the status of the agent and the status of the recipient. The recipient will be cast into an inferior role, so that the agent will neither value nor love the person in that role *as one loves oneself*.

Such an implication seems clear enough. Yet it is based on an understanding of self-love that is intuitive, and it is surprisingly difficult to *explain* the way that the qualification "as thyself" operates in this commandment. The Biblical parables that are designed to instruct us here awaken a *feeling* for what the law requires, but the connection between self-love and neighbor-love remains difficult to spell out. Numerous thinkers have tried to explain this connection, of course, and Gene Outka's discussion of the commandment in *Agape* is extremely useful in sorting out the tangles that one can get into. His suggestion that this commandment enjoins *equal regard* is particularly useful. One loves another as oneself when one's love is not conditioned by changeable circumstances or dependent on accidental features which the other might or might not possess. That is what ensures the equality of love's regard. An ideal Christian extends consideration to the neighbor regardless of the neighbor's qualifications, so that preferences are eliminated in choosing those who deserve to be loved. A person with such virtue, moreover, maintains this attitude through the willingness to forgive the neighbor's conduct.[2] This means that the believer values other people simply *as human beings*, treating them as individuals whose worth is established by their common status as creatures of God. In extending to them the same kind of regard that one has for oneself, the faithful Christian's concern goes out to meet the neighbor's needs, and it does so with unalterable respect for his or her freedom.[3]

I have little but admiration for the way in which Outka sustains this view in relation to fundamental moral issues. He shows, for example, that *agape* does not exclude special moral relations but rather undergirds them.[4] He argues, moreover, that it does not preclude moral agents from being more demanding of themselves than for others—from "going an extra mile" or from exhorting them to works of supererogation.[5] My only concern is the status that he accords the love commandment as a "substantive moral principle." This phrase suggests, too easily I think, that the *content* of the love commandment can be given in terms of specific actions, and that compliance with it can be measured solely on the basis of performance. I think that the matter is far more complicated than this.

The love commandment is a moral rule; that much is clear. But the conditions which must be met for an action-guide to count as a moral rule do not distinguish between rules which enjoin (or prohibit) specific actions and rules which enjoin (or prohibit) the disposition to act in a generally specifiable way.[6] Does the requirement that we love our neighbors as ourselves yield concrete directives when applied to particular moral issues? Can specific rules, adequate to our circumstances, always be derived from it? Or does it represent only a moral generality, clear enough for us to follow in many cases perhaps, but impossible to exhaust as an action-guide unconnected with moral feeling.

My view is that the second great commandment of Christianity does not offer specific guidance in *all* cases in which it applies—that it represents more of a dispositional guide than a rule for performance. The difference between a dispositional guide and a substantive moral rule would not be that important were it not for the relation of this commandment to the first commandment of Christianity—that we should love God. Yet one of the most distinctive features of Christian love is that it depends on this prior love. One who does not love God cannot rightly love oneself or one's neighbor. With this added requirement, we can see the love commandment begin to deepen. To get to the bottom of it we need to learn what it means to think of it as a dispositional guide.

1. PREFERENCE, FREEDOM, AND THE CONCERN FOR BASIC NEEDS

The difficulty in specifying the content of the *agape* principle comes from uncertainty surrounding the notion of loving ourselves. How can we love others as ourselves, and act accordingly, when we are not sure what loving ourselves means in the first place? Loving oneself might mean adopting a favorable attitude to those idiosyncracies that make one an individual. Or it might mean approving of those actions which express one's freedom. Or again, it might mean attending to the basic needs one has as a person and thus never neglecting oneself. All of these concepts of self-love, however, prove inadequate when taken as the basis of neighbor love.

Consider the first. In loving myself, do I treat my special properties as the object of my love? And do I attempt to use such preferences as a norm by which to assess the needs of others? Suppose that I am a homosexual. Do I invite my heterosexual friends to participate in gay activities simply because that is the way that I would like to be treated by others? Am I to assume that everyone wants what I want? The example hardly needs to be elaborated since the point is clear. We cannot rightly universalize our *preferences* as standards of correct behavior if this would mean imposing our own idiosyncracies on others. If loving ourselves means delighting in these idiosyncracies and favoring the accidental inheritances of our biological and cultural background, then the commandment to love our neighbor *as ourselves* quickly degenerates into a selfish, inconsiderate, and parochial rule.

Proper self-love, therefore, cannot be a matter of loving the idiosyncracies that make us unique. Approving such idiosyncracies in oneself is much closer to being *proud* of oneself; and however advisable it might be to instill such pride as a psychological antidote to self-doubt and defeatism, pride is still not the virtue from which Christian charity springs. The pride which I take in my individuality must not be confused with the way in which I love myself as a pattern for loving others. Otherwise, I will treat my neighbors in ways which do not sufficiently recognize their right to their own uniqueness and their own pride.

Since it is so inconsiderate, then, to assume that others ought to have the same preferences and idiosyncracies that provide self-satisfaction for us, one might interpret the commandment to love one's neighbor as oneself as a matter of respecting the neighbor's freedom. Knowing that others have their own preferences, should we not give the same weight to the satisfaction of their desires as we give to our own? Should we not afford them the same opportunities to take pride in themselves, recognizing the fact that their preferences, etc., will be different from our own? This interpretation of the love commandment comes much closer than the first to Outka's standard of equal regard. I love myself by exercising my freedom, defining myself through the choices that I make. Should I not love others by recognizing their freedom to do the same?

The trouble with this is that there are *limits* to the mutual support that people can offer in the encouragement of one another's freedom. One person's choices are frequently incompatible with another's moral standards, and it is asking too much to expect the second person to support the freedom of the first *by supporting his or her judgments*. Thus, if I set aside my own choices to support my neighbor's interests, I may be led to support aims which I morally abhor. After all, what are my neighbor's interests? Some are bent on world conquest. Some are anarchists. Some kill animals for sport. Some trade women like cattle, etc., etc. How can I support such aims without violating my own considered judgments of what is right or wrong?[7] How can I be sure that my neighbors' sense of themselves is not bound up with immoral exercises of freedom? Again, these examples need not be drawn out. It should be clear that loving another as oneself cannot be a matter of suspending one's moral opinions in order to support, indiscriminately, the neighbor's freedoms. That would lead to internal contradictions in an agent's own moral stance.

Perhaps, however, there are other ways to support one's neighbors' freedom without supporting their decisions indiscriminately. For example, one might support those governmental policies that emphasize a certain list of rights—educational opportunity, legal protection, etc. Such an interpretation of the love commandment would put restraints on the freedoms that we affirm in our neighbor by defining his or her rights. Thus, we would affirm those freedoms that the neighbor has a *right* to exercise. This would be compatible with Christian charity, no doubt. And yet if it means that the force of Christianity's second great commandment might be exhausted by governmental policies, one has to object. Those who endeavor to live a life of Christian love might well encourage their governments to protect people's freedom and to educate them for autonomous living, but the love commandment requires them to do more than this. It enjoins *personal* respect, not simply the support of general policies. In Outka's terms, identical treatment is always the result of following a general policy, but the love commandment requires equal regard, not necessarily identical treatment.[8] Adhering to general policies allows one to relate to the neighbor at a distance, where the neighbor's peculiar features as an individual do not count as much as the shared features by virtue of which the policy applies. One might even say that a policy-governed treatment, contrary to the intention of the love commandment, tends to depersonalize people by treating them categorically. Or, as I would prefer to say, it tends to reduce our moral obligations to specific "do's and don't's," to duties that might be fulfilled by mere deeds, unaccompanied by the feeling-guided flexibility that particular circumstances warrant.

Yet if one cannot fulfill the love commandment in this way—by sanctioning respect for the neighbor's freedom—what can one do? Is there another way in which my self-love might be extended from myself to my neighbor? Frequently, a distinction is drawn between people's spiritual life and their physical existence, or between the exercise of their higher freedoms and their basic needs as human beings. The love commandment can be interpreted in a parallel fashion, as if it required more attention to people's basic needs than to the exercise of their higher freedoms. And in fact, there seems to be considerable biblical warrant for doing so: Jesus cares for the sick, feeds the hungry, extends fellowship to the lonely and the outcast, and advises us to visit the fatherless and widows in their affliction. He does not worry as much about people's world views as he does about their worldly needs, and his own example serves as a guide in putting *agape* into practice. The needs that he addresses here might be defined as essential, or crucial, needs. None of us neglects such needs or treats their fulfillment as an optional matter. If we love ourselves by trying to satisfy our essential needs, then we might love our neighbors in the same way, never turning a deaf ear to the cries of human need around us.

One difficulty with this has already been mentioned, and that is the possibility that the welfare of others might be taken care of in a patronizing manner. That would violate the requirement that we love others *as ourselves*.[9] Equally serious is the underlying assumption that people's needs and their choices can be clearly distinguished. All of the needs just mentioned are needs that various people have at times *chosen* not to pursue. We have all heard of ascetics who deny themselves clothing, human company, speech, health, and all but the most minimal nourishment. Recently I read about a young man who learned to sleep in a squatting position—outdoors, in the rain—so that he would *never* need shelter. People, in short, *choose* to pursue or not to pursue the fulfillment of their most basic needs, so that there is no clearly marked difference between essential needs, which we all *must* pursue, and optional needs, which we are free to pursue or not. There is a gray area between these two sorts of needs, and it complicates the view that the love commandment enjoins equal regard for the basic needs of human beings. In many cases, we cannot be sure that our neighbor *wants* those needs that *we* regard as basic satisfied. Hermits are not likely to agree that people need community, celibates are not likely to agree that people must have a sexual life, certain religious extremists are not likely to agree that people need to worry over their health, and so on. The dying, to take another example, often have a radically altered sense of their priorities, in which the satisfaction of their ordinary needs occurs well down on the list.

So what does neighbor love require of us in these cases? It requires us to put ourselves in our neighbor's shoes, as Outka says, so that we might appreciate his or her point of view.[10] This helps us to avoid discounting the neighbor's opinions, as if they didn't count in deciding how we are to love him. But this simply takes us back to where we were before—to respecting the neighbor's freedom—and as I said, there are limits to the extent that we can do this. Too many of the neighbor's choices are morally abhorrent to us. One's neighbor may want to commit suicide, for example. Are we to love such a neighbor by respecting that need?

Inevitably, I think, we are thrown back on our intuitions. We are to show our love for the neighbor *however it seems appropriate*. In trying to practice the love commandment, we are to show *balance* in its interpretation. We are to show our neighbors the same respect that we show for ourselves by respecting their freedom to choose for themselves, *unless* their choices morally conflict with our own. Where their choices are morally abhorrent to us, we are to shift our concern to their needs; and where their outlooks discount their needs, we are to respect their freedom to think as they do—unless, of course, moral conflicts obtrude. The point here is not to blunt the force of the love commandment. It is to emphasize the fact that the love commandment enjoins a *disposition*. For that is exactly what the willingness to shift one's focus from needs to freedoms and back again reflects—an attitude which is prepared to *adjust* the way in which *agape* is put into practice.

2. SELF-LOVE

To this point, the conception of self-love that underwrites the commandment to love others as we love ourselves has remained implicit. It needs to become explicit, not only to strengthen the case for saying that love commandment enjoins a disposition, but also to enable us to recognize the connection between Christianity's two great commandments. The second commandment, that we love others as we love ourselves, depends on the first, that we love God; and the proper understanding of self-love depends on the connection between the two.

So how, then, do we love ourselves? My suggestion is deceptively simple. We love ourselves by wanting to be happy, to be fulfilled, to be complete. *And we do not abandon this wish.* The desire for such happiness is a universal, permanent, and inescapable feature of human life. That is why the love commandment speaks of the love that we have for ourselves without bothering about exceptions. There are none. We all *in some sense* want to be happy, or to be truly fulfilled.

Nevertheless, we do not seek our fulfillment in the same ways or identify our interest in being happy with the same objectives. Thus, we need to draw a distinction between two senses in which people seek happiness. In the first sense, we identify our happiness with something in particular, like wealth or pleasant experiences or contented states of mind, so that the pursuit of happiness becomes equivalent to the pursuit of these specific goals. The pursuit of happiness *in this sense* is a choice since one chooses to identify happiness with one end or another. One *invests* one's happiness in a certain end, that is, but one could have invested it in another aim. As a result, the desire for happiness *as an invested end* is variable, and we cannot assume that everyone has a common desire for the same sort of happiness. For convenience, let's call the desire for this kind of happiness—happiness invested in something specific—the desire for happiness in sense number one.

There is another sense in which we desire happiness (or fulfillment), according to which the desire for happiness is not invested in anything in particular but is a desire for something-we-know-not-what. Think of those people who seem irreconcilably unhappy, who do not want anything and who lack all passion. Such people do not have the desire for happiness invested in anything. They lack enthusiasm for doing anything. Instead, they seem to have abandoned the desire for happiness altogether. Rather than abandoning that desire, however, they have *withdrawn their interest from particular ends*. They simply have no desire for happiness in sense number one—*and yet they still care about their own fulfillment as an unfocused concern*. They just do not know where such fulfillment is to be found. Perhaps they have lost all hope, thinking that none of their specific goals can ever be realized. Yet the fact that they still desire *something* is shown by their misery; for if they did not care about happiness at all, they would not be made miserable by its absence. Their vulnerability to despair, in other words, proves their desire, which has merely lost its specific form. Such a desire is unfocused and therefore impossible to pursue as an end. It can only be manifested in a desperate, undirected, and hopeless way. Let us call the desire for happiness in this unfocused way sense number two.

The desire for happiness, therefore, is ambiguous. It can be a desire for something in particular, in which case it is focused or invested, or it can be a desire for something unknown, in which case it is unfocused and uninvested. That is why the truism that everyone wants to be happy is so often doubted. To say that everyone wants happiness in sense one is untrue—some have given up this desire; whereas it is safe to say that everyone desires happiness either in sense one or in sense two. As an uninvested longing, the desire for fulfillment is simply human care or concern. It is the inescapable medium of human existence, and its frustration is the source of all spiritual suffering.

Are either of these desires selfish? One might think that they both are, and yet it is only the desire for happiness in the first sense, as in invested desire, that can be selfish. Only those desires which are chosen are moral matters at all, and since the desire for something-we-know-not-what is not something that we choose, we cannot be held accountable for it. No one can avoid it. We could not get rid of it even if we wanted to, which means, again, that there is no point in calling it selfish. Selfishness, after all, is a pejorative idea. Selfish people go about trying to satisfy ends with two basic characteristics: 1) these ends are optional, and 2) they can be pursued without regard to the concerns of others. If one attaches supreme importance to such ends, one acts selfishly. The desire for happiness as a focused end easily qualifies here—but not the desire for happiness in sense two.

It is important to realize, however, that there are some optional ends—moral ends—which cannot be selfishly pursued, even if they become matters of supreme personal importance. If one invests one's happiness in such ends, so as not to expect a reward, one can hardly be accused of being selfish. One cannot possibly be selfish about this since these ends must be pursued by attending to the needs of others. True, one can relegate moral endeavors to a menial status by pursuing other goals on the far side of morality; but then one's moral endeavors would not be one's *true* goals. If, for example, one were to invest one's ultimate interest in eradicating poverty, one's fulfillment would consist of just that, since it would be found *in the eradication of poverty* rather than in any ulterior aim. Pursuing such an end would certainly not be selfish. The person who attempts it might feel guilty or inwardly unhappy for not doing more to reduce poverty, but such self-concern could hardly be described as selfishness in the pejorative sense. If this kind of inward self-concern represented selfishness, a person could not feel guilty about *anything*, including selfishness itself, without demonstrating more selfishness, which is absurd. Only if one's moral goals were the *means* of attaining more ultimate ends having nothing to do with one's relation to others could a person with moral intentions be described as selfish. But then, one's happiness would be invested in these ulterior ends, not in moral aims, which would only be the means of furthering one's true desires.

Putting aside this confusion about selfishness, though, still leaves us with our original question: how should the commandment to love others as ourselves be interpreted? Should it be interpreted to mean "love others as you love yourself when you pursue your happiness in the form of a focused aim" (i.e., in sense one). Or does it mean "love others as you love yourself when you desire your fulfillment in an unfocused way" (i.e., in sense two)? To interpret the commandment in the first way has a certain plausibility, since it mitigates the selfishness involved in pursuing definite ends. On this interpretation, what would otherwise be selfish desiring must be converted into moral desiring, since one would not be able to seek one's own happiness without at the same time seeking the happiness of others. Such a rule would make *joint* happiness—one's own as well as one's neighbor's—one's proper aim. This happiness would still have to be identified with something specific, like wealth or pleasure, otherwise we would not be presumed to love ourselves in sense one. Yet the words of Jesus on this view would prevent the selfishness involved in such desiring from getting out of hand. And for this reason, such an interpretation would seem to be acceptable.

The same might be said of making moral goals one's specific aims. Obviously, those who devote themselves to such goals cannot be accused of selfishness. They love themselves, yes, in the empty sense that they seek their own well-being, but they seek this happiness *in a moral life*. Couldn't others be loved in the same way—i.e., as people who should seek their happiness in moral endeavors? On this view, the love commandment would mean: "love your neighbor as you love yourself in seeking moral ends above all other goals." Applying the commandment would mean treating others as if their highest interest consisted in being moral. This interpretation would also seem to be acceptable.

Nevertheless, there are problems with these accounts. For one thing, there does not seem to be anything distinctively Christian about them. They turn the Christian ideal of neighbor-love into in straightforward morality, which has no essential relation to faith. For another thing, they presume that all people want the same *kind* of happiness. Some people seek their happiness in something like wealth; some others identify their happiness with moral aims. In either case, these accounts are inflexible in conceiving the neighbor's happiness. They tend to discount the relevance of the neighbor's own desires, which might be invested in quite different ends. It is as if the agent were to choose *for the neighbor*, deciding what the neighbor's happiness *ought* to consist in rather than allowing one's neighbors to decide for themselves. One who loves oneself in seeking moral aims, for example, will love others as potential moral agents; and that will disqualify those who do not fit into this category—retarded people, for example. So this interpretation of "loving oneself" will not do. It breeds too much parochialism.

What about the other alternative, though? We can interpret the love commandment as requiring us to love others in the same way that we desire our happiness in sense two—i.e., when we long for an unspecified fulfillment. Understood in this way, the commandment requires us to extend to others the same concern that we show for ourselves *when we do not know exactly what the fulfillment that we seek consists of*. Such an interpretation has the advantage of clarifying the categorical nature of the commandment, as the commandment applies to everyone without qualification on this view. One does not have to meet any prior conditions to be subject to it, for it does not say, "if you love yourselves (and you might not), then you must love your neighbors as you love yourselves." The commandment presumes that all people do love themselves, although the only sense in which they do is the sense in which they long for fulfillment of *some* kind, specified or unspecified.

This kind of self-love is not without implications when it comes to putting the commandment to love our neighbors into practice. These implications do not derive from the presumption that we all desire happiness of a certain sort but from the fact that our self-love represents a permanent bond of attachment to ourselves, a bond which survives in many different forms but which never wholly disappears. We change the ends in which we invest our hopes of happiness, sometimes identifying our fulfillment with one thing and sometimes with another. Yet even if we feel that we have made mistakes, overvaluing things like money or fame, we do not abandon the unfocused concern that we originally invested in these things. We have banked fires of passion which might be rekindled at any moment, simply by being invested in new aims. But the passion that we put into these new aims is already inside us waiting to be identified with something new. Such passion, as Kierkegaard said, comes from our interest in eternal or absolute happiness.[11] This kind of happiness cannot be identified with anything in particular, and though it remains something that we can never focus on as a particular goal, we never disown our interest in it. No matter how foolish we may have been in trying to find it in this form or in that—no matter how disappointed we might become in ourselves— we never lose our longing for it.

Precisely this, then, is the feature which can guide us in deciding how to practice *agape*: the refusal to abandon concern. For if we do not give up on ourselves, abandoning all interest in our true happiness, then we should not give up on others, simply because they seek their happiness in ways that we cannot support. We cannot decide for our neighbors what precise form their happiness is to take, and we cannot give blanket approval to their ultimate passions. But we can endeavor to show our regard for our neighbors *in one way or another*, which we can do by *maintaining* this regard unconditionally. They may be objectionable, but they are still human beings; and as Outka clearly states, they are entitled to our regard because of that.

The refusal to disregard our neighbor requires the willingness to forgive. We forgive ourselves, in effect, when we reinvest our ultimate desires in new aims, having become despondent with ourselves for seeking happiness in unfruitful ways. So if we forgive ourselves for the mistakes that we have made in pursuing our happiness, we should be willing to forgive others for making the same kind of mistakes. And since forgiveness means restoring relationships that have been broken, this means that we must be willing to preserve a relationship with a person even if we cannot approve of the way in which that person pursues happiness. We cannot always be expected to change our assessment of the neighbor's desires, just as we cannot be expected to approve of the wrongs that he or she has done. But we cannot take these wrongs as reason to discount the offender as a human being, as if his interest in fulfillment were not worthy of the same permanent respect that we show to our own. We cannot do this, that is, as long as we love our neighbors *as ourselves*.

In more traditional terms, this permanent concern for our neighbor as a human being might be described as a concern for the neighbor's God-relationship. This is actually the first of three ways in which Outka summarizes the content of *agape* as a substantive ethical principle. Ideally, Christians want for their neighbors the same absolute happiness that they believe God has promised to them, and it is part of their respect for the neighbor's interest in such fulfillment that they are willing to *witness* to them. Outka points out that this witnessing does not mean invading the neighbor's privacy or trying inconsiderately to alter the neighbor's life, nor does it mean patronizing people in the way one speaks to them. It means only that one who loves the neighbor as oneself must be *willing* to offer him that view in which one finds one's own fulfillment. Keeping one's own sense of salvation private, as if it had no relevance for others, or as if others could have no interest in it, would be to treat other people and their interest in happiness as unworthy of the highest respect. To witness merely out of a sense of duty, on the other hand, would not show this kind of respect. To treat the ideal of *agape* in that way would diminish the requirements of neighbor-love to mere performance, leaving it unrelated to any genuine interest in the hopes of other people.[12]

In any event, we can see more clearly why the love commandment does not specify precisely "what" must be done. One must love the neighbor as oneself, to be sure; but this offers few concrete directives. It means that one must be willing to support one's neighbor's freedom in seeking fulfillment, but only to the extent that the neighbor's choices are morally permissible. It means that one must be willing to support the neighbor's basic needs, but only to the extent that the neighbor acknowledges these needs. It means that one must be willing to forgive the neighbor, restoring a respectful regard wherever it has been destroyed by wrongs. And it means that one must be willing to share with one's neighbor those beliefs in which one finds one's own fulfillment. All of this grows out of the requirement to love our neighbors *as ourselves*. Yet just as we do not love ourselves in the doing of anything in particular, we are not to love others by indiscriminately supporting their freedom, or by assuming that we always know what they need, or by trying to force on them our more cherished beliefs. Rather, one conforms to Christianity's second great commandment by maintaining a certain disposition, struggling to sustain an accepting attitude toward others in the face of obstacles, extending approval to them as far as one can in good conscience, and preserving a willingness to forgive them for what one takes to be their wrongdoings. One tries to *balance* these approaches, relying on the one whenever the other proves difficult to put into practice. Such an attitude does not compromise the intent of neighbor love. One makes the same kind of adjustments in relation to oneself in trying first one thing and then another in the effort to realize one's fulfillment; and the love commandment enjoins the same disposition in our treatment of others.

Instead of weakening the love commandment, this interpretation of it actually strengthens it, since it explains why the commandment cannot be fulfilled in a hypocritical way. One cannot outwardly fulfill the law while inwardly violating its spirit, simply because the law applies first to attitudes, laying down no particular activity which one must perform in order to comply with it. Being a dispositional commandment, it requires a dispositional change, and the behavioral consequences of keeping the commandment flow from that disposition. One either fulfills the law inwardly in one's heart, therefore, or one does not fulfill it at all. One either has the proper disposition or one does not.

3. "AGAPE" AND THE LOVE OF GOD

One might say, therefore, that the love commandment represents a kind of "situation ethics" in which the particular injunctions of a moral law depend on the particular features of a moral situation. I have no objection to this way of putting the point, as long as one remembers that there are *some* guidelines for putting this commandment into practice.[13] One also needs to acknowledge the fact that a commandment to bear a certain disposition is generally much more difficult to satisfy than a commandment to perform a certain action. A commandment to *do* something can be fulfilled by the appropriate action, regardless of the feelings of the agent; whereas a commandment to do something *out of a certain disposition* cannot be fulfilled in a perfunctory way. The willful creation of an inward disposition is a difficult thing.

Yet if all people have within themselves the appropriate disposition to begin with—since they all love themselves—then the commandment to love one's neighbor as oneself should not involve the creation of a new disposition. It should involve no more than the extension of an existing disposition. Yet what then becomes of Kierkegaard's remark that one who tries to love others as one loves oneself will learn what proper self-love is? Will obedience to this law lead one to change one's self-regard?

That is one difficulty which we have yet to clear away. Another difficulty is that we have yet to capture anything specifically Christian in this commandment. Being a Christian entails the willingness to confess one's faith to those whose longing for happiness gives them willing ears—yes. But being a humanist and trying to practice neighbor-love means that one should be willing to share the humanist outlook also. The willingness to share the view in which one's happiness resides is a formal feature of the love commandment, regardless of what this view might happen to be. Christianity, however, seems to add something to the love commandment, so that it becomes a distinctively Christian ideal. And the explanation of this also concerns the dispositional side of *agape*.

To clear up these difficulties let's go back to the distinction between the desire for happiness as a desire for something specific and the desire for happiness as an unfocused aim. This distinction makes it easier to claim that everyone desires to be happy, if not in the first sense then at least in the second. Yet wanting to be happy is not necessarily the same thing as *pursuing* happiness. Does everyone *pursue* happiness? Or do they pursue it out of the same disposition? Obviously, they do pursue it when they identify it with a particular end. But it is unclear whether they pursue it when they do not equate it with anything. After all, how does one pursue something that one cannot even focus on? We need to think carefully about these matters—about what pursuing happiness means—because Christianity's contribution to the love commandment comes in just at this point.

Most people pursue happiness *as if it were something to be acquired*. Whether they identify their happiness with something in particular, or whether they hope that an unspecified sort of happiness will follow on the attainment of some other end, they remain preoccupied with the struggle for happiness. It doesn't much matter what form this desire takes; they feel responsible for its satisfaction. Happiness is something that one *must* pursue, since it is not a birthright and one doesn't get it automatically. One has to struggle for it.

This preoccupation with life's struggle, with achieving one's happiness as a prize, is not the attitude with which a Christian beholds the neighbor. The Christian does not simply lessen his or her preoccupation in order to attend to the preoccupation of others. There is nothing wrong with doing that, but it does not get to the bottom of the Christian view. Instead, Christianity promises to free one from this preoccupation—to teach one a new attitude toward happiness—by altering the disposition generated by looking on happiness as something that must be achieved. It thereby enables the love commandment to be fulfilled in the heart of the believer as well as in the treatment of others.

To appreciate this last thought, we need to realize that most people, even though they all love themselves, do not have the kind of loving disposition that extends itself to others. Usually, they are too caught up in their own projects for that; and usually, this means that they are selfish. Yet they can be caught up in the struggle for happiness even if this struggle is unselfish. They can be ruled by the idea that happiness must somehow be achieved, their own happiness along with that of their equally valued neighbors. That is the idea that Christianity undercuts. We do not have to labor under the terrible responsibility of having to achieve our truest happiness, either separately or jointly. Christianity relieves us of that misconception, and as a result we become less preoccupied with the *struggle* for happiness and more interested in conveying its promise.

In other words, we need only to acknowledge the commonplace truism that we must love ourselves before we can love others. Our concern with our happiness is not enough here; we need to add to this self-concern about fulfillment another kind of self-regard. We need a *positive* disposition toward the problem of securing this happiness, something that makes us feel secure. For without a feeling of security in our search for happiness, we cannot turn our thoughts adequately toward the needs of others. Otherwise our insecurities about our needs will interfere with our relation to others. In short, we have one kind of self-love which is manifested in our unshakable desire for happiness, but beyond this, we need another kind of love which is capable of freeing us from that very problem. Only when we have both can we love our neighbors as ourselves.

Those who are preoccupied with attaining their own happiness or the happiness of others might be described as being *bound* by this desire. To be bound by the desire for happiness, as one should be reminded again and again, is not necessarily to be selfish. People can pursue their happiness in sense one (as a focused desire) or they can pursue in sense two (as an unfocused desire). If they pursue it as an unspecified form of satisfaction to be discovered in moral ends, then their pursuit of it is unselfish. Nevertheless, they will remain *bound* by this pursuit as long as they hold themselves entirely responsible for achieving the goal. On the other hand, if they regard themselves as *graced* with perfect happiness, as if it had been provided for them without their having to work for it, then their desire for happiness might be described as an *unbound* desire. Such people are free of a terrible weight, free of its worry and free to devote themselves *dispositionally* to neighbor-love. To follow the love commandment, therefore, one needs to become *unbound* in the desire for happiness. One either has to finish the job of searching for perfect fulfillment, so that nothing of it remains, or failing that, one needs to trust that the unquenchable longing for such happiness has been answered in an unknown way, that one is an heir to ultimate well-being, and that one can rely on this hope even without knowing how to define its object.

Some people can draw all the assurance that they need here from the sheer fact of their birth. For them, nature gives rise to no being without first stamping it with approval. Feeling the goodness of the world or sensing an "OK" behind all natural things gives them the confidence that their search for fulfillment does not have to be crowned with success for them to feel a sense of underlying confidence about their lives. They possess their happiness in a natural way; it comes with the gift of life, neither being identified with anything nor being dependent on one or another form of success. Perhaps the people who have such a natural assurance of their well-being are rare, but even if they are, they are free of the obsessive sort of desire that stands in the way of neighbor-love.

Christianity, of course, denies that such natural happiness can survive the heartaches and disappointments of an earnest human life. True happiness comes from the love of God, which is not a natural fact to be taken for granted but a gift to be accepted with thanksgiving. God, as the faithful believe, does not assume that we know what happiness is, nor does he promise happiness in the form that we might imagine. Rather, he promises us satisfaction for the unfocused desire that underlies all our hopes, the desire for happiness of an unknown kind. The believer who trusts in that accepts a promise, but it is a promise which enables one to forgo the desperate struggle to achieve the goal of fulfillment. Paradoxically, in relinquishing this goal and living in trust, believers find much of that happiness that they had once felt responsible for securing on their own.

The believer's response to faith's assurance, then, is gratitude. Indeed, if one does not feel gratitude for the promise of God, then one does not know what the love of God is. The commandment to return God's love entails the obligation to be grateful for the assurance that God offers. Yet, while one is obliged in faith to feel gratitude, this is not something that one can do merely by performing an act. Acts are crucially important as signs of gratitude, but the outward performance of an act is not equivalent to the disposition from which it springs. One must *feel* grateful inwardly. This is not simply a matter of actively responding to grace, as Outka sometimes suggests.[14] It is a matter of having one's disposition altered, so that one is *moved* to act in thankful ways.

If the idea that gratitude might be commanded seems strange, that is because we generally think of moral principles as governing only our deeds, not our feelings. Yet there is nothing strange about telling our children that they should feel grateful on certain occasions, and there is nothing wrong with telling people that they should feel grateful on the occasion of receiving God's love. Gratitude is the fitting response, and we have every right to expect it whenever people are blessed with great gifts.

Gratitude, however, is an expansive attitude which seeks expression in outward acts. To feel grateful is to turn one's thoughts to others to whom one might show one's gratitude. If one's benefactor is unavailable, or if there are no people to be thanked for one's good fortune, one tries to acknowledge a gift by repeating the generosity in a gift to another. Since God is not a person one can thank directly, one must express one's gratitude to God in this way. One *shows* one's gratitude for the lifting of human responsibility in relation to happiness, and one shows it *in one's treatment of others*. Thus, the grateful disposition of a believer comes out in charity to one's neighbors—in acts that demonstrate one's willingness to love and to regard another's interest in happiness as equivalent to one's own. One cannot specify the requirements of neighbor-love any further precisely because it is a disposition, not a type of behavior, that is commanded.

In fact, as long as a grateful disposition underlies one's acts, it does not always matter what these acts are. A gift which is offered in the spirit of charity may be highly prized by the giver and yet unappreciated by the one who receives it. This often happens when those of another culture try to give us tokens of their affection, for example. An Eskimo offers us a piece of blubber, a Japanese offers us the fish's eye, and the Hindu offers us a special gift of pan. None of these things needs to be valued in itself to be appreciated as a sign of the giver's disposition. We realize that the givers are offering something precious to them, and though their gifts are not precious to us, we accept them as the charitable acts that they are. In so doing, we appreciate the attitude that underlies the gift more than the gift itself.

The same holds true, I think, of the love commandment. The acts that fulfill this commandment are born in the disposition of believers. Those who believe in the promises of God are unbound from the task of achieving their happiness. They have replaced the struggle for happiness with the trust that it will be given to them in God's way. Thus, they are free to show others a pale copy of the concern that they believe has been shown to him. Their fundamental disposition has changed from preoccupation into gratitude, the fountainhead of all Christian charity. This is the reason why the second great commandment of Christianity depends on the first. And it is the reason why there is something distinctively Christian in the ideal of *agape*.

NOTES

1. Sören Kierkegaard, *Works of Love*, Howard and Edna Hong, trans. (New York: Harper & Row, 1962), pp. 34-35.
2. Gene Outka, *Agape* (New Haven: Yale University Press, 1972), pp. 11-12.
3. Ibid., pp. 263, 265-66.
4. Ibid., pp. 268-74.
5. Ibid., pp. 277; 294-309.
6. Ibid., pp. 197-200.
7. The same difficulty arises in an utilitarian ethics. If one is to decide ethical questions solely on the basis of the amount of happiness one's decisions produce, then one has to "step aside" from one's own fundamental convictions and take up an ethically neutral attitude toward the projects of others. But this neglects the extent to which one's actions flow from one's own attitudes and, by requiring one to distance oneself from one's own moral disposition, violates one's integrity. See Bernard Williams, "A Critique of Utilitarianism" in *Utilitarianism: For and Against*, with J. J. C. Smart (Cambridge: Cambridge University Press, 1973), pp. 115-17.
8. *Agape*, pp. 19-21.
9. In part, Outka avoids the possibility that the love commandment might be fulfilled in a patronizing way by referring to the need of the neighbor to have his "welfare accounted as valuable as another's," including one's own. Such a need might exist, but it is not particularly helpful to refer to it in explanation of the force of "equal regard." It comes close to saying

that we ought to regard the needs of others as we regard our own, and that one of their needs is to have their needs so regarded. See p. 265.

10. *Ibid.*, pp. 262-63.

11. Sören Kierkegaard, *Concluding Unscientific Postscript*, Walter Lowrie, trans. (Princeton: Princeton University Press, 1972), see the chapter "Truth is Subjectivity," *passim*.

12. *Agape*, pp. 263-67.

13. My sympathies lie with a very conservative interpretation of situation ethics, in which rules have a presumptive validity and are not simply useful compendiums of past experience. Outka himself favors a view in which rules have "prima facie" authority, and he implies that Joseph Fletcher might be interpreted along these lines. His discussion of situation ethics in chapter 4 of *Agape* is very helpful.

14. *Agape*, p. 52.

Jean Porter*

Salvific Love and Charity: A Comparison of the Thought of Karl Rahner and Thomas Aquinas

Near the beginning of his journey among those who have lost the good of the intellect, Dante comes among the good pagans, whose only (only!) punishment is the grief of longing without hope, eternally prolonged. Virgil exclaims, ". . . I would have you know they sinned not; yet their merit lacked its chiefest fulfillment, lacking baptism. . . ."[1] In these lines, Dante expresses a dilemma that has haunted Christianity since its inception. Until comparatively recently, most Christians have held that baptism, or at least explicit faith in Christ, is a prerequisite for salvation; and yet, this conviction has been difficult to square with a belief in God's justice and the evident moral goodness of so many non-Christians. It is little wonder, then, that Karl Rahner's views on the relation between love of neighbor and love of God, which seem to many to resolve this dilemma, have proven to be so influential. Rahner holds that any other directed love of the neighbor, such as is expressed in genuine morality, is at the same time the deepest possible love of God, whether recognized as such by the subject or not. In other words, the neighbor-love that underlies genuine morality is itself a truly salvific love, in that it serves to unite the human spirit to God in such a way as to lead

---

*Earlier versions of this essay were read at the annual meeting of the International St. Thomas Society in Boston, December, 1986, and the annual meeting of the Society of Christian Ethics in Durham, North Carolina, January, 1988, and I benefitted greatly from comments offered at those meetings. In addition, Alasdair MacIntyre, Charlotte Martin, Thomas O'Meara, Gene TeSelle, William Werpehowski, and an anonymous reader for Georgetown University Press read earlier versions of the essay and made very helpful suggestions for its improvement. Any remaining errors are of course mine alone. J.P.

ultimately to salvation. Explicit or thematic Christian belief is not required for salvation, because the love of neighbor contains, in a pre-thematic way, all and more than explicit belief affirms. So Rahner's argument goes.[2]

The continuing interest in Rahner's account of salvific love is all the more remarkable when we consider that it was shaped in the context of debates over issues that have lost much of their interest today. (Although it may well be that these issues no longer interest us because he appears to many theologians to have resolved them successfully.) For him, the central questions, at least initially, were, "What is the relationship between nature and grace? And how can this relationship be explicated in such a way as to avoid an extrinsicism of grace, while yet preserving its absolute gratuity?" A full treatment of his resolution of these questions would take us far afield, but I believe that it may be fairly said that Rahner succeeds in developing a doctrine of grace, including an account of salvific love, that avoids any hint of extrinsicism and yet preserves the gratuity of grace. Nonetheless, his account of grace and salvific love, precisely because of its importance and originality, raises other issues that are not central to the debates in which that account was forged. In particular, it forces us to look again at the relation between the moral life and the life of grace, and to ask whether Rahner's account of salvific love clarifies or obscures this relationship.

In this analysis, I compare Rahner's account of salvific love with the parallel discussions of love and charity in Aquinas' *Summa Theologiae*. I choose this particular comparison because Aquinas does have a fully developed account of the relation and, specifically, of the distinction between the moral life and the life of grace. Hence, a comparison between Aquinas and Rahner clarifies Rahner's treatment of this issue. Furthermore, I contend that this comparison indicates that Rahner has not fully grasped the implications of his account of salvific love. Specifically, I argue that, by making his concept of salvific love so inclusive, Rahner empties it of much of its content, in contrast to Aquinas, whose concept of charity is much more concrete. I do not mean to suggest that Aquinas' account is preferable to Rahner's, for Rahner in his turn raises questions that Aquinas does not address. However, a comparison of their thought is useful in calling our attention to problems that need further work.

1. SALVIFIC LOVE

In order to understand Rahner's account of salvific love, it is necessary to place it within the context of his overall views. As is well known, Rahner attempts to bring Thomistic theology into the modern era by grounding it explicitly in a neo-Kantian "turn to the subject," that is, in a systematic display of the transcendental conditions for knowledge in general and for the knowledge of God in particular. The centrality of Rahner's anthropology to his overall work, and its consequent richness and complexity, make any attempt to summarize it risky at best. Nonetheless, following Anne Carr, I believe that we can state its central tenets as follows:

A. The human psyche is grounded in an experience of subjectivity. This experience becomes conscious through a process of radical questioning, in which we as human subjects become objects to ourselves and are forced to recognize that no explanation of human subjectivity is sufficient. Every normal adult human being experiences this process of questioning and is aware of some dissatisfaction with his or her self-awareness, although this knowledge may well be suppressed at the conscious level.

B. At the same time, each person becomes aware that her or his psychological processes have no fixed limits. We are always capable of questioning, knowing, willing, and loving more than we do. For each, this realization deepens his or her self-awareness as subject, or spirit, therefore reinforcing and deepening dissatisfaction with all attempts to understand one's self as subject.

C. Unless this process is willfully suppressed, these questionings lead to the further realization that one's experiences as a thinking, willing, and loving creature presuppose an infinite horizon of being, and therefore, that the experience of subjectivity is at the same time for each person an experience of self-transcendence toward the infinite, a *positive* infinity.

D. "And this it is that all call God"; that is, this experience of the positively infinite as the ground of all being is the presupposition for all further knowledge of God's existence and (so to speak) personality, whether that knowledge is philosophically derived or is revealed.[3]

This final point is crucial to Rahner's account of salvific love, and indeed, to his whole theology, and therefore calls for some elaboration. What Rahner is saying is that the human spirit, as a being capable of unlimited self-transcendence in knowledge and love, is always inescapably aware of infinite truth and goodness as the implicit horizon of any spiritual act. Thus, the human person can be said to approach God as Infinite Being asymptotically, as it were, through repeated efforts to know more and to love more perfectly. In and of itself, this process would not be sufficient to unite the human person directly to God as a loving, personal, and Triune reality.

Rahner, following the Catholic tradition on this point, insists that such a union requires God's own direct self-communication through a properly supernatural dynamism of justifying grace (which finds its ultimate fruition in the direct, beatific vision of God). For example, he says that "... the gratuitousness of creation, as a free act of God, and grace as a free gift to the creature, are not the one and the same gift of God's free act."[4] But Rahner also holds that God, who wills the salvation of all, does in fact communicate God's self through an offer of direct personal union that is active in the spiritual dynamism of every person, whether this offer is accepted or not.[5] Because this communication takes place at the depths of consciousness, it is pre-thematic; that is, it forms part of the horizon of all consciousness, without necessarily being itself an explicit object of consciousness. Moreover, while this dynamism of grace is formally distinct from the purely natural dynamism of the human spirit, and is affirmed as a matter of doctrine to be gratuitous, the two dynamisms are in fact always concretely united in the actually existing order of things. Indeed, even the formal distinction between the natural and the supernatural dynamisms of the human spirit toward God tends to disappear in Rahner's later writings: "The absolutely unlimited transcendence of the natural spirit in knowledge and freedom along with its term, the holy mystery, already implies by itself such an infinity in the subject that the possession of God in absolute self-communication does not really fall outside of this infinite possession of transcendence, although it remains gratuitous."[6]

Although Rahner has expressed reservations about the view of some neo-scholastics that there is a natural desire for God, present as a motive force in all persons, nonetheless his thought is in continuity with the spirit of this view, and he himself suggests the thesis that grace is ubiquitous as an alternative to this view.[7] His anthropology implies that a pre-thematic desire for God is intrinsic to human persons as we now are, and innate in the sense that God has implanted that desire in the depths of the human spirit. Each of us is subject, like it or not, to the pre-thematic awareness that our drive to know and act and love can never be satisfied except in an infinite object. While we can willfully suppress this restless yearning, we cannot put an end to it, nor exorcise the dissatisfaction that will result from our attempts to do so. On the other hand, if we follow this yearning through the stages of our growing self-knowledge as spirit, it will lead us progressively to an ever-deepening knowledge of God as the ground of our freedom.

Nonetheless, this yearning for God can be frustrated, suppressed, or finally rendered hopeless through the "no" of unrepentant sin. It is very important to realize that sin and damnation are real possibilities for Rahner, even though he also holds firmly to the real possibility of salvation for all. On a first reading, it is puzzling to find that this is Rahner's view. After all, on his own showing there is an orientation toward God in the depths of the human spirit, which expresses itself in every human act. Hence, it would appear that every human act necessarily involves at least a pre-thematic intentionality toward God as the horizon of our existence. How then is a sinful action possible at all, since such an action is nothing other than an act of refusal of God, whether it is explicitly understood as such, or not? Rahner is well aware of this paradox: ". . . there is in the act in which freedom says 'no' a real and absolute contradiction by the fact that God is affirmed and denied at the same time. . . . We have to affirm the real possibility of such an absolute contradiction."[8]

Even though Rahner thus emphasizes the paradoxical character of sin, his grounds for asserting its possibility are made clear in his account of morality. And it is important that we examine this assertion carefully, since it will provide the key for understanding his account of the relationship of salvific love to morality.

Let us begin this examination by putting a different, but related, question to Rahner: What is the point of morality? His answer is that morality is the means by which the human person attains (or at least approaches) self-realization as a self-transcending spirit.[9] At once, a further question arises: How is it possible to speak of attaining the full realization of that which one already is, namely, a self-transcending spirit? Rahner's answer goes as follows: There is nothing inappropriate in speaking of something as being, in some sense, what it is only potentially in another sense (for example, an acorn is truly an oak in one sense—that is, it is *specifically* an oak and not a daisy—but is an oak only potentially in another sense). So it is with the human spirit. Each of us must exercise some transcendence in order to act at all. But the full self-transcendence that alone can fulfill us perfectly is only potentially present in each human being, although this potency is formally the ground of any potentiality for human action whatever. (In somewhat the same way, the possibility for becoming a spreading oak is the formal condition for the process by which the nut becomes a sapling, and then a tree—although of course these processes may be terminated at any point before reaching the fruition of maturity.)

Moreover, the exigencies of the human spirit are such that the human person can only attain self-realization as a spiritual being through a conscious intentionality toward self-transcendence. But in what does this intentionality consist? Certainly not in the explicit desire for self-transcendence; otherwise, only a few philosophers would ever approach true human fulfillment. To the contrary, Rahner holds that this intentionality is present, although in a pre-thematic way, whenever a person goes out of himself or herself in genuine love to affirm the reality and integral value of another person. It is only through such an act that the individual encounters an Other that is personal, and therefore truly Other. Hence, in an act of this sort, and only in such an act, the human person recognizes the true freedom of self-disposal that is his or hers (potentially) as transcendent spirit. As Rahner says: "The only way in which man achieves self-realization is through encounters with his fellow man, a fellow who is rendered present to his experience in knowledge and love in the course of his personal life, one, therefore, who is not a thing or a matter, but a man."[10] And it is just such an act, which Rahner describes as an act of genuine neighbor-love, that is truly a moral act.

At the same time, an act of genuine neighbor-love is truly an act of salvific love in which the human person says "yes" to God in the depths of his or her personal being. Precisely because any act of genuine neighbor-love is *ipso facto* an act of supreme freedom, it is also the supreme act of self-affirmation of the human spirit as spirit, that is, as a being capable of unlimited self-transcendence. And because God is the ultimate source of this potentiality, such an act is at the same time the fullest and most complete act of openness to God that a human being can perform. Conversely, an immoral act, that is, a refusal to go out of one's self in genuine neighbor-love, is implicitly yet truly a refusal of freedom and of God, who offers God's self to each person in the invitation to freedom. Hence, although every human act is an affirmation of God in one sense, not every human act affirms God in the more proper sense of claiming fully one's own freedom. And this possibility, that is, that we might fall short of a full affirmation of our own freedom in a given action, is the ground of the possibility of sin.

Even more important for our purposes, our ability *not* to sin, to affirm our full freedom in true neighbor-love, is the ground of the salvific significance of the moral life for Rahner. To repeat: for Rahner, the human person cannot make a more radical act of openness to God than that which is made implicitly by claiming one's full freedom in an act of neighbor-love. All that remains for this act to be salvific is for God to endow it with the character of saving faith:

> ... whenever man posits a positively moral act in the full exercise of his free self-disposal, this act is a positive supernatural salvific act in the actual economy of salvation even when its *a*

posteriori object and the explicitly given *a posteriori* motive do not spring tangibly from the positive revelation of God's Word but are in this sense 'natural.' This is so because God in virtue of his universal salvific will offers everyone his supernatural divinizing grace and thus elevates [moral action]. Furthermore, the thereby already given, supernatural transcendent although unconscious horizon of the spirit (its *a priori* orientation towards the [Triune God]), includes an element of (transcendental) revelation and possibly of faith which also gives such an act that sufficient character of 'faith' necessary [for it to be salvific].[11]

Hence, Rahner asserts that not only is every act of genuine love of neighbor also an act of love of God, but conversely, every act of the love of God is also formally an act of the love of the neighbor. Hence, the two can never really be separated: ". . . whenever a genuine love of man attains its proper nature and its moral absoluteness and depth, it is in addition always so underpinned and heightened by God's saving grace that it is also love of God, whether it is explicitly considered to be such a love by the subject or not."[12]

When we turn to Aquinas' discussion of love of God and neighbor in the *Summa Theologiae*, we will see that there are at least apparent similarities between Rahner's account of salvific love and Aquinas' account of charity. But underneath these *prima facie* similarities there are more basic, and instructive, differences between the two accounts. We now turn to a consideration of Aquinas' account of charity and a comparison of that account to Rahner's account of salvific love.

2. CHARITY

As we have just seen, Rahner holds that there is a supernatural and graced, yet ubiquitous, yearning toward God that is present, however inchoately, in each person. Aquinas, on the other hand, is often taken as an example of those who hold that there is a natural desire for God present in all. This interpretation would suggest that, at least, he and Rahner agree that there is *some* sort of desire for God present as a motive force in all persons. And at first glance, it would seem that this interpretation is justified, for the *Summa Theologiae* contains numerous references to a natural desire or love for God.[13] On closer examination, however, we find that when Aquinas uses this expression, generally he refers explicitly to the natural desire of *all creatures* for God; indeed, there seems to be no place in the *S.T.* where Aquinas speaks of a natural love for God on the part of human beings specifically. (Elsewhere, he does, for example, in the *Summa Contra Gentiles* III. I, 48). And so, before we conclude too quickly that we understand the relation of nature and grace for Aquinas, it will be well to ask what he means by asserting that all creatures have a natural desire for God. In order to make sense of this claim, it will be necessary to place it in the overall context of his doctrine of creation.[14]

Certainly, when Aquinas speaks of the natural desire or love of the creature for God, he does not mean to say that every creature has a conscious yearning for the Almighty. Rather, he uses this expression to point toward one important aspect of his doctrine of creation, which is an account of the world and all that in it lies, considered as creatures.[15] According to Aquinas, God, as Creator, is the ultimate final cause of all things (as well as the ultimate formal and efficient cause). Hence, everything that exists may be said in some sense to be moving toward God, because a final cause is by definition the purpose or goal of some process.[16] And logically so, since if God creates, God must have a purpose in doing so, which purpose can only be the communication of God's own goodness. But the term "good" and its derivative forms are nothing other than ways of describing existence itself under the formal aspect of desirability.[17] Hence, to say that God bestows goodness on creatures is in effect to say that God creates, taking the act of creation under the specific logical aspect of bringing something desirable into being.

Correlatively, when Aquinas says that the creature desires God, he is saying that it desires its own actual perfection, since all created goodness is (somehow) a similitude of divine goodness.[18] Similarly, God directs irrational creatures toward God by building into them, so to speak, dynamisms toward their own specific perfection[19]—which is the same thing as simply creating them as creatures of specific kinds with their own proper principles of operation. Nothing in the *S.T.* suggests that the natural desire for God on the part of creatures is anything more than this natural inclination of all creatures toward their own specific perfection.

In what sense, then, are we to understand the natural desire of the human person for God in Aquinas' system? As was noted above, Aquinas is very reluctant even to speak of such a desire, at least in the *S.T.* I believe that this reluctance stems from his desire to avoid confusion between two senses of "natural," which can mean "proper to a given species," or can serve as a contrast term to "rational." For Aquinas, what is distinctive about human beings is that we must direct ourselves toward our specific perfection through conscious and rational choice; in *this* sense, we do not attain our final end naturally (as irrational creatures do).[20] Since the natural desire for God and the desire for one's specific perfection come to the same thing for Aquinas, we can readily appreciate his reluctance to speak of a natural desire for God on the part of human beings. Nonetheless, even in the *S.T.*, the existence of a human directedness toward God that is natural in the sense of being innate may fairly be assumed from what Aquinas says repeatedly about the natural/innate desire of all creatures for God.

So far, it would seem that Aquinas and Rahner do at least agree that there is some sort of desire for God present as a motive force in everyone. But more careful reflection indicates that their similarities on this point are not so great as we might at first be inclined to suppose. For Rahner, an innate directedness toward God is built into the self-transcending structure of the human mind in such a way that it can be revealed through the gradual process of coming to know oneself as a thinking and willing subject. But I have not been able to find any evidence that Aquinas also holds that a desire for God is built into the structures of the mind in such a way that that desire can become explicit through a phenomenological reflection on one's own mental processes. To the contrary, Aquinas denies that the explicit knowledge of God is innate in all persons.[21] He explains that a knowledge of God can be said to be innate in a certain sense, in that all persons desire happiness, and true happiness consists in union with God. However, this does not mean that all persons know God in a proper sense of "know," since there are many who believe that ultimate happiness consists in the enjoyment of some finite good. The point that Aquinas makes here depends on a familiar observation about the ambiguity of "knowing." In an absolute sense, I can be said to know X only if I know it *as* X. If X = Y, but I do not know that, then in a derivative sense I may be said to know Y, because I know what is *in fact* equivalent to X—but if I were asked if I knew Y, I would deny it. If I know Mr. Smith who, unknown to me, is my long-lost father, then in a derivative sense I may be said to know my father, but not in the proper sense that counts for me.[22]

In what sense, then, *are* we to understand the human directedness toward God, as Aquinas would construe it? The most likely interpretation will be guided by what he says explicitly about the desire, or directedness, of all creatures toward God. Understood in this sense, the human person's natural desire for God is nothing other than a desire for one's own perfection as a human person, that is, as a rational animal. There is no need to introduce the postulate of a conscious, intentional human orientation toward God, pre-thematic or otherwise, in order to extend what Aquinas says about the natural desire for God to human creatures. In other words, Aquinas sees the innate human desire for God as being equivalent to a desire for one's own specific good as a human being; in turn, this specific good, seen from the standpoint of the Christian believer, is in fact a created similitude of God's goodness.[23] Hence, human beings are not distinguished from the rest of creation by the natural, creaturely desire for God, understood as a desire for specific perfection as a creature of a certain kind. There is, however, one important difference between human persons and the rest of creation, still considered as purely rational beings: We, as rational animals, must direct ourselves toward our own specific perfection by a series of conscious choices, informed by a rational plan for attaining our own perfection.[24] In other words, the human person is able to grasp the rational principles and exigencies of human existence and flourishing, and to act accordingly. These principles are nothing other than the proper external and internal principles of human action, or, as we would say, the principles of morality.[25] If we recall that a creature's desire for its own perfection can be equated with its desire for God, understood as the desire for a created similitude of God's goodness, then we may say in this sense, the natural desire for God is the ground of the moral life for Aquinas. But note once again that, properly understood, this claim does nothing more than to redescribe, under a different formal aspect, the claim that our natural desire for our specific perfection is the ground of the moral life.

Contrast the natural desire for God, understood in this sense, with justifying grace and its operative principles, the theological virtues of faith, hope, and charity. The theological virtues are distinguished from the cardinal (moral) virtues precisely in the fact that whereas the cardinal virtues, taken alone, direct us toward our natural perfection, the theological virtues direct us toward union with God as God is in God's self.[26] Aquinas describes the union between God and the human person brought about by the theological virtues in the strongest terms, short of the hypostatic union, that he can find: The justified are united to God without any intermediary;[27] enjoy "a certain intimate conversation" with God;[28] are connatural with God;[29] partakers of the divine nature;[30] even deified (*deificet*).[31] In short, the theological virtues, when perfected in charity, transform their subject into a true friend of God who participates intimately, through the transformation of the inmost mind, in the mind of God.[32] At the same time, Aquinas insists just as strongly that the direct union with God to which the supernatural virtues direct the justified completely exceeds all the potentialities of human nature.[33] Hence, he insists that the supernatural virtues are bestowed entirely from without.[34]

At the same time, the justified, who are given a new orientation toward God as a personal reality, also find a new orientation toward God in their moral life. In contrast with Rahner, who holds that the directedness toward God that underlies the moral life may not come to explicit consciousness at all, Aquinas sees the theological virtues as transforming the moral life precisely in and through the introduction of a new, conscious orientation toward God, which transforms both mind and will.[35] Just as the justified once attempted to direct themselves toward their natural perfection as human persons (assuming that they were naturally just), so now, based on the new life bestowed in faith, hope, and charity, they act in such a way as to grow in union with God. The moral life now takes on a subordinate, although necessary role in these efforts: They now behave morally in order not to hinder their progress toward full union with God, which would be hindered or even rendered impossible by the contempt for God's creation, and especially for their fellow men and women, that deliberate immorality would require.[36] It is true that the object of the moral life, as it would be lived outside the order of grace, and the object of the truly salvific love of charity are materially one and the same. That is, because the moral life directs us toward our specific perfection as human beings, it is directed toward God as the supreme final cause, just as the development of any other kind of creature toward its own specific form of perfection is directed toward God as final cause. And as we know through revelation, this universal final cause is in fact identical with the God of Jesus Christ.[37] For this reason, the sublimation of the moral life, so to speak, into the life of progressive union with God in charity is logically possible. But it does not follow that these two kinds of desire for God are qualitatively the same, or even have the same formal object. In fact, for Aquinas, they are not and do not. There is a complete qualitative difference between our natural orientation toward goodness and the orientation toward God bestowed in grace.[38]

It follows that Aquinas distinguishes between two senses in which the human person can be said to know and to love God. And he appeals to this distinction in order to explain how it is possible to attain genuine knowledge of God and a limited but real sort of moral goodness apart from grace. Genuine knowledge of God is possible apart from grace through philosophical speculation, but what the knowledge in question amounts to is nothing more than knowledge of the existence of a first and final cause.[39] Knowledge of this sort is appropriate to our nature, he says, but it is qualitatively different from the knowledge of God as God is in God's self that is attained inchoately through faith and perfected in the beatific vision.[40] In itself, such philosophical knowledge of God is not even partially sufficient for true happiness or salvation. Furthermore, our natural knowledge of God, far from being a built-in feature of human consciousness, is attained only after much difficulty by the wise, in contrast to faith, which is possible to all, wise or simple.[41] Similarly, the moral virtues by themselves are capable of directing us toward a natural happiness which is in fact our created participation in God's goodness.[42] While Aquinas holds that perfect natural goodness is now impossible, due to original sin, he nonetheless maintains that we are capable even now of real, although imperfect, moral goodness without charity.[43] However, he says, since we are in fact called to a happiness that exceeds our natural capacities, it is appropriate to reserve the name of virtue in its fullest sense to the theological virtues which direct us toward that goal.[44]

We are now in a position to compare Aquinas' account of charity with Rahner's account of salvific love. Note first of all that Aquinas agrees with Rahner that love of God and love of neighbor are always linked together, at least (according to Aquinas) potentially so.[45] Aquinas does assert that the love of God is formally prior to the love of neighbor in charity,[46] but Rahner would not necessarily disagree with that claim, since he holds that God's offer of God's self is always formally (although not temporally) prior to the person's 'yes' to God in an act of true neighbor love.

Nonetheless, the two theologians do differ in one crucial respect: Aquinas holds that charity adds something qualitatively different to the moral life as now experienced, whereas Rahner holds that salvific love does not necessarily add any new element to the moral life as now experienced. Certainly, Rahner does hold that God must add an element of sanctifying grace to the moral act in order to elevate it to an act of salvific love. But his point is precisely that this element of sanctifying grace is present whenever the moral life is lived with integrity. For him, there is concretely no such thing as a life of moral goodness lived without grace, distinct from the life of grace on the one hand, and the life of actual sin on the other. But for Aquinas there is such a thing as moral rectitude without grace, and correlatively, the theological virtues do add something qualitatively new to the moral life. And this new element makes a difference to the way that the moral life is conducted and experienced. That is to say, the life of the justified person looks different from the life of the morally good person; the former acts in different ways and expresses different motivations and feelings than does the latter.

Admittedly, this is not immediately apparent. Aquinas does say that genuine moral virtue and really good actions are possible without grace; genuinely good, that is, in the sense of corresponding to the exigencies of our human nature, although not even partially sufficient to unite the individual to God.[47] In other words, for Aquinas it is possible to identify a kind of moral goodness that exists apart from grace, and to tell the difference between it and the life of charity. But he also says that charity is the form of all the moral and theological virtues, as they exist in the justified individual, and correlatively, charity cannot exist without the other virtues.[48] Might this not imply that charity (and faith and hope) simply supervene on the moral life, so to speak, adding a specifically religious motivation, or even a new set of duties, without changing the substance of the moral life *per se*?

I think not. What this suggestion overlooks is that fact that for Aquinas, charity is an architectonic virtue. That is, charity integrates the other virtues and capacities of the person into a unified personality, in and through orienting that person's actions and reactions to a particular end. We read that charity (which presupposes faith and hope) serves to direct the individual to the happiness of the beatific vision, which is recognized to be true happiness.[49] Hence, while charity does add some new duties to the moral life (for example, fraternal correction),[50] that is not the essential change that it brings about. Rather, its most significant impact is to be seen in the way in which the moral life is conducted. What the charitable person does may be the same as what the naturally good person does in a particular instance, but the way in which it is done will be different. The charitable person does the right thing for the right reason, that is the love of God; it is in this sense that charity is the form of all the other virtues, bestowing on them their proper objects.[51] Because the personality of the charitable person has been unified by an aspiration toward the supreme joy of union with God, she or he will do the right thing readily and gladly, without suffering the inner conflicts of the individual who is devoted to the conflicting goods of human life (as Aquinas thinks the person without grace inevitably will suffer them).[52] Furthermore, the charitable person will exhibit capacities that the ungraced person will not have, most important, the ability to grasp intuitively what devotion to God requires in a particular instance and to act accordingly.[53] Hence, because charity serves to coordinate the virtues and capacities of the individual over the course of a whole life, its effects will be most evident when we look at that life taken as a whole.[54]

3. MORALITY AND GRACE

My purpose in comparing Aquinas and Rahner with respect to their accounts of charity/salvific love is not to adjudicate between the two accounts, and it is certainly not to advocate that we jettison Rahner's account in favor of Aquinas'. Even if we were prepared to accept the full implications of Aquinas' account of grace and its dependence on explicit beliefs, there have been too many intellectual and social changes since his time to make his theology a viable contemporary option as it stands. Nonetheless, by comparing Rahner to one of his most important pre-modern sources, we may be able to see something about the distinctive contours of Rahner's thought that would otherwise not have been apparent to us. Such a comparison may suggest that Rahner's account has not adequately dealt with questions that must be addressed in any fully adequate account of salvific love. At least, that is the argument that I will offer in this section.

Specifically, I will argue that it is an advantage of Aquinas' account, as compared to Rahner's, that the former preserves the specificity and concreteness of the concept of charity/salvific love, whereas the latter does not. I realize that this claim is bound to seem strange at first. After all, Rahner deliberately strips the concept of salvific love of the elements that particularize it for Aquinas, namely, its relation to a conscious, explicit orientation to the God of Jesus Christ, and he does so for reasons that are bound to engage our concurrence. He is firmly committed to the claim that in view of the universal salvific will of God, salvation is a real possibility for all men and women, including non-Christians, and even atheists. And he naturally concludes that as long as salvific love presupposes specifically Christian beliefs, that claim cannot be made. Hence, he detaches salvific love from any essential connection to Christian beliefs, or any other specific beliefs whatever. In the process, he empties the network of concepts associated with the doctrine of grace of any independent content. Rather, for Rahner these concepts become alternative ascriptions for states of affairs that could also be adequately described through the language of morality, broadly understood. Indeed, at least one theologian has suggested (approvingly) that a radical appropriation of Rahner's thought may lead us to "the abandonment of the entire framework of nature and grace as it has been handed down to us through the ages."[55] And while such a move would have the advantage of freeing us from a conceptual framework that has become increasingly problematic, it would also seriously impoverish the language of Christian moral discourse in at least one respect.

In order to see the implication of Rahner's account of salvific love for Christian moral discourse, it must be noted that the concepts by which the doctrine of grace is applied to persons—faith, hope, charity or salvific love, and sinfulness—are concepts of virtues or vices, whatever else they are. That is, they are meant to describe enduring traits of character, which are manifested by characteristic kinds of actions and patterns of behavior and sometimes also by sets of emotional dispositions. Now, since this is the case, it is clear that if we claim to have a concept of, say, charity, at all, then we must be able to say what charity looks like—what the charitable person characteristically does, what sorts of actions count as charitable actions, what sort of evidence would count as *prima facie* evidence that a person is not charitable, and so forth.

My point here is quite general and does not depend on the specifically theological quality of these particular character traits. Therefore, it may be clearer if we consider a second, more ordinary example. Consider, then, what is involved in formulating a concept of the vice of greed. No doubt it would be possible to formulate a definition of greed, or to find it in the dictionary. But I have not bothered to try, because we generally know well enough what greed means. What we know, specifically, is what greed looks like, that is, what kinds of things the greedy person does, and what sorts of actions count as greedy actions. We can distinguish greediness, in persons or actions, from other kinds of deficiencies. Our discriminating capacities in this regard will not be infallible. But then, our capacities for discrimination never are infallible, and when we make a mistake, we can normally give an account of what went wrong in our evaluations. ("We all thought she was greedy, but now we know that she was suffering from diabetes.") In fact, any general definition of greed that we may propose will depend on these capacities for recognizing greed when we see it. Possession of such a definition will never replace these capacities. Rather, these capacities enable us to apply, extend, and where necessary correct such a definition.

The example of charity is not quite parallel to that of greed, but the difference between them is not primarily theological. Rather, the salient difference between them lies in the fact that greed is associated with specific kinds of situations and particular appetites, whereas charity, as an architectonic virtue, is not so particularized. Nonetheless, Aquinas indicates sufficiently how we are to recognize charity as an enduring trait of character, by spelling out the kinds of dispositions and enduring orientations that it produces. Although we may not be able to distinguish a particular act of charity from a particular act of an acquired virtue in every case, nonetheless, on Aquinas' showing, we can recognize a charitable life with tolerable accuracy. Specifically, what we observe, over the course of a lifetime, is the way in which the various actions and character traits of an individual are brought into a unity by a conscious orientation toward the God of Jesus Christ. And that unity looks different from the life of the upright pagan, or indeed, that of the unloving Christian.

Rahner, on the other hand, deliberately empties the concept of salvific love of anything that would distinguish it from the genuine love of the neighbor that, for him, is proper to morality. For Rahner, salvific love is no longer a virtue, that is, a trait of character at all. Rather, he holds that salvific love is concretely present in *every* moral act, just insofar as the latter *is* a moral act. Certainly, Rahner recognizes the possibility that an unloving person might preserve outward conformity to the moral code, but in his view, the actions of such a one would not be true moral acts.[56] In other words, for Rahner there are finally only two possibilities: an action of true morality which is always graced, or actual sin (in contrast to Aquinas, who recognizes the possibility of ungraced actions that are nonetheless not positively sinful).[57] Hence, as Rahner treats it, "salvific love" becomes a theologically motivated ascription, rather than a concept of a recognizable quality of character. That is, when applied to a person or an action, the concept of salvific love does not add anything to the account of that person or action, which, on Rahner's hypothesis, could already be described adequately in terms of moral evaluation. What it does do is indicate the significance of that person or action in terms of a set of concepts and concerns, namely, those having to do with God and our relation to God. In other words, for Rahner, the notions of "moral goodness" and "salvific love" become co-extensive (and equally general); the latter term can be applied if and only if the former can, and it is distinguished from the former only to indicate that the subject matter of morality is now being considered under a different formal aspect.

And why not? There is nothing necessarily illegitimate about such a move. Indeed, as we have seen, Aquinas does about the same thing in his treatment of the general notion of the desire for God. The difficulty is that once we turn charity or salvific love into this sort of ascription, then the concept is no longer available to us as a way of conceptualizing *discriminations* that we may still need or want to make. And in this particular case, I would argue, we still do need to be able to make the relevant discriminations that separate out charity (and faith and hope) from otherwise similar qualities.

What follows is a large topic, and I do not pretend to be able to treat it adequately. I only hope to be able to show what the issues are. My central point is this: If my account of virtue concepts is correct, and if charity is truly a concept of a virtue, then it follows that it is, in a broad sense, an empirical concept. That is, it reflects discriminations that we actually do make between the life of charity, and other, perhaps quite attractive ways of life. I am not saying that we simply read off the existence of charity from the evidences of experience. We would not have a concept of this particular virtue if we did not approach experience from within a framework of Christian beliefs and practices.[58] But given that we do, the concept of charity has emerged from the discriminations that we find it necessary or at least helpful to make, as we try to direct our lives in accordance with those beliefs and practices. Specifically, the traditional concept of charity has emerged from our shared reflection on what counts as a successful Christian life. As such, it serves to indicate the point of being a Christian, to set criteria for success or failure as a Christian, and finally to formulate guidance and to offer remedies when things go wrong. Note further that these experiences and shared reflections can always modify the concept of charity (as is true of all virtue concepts). Hence, just as the notion of charity is an empirical notion, so certain theological questions that depend on our interpretation of charity are, at least in part, empirical questions. (For example, can the justified attain perfection in this life? John Wesley concluded that they could, in large part because he met people who in his opinion were living out of perfect Christian love.[59])

Note that I say that we *did* make these kinds of discriminations. But my chief objection to Rahner is that we still *do* find it necessary to make them. And yet, his reinterpretation of the notion of salvific love empties out the very conceptual framework within which they are to be made. As I see it, Rahner's account leaves us with only two options. On the one hand, we can just stop making the relevant discriminations; that is, we can deny that being a Christian matters in such a way that it is of interest to us to discern what a successful Christian life looks like. But in that case, it is difficult to see why we should bother with Christianity at all.

On the other hand, we might still try to discern what counts as a successful (explicitly) Christian life, but deny that there is any necessary connection between living a successful Christian life and entering into union with God. That is Rahner's approach. But this approach, too, involves difficulties. For one thing, it still leaves us wondering whether there is any good reason to want to be a Christian. This objection is not as serious as it may appear at first to be, because even if one holds that the essential character of salvific love does not require explicit faith, it is still possible to argue that the fullness of salvific love requires that it be expressed in historical Christianity (as Rahner in fact does).[60] However, a more serious difficulty remains. For not only did the traditional concept of charity emerge in the context of a set of beliefs about God and his plan for the world, but it has served in turn to provide those beliefs with a central component of their content.

Throughout the Christian tradition, charity has consistently been held to be necessary for salvation. Well and good; but what do we mean by salvation, and why should we want it? It is easy to answer this question in formal theological terms: Salvation is the beatific vision, direct union with God, and so on. The difficulty is that in themselves, these concepts are remote from our everyday ideas of happiness and misfortune. Indeed, we may agree with Aquinas that we cannot properly form *concepts* of God or the beatific vision at all, although we can provide such terms with a sort of derivative intelligibility.[61] But even if we do not want to go that far, the fact remains that claims about salvation have very little concrete meaning and practical significance unless they can be tethered to day-to-day life in some way. And the traditional concept of charity served as one critical point at which that tethering took place. What do we mean by salvation? For centuries, Christians have not only answered this through theological formulae; we have also pointed to examples of the life of charity, in order to indicate something of the quality of the new life. (Hence, charity has traditionally been said to be the inchoate but real beginning of the life of glory.) Why should anyone want salvation? We point to examples of those who are living the life of charity in order to show that they have something that other people might reasonably want; or conversely, we point to examples of sinfulness in order to show that sin is really a misfortune, even though appearances are sometimes to the contrary.

Moreover, I would suggest that one of the central reasons that Christianity has been able to sustain itself as a religion lies in the fact that these discriminations continue to have at least some plausibility and point. For many of us, the life of sin *is* a misfortune, and even more important the life of charity *does* have something to offer that decent good living alone cannot supply. The distinctions that the traditional doctrine of the theological virtues attempted to capture were not simply forced upon us by the logic of an abstract theological system. Rather, these distinctions have been forced upon us, so to speak, at least in part by the discriminations that we do in fact make. Hence, it is a serious weakness in Rahner's account of salvific love that it cannot account for these discriminations.

And yet, in another respect Rahner's account of salvific love does reflect a very widespread perception about charity as we use the concept today. Specifically, Rahner's theory accurately reflects the fact that we do not in fact find that charity is always linked with

Christian belief or participation in the life of an institutional church. And in my view, it would be a very great mistake to deny this perception by attempting to argue that charity, or final salvation, necessarily presupposes explicit Christian belief. The challenge that Rahner sets for us, then, is to discern how we do in fact make the necessary discriminations between charity and other desirable qualities, and to give some account of these discriminations that integrates them into the wider context of contemporary Christian belief, without forcing us to the conclusion that salvific love is always necessarily linked to explicit belief. But, happily, that is not the task of this essay.

NOTES

1. *The Divine Comedy I: Inferno* IV 33-35. The translation that I use is that by Dorothy Sayers (Harmondsworth, Middlesex: Penguin Books, 1949).
2. For this essay, I relied especially on Rahner's remarks in three works: *Foundations of Christian Faith: An Introduction to the Idea of Christianity* (New York: Crossroad, 1985); "The 'Commandment' of Love in Relation to the Other Commandments," *Theological Investigations* 5 (New York: Crossroad, 1966), pp. 439-59, and "Reflections on the Unity of the Love of Neighbor and the Love of God," *T.I.* 6 (New York: Crossroad, 1969), pp. 231-52. Additionally, I have drawn on the following: "Concerning the Relationship Between Nature and Grace, *T.I.* 1 (1961, 1965), pp. 297-318, "Nature and Grace," *T.I.* 4 (1966), pp. 165-88, "Experience of Self and Experience of God," *T.I.* 13 (1975), pp. 122-32, "Observations on the Problem of the 'Anonymous Christian,'" *T.I.* (1976), pp. 280-94, "Anonymous and Explicit Faith," *T.I.* 16 (1979), pp. 52-59, and *The Love of Jesus and the Love of Neighbor* (New York: Crossroad, 1983).
3. Anne E. Carr, "Starting with the Human," in *A World of Grace: an Introduction to the Themes and Foundations of Karl Rahner's Theology*, Leo J. O'Donovan, ed. (New York: Crossroad, 1981), pp. 17-30. Rahner himself offers a summary discussion of these points in *Foundations*, pp. 51-71.
4. "Nature and Grace," p. 185; compare also the extended discussion of the gratuity of grace in "Concerning the Relationship between Nature and Grace."
5. This is the supernatural existential; see *Foundations*, pp. 126-133.
6. *Foundations*, pp. 129-130.
7. See "Concerning the Relationship Between Nature and Grace."
8. *Foundations*, p. 99.
9. In what follows, I rely especially on "The 'Commandment' of Love in Relation to the Other Commandments" and *Foundations*, pp. 90-133.
10. "Experience of Self and Experience of God," p. 127.

11. "Reflections on the Unity of the Love of Neighbor and the Love of God," p. 239.
12. "Reflections of the Unity of the Love of Neighbor and the Love of God," p. 237.
13. See, for example, *S.T.* I 6.1; I-II 26.2, 109.3, 7.
14. *S.T.* I 44, 45.
15. For my interpretation of Aquinas' account of creation, I am indebted to David B. Burrell, *Aquinas: God and Action* (Notre Dame: University of Notre Dame, 1979), especially 135-40. I discuss the relation between the natural desire for God and the moral life in Aquinas in more detail in "Desire for God: Ground of the Moral Life in Aquinas," *Theological Studies* 47 (1986), 48-68.
16. *S.T.* I 44.4.
17. *S.T.* I 5.1.
18. *S.T.* I 6.1 *ad* 2.
19. *S.T.* I 22.2, 103.1; I-II 93.5.
20. *S.T.* I-II 1.2.
21. *S.T.* I 2.1.
22. See *S.T.* I 2.1 *ad* 1; cf. I-II 5.8.
23. I discuss Aquinas' views on the natural end of the human person in some detail in *The Recovery of Virtue: The Relevance of Aquinas for Christian Ethics* (Louisville: Westminster/John Knox Press, 1990), 63-8.
24. *S.T.* I-II 1.2, 1.8.
25. For example, see *S.T.* I-II 19.3, 62.2, 64.1,2.
26. *S.T.* I-II 62.1.
27. *S.T.* II-II 23.6, 27.4; I-II 66.6.
28. *S.T.* I-II 65.5; (my translation).
29. *S.T.* II-II 23.2.
30. *S.T.* I-II 62.1.
31. *S.T.* I-II 112.1.
32. *S.T.* II-II 23.1, 2.
33. *S.T.* I 12.13; I-II 5.5, 62.1,2, 109.5, 110.1.
34. *S.T.* I-II 63.1; cf. I-II 62.1.
35. *S.T.* I-II 62.4.
36. *S.T.* I-II 4.4, 71.6, 72.4, 73.1; cf. 65.3.
37. *S.T.* I 2.3.
38. *S.T.* I-II 4.4, 71.6, 72.4, 73.1; cf. 65.3.
39. *S.T.* I 2.3; II-II 2.3.
40. *S.T.* I-II 109.3 *ad* 1; II-II 2.3.
41. *S.T.* I-II 109.2.
42. *S.T.* I-II 62.1.
43. *S.T.* I-II 109.2.
44. *S.T.* I-II 65.2.
45. *S.T.* II-II 25.1, 27.8.
46. *S.T.* II-II 26.2.
47. *S.T.* I-II 100.10, 109.2.
48. *S.T.* I-II 65.2,3.

49. *S.T.* I-II 62; II-II 23.4,6.
50. *S.T.* II-II 33.
51. *S.T.* II-II 23.8.
52. *S.T.* II-II 29.
53. *S.T.* II-II 45.
54. I am grateful to Stanley Hauerwas for pointing this out to me.
55. George Vandervelde, "The Grammar of Grace: Karl Rahner as a Watershed in Contemporary Theology," *Theological Studies* 49.3 (September 1988), pp. 445-459, at 459.
56. For example, see *Foundations*, p. 102.
57. See *S.T.* I-II 100.10.
58. For further discussion of this point, see George Lindbeck, *The Nature of Doctrine: Religion and Theology in a Postliberal Age* (Philadelphia: Westminster Press, 1984), pp. 30-45.
59. John Wesley, "A Plain Account of Christian Perfection," in Frank Whaling, ed., *The Classics of Western Spirituality: John and Charles Wesley* (New York: Paulist Press, 1981), pp. 297-378.
60. "Anonymous Christianity and the Missionary Task of the Church," *Theological Investigations* 12 (New York: Crossroad, 1974), pp. 161-178.
61. *S.T.* I 13; cf. Burrell, pp. 12-54.

RONALD M. GREEN

Kant on Christian Love

If one were seeking insight into the nature and meaning of Christian love, Immanuel Kant would hardly seem to be the first philosopher one would consult. Kant, the rationalist foe of all religious enthusiasm and emotion in the moral life, the advocate of unflinching devotion to duty, does not strike one as a thinker likely to understand the meaning of religiously inspired, self-emptying love. Indeed, there is some basis for the intuition that Kant's moral thinking may not be the best introduction to Christian ethics, and that the Categorical Imperative and the Christian idea of *agape* may be fundamentally different guides to moral conduct. Nevertheless, Kant did write about Christian love. His reflections on its meaning remain of interest, and those seeking to understand the nature and limits of *agape* can still perhaps learn from Kant.

In what follows, I want to explore Kant's specific efforts to interpret the love commandment found in Matthew 22:37-40 and in Mark 12:30-31. These efforts, often brief and always undertaken in the context of other discussions, form the principal resource for anyone wishing to comprehend Kant's understanding of *agape*.[1] In addition, Kant's writings contain several extended discussions of benevolence and beneficence, duties that he sometimes equates with Christian neighbor-love. For this reason, I propose to examine these discussions as well. But before turning to either matter, it is important first to dispel a popular misconception of Kant's ethics that renders his thinking not merely distant from the idea of *agape* but absolutely hostile to any ethic involving human sympathy and fellow-feeling.

The misconception derives from Kant's well-known discussion of the (morally good) will at the beginning of his *Foundations of the Metaphysics of Morals*. In the effort to develop the idea of action done *from* duty, Kant dismisses as having "no moral worth" a kindly deed performed by a person who finds "inner satisfaction in spreading joy" to others. In contrast, Kant holds up the example of an individual with little sympathy in his heart, "by temperament cold and indifferent to the suffering of others," who nevertheless is able out of duty to benefit others in distress. Such a person, Kant maintains, finds in himself a far higher source of moral worth than can be gained through a good-natured temperament.[2]

This passage has disturbed or angered generations of readers. The poet Schiller used it to characterize Kant as a philosopher who regarded the malign performance of outwardly moral acts as superior to generous compassion for one's fellow human beings.[3] If Schiller and others who have read the passage this way were right, Kant's ethics would be infinitely remote from anything like the kind of other-regarding compassion that many believe to be an important part of Christian love.

But Schiller and others miss Kant's point here. Kant's aim, after all, is to illustrate what it means to act *from* duty, to be essentially motivated by moral concerns, and he wishes to distinguish such action from that which happens to conform to duty but is without genuine moral motivation, what he calls action *in accord with* duty. To this end, Kant performs a thought experiment in which he offers what today might be called a "controlled sample" of genuine moral motivation.[4] For this purpose, actions motivated by feelings of sympathy and benevolence to others will not do. They represent "tainted" specimens since it is difficult in such cases to determine whether the action is motivated by sentiment and feelings or by a genuine respect for duty. Kant finds his 'pure' instance of moral conduct, therefore, in the case of an individual respectful of the moral law and of whom one can predicate no emotional or self-oriented reasons for conduct. Here there is no doubt, Kant concludes, that respect for duty is present.

What Kant clearly is *not* doing in this passage is holding up as the paragon of moral virtue someone who dislikes or hates those he helps. Nor is he in any way belittling the conduct of individuals whose sense of duty is supplemented and enhanced by feelings of sympathy and love. Indeed, we shall see later that Kant believes it is our duty to encourage and to develop such benevolent feelings. Instead, what Kant is trying to do is clarify what he believes to be the essential basis or determining ground (*Bestimmungsgrund*) of moral worth. For reasons we shall soon explore, he insists that this cannot be found in emotional states or preferences, but must be rooted in a reasoned commitment to duty. The purpose of his thought experiment, therefore, is to separate a genuine moral motivation from adventitious motives that can obscure its presence or its absence. How unfortunate that for many readers, this "pure" case should be taken as Kant's moral ideal.

Kant's point in this passage will not, of course, entirely make sense to those who believe that various emotional states—sympathy, compassion, or love—are properly the basis of moral conduct and moral worth. Why Kant dismisses these states as bases for morality, as appropriate determining grounds for the will, requires further explanation. As a topic, it also serves as introduction to Kant's own conception of Christian love. A brief passage in the *Foundations* is crucial for our understanding of Kant's perspective. Continuing his effort here to distinguish between illegitimate motives based on feelings and the only valid motive based on duty, Kant reasserts his conviction that only an action done out of respect for the moral law has moral worth. He comments:

> It is in this way, undoubtedly, that we should understand those passages of Scripture which command us to love our neighbor and even our enemy, for love as an inclination cannot be commanded. But beneficence from duty, when no inclination impels it and even when it is opposed by a natural and unconquerable aversion, is practical love, not pathological love; it resides in the will and not in the propensities of feeling, in principles of action and not in tender sympathy; and it alone can be commanded.[5]

It alone can be commanded. These words express the heart of Kant's objection to any ethic based on emotional preferences and to any understanding of Christian love which would interpret it in terms of emotional states. For Kant, a defining feature of morality is its imperatival force: we encounter moral rules or principles as commands which we are called on to obey. Moreover, the whole language of moral praise and blame expresses this same understanding. We commonly exhort one another to moral conduct and we condemn and discourage immoral behavior. But what is commanded must be capable of being done. "Ought implies can" because it makes no sense to demand what is beyond a person's power. For Kant, it follows that duty cannot depend on or proceed from emotional states—however refined or lofty these might be—because he believes that emotions are essentially beyond our control. I feel sympathy for another or I don't; I love or don't love. As emotions, these are states I experience, suffer or enjoy, but I cannot simply elicit them by acts of will.

For this reason, Kant believes that the command to love the neighbor, understood as a command to develop feelings of compassion or concern, would be nonsensical—like a command to enjoy food or music that one finds distasteful. In Kant's view, an ethic based on feelings would not only run counter to our shared conviction that moral duties are something we can be called on to obey, but it would also end by violating some of our deepest beliefs about moral praise or blame. Such an ethic would lead us to praise persons for harboring feelings as natural to them as their tastes and for which they are not really responsible, while we might be led to condemn individuals of a different make-up unlucky enough not to enjoy or experience these feelings. For Kant, these absurdities lead to the conclusion that where love is regarded as a matter of feeling, "a duty to love is logically impossible."[6]

Nevertheless, the fact that the injunction to love the neighbor cannot be understood as a requirement of emotional concern for that neighbor, does not mean that the Gospel requirement lacks sense in Kant's eyes. In place of such a "pathological" or feeling-based idea of love, Kant interprets the Gospel command as involving "practical love." This resides in the will, not the feelings, and calls forth action instead of sympathy. In the *Foundations* Kant states matters this way, but he does not really develop the idea. Not until the *Critique of Practical Reason* do we encounter a fuller discussion of the commandment to love God above all and the neighbor as oneself.[7] Commenting on this, Kant begins by insisting that love of God as an "inclination" or state of emotional desire is impossible since God cannot be an object of the senses. Presumed here is Kant's belief that all such desiring love has a sensual or sensory basis. But since God cannot possibly be loved in this way, to love God can only mean that we endeavor to fulfill all His commandments (which Kant everywhere equates with obedience to the dictates of the moral law[8]). While it is possible to love one's fellow human being in a 'pathological' or feeling-determined way, such feelings cannot be commanded. This means that love involves the requirement that we try to practice all our moral duties with respect to the neighbor. In sum, Christian love for Kant represents an injunction to the most perfect fulfillment of rationally understood moral duty. It involves respecting the dictates of the Categorical Imperative in their fullest and most complete sense.

Anyone nourished by the tradition of modern Christian reflection on *agape* might well find this an impoverished account of the love commandment. Altogether lacking in Kant's thinking is any sense that love might involve the kind of unnecessitated and overflowing regard for the other that is emphasized by a writer like Nygren. Also missing are the themes of self-sacrificial devotion stressed by writers like Kierkegaard or Niebuhr. Nor does Kant appear to discern any complexity in the relationship between the twin commandments of love of God and love of neighbor, since he collapses both commandments into the same requirement of respect for rational duty. Within this scheme, for example, the vertical element of relationship with God does not significantly inform the horizontal realm of the ethical. In the manner lamented by Kierkegaard, God becomes an "invisible vanishing point."[9]

These are possibly serious limitations in Kant's view. But it would be wrong to characterize his interpretation of the love commandment as either ethically or religiously impoverished. On both the moral and religious planes, Kant's perspective has a dimensionality and depth that merits attention. Morally, for example, there is abiding validity in his critique of any interpretation of Christian love that renders it a matter of sentiment rather than a practical commitment to forms of conduct. On the moral level, as well, Kant's equation of Christian love with duty in its fullest sense also represents a response to the many problems that accompany alternative interpretations. Gene Outka has identified a number of these problems.[10] How do love and justice relate to one another? When do the needs of the person who stands before me take precedence over those of the community as a whole? What degree of self-regard is permitted to one committed to altruistic concern for others? Is it possible for totally selfless devotion to others to violate valid requirements of self-respect and specific duties to oneself? While the equation of Christian love with full obedience to the moral law may not immediately answer all of these questions, it does point to their solution. Viewed this way, the agapistic response would not be one-sidedly altruistic, individualistic, or self-sacrificial, but would rather conform to that fair and reasonable reconciliation of competing interests at which morality aims.

Religiously, as well, Kant's discussion of love merits attention, because it forms the basis for an important effort on his part to provide a philosophical understanding of the problem of sin. Kant's development of this theme does not occur until his *Religion within the Limits of Reason Alone*. There, to the surprise of many readers who regard him as an optimistic enlightenment philosopher, Kant introduces the idea of "radical evil" in human nature, and he goes as far as to suggest a role for divine grace in the economy of human moral redemption.[11] This mature treatment of sin is given its earliest expression by Kant in the *Critique of Practical Reason*, where it is intimately connected with Kant's treatment of Christian love.

Kant's discussion here anticipates in many ways Reinhold Niebuhr's understanding of love as an "impossible possibility." On the one hand, says Kant, because of the unyielding stringency of its demand for full moral obedience, the love commandment provides a stimulating challenge to the moral life. The Matthean commandment, he states, presents an "ideal of holiness" so perfect that it is "unattainable by any creature." Nevertheless, in this very purity, the commandment is an "archtype which we should strive to approach and to imitate in uninterrupted infinite progress."[12]

On the other hand, this lofty ideal not only stimulates and challenges, it also places human striving under judgment and brings a proper sense of humility to the committed moral agent. In this connection, Kant criticizes the fancied moral perfection and "self-conceit" of those who believe love to involve a spontaneous goodness of heart. Such persons, Kant says, think that they can fulfill the moral law by an intensity of feeling and by occasional acts of self-sacrifice. But duty has nothing to do with feelings, and its dictates are not fulfilled by fleeting instances of generosity. Instead, duty places a stern and unremitting discipline on the whole of life.[13] This discipline runs counter to many of our ordinary desires and to our natural forms of self-love. The immediate effect of the love commandment, therefore, is to humble and chasten us. More profoundly, it drives us to repentance for our repeated moral failures and to a sense of dependence on God's mercy (combined with our own striving) for the perfection of our moral natures.

In a long footnote near the end of the second *Critique*, Kant highlights this last theme by contrasting Greek ethics, marked as it is by a confidence in human beings' this-worldly attainment of the good, with Christian ethics and its reliance on a transcendent religious fulfillment of human's destiny. The difference between these ethics, he remarks, follows strictly from the stringency of Christianity's commitment to love:

> Christian ethics, because it formulated its precept as pure and uncompromising (as befits a moral precept), destroyed man's confidence of being wholly adequate to it, at least in this life; but it reestablished it by enabling us to hope that, if we act as well as lies within our power, what is not in our power will come to our aid from another source, whether we know in what way or not.[14]

The concluding note of hesitation here about the extent to which human beings can understand God's morally redemptive grace is typical of all Kant's thinking on this matter. Even in the *Religion*, where the second *Critique*'s idea of reliance on an infinitely prolonged afterlife as a means of attaining perfect virtue seems to be replaced by the idea of a more direct and immediate divine act that heals the will, Kant always appears uneasy with the direction in which his rigorous analysis is taking him. As commentators have noted,[15] his discussion there wavers between a stress on man's clear and unaided duty to do all that is in his power on behalf of the moral law and a qualified reliance on God's aid. The details of Kant's agonizing engagement with the problem of divine grace need not concern us here. What is important is that a thinker, who many have characterized as hostile to Christian theology, is, in some ways, one of the great philosophical interpreters of the Christian doctrine of sin. What is also especially noteworthy in this context is that his development of these ideas builds directly on his understanding of Christian love.

So far, I suggest that Kant equates Christian love with strict respect for duty. This presumably means a firm resolve never to do what duty prohibits as well as a commitment to some positive duties. In addition to this general position, however, there are passages in Kant's writings where, in a more focused way, he equates love of neighbor with a very special positive duty that he calls "benevolence" or "beneficence." Kant's terminology here is not always clear. On some occasions he speaks of the duty he has in mind as benevolence, although, in clear discomfort with this word's dispositional connotations, he sometimes calls it "benevolence as conduct."[16] Elsewhere, he resorts to the more action-oriented term "beneficence."[17]

In all these references, what Kant has in mind is not merely sympathetic concern for others—since that involves uncommandable feelings—but an active, willed effort on our part to aid our fellows. In Kant's view, beneficence involves our making others' happiness our end. It finds concretion in the duty "to promote, according to [our] means, the happiness of others who are in need, and this without hope of gaining anything by it."[18] So understood, this is a positive duty without fixed limits. Along with other acts of indefinite obligation, like the requirement of self-development, it belongs to the domain of "meritorious" duty. In this respect it differs from an "imprescriptible" duty like promise-keeping whose violation is always clear and specifiable.[19] But the fact that we cannot in a general way identify violations of this duty does not make it purely supererogatory. Within the limits of our means and abilities, we are each morally required to benefit and aid our needy neighbor. We may not be required to impoverish or kill ourselves in this effort,[20] but we are called upon as a matter of moral obligation to check our pursuit of self-interest when others' welfare can reasonably be served.

What does Kant believe to be the moral and conceptual basis of this duty? How is it justified? Expectedly, Kant makes no reference to specifically religious justifications in answering these questions. "Love of neighbor" as beneficence is not, for him, a consequence of a special religious perspective, nor is it the special property of any self-designated community of saints. Instead, beneficence is an aspect of rationally defensible moral obligation and, as such, is incumbent on all who are human. Interestingly, however, Kant's specific efforts to develop the rational basis of this duty form one of the most problematical aspects of his moral theory. A brief look at these efforts helps shed light on the strengths or weaknesses of Kant's moral theory as a whole.

It is well known that for Kant, all conduct must conform to the dictates of the Categorical Imperative. This, in turn, involves the requirement that all proposed policies of action (or what Kant calls "maxims") be capable of becoming universal law. (Kant states this Imperative formally as follows: "Act only according to that maxim by which you can at the same time will that it become universal law."[21]) However, this is largely a negative test: we may do whatever we please as long as it is not incapable of becoming universal law. To establish whether there is a duty of beneficence, therefore, one need only put the contrary maxim to the test. Is a policy of non-beneficence (of resolutely denying others needed aid when it is in our power to give it) capable of becoming universal law? If the answer to this is "no," then beneficence is in fact a basic moral obligation.[22]

Obviously, the answer to this question will depend upon what is meant by "universal law" and what further test is involved in determining whether a maxim is capable or incapable of becoming such a law. Commonly, both these matters are interpreted in terms of the test of "universalizability" or "generalizability."[23] This involves two things. First, there is the requirement that I think of what I propose to do as open to all other, similarly situated moral agents. This implies that the action involved is of the sort that can logically be conceived as acted on by everyone. Second, once this is done, I must consider whether *I* would personally be willing to put up with others' acting in this way with respect to me. Since a maxim permitting nonbeneficence can logically be thought of as acted on by all persons, the Categorical Imperative seems to yield the following concrete question as a final test for this maxim: Would I be prepared to live in a world in which persons were morally permitted casually to deny others (including myself) needed aid when it is otherwise in their power to give it? If the answer to this is "no," then beneficence becomes a moral obligation.

This, in fact, seems to be the shape of Kant's own efforts to justify the duty of beneficence. In the *Doctrine of Virtue*, for example, he observes that "every man who finds himself in need wishes to be helped by other men." But if anyone denies the obligation to beneficence, says Kant,

> if he lets his maxim of not willing to help others in turn when they are in need become public, i.e. makes this a universal permissive law, then everyone would likewise deny him assistance when he needs it, or would at least be entitled to.

Hence, Kant concludes,

> the maxim of self-interest contradicts itself when it is made universal law, that is, it is contradictory to duty.[24]

In the *Foundations* a very similar argument is set forth. There we read that since instances can arise in which one needs "the love and sympathy of others," a person who denied the obligation to mutual aid would effectively rob himself of desired assistance and his will would be "in conflict with itself."[25]

On the surface, these are convincing arguments. But, as many critics have noted, they do not withstand close scrutiny. Granted that if I choose to reject a duty of beneficence, in keeping with the requirement of universalization, I thereby deny myself the assistance of others in moments of need. But why can't this sometimes be a reasonable choice? After all, life is a matter of choice among competing objectives. We cannot have everything we wish and we must often trade off one valued good for another. If I choose to become a professor of ethics, for example, I probably cannot at the same time be an astronaut. Why, then, can't I, as a cold and self-sufficient person, choose to forgo aid from others in order to free myself from a similar responsibility to them and thereby to better pursue my other goals?[26]

Kant's efforts rationally to justify this duty, therefore, seem to fail. What are we to conclude from this? There are several possibilities. One is that Kant is simply mistaken: beneficence is not a universal moral obligation. This might suggest that beneficence properly finds grounding only in the select domain of a religious ethic, where individuals evidence their gratitude for God's generosity by rendering assistance to the neighbor. For Christians, the failure of Kant's argument would thus serve as point of departure for a demonstration of the special link between Christian faith and neighbor-love.

A second possibility is to conclude that Kant has not here really developed his argument for beneficence in the most complete way. It is common to note that there are at least three different formulations of the Categorical Imperative in the *Foundations*. The first, and the one we have looked at, stresses a maxim's capability of becoming universal law. The second stresses the requirement that we treat humanity, whether in our own person or that of another, "always as an end and never as a means only."[27] The third asks us to view each moral agent as a legislator in a hypothetical "realm of ends" in which that agent is both the subject and object of universal laws.

Of these three formulations, it is sometimes argued that the second one best expresses Kant's understanding of the conceptual basis of moral responsibility. If we are to make sense of his assertion of a universal obligation to beneficence, therefore, it might be that we should look to its possible justification in terms of this second formulation. In fact, there is some support for this suggestion in the *Foundations*. There Kant rehearses his four famous examples in the course of a discussion of the second formulation. He concedes that "humanity might, indeed, exist if no one contributed to the happiness of others," but he adds that for the conception of humanity as an end in itself "to have its full effect upon me," the ends of every person must as far as possible be my ends. Thus, it seems that a full regard for the humanity of other persons, not any narrowly self-protective concern for one's own welfare in light of the requirement of universalization, is what yields, the duty of beneficence.

Further supporting this suggestion is a footnoted remark made by Kant at this point in his discussion. This remark rejects as an adequate guide to moral conduct the simple universalization formula represented by the so-called "negative golden rule" and it suggests that this formula is at best somehow a derivative of the more comprehensive "humanity" formulation. Kant's remark here also illustrates the extent to which he believed the Categorical Imperative was a more reliable way of thinking about moral responsibility than this variant formula for the Christian love ethic:

> Let it not be thought that the banal "*quod tibi non fieri, etc.*" [What you do not want done to you, etc.], could here serve as guide or principle, for it is only derived from the principle [of not using others as means] and is restricted to various limitations. It cannot be a universal law, because it contains the ground neither of duties to oneself nor of the benevolent duties to others (for many a man would gladly consent that others should not benefit him, provided only that he might be excused from showing benevolence to them). Nor does it contain the ground of obligatory duties to another, for the criminal would argue on this ground against the judge who sentences him. And so on.[28]

There is some reason to believe, then, that Kant regarded the second formulation as adding a critical element to the justification of beneficence beyond that afforded by the requirement that one be willing to put up with one's maxims acted upon by others. Nevertheless, for several reasons, I am personally hesitant to read Kant this way. For one thing, there is the consideration that Kant insists that each of the three formulations of the Categorical Imperative "are fundamentally only so many formulas of the very same law, and each of them unites the others in itself."[29] That is, they represent not three partial expressions of morality's rule that require mutual supplementation, but each is a complete guide to conduct in and of itself that merely expresses an identical idea in a different way. Second, I find it hard to believe that a thinker as demanding as Kant, one whose every sensitivity is to give moral argument the rigor of a quasi-mathematical proof, would settle for a test of maxims that seems to amount to nothing more than a poetic encouragement to respect for others. What, after all, does it mean to treat other persons as means and not as ends? Do I treat my butcher as a "means only" when I ask him to perform some menial task for me? Do I use a criminal as a "means only" when, for the sake of everyone's safety I ask that he be incarcerated or executed? Interestingly, Kant does not believe this last case represents an instance of using someone as a "means only."[30] The additional fact that on more than one occasion Kant appears to suggest that there is some kind of exact decision-procedure for applying the second formulation suggests that this formulation is closely related to the other more precise formulations of the Imperative. Third and finally, there is the fact that Kant himself characterizes the simple universalization or generalization argument represented by the negative golden rule as banal, while he never characterizes the first formulation of the Imperative in this way. This suggests that the first formulation involves more than a requirement of universalization and a test of the resulting maxim in terms of the agent's wishes. It further indicates that Kant believes his justification of beneficence by means of the first formulation is adequate in itself.

This suggests to me yet another way of interpreting Kant on beneficence. It may be that the first formulation is meant to involve more than a rule of universalization and a test of the resulting universalized maxim in terms of the agent's preferences. Various commentators have explored this possibility. H. J. Paton, for example, has argued that underlying Kant's vision of what can become universal law is a teleological conception in keeping with which there are certain modes of conduct most appropriate to the fulfillment of human life.[31] On this reading, some logically universalizable maxims (such as the refusal either to aid others or to develop one's abilities) would be incapable of being willed as universal law, not just because I would not like to see them practiced with respect to me, but because they contradict certain ends we all intuitively recognize as "human."

The problem with this reading of Kant is that with little evidence for doing so, it converts his ethic into a teleological perspective more akin to Aristotle's or Aquinas's. It also replaces an ethical theory alleged to have a quasi-mathematical precision with one proceeding from a highly intuitive perception of humanity's essential ends and nature. Paton's effort to rehabilitate the first formulation is understandable. But the specific proposal he makes looks distinctly unKantian.

Other commentators have suggested a second and far simpler route to the interpretation of Kant's thinking about the Categorical Imperative. We just saw that when it is interpreted as a rule of universalization, the Categorical Imperative has two parts: a requirement that the proposed policy be open to all other persons (and logically conceivable as such) and the test of the resulting maxim in terms of *my* willingness to put up with its consequences. But what if the second part of this procedure is not meant to be rooted in the conditions and needs of the specific willing agent? What if, in considering a maxim, I as the agent must also take into account the impact of that maxim on other persons with possibly different needs or in different circumstances? In other words, what if I had to assess my universalized maxim in an *impartial* way, as though I could be any one of the persons (including myself) who might be affected by it? In that case, the results of the reasoning process might be far different from that obtaining when a purely subjective test is imposed.

Let me illustrate. We have already seen that it is entirely possible for me as a self-sufficient, cold-tempered individual who clearly knows my own interests to dispense with a rule requiring mutual aid. But is this possible for me as a person who must reason impartially and take into account—literally step into the shoes of—every other member of society? Reasoning this way, it is true, I might impartially acknowledge that there are some persons like me who might reasonably dare to dispense with a duty of mutual aid. But we are rare creatures. Most human beings occasionally need assistance from others and are more than willing to put up with the slight inconvenience of providing it in order to be able to rely on aid when we need it. Not knowing which of these many possible persons I am (in the fashion of the hypothetical contractors of Rawls's "original position"[32]), isn't it rational for me to select a rule of beneficence, especially if this is construed so as not to require me normally to undergo great risk? I think so. In this respect, the duty of beneficence is somewhat like the purchase of insurance, whereby one hopes that repeated small disbursements may protect one against the harm of catastrophic loss. Although some particular persons who are able accurately to predict their future experiences may find it rational to decline insurance or to self-insure, anyone rendered less knowledgeable (or "impartial") before the future will find insurance a rational purchase.

On this interpretation, then, we have a reading of the first formulation which, just as Kant says, yields the duty of beneficence. Moreover, it does so with the relative precision one would expect from Kant's ethics and without any need for supplementation by the other formulations of the Imperative. Furthermore, the suggestion that reasoning about morality takes place under conditions of impartiality has deep roots in Kant's ethics, especially in connection with his important distinction between the Categorical and hypothetical imperatives.[33] The former is distinguished by the fact that it does not permit merely particular desires—as opposed to generalized human needs—to be made determining considerations of the will. A number of writers—including Rawls, Hill and Murphy[34]—have regarded impartiality as a key feature of Kant's ethical theory. Applied to the first formulation and to its justification of the duty of beneficence, this interpretation makes good sense.

As powerful as it may be, however, this reading of Kant has some problems. The principal one is that Kant never tells us that the first formulation involves an impartial test of generalized maxims. He says only that a morally suitable maxim must be capable of becoming universal law. While it may be possible to see a requirement of impartiality as implicit in this test, it is never openly said to be so. Does this mean that we must reject the interpretation I have just outlined?

Not necessarily. There is another way of reading the first formulation that gives impartiality an important role in its application and that is more directly suggested by the wording of the formulation itself. This involves taking the phrase "universal law" in its fullest and most explicitly *legislative* sense. Commonly, this phrase is taken to mean that a proposed maxim be universalized as *binding* on all persons—a law for them. But we might here recall Lincoln's observation that a republic is not just *for* the people but *of* them and *by* them as well. This suggests that a universal law may not just be applicable to and binding on all rational persons, but may also be a law that has been freely accepted by, even voted for, by all such persons. It is *their* law in the sense that they have helped will it into existence—or could be expected to do so. With this explicitly legislative metaphor in mind, therefore, we may think of universalized maxims as having to pass a test in which they they must receive not just my approval but that of all other rational persons convened in a hypothetical democratic assembly.

I would point out that this interpretation of the first formulation is directly picked up (Kant would say it is merely reexpressed) in the third formulation which renders every moral agent a legislative member (maker and subject of laws) in a hypothetical realm of ends. It may also express the deeper and more rigorous content of the second formulation: to respect someone as an end is not to regard his empirical will (e.g., the criminal's wish to escape punishment) but his considered willing as a member of a hypothetical universal assembly making general laws for the human community. Most importantly, this legislative interpretation has the effect of picking up the working implications of the concept of impartiality we have just explored. To reason impartially, after all, is not to ignore persons' interests but is rather to set individual interests (including one's own) in the context of an array of competing interests and then, on this basis, to select a course of action most likely to serve the community's welfare as a whole ("the common good" in its classical sense). But this is precisely what the legislative interpretation I am proposing involves. As a moral agent reasoning this way, I must mentally "poll" the variety of interests in the hypothetical legislature as I reason toward what would be the likely outcome of a voting procedure in this context. I must effectively think like an impartial—or, better, omnipartial—spectator and ask which forms of conduct would reasonably be accepted as abiding rules of conduct ("laws") in the give and take of a legislative assembly where each person can be thought of as possessing a decisive vote.[35] Thus, by taking Kant's phrase "universal law" in its most naturally legislative sense, we are led to the impartiality procedure which, as we have seen, is perhaps the only way of making sense of the first formulation.

I might add here parenthetically that these considerations render questionable the common classification of Kant as a deontological as opposed to a contractualist or even teleological ethical thinker. In fact, elements of all three approaches have their place within a legislatively construed Categorical Imperative. The contractualist dimensions are evident, as is a teleological concern with the impact of various legislative proposals on the welfare of persons. Since the resulting laws are arrived at impartially in a way that overrides a decisive role for considerations of any single persons or subgroup's happiness, however, this Imperative has a distinctly deontological quality. Indeed, because the implicit legislative community ideally comprises all *rational* beings whose legislative activity is never determined by personal interests, the rules it selects are properly thought of as objective rational laws, not in the sense that they neglect persons' needs but because they do not arise from merely subjective considerations.

If I am right about this interpretation, what does it tell us about the duty of beneficence? Nothing more, perhaps, than was already said in connection with the view that sees the first formulation as involving universalization plus impartial assessment of the resulting conduct. Both of these interpretations yield the same decision process, although the legislative interpretation, I would argue, does so more naturally and more in keeping with Kant's explicit remarks. In either case, however, beneficence emerges as an important human obligation, just as Kant says it is. Reasoning impartially and taking into account all possible interests, any of us would be foolish to dispense with a duty of mutual aid. Similarly, we must expect that a community of hypothetical legislators would readily "pass" a moral law establishing this duty since the vast majority of human beings are benefited by it and even a minority that might be inconvenienced is not seriously disadvantaged by its establishment. On either account, therefore, Kant is right.[36] There is such a duty incumbent on us all. Beneficence and mutual aid need not be regarded as the moral property of any special religious group. And to the degree that active regard for the neighbor is morally a part of *agape*, we can say that Christian ethics here shares a commitment with an ethics based on reason and open to all who are human.

Much of what I have said to this point should be somewhat chastening to those who hold a high-flown conception of Christian love. Kant shows us, I think, that interpretations of Christian love which stress its affective dimension can both violate our understanding of moral obligation and can trivialize the moral and religious depths of this requirement. He also shows us that active commitment to others' welfare may not be a uniquely Christian requirement. If not construed to require completely sacrificial devotion, it can be rationally justified as an obligation for all who are human. He further suggests the difficulties of the golden rule as a moral principle, and, perhaps more importantly, he shows that full regard for all our neighbors' welfare requires a structured way of thinking in which valid but competing claims can be adjudicated and assessed.

If this was all that Kant had to say about neighbor-love, I believe his contribution would be substantial. Before concluding, however, I might mention one further idea of Kant's that helps deepen his understanding of the extent of our duties to others. I began this essay by observing how strenuously Kant denies that neighbor-love can be regarded as a matter of holding or expressing feelings of love, compassion, or sympathy. But now I must add that in several almost casual remarks in *The Doctrine of Virtue*, Kant suggests that it is precisely our duty to try to develop these feelings. One of these remarks occurs in the context of a denial that benevolence be thought of as involving emotional love of neighbor. Contrasting this with active efforts at neighbor-love, Kant observes:

> *Helping* others to achieve their ends is a duty. If a man practices it often and succeeds in realizing his purpose, he eventually comes to feel love for those he has helped. Hence the saying: you *ought* to *love* your neighbor as yourself, does not mean: you should immediately (first) love him and (afterwards) through the medium of this love do good to him. It means, rather: *do good* to your fellow-man, and this will give rise to love of man in you (as an aptitude of the inclination to beneficence in general).[37]

Somewhat later, in the context of a discussion of sympathy, Kant gives further concretion to this suggestion:

> [W]hile it is not in itself a duty to experience sadness, and so also joy, in sympathy with others, it is a duty to participate actively in the fate of others. Hence we have an indirect duty to cultivate the sympathetic natural (aesthetic) feelings in us and to use them as so many means to participating from moral principles and from the feelings appropriate to these principles—Thus it is our duty: not to avoid places where we shall find the poor who lack the most basic essentials, but rather to seek them out; not to shun sick-rooms or debtors' prisons in order to avoid the painful sympathetic feelings that we cannot guard against. For this is still one of the impulses which nature has implanted in us so that we may do what the thought of duty alone would not accomplish.[38]

Our appreciation of the depth of these remarks is enhanced when we recall that Kant was no friend of a social order based on great inequalities in income and that he occasionally even condemned economic philanthropy because of the injustices on which it depends.[39] Kant would never have us "use" the suffering of others as a means to our moral elevation, but he would call us to an active involvement in whatever unavoidable suffering our neighbors experience, both as a means to our moral growth and as an encouragement to continually active neighbor-love.

We therefore come full circle. The philosopher who had initially banished compassion and feeling from the moral life now appears, against the background of a rigorous understanding of concepts, as a proponent of sacrificial altruism and compassionate involvement with the suffering of others. Does this, then, express some of the very central ideas of the Christian conception of *agape*? Perhaps not. There may be specifically religious dimensions of *agape* and possibly also extreme elements of supererogation missed by Kant. Nevertheless, I believe there is ample reason to reaffirm what I said at the outset: those interested in deepening their understanding of the meaning of Christian neighbor-love will not do badly by starting their reading with Kant. His views may not only chasten the excesses to which *agape* has sometimes been subjected, but may also express some of the rational considerations on which Christians have implicitly drawn in trying to make their ethic a practical guide for conduct in society.

NOTES

Note: page references to various other-than-English editions are in brackets and follow the translation page references.

1. Although Kant refers on several occasions to the love commandment found in Matthew 22:37-40, he never actually uses the term *agape* in discussing Christian love.
2. *Foundations of the Metaphysics of Morals*, Louis White Beck, trans. (Indianapolis: Bobbs-Merrill, 1959), p. 15. [Edition of the Preussischen Akademie der Wissenschaft, s. 398.]
3. *Über Anmut und Werde*. For a fuller discussion of the relations between Schiller and Kant see Lewis White Beck, *A Commentary on Kant's Critique of Practical Reason* (Chicago: University of Chicago Press, 1960), pp. 120. n. 231.
4. In the *Critique of Practical Reason*, Lewis White Beck, trans. (Indianapolis: 1956), pp. 164f. [160f.] Kant refers to this moral stance as one involving "negative perfection" and he explicitly advocates its use in illustration as a method of moral pedagogy.
5. *Foundations*, pp. 15f. [399].
6. *The Doctrine of Virtue*, Mary J. Gregor, trans. (Philadelphia: University of Pennsylvania Press, 1964), p. 62 [401].
7. *Critique of Practical Reason*, pp. 85f. [83f.].

8. *Religion within the Limits of Reason Alone*, Theodore M. Greene and Hoyt H. Hudson, trans. (New York: Harper & Row, 1963), p. 148 [124].

9. *Fear and Trembling*, Walter Lowrie, trans. (Princeton: Princeton University Press, 1941), p. 78.

10. *Agape: An Ethical Analysis* (New Haven: Yale University Press, 1972).

11. In *The Nature and Destiny of Man*, (New York: Charles Scribner's Sons, 1941), Vol. I, p. 120, n. 12, Reinhold Niebuhr takes note of Kant's discussion of "radical evil" but dismisses this as "contradictory" to Kant's whole scheme of thought and as a pietistic intrusion in the thought of an Enlightenment optimist.

12. *Critique of Practical Reason*, p. 84 [83].

13. Ibid., p. 85 [83]. Also, *Lectures on Ethics*, Louis Infield, trans. (New York: Harper & Row, 1963), pp. 135-37.

14. *Critique of Practical Reason*, p. 132, n. 2 [127].

15. See, for example, the discussion of Kant's doctrine of grace in Alan Wood, *Kant's Moral Religion* (Ithaca: Cornell University Press, 1970), Chap. 6.

16. *Doctrine of Virtue*, p. 62 [400].

17. Ibid., p. 53 [392].

18. Ibid., p. 120 [452]; see also p. 62 [401].

19. *Foundations*, p. 42 [424].

20. *Doctrine of Virtue*, p. 122 [453].

21. The translation here is my own. I believe both Beck and Paton mistranslate this formulation by interpreting the German *werde* as *should become*, a reading which is a valid English subjunctive but which also has the sense of making universal law dependent upon the willing agent's wishes, in keeping with a generalization view of the formula. Kant' s own wording is as follows: "*handle nur nach derjenigen Maxime, durch die zugleich wollen kannst, dass sie ein allgemeines Gesetz werde.*"

22. For a discussion of the logic of moral permissions and requirements in a Kantian framework, see Onora Nell, *Acting on Principle* (New York: Columbia University Press, 1975), p. 77.

23. A list of those commentators who have read the first formulation as involving only universalization or generalization would include the great majority of Kant's commentators. More remarkable than the number who have read Kant this way, however, is the way in which even sophisticated commentators slip into this reading of Kant without realizing that it may not be the only interpretation of the imperative. Two examples will suffice:

"I shall assume that what Kant means by saying that we cannot will that a maxim should become universal law is that, if it were in our power to bring about a state of affairs in which everyone acted on our maxim, we could not bring ourselves to do it."—Jonathan Harrison, "Kant's Examples of the First Formulation of the Categorical Imperative," *The Philosophical Quarterly* 7 (1957): 50-62, p. 52.

* * *

"The principle we have just quoted (the first formulation), means that people should only adopt as rules of living for themselves rules they can will should always be followed by everyone else."—H. B. Acton, *Kant's Moral Philosophy* (London: Macmillan, 1970), p. 21.

24. *Doctrine of Virtue*, p. 121 [452].

25. *Foundations*, p. 41 [424].

26. In his *Generalization in Ethics* (New York: Russell & Russell, 1961), pp. 269ff. Marcus Singer claims that "no one, no matter how wealthy, strong or self-sufficient can so order and determine things as never to be in need of help of any kind or degree" (p. 269). This may be true, but it does not follow that some rational persons might not choose to forgo help of any kind if they could best serve their foreseeable interests by doing so. For a more recent, but similar effort to affirm the irrationality of a rule denying mutual aid, see Barbara Herman, "Mutual Aid and Respect for Persons," *Ethics* 94 (July 1984), 577-602.

27. Ibid., p. 47 [429].

28. Ibid., p. 48 [430].

29. *Foundations*, 54 [436].

30. See, for example, his discussion of capital punishment in *The Metaphysical Elements of Justice*, John Ladd, trans. (Indianapolis: Bobbs-Merrill, 1965), p. 102 [333].

31. *The Categorical Imperative* (London: Hutchinson University Library, 1947), pp. 153ff. See also Keith Ward, *The Development of Kant's View of Ethics* (Oxford: Basil Blackwell, 1972), pp. 107-13.

32. *A Theory of Justice*, Chapter 3.

33. *Foundations*, pp. 31ff. [414ff.].

34. Rawls, *A Theory of Justice*, Section 40; Thomas Hill, "The Kingdom of Ends," *Proceedings of the Third International Kant Congress* (Dordrecht: D. Reidel, 1972), pp. 310f.; Jeffrie G. Murphy, *Kant: The Philosophy of Right* (London: Macmillan, 1970), p. 94 stresses the way in which Kant's view rests on rational choice utilizing the "essential ends" or common basic interests of humankind, an interpretation that relies on an impartial assessment of human values.

35. It might appear that this requirement of universal assent to principles would frustrate social agreement. However, the long-term perspective of a hypothetical universal legislature and the need for agreement on rules exerts a counterpressure toward agreement. The resulting legislative process corresponds to the thinking of a single impartial person who, in view of the stakes involved on each issue, occasionally chooses to respect or override individual interests. For a fuller discussion of this idea, see my "The First Formulation of the Categorical Imperative as Literally a 'Legislative' Metaphor," *History of Philosophy Quarterly* 8:2 (April 1991), 163-79.

36. It might be objected that this way of thinking seems to make basic moral rules depend on the empirical facts of human valuation in ways that Kant, with his insistence on morality as involving universality and necessity,

would not permit. However, the fundamental formal rule being applied in this case—the rule of universal acceptability as law—has just the necessity Kant claims for it. As the supreme moral principle, it defines the unique condition of a free harmony of wills, and, as such, the unique condition of morality. As far as derivative rules like mutual aid are concerned, they have derivative necessity given the facts of human nature. Kant does not appear to claim that these specific items of moral legislation necessarily extend beyond the community of rational *human* beings. Apart from the Categorical Imperative, he seems to ascribe universality only to those derivative moral rules—such as promise-keeping—whose universalized maxims involve logical contradiction. For a more compete discussion of this, see Ibid.

37. *Doctrine of Virtue*, pp. 62f. [401].
38. Ibid., p. 126 [456].
39. In the context of a discussion of casuistical questions connected with beneficence, Kant remarks: "The ability to practice beneficence, which depends on property, follows largely from the injustice of the government which favours certain men and so introduces an inequality of wealth that makes others need help. This being the case, does the rich man's help to the needy, on which he so readily prides himself as something meritorious, really deserve to be called beneficence at all?" Ibid., p. 122 [453].

John P. Reeder, Jr.

Analogues to Justice

Of the Golden Age, Hume remarked:

> . . . Cordial affection, compassion, sympathy, were the only movements, with which the human mind was yet acquainted. Even the distinction of *mine* and *thine* was banish'd from that happy race of mortals, and carry'd with them the very notions of property and obligation, justice and injustice (Hume, 1967: 494).

And he suggests that we might again have no need for justice:

> Again: suppose that, though the necessities of the human race continue the same as at present, yet the mind is so enlarged and so replete with friendship and generosity that every man has the utmost tenderness for every man, and feels no more concern for his own interest than for that of his fellows: It seems evident that the *use* of Justice would, in this case, be suspended by such an extensive benevolence, nor would the divisions and barriers of property and obligation have ever been thought of. Why should I bind another, by a deed or promise, to do me any good office when I know that he is already prompted by the strongest inclination to seek my happiness and would of himself perform the desired service, except the hurt he thereby receives be greater than the benefit accruing to me; in which case he knows that, from my innate humanity and friendship, I should be the first to oppose myself to his imprudent generosity? Why raise landmarks between my neighbor's field and mine when my heart has made no division between our interests, but shares all his joys and sorrows with the same force and vivacity as if originally my own? Every man, upon this supposition, being a second self to another, would trust all his interests to the discretion of every man without jealousy, without partition, without distinction. And the whole human race would form only one family where all would lie in common and be used freely, without regard to property; but cautiously too, with an entire regard to the necessities of each individual, as if our own interests were most intimately concerned (Hume, 1957: 16).

Hume recapitulates an ancient motif of Western thought in the suggestion that in a Golden age humans did not need justice. And in his suggestion that were human nature changed, we would not need it again, he echoes the belief that in the eschaton humans will transcend justice. But could extensive benevolence really supplant justice? There is indeed a long tradition in Western thought that holds that concepts of distributive justice are forms of morality that arise in light of regrettable features of the human condition; if only these features could be eliminated, then justice could be replaced by something else, often said to be love, caring, or extensive benevolence. We are familiar with this argument in theological traditions: the creature who is enmeshed in sin, the defensive self-regard that is the result of a failure to trust the Creator, needs justice. As Reinhold Niebuhr put it, "history" is the realm of conflicts of interests restrained by justice. More recently, feminist writers explain the emphasis on justice as the product of male experience where the capacity for caring or benevolence has been reduced due to social conditioning or patterns of early childcare.

Now while each of these accounts has common features, their explanatory frameworks obviously differ. I will not focus on the differences in these diagnoses, but on the prescription that justice could and should be replaced by some form of love of neighbor or benevolence. Reinhold Niebuhr, of course, thought that *agape* could flourish only "beyond history" but other theologians, like some feminists, look for a morality of love in this world. I will argue that love (extensive benevolence) could replace justice but that analogues to principles of justice, distributive policies if you will, would be necessary. In order to show in what sense love could render justice unnecessary, I will discuss the social order on the planet Anarres in Ursula LeGuin's novel, *The Dispossessed*, and then argue that in this society essential features of what John Rawls called the "circumstances of justice" do not obtain. Then, also using Anarres as an example, I will try to show how notions of liberty and well-being are at work there, and how this ethos illustrates the way in which love needs distributional specification.[1] My aim is to clarify one sense in which love transcends justice.[2]

1. THE MOON ANARRES

Could one argue that justice could be dispensed with on a large scale?[3] The society on the moon Anarres seems to represent just such an attempt. Notions of justice or rights do not figure centrally in normative discourse. The settlers do not talk a lot about what is due or owed, what they deserve, or what they have a right to. Although the novel in part is concerned with flaws in this utopia—it unwittingly apes the exploitative and dominance-seeking society it rebelled against and fled—Anarres as a sexually egalitarian, property-rejecting, and anarchist society is said to rest on "mutual aid."[4] Mutual aid is not limited to families or friends, but is extended to everyone in the social body. Out of compassion one comes to desire to prevent suffering and to promote the good of all.[5]

"... You're denying brotherhood, Shevek!" the tall girl cried.

"No—no, I'm not. I'm trying to say what I think brotherhood really is. It begins—it begins in shared pain."

"Then where does it end?"

"I don't know. I don't know yet." (LeGuin, 1975: 50)

One desires one's own good but one also desires the good of others and one has the same degree of concern for the interests of others as for one's own; one has in effect what Hume called "extensive benevolence." The Anarresti simply contribute to the social product *both* for their own sakes and for others, and they take without thought of shares; one shares—contributes and uses—without claiming one's fair share. The basic principle is "mutual aid" where this means mutual extensive benevolence, not a claim based on justice.

But what is the "justice" that Anarres apparently tries to do without? There are various ways to identify or define concepts of justice in contrast to other sorts of moral norms: e.g., 1) norms of justice are those that prescribe a morally correct distribution of goods in some form of social interaction, more narrowly, exchanges, or, more broadly, the allocation of the benefits and burdens of cooperative effort; 2) norms of justice are those that have a particular sort of normative content or vocabulary, e.g., rights, or, as I will say here, a system of rightful claims or shares, of what is due or owed; 3) norms of justice are those that have a certain sort of rationale or justification, e.g., reciprocal self-interest, a Kantian veil, an Aristotelian common good. In this essay, I identify norms of justice in terms of 1) and 2) as a set of defining conditions: norms of justice are those that prescribe a morally correct distribution of the benefits and burdens of social cooperation, and do so through notions of rightful claims or shares that are due or owed. 1) in itself is not sufficient to identify a system of justice, for the analogues to principles of justice on Anarres, as I will argue, also prescribe a morally correct distribution of benefits and burdens. 3) is not necessary because the moral starting point from which a system of justice is launched can differ. What happens on Anarres, as I interpret it, is that its members attempt to live directly out of love, without using a system of justice.

How does this work? One chooses one's social contribution, not only according to ability, but according to interest; one considers social needs but one's own enjoyment is also a criterion. One draws on the social product according to need and desire, but one would not eat more than one needed if others would go without; the only institutionalized inequalities are those that are functionally justified, e.g., special quarters or rations for scientists. The individual does not sacrifice himself or herself completely for others but seeks to further the good of the self as well as the good of others. One expects others to further one's good as well but one does not love in order to be loved. One freely chooses how to contribute and what to appropriate without legislation or coercion.

LeGuin's society has defects; old evils break out in unexpected forms. There is the ordinary will-to-power; there is ideological stagnation and the oppression of the creative. There is a refusal to recognize moral connections between Anarres and the society it rejected. There are normative ambiguities as well, e.g., if one does not usually call one's hand one's own, does this mean that one does not have even a prima facie title to one's bodily organs or sexual capacities? Despite an apparent abandonment of rights, the settlers sometimes seem to assume a right of self-determination that may include aspects of the body. But in the main, Anarres is an attempt to transcend structures of justice.

2. THE CIRCUMSTANCES OF JUSTICE

Let us focus on the fact that the Anarres experiment seems to involve a reliance on mutual love instead of justice. Do we want to say that on Anarres the settlers have no need of justice? I think it is the case that the situation on Anarres does not represent what John Rawls, in the tradition of Hume, calls the "subjective circumstances of justice." Michael Sandel imagines a family falling, if you will, from "spontaneous affection" or "generosity" to the "circumstances of justice":

> Consider for example a more or less ideal family situation, where relations are governed in large part by spontaneous affection and where, in consequence, the circumstances of justice prevail to a relatively small degree. Individual rights and fair de-

cision procedures are seldom invoked, not because injustice is rampant but because their appeal is pre-empted by a spirit of generosity in which I am rarely inclined to claim my fair share. Nor does this generosity necessarily imply that I receive out of kindness a share that is equal to or greater than the share I would be entitled to under fair principles of justice. I may get less. The point is not that I get what I would otherwise get, only more spontaneously, but simply that the questions of what I get and what I am due do not loom large in the overall context of this way of life.

Now imagine that one day the harmonious family comes to be wrought with dissension. Interests grow divergent and the circumstances of justice grow more acute. The affection and spontaneity of previous days give way to demands for fairness and the observance of rights. And let us further imagine that the old generosity is replaced by a judicious temper of unexceptionable integrity and that the new moral necessities are met with a full measure of justice, such that no injustice prevails. Parents and children reflectively equilibriate, dutifully if sullenly abide by the two [Rawlsian] principles of justice, and even manage to achieve the conditions of stability and congruence so that the good of justice is realized within their household (Sandel, 1982: 33).[6]

Thus, where familial benevolence prevails, the "subjective" circumstances of justice do not obtain. Although the "objective" circumstances with regard to resources remain constant ("moderate scarcity"), we do not have to do with the "subjective" circumstances where "the parties take no interest in one another's interests" and society is conceived as a "cooperative venture . . . typically marked by a conflict as well as an identity of interests" (Rawls, 1971: 126-130). According to Rawls, cooperation is mutually beneficial—the identity of interests—but until some norms of justice are adopted, people will differ as to how the fruits of cooperation are to be divided—the conflict of interests. The subjective circumstances of justice, says Sandel, obtain only when the "spirit of generosity" fails; there is now a "conflict of interests" in the sense that people are assumed to desire a greater rather than lesser share of the fruits of cooperation.

The situation on Anarres also does not resemble what, in contrast to Rawls's "liberal" view of the subjective circumstances, we might call a neo-Aristotelian conception. For Alasdair MacIntyre, for example, we do not experience conflicts of interest in Rawls's sense, for the members of a community value *ab initio* a way of life (specified by their view of the "good for man") that includes the well-being of self and other (1984). Self and other are presumed to value their relation with one another and this good, which is not privately possessed but shared, constitutes the basic bond of their common life. But how individuals will contribute to and receive from this common life will be determined, MacIntyre argues, by a system of justice; the virtue of justice refers to a disposition to render what is owed or due, what is deserved according to one's contribution to the common good (such a disposition being not only instrumental to but ingredient in the good of the common life). Thus, MacIntyre would not accept Rawls's view of the circumstances of justice, which does not presuppose a thick neo-Aristotelian good; but MacIntyre as well does not rely on extensive benevolence; even where a virtue of love is also assumed, justice still is required.

The crucial contrast seems to be between a view in which mutual love is seen as sufficient and those in which it is not. For Rawls, no bond with the other is assumed until the veil of ignorance (the crucial moral assumption) comes down and principles of justice for mutual advantage are devised. For MacIntyre, the basic bond of a commonly valued way of life is assumed but the distribution of the benefits of the common life requires a system of shares that specifies who *owes* what to whom. Even members of MacIntyre's neo-Aristotelian communities find it necessary to be able to insist on their due share. Where mutual extensive benevolence is assumed as sufficient, not only is a bond between self and other established, but it is also not necessary to express that bond in terms of rightful claims or shares. Where benevolence is mutual, one can rely entirely on the neighbor's love.

Thus, on either a liberal or neo-Aristotelian understanding of the circumstances of justice, there would be no occasion for *justice* on Anarres since mutual benevolence can be relied on. Benevolence (extensive because of its scope and degree, mutual because it is shared) would obviate the need for justice. Benevolence on Anarres is presumably neither too unevenly distributed, too capricious, nor too weak. The settlers on Anarres do in one sense experience conflicting needs and desires; during a famine, they need and want more food and water than is available if each are to have enough to live. But they are mutually benevolent. In one sense I want as much food as I can get, but in another sense I do not desire to "maximize" my good because I also want you to survive. One could put it counterfactually: if I did not want you to survive, I would want a lot more. Although, as I will argue shortly, the Anarresti do need distributive policies, they do not need justice in order to protect and promote the good of each.

It would be conceivable that the Anarresti love each other, but that their love could suffer from one or more of the characteristic weaknesses noted above, and thus they might be forced to express their love in a system of justice. Their love would be sufficiently robust to function as a distinctive *starting-point*, in contrast to, say, a Kantian veil or a neo-Aristotelian commonly valued way of life, but they might have to judge love insufficiently reliable to serve directly as the "only law" structured merely by broad distributional policies and not by a more definite system of claims and shares. But the supposition on Anarres is that love can be sufficiently reliable when human beings are not socialized so as to need a system of claims and shares in order to protect and promote their basic interests.

The point, then, is that the problem of justice on the side of the subject includes the stipulation that agents are not expected, for whatever reason, to get along only with love; they regulate their desires with the superimposition of another structure of motivation: the desire to do what is just. Hume's assumption was that benevolence is strong only in the circle of family and friends, and weakens toward strangers; to have a system of production and distribution (or at least one that is sufficiently stable) some other motivation must be established. One need not, however, assume that justice must take the form of an actual agreement based on self-interest or even the form of an agreement from a hypothetical starting-point such as Rawls proposes; the alternative to benevolence could take the form of a neo-Aristotelian theory of justice as part of an intrinsic good of relation that human beings naturally desire. Any such alternative, whatever content and rationale we give it, that provides distributional policies that specify rightful claims or shares, what is due or owed, we can call justice. It is justice that we characteristically express in Western traditions as what is owed or due and hence it is no accident that the settlers on Anarres reject not only property, but do not as a rule interpret their persons or the social product in the vocabulary of justice.[7]

Now, it may be the case that the background of capitalism led some thinkers in the liberal tradition to believe that benevolence was unreliable in human nature generally or that justice must be normatively conceived as an actual or hypothetical agreement between self-interested agents. It also seems to be the case that a patriarchal division of labor, which relegates women primarily to the "private" side of life, will tend to limit to the familial sphere the virtue of nurturing or caring that has had a special role in women's experience. However one accounts for the present situation, one can nonetheless conceive of circumstances in which mutual love would render justice otiose.

3. WELL-BEING AND LIBERTY ON ANARRES

But what of the claim that extensive benevolence needs justice? My thesis is that mutual love must receive the sort of distributive specification justice provides even if it does not need justice.[8] To see how this is the case, consider again the society of Anarres. On Anarres, concern for others is not based on self-interest, but self-interest is legitimate: love your neighbor as you legitimately love yourself. Thus, the question is not simply how does love defined as other-regarding concern deal with the multiplicity of neighbors, but how shall the good of all including the self be protected and promoted.[9]

The distribution of goods and services and the assignment of work seems to be governed on Anarres by a version of the principle, from each according to ability, to each according to need. One gives to the group the work one has the ability to do, one is interested in doing, and one believes needs doing; the assumption is that this will work out, if not for the most efficient production of goods and services, at least for a tolerable level; there is a central administrative body that matches skills, interests, and available positions; in emergencies, e.g., a famine, this organ can issue "levies," but there is no coercion; the individual must be prepared to compromise between individual predilection and social need.

As for benefits, one takes what one needs and wants; some basic goods such as food are regulated through communal kitchens so that individuals do not make distributive choices with every meal; for other products, one goes to depositories and makes a choice as to what and how much to take; the individual chooses so as not to deprive others of "as much and as good." If there is not enough for everyone, then, I suppose, first come, first served, or where life is at stake, as we will see, a utilitarian criterion is invoked. In any case, even when one takes, one does not own; the coat on one's back is a communal product that one is "using."

Would we say then that from each ... to each ... is the principle of contribution and reward on Anarres? This formula, at least for Anarres, seems to express a notion of equal contribution and appropriation. Each person, out of concern for his or her own good and the good of others, is supposed to contribute, matching talents, interests, and social need. Each person is supposed to make the same degree of effort. Even if there are residual variances in socialization or genetic inheritance that lead to different capacities to make an effort, I believe that on Anarres differences in this capacity are assumed to be slight, and if there are cases that vary widely from the norm, these individuals would be treated as exceptions and excused. The assumption is that individuals are similar in their capacity to make an effort, although their actual contribution will reflect talents and interests.

In turn, each person is supposed to receive from the social product a portion such that his or her basic well-being—a range of goods such as health and education—can be sustained in a roughly equal way. This does not mean that each individual is capable of exactly the same well-being or that each receives identical treatment; the equality of appropriation that is aimed for lies not in what is achieved or given in itself, but in the relation between what is required and what is given. Even if everyone were capable of the same state of health, for example, not everyone would need the same treatment; equality of access to health care would be seen in terms of what is necessary to bring each person up to what is possible (and desired), given the overall allocation of social resources.[10]

In education, because of variations in intelligence, not everyone is capable of the same educational achievement, and in addition, some have handicaps that prevent them from reaching the level they are capable of; equal access would consist of each person receiving the educational resources necessary to bring them up to the level of their capability and interest, eliminating handicaps if possible, provided that a decision about the distribution of the overall social product allows one to aim for full development.

The operative principle of equal appropriation on Anarres is similar to W. K. Frankena's notion of justice as equal attention to the good life of each: "Although C, D, and E are treated differently, they are not dealt with unequally, since their differing needs and capacities so far as these relate to the good life are equally considered and equally cared for" (1962: p. 15; cf. 19ff.). This does not mean that everyone is capable of an equally good life, only that everyone's good life must be equally protected and promoted; to do so, society should make *"the same relative contribution* to the good life of every individual" (1962: pp. 20-21; cf. p. 15).

Rawls calls Frankena's idea the "principle of equal proportionate satisfaction"; all conceptions of the good are to receive what is required for their satisfaction (1980: p. 551ff.). Rawls raises the objection that some people's notion of the good, e.g., a desire to study quasars with radio telescopes, would be much more costly than others and therefore the overall allocation would be dependent on the contingencies of particular plans of the good. It seems to me that Rawls's objection holds only if one applies the principle to the entire range of individuals' desires and aims. Applied to basic goods, the distortion Rawls fears would not occur. To avoid that outcome, it is not necessary to bypass our desires for basic goods such as food or health, and the relative costs of satisfying them, and to adopt the idea of "primary goods" as all-purpose instruments for the pursuit of any plan of the good (see 1980: p. 554). As far as I can tell, it is assumed on Anarres that basic human goods are somewhat fixed by physiological and psychological parameters, but that there is room for preference and taste about other goods. It is true, therefore, that in a society such as Anarres some policy would have to be devised for the distribution of goods required for the satisfaction of desires over and above a basic or "welfare" range of goods.[11] Given limited resources, the ideal of the full realization of plans of life will not be possible; some procedure for the appropriation of instrumental goods would be needed.

Thus, the underlying principle on Anarres is the notion of equal contribution and return, suitably adjusted for individual capacity, need, and interest. Note that the principle is not utilitarian. On Anarres, a lower level of overall good would be tolerated in order to include everyone in the distribution; *counting* each as one as utilitarians do would not be enough. But in extreme scarcity, where there is not enough even for everyone to have some of what they need and want, and where life itself is at stake, the society does seem to use a utilitarian standard. During the famine on Anarres, a train has to stop because of a wreck; it halts near a small town where the food supply is barely adequate:

> If the four hundred and fifty people on the train ate, the one hundred and sixty local people would not. Ideally, they would all share, all half-eat or half-starve together. If there had been fifty, or even a hundred, people on the train, the community probably would have spared them at least a baking of bread. But four hundred and fifty? If they gave that many anything, they would be wiped out for days. And would the next provisions train come, after those days? And how much grain would be on it? They gave nothing (1975: pp. 205-206).

The train with its four hundred and fifty eventually goes on and then, after sixty hours of hunger, the passengers eat one hundred and fifty miles down the line. In this case no redistributive solution was worked out and violence was clearly possible. In other cases the Anarresti rationed food so that it would in fact contribute to the food-producing capacity of the society and save more lives in the long run:

> ... the mill syndicate cut rations. People doing six hours in the plant got full rations—just barely enough for that kind of work. People on half time got three-quarter rations. If they were sick or too weak to work, they got half. On half rations you couldn't get

well. You couldn't get back to work. You might stay alive (1975: 250).

More harshly, mills were kept running even when it was clear that some would die because a provisions train was delayed:

> ... when the provisions train was stopped..., they kept the mills going, and people died of hunger on the job. Just went a little out of the way and lay down and died (1975: 249-250).

One character says that "making lists" is wrong, but evidently this is not a view widely shared; a utilitarian criterion of contribution and appropriation is adopted as a strategy in extremis.[12]

The principle of equal appropriation is qualified in a more routine way as well. Some inequalities are justified when they work out for the benefit of everyone, but these do not seem to be the sort of differences in reward that Rawls thinks one of his principles of justice, the so-called difference principle, would legitimate. Joel Feinberg puts Rawls's thinking as follows:

> Surely any reasonable person, Rawls argues, would prefer a system that gives him a larger amount of goods, though a smaller portion than his neighbor's, to a system that gives him a smaller absolute amount, though one that is an equal share (1978: 805).[13]

But what is unreasonable for Rawls is exactly what is preferred on Anarres, with the exception that functional inequalities that redound to the benefit of all are acceptable, e.g., physicists get private rooms or more desserts.[14] The Anarresti apparently could not accept Feinberg's statement of the difference principle, for it is broad enough to allow differential rewards as incentives. The Anarresti accept an analogue of the principle, but one that makes clear that only functional inequalities are allowed. To allow others based on the incentive of personal gain, even if the Anarresti believed that such incentives would raise the "absolute amount," would violate the commitment to "solidarity," the equality of contribution and appropriation.

There are not only parameters of contribution and appropriation for the social product on Anarres, but there would also have to be decisions about giving aid in situations that fall outside the basic distributional structure, e.g., natural disasters or accidents (see Reeder, 1982: p. 84ff.). I would assume that for the citizens of Anarres, given the commitment to equality, the consensus would be that one is expected to aid others up to the level of comparable cost; one is expected to give one of one's kidneys to save the life of another, but not two kidneys even to save two others. Shevek's father exceeded this standard when he returned to a burning building to save a child's life. (His act was what would be called supererogation in an ethic of duty.) On Anarres, mutual benevolence would underwrite aid only up to the level of comparable cost to the self; this standard of aid would correspond to the principle of equal contribution and return that regulates the basic structure.[15] The ethic does not call for "self-sacrifice" in the sense of going beyond comparable cost to aid the neighbor.[16] Furthermore, just as the norm of equality for the structure of society has to do with basic or "welfare" goods, so the notion of aid up to comparable cost in extraordinary situations concerns goods such as health or life. One is at liberty, as far as I can tell, either to augment or not the well-being of others above the level of basic goods; e.g., I am to give you a kidney if you need it, but I need not forgo building wooden boats so that you can build radio telescopes.

On Anarres, it also seems to be assumed that biological parents or others who assume child-rearing roles have special responsibilities. On the basis of an apparent consensus on child psychology, the infant remains in the nuclear family for a certain period and then goes on to a communal nursery-dormitory facility. There is tension in the novel about the adequacy of these arrangements, and there is room for parental judgment, but nurture is not seen as some species of moral responsibility independent of one's general concern for the neighbor. Rather, the grounds for special responsibilities are functional: one wants to promote and protect everyone's basic interests; children have special needs: how best can these needs be met?

In addition to equality of contribution and appropriation, Anarresti uphold a notion of equal liberty. The Anarresti are anarchists (no law or state); the individual chooses how to contribute and for the most part how to draw his or her portion. Anarresti also have the liberty to stand against current social policy in the name of the community's deepest traditions; only under conditions when this liberty is no longer authentically affirmed by the community does Shevek claim it as a "right of self-determination."

Equality of basic well-being puts limits on freedom, however; one is not morally free to work on pleasure boats while others starve; one is not free to hoard one's kidneys.[17] One is also limited in regard to the sort of preference one can give to the near and dear. One can give psychological or material support beyond what one's child-rearing responsibilities call for, for example. As long as one did not take all the relevant materials from the goods depository, and hence deprive others of a similar opportunity, one could spend one's extra time making toys for one's child. But it would not be right to devote special attention or goods to one's child if these resources are needed for famine relief. When a range of basic goods is endangered, then the effort to secure these goods for all takes priority; that all survive takes precedence over nonessential aspects of a particular child's well-being. Only when basic or essential goods are relatively secure can one devote surplus resources to "special relations." On Anarres, I believe, one would be permitted to feed one's starving child before the stranger's should the choice be necessary; and one would not be prohibited from preferring the well-being of near and dear when all have basic goods; but it would be wrong to augment one's child's well-being above the level of basic goods when others lack these necessities.[18]

It is also important to note that one's freedom is limited in regard to what one receives from the community as well as in regard to what one gives. Shevek, a central character, comes down with a fever and reports to the hospital. Diagnosed as a light pneumonia, he is told to go to bed.

> He protested. The aide accused him of egoizing and explained that if he went home a physician would have to go to the trouble of calling on him there and arranging private care for him (1975: 96).

Shevek agrees to go to bed, but he refuses an "antipyretic" to bring down the fever. Later when a doctor appears with a needle, he says again, "I don't want it," but the doctor says to stop "egoizing" and tells him to roll over (1975: 97).

Now, there are a number of things to say about this incident. First, Shevek, at least by the time the doctor arrives with the needle, is clearly incompetent; he is raving with fever, does not know where he is. But second, even assuming competence, it would be incumbent on Shevek to consider the cost to others of his recovery; staying in the hospital and taking the drug not only make him feel better, but lessen the burden on others. Even sick, he would have to make decisions that take into account the distribution of benefits and burdens generally. He does not possess, normatively speaking, a liberty that would enable him to treat himself or be treated as he would perhaps prefer. Third, one can speculate that on Anarres one's freedom is limited not only in regard to the mode of treatment, but as to whether to be treated. Suppose Shevek had to receive a series of painful treatments to attack a life-threatening disease. Does he have the "right" to refuse treatment? If Shevek's recovery would allow him neither to give to nor to receive from society (according to Anarresti conceptions), then, one supposes, he would be permitted to refuse treatment. He could also refuse treatment if the recovery would allow him only to give or only to receive, for he is not required simply to give with no provision for the self nor would he be required to continue to exist merely as the recipient of the aid of others. But if Shevek could recover so that he could not only receive but have something to give, then I assume it would be wrong for him (as long as he adheres to the Anarresti ethic) to refuse treatment and cut off his usefulness. If one has some prospect of giving and receiving, then to choose death to escape painful treatment or a reduced quality of life might count as "egoizing."

This speculation may go too far in restricting self-determination, of course. One would certainly think that the Anarresti would allow refusal of treatment in cases where death can only be delayed a short time. The individual must decide in any case, but the fever incident reveals the way in which Anarres generally makes trade-offs between well-being and liberty. Extensive benevolence is structured by distributive policies which balance access to basic well-being and various expressions of self-determination (see Baier, 1992).

4. EXTENSIVE BENEVOLENCE AND DISTRIBUTIONAL POLICIES

I have tried to show that there are distributional principles in regard to well-being and liberty on Anarres.[19] Just how are they *related* to mutual extensive benevolence? I defined mutual extensive benevolence as a shared disposition to desire the basic good of others as one's own. One is now prepared to act to protect or promote a good whether it is in one's own person or another. The thrust of extensive benevolence in this sense is universal—the good of any neighbor—but in practice it is limited to an environment of trust in the benevolence of others, at least insofar as it is lived out directly without recourse to a system of justice. Even the Anarresti have "defense" forces for relations with the outside world. On Anarres "mutual aid" is limited to Anarresti society, but theoretically it could extend to all persons; Shevek believes that Anarres is the "future."

Furthermore, one is prepared to protect or promote a basic good, whether it is one's own person or another's, to an equal extent or degree; my good (or my friend's or family's or ethnic group's) has no privileged position over yours. In other words, even if I desire the good of others as well as my own, I might desire my own good or the good of some people more than the good of some others; but I now conceive of myself desiring in the same way the good of all. Thus, mutual extensive benevolence is egalitarian or universal in two respects: one desires the basic good of every neighbor (persons or even sentient beings) and one desires the good of others with the same intensity as one desires one's own. The extensive benevolence that Hume thought to be inadequately present in human nature is the basis of the Anarresti ethic.

However this benevolence or love is to be explained, on Anarres it is simply taken for granted. It provides an analogue to the doctrine of objective reasons that Thomas Nagel attempts to ground in our very conception of ourselves as agents: "If one acknowledges the presence of an objective reason for something, one has acknowledged a reason for *anyone* to promote or desire its occurence...."; if we have reason to prevent our own suffering and secure the conditions of well-being and freedom for ourselves, then we have reason to desire and try to achieve these ends for anyone.[20] Extensive benevolence therefore provides for Anarres what neo-Kantians (like Nagel) attempt to supply as a demand of rational agency, or some neo-Aristotelians try to secure in a commonly valued relationship, namely, a basic bond of concern for self and other. That I affectively affirm the good of all with an equal intensity does not mean, however, that I endorse in my own view of the good the particular projects or life-plans adopted by individuals. I might not think, for example, that building radio telescopes is as good as building wooden boats. But I would be prepared on Anarres to affirm to an equal extent not only the basic liberty and well-being of all, but everyone's opportunity to pursue their projects (provided resources are available). In this sense, I affirm to an equal extent everyone's overall good. As Nagel puts it, everyone is as "important" as everyone else.[21]

But as Nagel points out, his "objective reasons" need still more specific "combinatorial principles" that establish how the good of others and the good of the self are to be related in practice (1970: 133-134). And similarly another level of specification is required for extensive benevolence. Extensive benevolence as equal concern for the basic interests of all does not necessarily translate into utilitarianism, for we have as yet no doctrine of basic human (or non-human) interests such that we know whether they are commensurable or whether there are values that should not be summed in a utilitarian calculus (as Thomists traditionally insist). One would have to choose whether extensive benevolence is satisfactorily expressed, for example, in utilitarianism that "counts each as one" but can allow gross inequality, in the equality of Anarres that may result in a lesser overall distribution, or in a system such as Rawls's that requires certain equalities but also justifies inequalities if they improve the position of the worst-off. In other words, the initial egalitarian starting point does not tell you which "principles of justice," or their analogues, to adopt; the Anarresti go in one way, another society based on extensive benevolence might make different choices.

Thus, extensive benevolence is specified so that it becomes a distributional policy. Where the objective circumstances of justice obtain, that is, under certain conditions of scarcity where humans cooperate and distributional policies are required, then this love that includes self and neighbor needs analogues to principles of justice. Just how this specification would be accomplished I am uncertain. Perhaps elements of neo-Aristotelian theories of the good would be employed (loving persons *value* certain social relations; the Anarresti value a rough equality of result more than the higher standard of well-being that a Rawlsian set-up might provide) or perhaps elements of Kantian theories could be employed (what, regardless of their specific view of the good, *anyone* needs and wants) (Wong, 1984: 175-76).

In any case extensive benevolence furnishes a different motivational structure than the one we associate with justice, at least in major Western traditions. One lives directly out of a mutual and extensive benevolence that is distributively structured but that does not require a system of justice. The indication that one is dealing with a system of love is that although on Anarres there are broad parameters of equal well-being and liberty, one does not insist on exact or measured shares. Within a framework where one trusts the benevolence of others, one does not have to insist on exactly what would be one's due in a system of justice. This does not mean that one is prepared over time to ignore the good of the self; it simply means, as Sandel put it, that one is not preoccupied with getting one's due. Or in a classic statement: ". . . love does not insist on its own (I Cor. 13:5).[22]

5. UTOPIAS AND OPTIONS

I have tried to show that extensive benevolence could make justice unnecessary. But such a love is itself distributively unspecified and under certain circumstances it needs decisions about how the good of each is to be understood and related to the good of others. These policies may resemble principles adopted for a system of justice, e.g., Rawls's, but they are put to work in a different framework.

What determines whether we can live directly out of extensive benevolence? Our views about what people are capable of, ideally or realistically, in the short or long term. In order for extensive benevolence to serve as the basis of the Anarres ethic it must be mutual; the citizens must be able to trust one another's benevolence. Thus, the ethic of mutual aid is limited to Anarres. With the home planet Urras, Anarres makes self-interested bargains: in return for metals, Urras will leave Anarres in peace.

What are some options? Patriarchal and capitalistic socialization incline many people in our society to think that the virtue of benevolence should be primary in the "private" sphere of the family and personal relations, while the virtue of justice must be primary in the "public" world. Benevolence remains, but mainly in the form of concern for particular others; the only role extensive benevolence plays in the public sphere is as a supplementary virtue, one which is ennobling perhaps but not required. We can perhaps explain the emergence of this paradigm as follows: the industrial revolution and the rise of capitalism produced an economic ethic of negative rights and only those positive obligations created by contract or promise; this ethic comes to dominate conceptions of public morality or is even projected over morality as a whole; whereas "charity" earlier referred to a general positive requirement to assist others, it now signals supererogation. At roughly the same time, production is taken from the home and women are allocated a "private" sphere in which the love or caring which is optional in the public world is required.[23]

Even if we no longer think of benevolence and justice as traits necessarily related to gender, however, and even if we conceive of alternatives to current systems of justice, pessimism about human nature might still lead us to retain the private-public dichotomy and to construct an ethic of justice for the public world. We could include sexual-familial relations in the basic structure covered by justice and, e.g., insist on a positive right to subsistence (and other essential goods) in addition to negative rights of noninterference, while still distinguishing a special sphere of caring for kin and friends. Nel Noddings (1984), for example, effectively confines caring (in her full sense) to a limited circle of kin and co-workers and hence she could be said to put the basic framework of sexual, economic, and political life under some other moral category. One can, but need not, love the stranger. For Noddings, caring requires awareness of the giver by the recipient, which is not always possible in dealings with the stranger, and in any case, caring as she defines it demands a degree of psychic expenditure that we cannot extend beyond a small circle. Thus, Nodding's confinement of caring seems rooted in her view of the finite resources of the human animal.

Alternatively we could operate with two distinct moral considerations in all spheres of life: extensive benevolence, and a desire for justice based perhaps on a neo-Kantian or Aristotelian link between self and other, would function as irreducible yet equally necessary perspectives that we bring to all moral situations. Carol Gilligan, for example, wants a contemporary ethic comprising both "rights" and "caring"; she does not mean that rights and caring belong principally in different spheres; nor does she seem consistently to say, although she earlier seemed to suggest (1982), that rights and caring combine into some kind of synthesis (rights providing a legitimate concern for self that caring, defined as concern for others, needed, while caring roots ethics in affective relationships deeper than mere rights and rules; each is the remedy for the deficiency of the other.)[24] Her considered view (1987) seems to be that the "justice perspective" and the "care perspective" (which I take to signify not only caring for particular others but for all who suffer) are two "moral orientations" sufficiently different that they cannot be "integrated" or employed "simultaneously" (1987: 19-20; 22-23); yet these perspectives illumine "different dimensions of the situation" (25) and hence both are part of the "moral domain" (26). Although Gilligan resists the idea of integration or synthesis, her basic theme seems to be that the moral life is twofold and that its dimensions are equally necessary; the "moral domain" is in effect a combination of two different "perspectives."

Lastly we might find ourselves retracing the steps of many Judaic and Christian theologians who believe that love must adopt principles of justice so long as the world remains finite and sinful.[25] Since even the extensive benevolence of believers can't entirely be trusted, those who love must express that love indirectly in a system of what is due or owed. Sanctification is not complete in this life; grace does not sufficiently heal nature. Those who love will desire to do justice, and justice is necessary not only in the economic and political world, but in sexual-familial relations as well.[26] While relations based directly on love may occasionally be possible in various spheres, we generally need justice. Extensive benevolence would not operate directly in society at large as it does on Anarres; love would now function as the motivating rationale for a system of justice that embraces both the mistakenly dichotomized "public" and "private" spheres. Given the deficiencies in their love, the parties find that on many occasions they make conflicting demands on scarce resources; not only do they need distributive policies (which they would require in any case), but they need a system of justice, of rightful claims and shares, on which they can rely.

My own leaning is toward alternative three. Nodding's model stipulatively defines caring as the sort of psychic expenditure that is necessarily limited to a few neighbors. I would also claim that we are capable of extensive benevolence as well; our *concern* for others is not necessarily a zero-sum game although our psychic and material resources are limited. We should distinguish caring and taking care of; once we care, we have to decide, as I argued above, how to distribute our resources.[27] And while Gilligan would be correct to say that extensive benevolence needs "justice" in the sense of distributional specification—this theme is implicit I think in her works—I do not believe that it requires justice as an element in a synthesis or as one of two irreducible perspectives; as I have argued, under certain historical circumstances (Anarres), extensive benevolence can render justice otiose. However, our present relations within and between nations are like Anarres's relations with Urras: we cannot trust ourselves or our neighbor to be benevolent. Even where extensive benevolence arises, it does not sufficiently overcome the classic difficulties; it is not sufficiently well distributed, and even where it appears it is often weak, capricious, or both. Thus, even for "believers" extensive benevolence will for the time being have only a grounding function; it is not acted on directly as on Anarres, but underlies a commitment to justice. The third alternative wagers that love is or could be sufficiently well distributed, steady, and strong to ground, to serve as the fundamental motivation for, say, a system of human rights; but there is not enough confidence in human improvement to attempt Anarres now.

How can this be? If we remember Sandel's family, the wager is that mutual extensive benevolence remains even when the family members find themselves unable to rely directly on their mutual love. Their bond of love is intact at a deep level, but on many occasions self-regarding desire overwhelms love for the other. Because the family members know their love is flawed, they adopt a system of justice. It is not that they have fallen back into the circumstances of justice altogether, and lacking any bond of love, experience a conflict of interests that requires justice as its remedy. They still have their bond of mutual love; but since it is ill-distributed, inconstant, or weak, they need a system of fair shares, of what is owed and due, of claims they can make on one another. In theological language, given finitude and sin, love needs justice. Love remains, and is sufficient to ground a desire to do justice.[28]

NOTES

1. See David Wong (1984) who distinguishes the starting point of compassionate identification and the social structure built upon it (206ff.).

Wong does not suggest that *tz'u*, "compassion" or "deep love," will provide a basis from which principles of justice, for example, can be deduced. But as the basis of our respect for others—a respect which does not rest on a comparison or evaluation of their qualities—it can shape social structure. For example, it would encourage "diversity of moral perspectives" and hence increase tolerance (208ff.), and it would promote the "decentralization of power and authority" (210). Cf. Victor Turner (1974) on the relation of anti-structure ("communitas") and structure, and Rawls (1971) on the relation of the original position, in particular the veil of ignorance, to principles of justice for the "basic structure." On Turner and Rawls, see Reeder (1980). On Hume, see Baier (1987) and MacIntyre (1988).

2. On various meanings of the contrast between love and justice, see Outka, 1972: Chapter 3 (Agape and Justice) and pp. 309-313; Childress (1985); and Williams (1990). See also Hauerwas, 1974: Ch. 6, and Meilaender, 1981. I am speaking in this paper of distributive justice but I believe that the mutual love of Anarres is also expressed in other ways associated with justice, e.g., reparations. I am grateful to Lee Yearley on this point.

3. Some writers have proposed that we could do without justice or rights in specific areas of life. For example, Jane English argued that there is no moral basis for the idea that grown children owe their aged parents support as a debt. Rather the relation ought to be seen as one of friendship: ". . . friendship ought to be characterized by *mutuality* rather than reciprocity: friends offer what they can give and accept what they need, without regard for the total amounts of benefits exchanged. And friends are motivated by love rather than by the prospect of repayment. Hence talk of 'owing' is singularly out of place in friendship" (1979: p. 353; cf. 354). John Ladd makes a similar proposal for the doctor-patient relation. Although patients may have a right to refuse treatment and a doctor the right to refuse to treat, the parties should construe their moral relationship in other categories and "bypass" rights (1978: pp. 18, 19, 22). Doctors, nurses, and patients can be friends, and following Aristotle, "friends . . . have no need of justice" (1978: p. 19; n. 47; n. 48). Ladd has in mind an ethic of responsibility that rests on need, ability to meet the need, and the existence of a "relationship" (pp. 24-26); while this moral category is not reducible simply to benevolence, it does assume "attitudes of concern, of caring . . ." (1978: pp. 26-28).

4. The aid Anarresti extend to one another can be referred to as giving, but it should carefully be distinguished from the "giving" that presupposes the idea of what is owned or to what one has a right.

5. There is some textual evidence against my interpretation. A character says "The reality of our life is in love, in solidarity . . . Love is the true condition of human life" (49). But someone else says "Love's just one of the ways through. . . ." This last character, however, may be referring to sexual love or friendship, whereas mutual benevolence as I characterize it is a desire to relieve suffering, based on compassion or sympathy: "shared pain." Cf. 228-9. One could argue that this recognition of shared pain should be interpreted in terms of Nagel's (1970) neo-Kantianism, or MacIntyre's notion of a neo-Aristotelian good of a way of life (1984). I take it as an independent starting-point on Anarres.

6. Sandel speaks of the "circumstances of benevolence." On Anarres trust in each other, as in Sandel's family, replaces trust in God. "Faith, that is, trust in the faithfulness of the covenanting God, frees a person from the kind of self-concern that would lead to defensiveness or even to worry about getting an equal share, at least where justice to others does not depend on justice for the self. From faith one is not anxious about one's own life and possessions (Matt. 6:25)" (Allen, 1984: 114).

7. As I noted, Anarresti do not usually appeal to notions of a fair share, what is owed or due, or what they have a right to. There are places in the novel, however, where Anarres is referred to as the "just" society. At some points, especially in regard to liberty, "rights" are appealed to.

8. Rawls (1971: 191) argues that "if the claims of these goods [of beloved individuals] clash, benevolence is at a loss as to how to proceed, as long anyway as it treats these individuals as separate persons. These higher-order sentiments do not include principles of right to adjudicate these conflicts. Therefore, a love of mankind that wishes to preserve the distinction of persons, to recognize the separateness of life and experience, will use the two principles of justice to determine its aims when the many goods it cherishes are in opposition. This is simply to say that this love is guided by what individuals themselves would consent to in a fair initial situation which gives them equal representation as moral persons. We now see why nothing would have been gained by attributing benevolence to the parties in the original position." In my view, mutual extensive benevolence of a certain sort renders the presupposition of conflicting desires counterfactual. But I agree that such benevolence needs distributive principles. On Anarres, as I will argue, principles of equal liberty and well-being are at work, but they are not the same as Rawls's. Cf. Sandel, 1982: 168-73 and Beckley (1986).

9. Cf. Paul Ramsey (1950). Allen (1984) argues that believers should give priority to the needs of others, even to the point of self-sacrifice, but never fail to respect, to value themselves as children of God (96; 112-120). Farley (1986: 104-109) argues that one can gain union even in self-sacrifice but that one is never to destroy one's personhood, one's autonomy and capacity for union. Both Allen and Farley identify other cases of bad self-sacrifice: false needs of the other, sacrifice as an end in itself, unreasonable expenditure, devaluation of the self's material well-being, sacrifice as a way to punish the self(Farley, 1986: 106; Allen, 1984: 119). Cf. Hallett (1989) on "self-subordination."

10. Cf. Veatch's principle of "equality of net welfare," which yields a "right to health care equal in proportion to need" (1981: p. 264ff.; p. 270ff.; cf. 1976).

11. See. Outka (1976: 89-90) on essential psychophysical needs, and Little and Twiss (1978: 37-38) on "welfare" in contrast to well-being.

12. The novel internally draws attention to morally problematic occurrences, e.g., regarding extreme scarcity, or the implied critique of certain forms of communal child rearing.

13. See Allen Buchanan's distinction between two versions of the difference principle: 1) if any inequalities are permitted they must maximize the prospects of the worst-off; 2) the prospects of the worst-off must be max-

imized (1980: 31-2). According to Buchanan, 1) could allow an equal distribution, even if the shares would in fact be smaller than under a nonequal distribution. But Buchanan says Rawls is arguing for 2) in accordance with the maximin principle. The parties in the original position want to maximize the minimum, and thus on the assumption that incentives are necessary to that end, they adopt the principle that the resultant inequalities should benefit the least advantaged. Buchanan argues that it is "extremely implausible" that "distributive justice could require *more* than perfect equality" (1980: 32). Sticking to justice as equality, Buchanan argues that it still might be morally required to go beyond justice and accept inequalities if equal shares were "lean" (32). But Rawls, he says, insists on accepting inequalities even if equal shares were "substantial or even bounteous" (33); for Rawls equality is justified only if it maximizes the minimum, and this Buchanan rejects as counterintuitive to his views about justice. But for Rawls justice is what the contractors say it is and "considered judgments" would have to be revised. To know that one would not want to go beyond equality as long as a certain level of good were reached is to put more information in the original position than Rawls allows.

14. There is the suggestion in the novel that some privileges may not in fact be functionally required, but if they were, they would be justified.

15. For feminist criticisms of self-sacrifice, see Andolsen (1981).

16. The basic norm I propose here resembles what Hallett calls the "parity" version of *agape* or Christian neighbor-love: *"equal benefit, whether to oneself or another, should receive equal weight, and unequal benefit unequal weight, without preference either way"* (1989: 3-4). This formulation, however, may blend together the equal concern of extensive benevolence (or the Rawlsian veil) and a utilitarian standard of distribution for situations in which there are competing goods (22-3; 38ff.). Some contemporary notions of *agape* as "equal regard" combine the egalitarian starting point but like Rawls see it specified in principles of equality (in regard to freedom and well-being) that cannot be overridden by utilitarian considerations (see Outka, 1972). See Hallett's useful typology of distributional norms (self-preference, parity, other-preference, self-subordination, self-forgetfulness, and self-denial); he argues that the scriptural standard is self-subordination, i.e., when goods compete, disregard one's own good; seek one's own good only in the absence of conflict (53-62).

17. But if one's labor and one's bodily parts are at the disposal of the community, subject only to one's decision as to where and when one makes the contribution, is the same true of one's sexual parts? Apparently not, for others do not expect to use one's body simply because they need or want it. One is not "egoizing" if one refuses a sexual liaison. One does not merely choose when and where to contribute to the goal of sexual satisfaction for all. One could see this limitation simply as an inconsistency, a failure to follow the implications of a general doctrine. More likely it is assumed on Anarres that to give the "freedom of the flesh" is to give the self; perhaps sexual parts are seen as integral to the self whereas a kidney is not. If so, then sexual giving and receiving constitute a sphere outside of the social product and the bodily parts covered by the norm of equality of well-being.

18. Contemporary attacks on neo-Kantians or Kantian interpretations of Christian *agape* often focus on two objections (see, e.g., Post, 1988, 1990, and Sandel, 1984): 1) the agent is conceived ahistorically; 2) no place or no important place remain for duties of special relations; one's duty is wholly or at least principally to persons as such. Contemporary neo-Kantians, however, e.g., Rawls, make a moral not a metaphysical point; the veil of ignorance is a moral point of view, not a thesis about personhood or personal identity (see Rorty, 1988 and Reeder, 1990); furthermore, from the perspective of the veil, the contractors, in the Rawlsian idiom, might be said to assign special duties to kin as a way of securing the basic principles of justice in the sexual-familial sphere; the contractors can also allow and even encourage preference for the near and dear provided that general duties of justice are satisfied. Critics however may want to claim that duties to children, for example, are not an expression of a more general duty to the neighbor, or that such duties can override obligations to the stranger. The Anarresti allow me to prefer the near and dear when there are not enough basic goods for all; but I may not fail to provide the stranger with a basic good in order to increase the well-being of the near and dear beyond the basic level. Cf. Sher, 1987: 184-86; Stocker, 1987: 66; Held, 1987: 111-119; Friedman, 1987: 195ff.; and in this volume, Outka and Werpehowski.

19. Note that where the objective circumstances do not obtain, benevolence could be expressed without the structure of distributional policies. Love could be "heedless" because it would not have to be restricted in order to provide for the self. I am indebted to discussions with Diana Fritz Cates on this point. See Reeder (1980) where the Kingdom of God is seen as a state where both the objective and subjective circumstances are transcended. For an analysis of Hume and Rawls, see Hubin (1979).

20. 1970: 119, 127. Nagel explicitly contrasts his theory with one that would "rest the motivational influence of ethical considerations on fortuitous or escapable inclinations" (p. 6), e.g., those stemming from sympathy (p. 11). Thus, he argues that "one has a *direct* reason to promote the interests of others—a reason which does not depend on intermediate factors such as one's own interests or one's antecedent sentiments of sympathy and benevolence" (pp. 15-16). Nagel's view is thus explicitly Kantian. I am indebted to Lawrence Blum's (1980) contrast of the altruistic emotions and Nagel's theory of objective reasons.

21. See Nagel (1980, 1986) on the goods that are agent-neutral, in contrast to agent-relative "autonomy" goods.

22. Cf. Outka (1972: 309-310).

23. See Sandra Harding (1987) for a critique of the sort of psychoanalytic explanation offered by Chodorow (1978) and others, and utilized by Gilligan (1982), Keller (1986), etc., to account for gender differences in thinking generally and moral perspectives especially. Harding's thesis is that the root causes for the difference between the "justice" and the "caring" perspectives lie in early modern economic and political developments; a "public" ethos of individual rights is developed and allocated along preexisting gender lines and caring is banished to the "private" world of women; new generations are socialized into this construction, as opposed to the view

that it originates in early infantile experiences. Thus, as Harding remarks, "Perhaps the dichotomy we need is one between modern, Western men, and the rest of us [Western women *and* African men, e.g.] (1987: 305). Cf. Meyers (1987: 142-44. Gilligan and Wiggins (1988: 114-16) root justice and care first in early experiences of inequality and attachment (see also Gilligan, 1987).

24. Cf. also Farley (1986: 80-82) on how love must not distort the reality of others, their equality and difference, their needs for autonomy and relation. A "'just love'" is one that "aims to affirm truthfully the concrete reality of the beloved" (1986: 82). Farley distinguishes this qualified notion of love from her general definition (affirmation, union, response) but it seems to me that the basic notion of an affective affirmation of the other's well-being means that I "say yes to you according to my understanding of your truest reality" (30). Perhaps the contrast is between wanting the good of the other and really attending to what that good is. And even if one truly attends, one has to face the distributional question: how is the true good of self and other to be achieved.

25. Farley, for example, argues that love not only needs obligation but a "framework" of principles and practices "subject to norms of justice" (1986: 35-7; 13); out of love one desires justice. Also see Heyward (1982).

26. Ketchum and Pierce argue that since the model of competition for unequal wealth and power is taken for granted in American society, including medicine, then justice and rights are necessary (1981: 20). Cf. Ladd (1978: 137; cf. 1982) who argues that the competitive model should not be taken as an essential truth of human nature.

27. Noddings says that we can "care about everyone" in the sense of "an internal state of readiness to try to care for whoever crosses our path;" this however is not equivalent to actual "caring-for" (1984: 18). If Gilligan's or Noddings's "caring" were inherently particular, then "justice" would presumably carry the whole weight of universality. I hope in a subsequent paper, drawing in part on Gilligan and Noddings, to show how love of particular others can develop into extensive benevolence. And while I have suggested how the Anarresti relate care for the near and dear to care for brothers and sisters generally, I have not tried to settle this normative issue. I am grateful to Julia Judish for conversation on these points.

28. I am grateful to a number of colleagues, among them Paul Lauritzen, Gene Outka, Sumner Twiss and Lee Yearley; Zachary Lesser and Wayne Wilson helped to improve the manuscript at a number of points.

REFERENCES

Allen, Joseph L. 1984 *Love and Conflict: A Covenantal Model of Christian Ethics*. Nashville: Abington Press.

Andolsen, Barbara Hilkert 1981 "Agape in Feminist Ethics," *The Journal of Religious Ethics* 9 (Spring): 69-83.

Baier, Annette, C. 1987 "Hume, the Women's Moral Theorist?" in Kittay, Eva Feder, and Meyers, Diana T., eds., *Women and Moral Theory*. Totowa, N.J.: Rowman and Littlefield: 37-55.

_____. 1992 "Claims, Rights, Responsibilities," in Gene Outka and John P. Reeder, Jr., eds., *Prospects for a Common Morality*, Princeton, N.J.: Princeton University Press: 149-69.

Beckley, Harlan R. 1986 "A Christian Affirmation of Rawls's Idea of Justice as Fairness: Part II," *The Journal of Religious Ethics* 14 (Fall): 229-46.

Blum, Lawrence 1980 *Friendship, Altruism, and Morality*. London and Boston: Routledge and K. Paul.

Buchanan, Allen 1980 "A Critical Introduction to Rawls' Theory of Justice," in Blocker and Smith, eds., *John Rawls' Theory of Social Justice*. Athens: Ohio University Press: 5-41.

Childress, James F. 1985 "Love and Justice in Christian Bio-medical Ethics," in Shelp, Earl E., ed., *Theology and Bioethics*. Dordrecht, Holland: D. Reidel Publishing Co.: 225-244.

Chodorow, Nancy 1978 *The Reproduction of Mothering: Psychoanalysis and the Sociology of Gender*. Berkeley: University of California Press.

English, Jane 1979 "What do Grown Children Owe Their Parents," in O'Neill, Onora, and Ruddich, William, eds., *Having Children: Philosophical and Legal Reflections on Parenthood*. New York: Oxford University Press: 351-56.

Farley, Margaret A. 1986 *Personal Commitments: Making, Keeping, Breaking*. San Francisco: Harper and Row.

Feinberg, J. 1978 "Justice," in Reich W., ed., *The Encyclopedia of Bioethics*. Vol. 2. New York: Macmillan Publishing Co., and The Free Press: 802-811.

Frankena, William K. 1962 "The Concept of Social Justice," in Brandt, Richard, ed., *Social Justice*. Englewood Cliffs, N.J.: Prentice Hall, Inc.: 1-29.

Friedman, Marilyn 1987 "Care and Context in Moral Reasoning," in Kittay, Eva Feder, and Meyers, Diana T., eds., *Women and Moral Theory*: 190-204.

Gilligan, Carol 1982 *In a Different Voice*. Cambridge: Mass.: Harvard University Press.

_____. 1987 "Moral Orientation and Moral Development," in Kittay, Eva Feder, and Meyers, Diana T., eds., *Women and Moral Theory*. Totowa, N.J.: Rowman and Littlefield: 19-33.

_____ and Grant Wiggins 1988 "The Origins of Morality in Early Childhood Relationships," in Carol Gilligan, Jamie Victoria Ward, Jill McLean Taylor, with Betty Bardige, eds., *Mapping The Moral Domain: A Contribution of Women's Thinking To Psychological Theory and Education*. Cambridge, MA: Harvary University Press, 1988: 111-38.

Hallett, Gareth 1989 *Christian Neighbor Love: An Assessment of Six Rival Versions*. Washington: Georgetown University Press.

Harding, Sandra 1987 "The Curious Coincidence of Feminine and African Moralities: Challenges for Feminist Theory," in Kittay, Eva Feder and Meyers, Diana T., eds., *Women and Moral Theory*: 296-315.

Hauerwas, Stanley 1974 *Vision and Virtue: Essays in Christian Ethical Reflection*. Notre Dame, Ind.: Fides Publishers, Inc.

Held, Virginia 1987 "Feminism and Moral Theory," in Kittay, Eva Feder and Meyers, Diana T., eds., *Women and Moral Theory*: 111-128.

Heyward, Carter 1982 *The Redemption of God*. University Press of America.

Hubin, Clayton D. 1979 "The Scope of Justice," *Philosophy and Public Affairs* 9 (Fall): 3-24.

Hume, David 1957 In Hendel, Charles W., ed., *An Inquiry Concerning the Principles of Morals*. New York: Liberal Arts Press.

———. 1967 In Selby-Bigge, L. A., ed., *A Treatise of Human Nature*. Oxford: Clarendon Press.

Keller, Catherine 1986 *From a Broken Web: Separation, Sexism, and Self*. Boston: Beacon Press.

Ketchum, Sara Ann, and Pierce, Christine 1981 "Rights and Responsibilities," *Journal of Medicine and Philosophy* 6 (August): 271-80.

Ladd, J. 1978 "Legalism and Medical Ethics," in Davis, J. W.; Hoffmaster, Barry; and Shorten, Sarah; eds., *Contemporary Issues in Bioethics*. Clifton, N.J.: The Humana Press: 1-35.

———. 1982 "The Distinction Between Rights and Responsibilities," *Linacre Quarterly* (May): 121-42.

LeGuin, Ursula 1975 *The Dispossessed*. New York: Avon Books.

Little, David, and Twiss, Sumner B. 1978 *Comparative Religious Ethics*. San Francisco: Harper and Row.

MacIntyre, Alasdair 1984 *After Virtue*, 2nd ed. Notre Dame: University of Notre Dame Press.

———. 1988 *Whose Justice? Which Rationality?* Notre Dame, Indiana: University of Notre Dame Press.

Meilaender, Gilbert C. 1981 *Friendship: A Study in Theological Ethics*. Notre Dame, Indiana: University of Notre Dame Press.

Meyers, Diana T. 1987 "The Socialized Individual and Individual Autonomy: An Intersection Between Philosophy and Psychology," in Kittay, Eva Feder and Meyers, Diana T., eds., *Women and Moral Theory*: 139-153.

Nagel, Thomas 1970 *The Possibility of Altruism*. Oxford: The Clarendon Press.

———. 1980 "The Limits of Objectivity," in McMurrin, Sterling M., ed., *The Tanner Lectures on Human Values*. Salt Lake City: University of Utah Press.

———. 1986 *The View from Nowhere*. New York: Oxford University Press.

Noddings, Nel 1984 *Caring: A Feminine Approach to Ethics and Moral Education*. Berkeley: University of California Press.

Outka, Gene 1972 *Agape: An Ethical Analysis*. New Haven: Yale University Press.

———. 1976 "Social Justice and Equal Access to Health Care," in Veatch, R. M., and Branson, Roy, eds., *Ethics and Health Policy*. Cambridge, Mass.: Ballinger.

Post, Stephen G. 1988 "Communion and True Self-Love," *The Journal of Religious Ethics* 16 (Fall): 345-62.

―――――. 1990 *A Theory of Agape: On the Meaning of Christian Love*. Lewisburg: Bucknell University Press.

Ramsey, Paul 1950 *Basic Christian Ethics*. New York: Charles Scribner's Sons.

Rawls, John 1971 *A Theory of Justice*. Cambridge, Mass.: Harvard University Press.

―――――. 1980 "Kantian Constructivism in Moral Theory," *Journal of Philosophy* LXXVII (September): 515-72.

Reeder, John P., Jr. 1980 "Assenting to *Agape*," *The Journal of Religion* 60 (January): 17-31.

―――――. 1982. "Beneficence, Supererogation, and Role Duty," in Shelp, Earl E., ed., *Beneficence and Health Care*. Dordrecht, Holland: D. Reidel Publishing Co.: 83-108.

―――――. 1990 "Individualism, Communitarianism, and Theories of Justice," in Sizemore, Russell, and Swearer, Donald, eds., *Ethics, Wealth, and Salvation: A Study in Buddhist Social Ethics*. Columbia: University of South Carolina Press: 235-52; 273-80; 291-96.

Rorty, Richard 1988 "The Priority of Democracy to Philosophy," in Patterson, Merrill A., and Vaughn, Robert C., eds., *The Virginia Statute for Religious Freedom*. Cambridge: Cambridge University Press: 257-82.

Sandel, Michael J. 1982 *Liberalism and the Limits of Justice*. Cambridge: Cambridge University Press.

―――――. 1984 "The Procedural Republic and the Unencumbered Self," *Political Theory* 12: 81-96.

Sher, George 1987 "Other Voices, Other Rooms? Women's Psychology and Moral Theory," in Kittay, Eva Feder and Meyers, Diana T., eds., *Women and Moral Theory*: 178-89.

Stocker, Michael 1987 "Duty and Friendship: Towards a Synthesis of Gilligan's Contrastive Moral Concepts," in Kittay, Eva Feder and Meyers, Diana T., eds., *Women and Moral Theory*: 56-68.

Turner, Victor 1974 "Metaphors of Anti-structure in Religious Culture," *Dramas, Fields, and Metaphors: Symbolic Action in Human Society*. Ithaca and London: Cornell University Press: 272-99.

Veatch, Robert M., 1976 "What is 'Just' Health Care Delivery," in Veatch, R.M., and Branson, R., eds., *Ethics and Health Policy*. Cambridge, Mass.: Ballenger: 127-53.

―――――. 1981 *A Theory of Medical Ethics*. New York: Basic Books, Inc.

Williams, Preston N. 1990 "An Analysis of the Conception of Love and Its Influence on Justice in the Thought of Martin Luther King, Jr.," *The Journal of Religious Ethics* 18 (Fall): 15-31.

Wong, David B. 1984 *Moral Relativity*. Berkeley: University of California Press.

www.ingramcontent.com/pod-product-compliance
Lightning Source LLC
Chambersburg PA
CBHW050618300426
44112CB00012B/1553